MIGRANT AESTHETICS

LITERATURE NOW

LITERATURE NOW

Matthew Hart, David James, and Rebecca L. Walkowitz, Series Editors

Literature Now offers a distinct vision of late-twentieth- and early-twenty-first-century literary culture. Addressing contemporary literature and the ways we understand its meaning, the series includes books that are comparative and transnational in scope as well as those that focus on national and regional literary cultures.

John Brooks, *The Racial Unfamiliar: Illegibility in Black Literature and Culture*

Vidyan Ravinthiran, *Worlds Woven Together: Essays on Poetry and Poetics*

Ellen Jones, *Literature in Motion: Translating Multilingualism Across the Americas*

Thomas Heise, *The Gentrification Plot: New York and the Postindustrial Crime Novel*

Sunny Xiang, *Tonal Intelligence: The Aesthetics of Asian Inscrutability During the Long Cold War*

Jessica Pressman, *Bookishness: Loving Books in a Digital Age*

Heather Houser, *Infowhelm: Environmental Art and Literature in an Age of Data*

Christy Wampole, *Degenerative Realism: Novel and Nation in Twenty-First-Century France*

Sarah Chihaya, Merve Emre, Katherine Hill, and Jill Richards, *The Ferrante Letters: An Experiment in Collective Criticism*

Peter Morey, *Islamophobia and the Novel*

Gloria Fisk, *Orhan Pamuk and the Good of World Literature*

Zara Dinnen, *The Digital Banal: New Media and American Literature and Culture*

Theodore Martin, *Contemporary Drift: Genre, Historicism, and the Problem of the Present*

Ashley T. Shelden, *Unmaking Love: The Contemporary Novel and the Impossibility of Union*

Jesse Matz, *Lasting Impressions: The Legacies of Impressionism in Contemporary Culture*

Jeremy Rosen, *Minor Characters Have Their Day: Genre and the Contemporary Literary Marketplace*

Sarah Phillips Casteel, *Calypso Jews: Jewishness in the Caribbean Literary Imagination*

Carol Jacobs, *Sebald's Vision*

Rebecca L. Walkowitz, *Born Translated: The Contemporary Novel in an Age of World Literature*

Héctor Hoyos, *Beyond Bolaño: The Global Latin American Novel*

Mrinalini Chakravorty, *In Stereotype: South Asia in the Global Literary Imaginary*

Heather Houser, *Ecosickness in Contemporary U.S. Fiction: Environment and Affect*

Caren Irr, *Toward the Geopolitical Novel: U.S. Fiction in the Twenty-First Century*

Migrant Aesthetics

CONTEMPORARY FICTION, GLOBAL MIGRATION, AND THE LIMITS OF EMPATHY

Glenda R. Carpio

Columbia University Press
New York

Columbia University Press
Publishers Since 1893
New York   Chichester, West Sussex
cup.columbia.edu
Copyright © 2023 Columbia University Press
All rights reserved

Library of Congress Cataloging-in-Publication Data
Names: Carpio, Glenda, author.
Title: Migrant aesthetics : contemporary fiction, global migration, and the limits of empathy / Glenda Carpio.
Description: New York : Columbia University Press, [2023] | Series: Literature now | Includes bibliographical references and index.
Identifiers: LCCN 2022059810 (print) | LCCN 2022059811 (ebook) | ISBN 9780231207560 (hardback) | ISBN 9780231207577 (trade paperback) | ISBN 9780231557023 (ebook)
Subjects: LCSH: American fiction—21st century— History and criticism. | Immigrants in literature. | Emigration and immigration in literature. | Empathy in literature. | LCGFT: Literary criticism.
Classification: LCC PS374.I48 G54 2023 (print) | LCC PS374.I48 (ebook) | DDC 813/.6099206912—dc23/eng/20230309
LC record available at https://lccn.loc.gov/2022059810
LC ebook record available at https://lccn.loc.gov/2022059811

Cover design: Julia Kushnirsky
Cover image: Detail of Tony de los Reyes, *Border Theory (rio grande/colorscale 7)*, 2014. © Tony de los Reyes

For Andrea

CONTENTS

ACKNOWLEDGMENTS ix

Introduction: Migrant Aesthetics 1

Chapter One
Migrant Anonymity: Strategic Opacity in Dinaw Mengestu and Teju Cole 33

Chapter Two
Migrant Refraction: Aleksandar Hemon's Anti-Autobiography 68

Chapter Three
Migrant Solidarity: Valeria Luiselli's Echo Canyon 95

Chapter Four
Carceral Migration: Julie Otsuka's Internment Novels 128

Chapter Five
Apocalypse and Toxicity: Junot Díaz's Migrant Aesthetics 159

Chapter Six
Carceral Migration II: The Flores Declarations and
Edwidge Danticat's *Brother, I'm Dying* 195

Epilogue
"Chinga La Migra"—Karla Cornejo Villavicencio's
The Undocumented Americans 221

NOTES 237

INDEX 273

ACKNOWLEDGMENTS

This book took me a long time to write and almost drove me mad. Its subject is too close to my heart; its form proved elusive for years and made me wonder if I could write it at all. And it is no exaggeration to say that my chosen family saved me and helped me believe that I could. Namwali Serpell: "She is a friend of my mind . . . The pieces I am, she gather them and give them back to me in all the right order." How fitting to find in Morrison's *Beloved* the words to describe what you have meant to me in this arduous battle, my sister, my brilliant friend. Anyone who has ever had the pleasure to have your eyes on their work knows that, beyond being a force of nature as a scholar and a writer, you are the best reader one could ever hope for. My gratitude to you knows no bounds.

Ajantha Subramanian and Vincent Brown nurtured my mind and soul. With Rachel St. John, they read every chapter with a precision characteristic of their own brilliant work. And with their children, Zareen and Anisa, they sheltered me through many storms. The writing group you constituted, Ajantha, Vincent, and Rachel, was my bloodline. My thinking and writing were vastly improved by your generous and incisive feedback.

For the soul-searching and funny chats about the creative process, for the collaboration on "This Little," using the Flores testimonies, and for your deep and generous sense of friendship, I thank my other sister and brilliant friend, Michele Asselin. Your curiosity, your kindness, your capacity for tenderness makes me feel the awe I feel when I encounter art at its best. With your family, Joseph, Simone, and Wren Meltzer, you have given me so much joy and love as I wrote this book.

And for our lovely 10 Maple Street dinners (and other such gatherings), where you have heard the ups and downs of this and other projects, I am eternally grateful to you, Julian Lucas and Christopher Alessandrini. Every time I read your work, my heart skips a beat. The same is true of your work, Ernest Mitchell. You, along with Namwali, Julian, and Christopher, are among those stars I once had the pleasure and honor to teach and whose brilliance now illuminates my way. I am looking at you, Nicholas Rinehart and Isabel Duarte-Gray.

My comadres, Marissa Sanchez and Cristina Salas-Porras Hudson, reminded me to laugh from the heart. And so did Deborah Wafer and Brooke Minters. Kelly Duane de la Vega and her lovely family, Mario, Lila, and Pablo de la Vega, kept me strong with their own clear and fierce political commitments. Ramie Targoff kept the bar high with her elegant ways and her fierce productivity. *Sei una stella cometa, carissima amica.*

Mentors and colleagues, among whom Werner Sollors looms large, were the models and fire that kept this project going. As a fellow migrant, and scholar extraordinaire, you have shown me, dear Werner, how to ask the most probing questions about what it means to be a migrant in America. Thank you for incisive readings of each chapter. Other colleagues have been indispensable. David Alworth believed in this book from its fledgling beginnings and offered excellent suggestions and support. The late Lauren Berlant and Sianne Ngai edited an article for *Critical Inquiry* that informs the chapter on Aleksandar Hemon and the whole book. Their sharp feedback and support, especially from Sianne, made it possible to surmount one of the toughest hurdles along the way. My colleagues and the staff in the English Department at Harvard have provided the intellectual and material conditions to see this work to completion. I am particularly grateful to Deidre Lynch, Stephen Greenblatt, Louis Menand, and Jesse McCarthy, with whom I have shared my work on Valeria Luiselli's *Lost Children Archive* for Humanities 10. My thanks too to other members of that course, particularly Alison Simmons, Jill Lepore, and Matthew Ocheltree. Our students for Humanities 10 have been a great source of inspiration for this and other projects to come. I thank Stephen too for first introducing me to Kafka's "A Report for an Academy," long ago at UC Berkeley and for his friendship throughout the years. My warmest thanks go to the English department staff, especially to Anna McDonald, Sol Kim-Bentley, Lauren Bimmler, Case Kerns, Gwen Urdang-Brown, and Lee Marmor for supporting a rookie chair as she finished this book. Thanks also to Kailey Bennett, Daniel Hegarty, and Henry Vega Ortiz. I also thank my colleagues in the Department of African and African American Studies, particularly Tommie Shelby and the indomitable Henry Louis Gates Jr.

My gratitude goes to all the students. My favorite part of being at Harvard is meeting and learning with and through you. Special thanks go to Dena Fehrenbacher, Janet Zong York, Sophia Mao, and Zhe (Carrie) Geng, with whom I had vibrant discussions on contemporary immigrant fiction. I also thank Maria Zymara, who invited me to present the book to the Poggioli Colloquium, where I benefited from the piercing questions and comments from the Comparative Literature community at Harvard. And I'm grateful to you, Jordan Virtue, for the precision with which you read the final draft of this book.

I am lucky that I have been able to meet many of the writers in *Migrant Aesthetics* at Harvard and its peripheries. Long before I met Teju Cole, I started working on *Open City*; I am so grateful to now count him as my colleague. Thank you, Valeria Luiselli, for *The Lost Children Archive*, a book that helped me write and see my own design. It's been a dream to have you at Harvard. My gratitude also goes to you, Junot Díaz, for the decades of work on us migrants. And to you, Karla Cornejo Villavicencio, for your fierceness.

My gratitude extends to the generous and incisive readers at Columbia University Press, and to Philip Leventhal, who listened to early, murky ideas about what this project could be and believed that there was potential. I am grateful for his patience and support. And to the rest of the team at the press, especially David James, Adriana Cloud, Kathryn Jorge, Monique Briones, my deepest gratitude.

Italy and my loved ones there have helped me keep perspective. I am grateful to the Fulbright fellowship for affording me the opportunity to teach at Ca' Foscari University in Venice, Italy, where I first essayed some of the ideas in this book. Alide Cagidemetrio's formidable role as a model of scholarship at Ca' Foscari and beyond and her role in nurturing the Harvard-Ca' Foscari Summer School have been central in my thinking about America and migration from abroad. Thank you, Stefania Piferi, Fabio,

Riccardo, and Andrea Menon for our adventures, which kept me balanced and joyful. I am also lucky beyond measure to have had the love and support of my adoptive family, Arnaldo, Franca, Matteo, and our late and beloved Andrea Bardi. Dedicating the book to you, Andrea, is but a small measure of the love I hold in your memory. When we met, long ago, you told me that I was easy to love, and this was no small gift to a girl who felt alien everywhere. I hold your memory and your family, Daniela, Carlotta, and Maria Vittoria, close to my heart.

I have thanked my goddaughters with their families, but I would be remiss if I did not do so in a category of their own. Zareen and Anisa Subramanian Brown, you have listened to endless shoptalks and grown up alongside first and second book projects and you still love me and your parents! What a blessing! Simone and Wren Meltzer, your joy and wit, your curiosity and sharp intelligence have kept me honest and quick on my feet. Lila de la Vega, your brilliance and commitment to justice gives me hope in this dark world. All my goddaughters—with their razor-sharp questions and unwillingness to take easy answers—remind me constantly to stay the course. I trust that they will knock the walls of injustice down and stay committed to truth.

I thank you, Dr. Ralph Klein, for being my anchor and my guide. And, finally, my gratitude and love goes to you, Federico Ferro. You listened to my ideas patiently (even while trying to alert me that there were bears in our midst!). You held me tight when I felt the sharpest pangs of doubt and made me laugh (sei il ballerino più bello del mondo!) when I had to be reminded of that world we call "Agrigemento." Our life with our beloved Mina has nurtured and sustained me. I thank you both for granting me so many moments of joy, especially as I worked on this book.

MIGRANT AESTHETICS

INTRODUCTION
Migrant Aesthetics

Franz Kafka's "A Report for an Academy" (1917) is a short story about an ape who learns to behave like a human, and who later gives an account of his transformation. The ape, speaking to an audience of human gentlemen at the titular academy, describes his origins in Africa, where he was shot, captured, caged, and sent off as cargo on a ship bound for Europe. Finding himself, for the first time, without the freedom to move at will, he began to study human behavior, seeking to transform himself into a human as a way out of his predicament. The process was painful, requiring him to shed all prior memories and identity, but, in time, he was so successful that he could no longer access his emotions and experiences as an ape.

This story has always struck me as a brilliant exposition of the pain of transculturation. The protagonist not only suffers a violent deracination but must also mask his pain with a narrative of successful acculturation, since his psychic and social survival depends on it. The academy, meanwhile, looks on—in amusement? in pity? When I first read the story, I was in graduate school and still processing my own uprooting. I wanted to give my past a narrative shape, and almost everyone I met—everyone who was not an immigrant, that is—thought I should tell my story. I came to the United States when I was twelve years old, the daughter of a woman who crossed the border hidden in the back of a truck and later found work with a wealthy couple who sponsored my family. I did not speak English. Yet here I was, years later, getting a PhD in English at UC Berkeley.

Their enthusiasm for this narrative always made me cringe. I wanted to tell the story *behind* that ostensible advertisement for American self making. Then, eventually, it dawned on me: Why should I make myself vulnerable to the kind of double-layered pain that Kafka's ape suffers? What about all the other migrants whose stories do not end in success, at least by the standards of the mythical American dream? What about all the migrants who struggle or perish? And what about the larger story about the political and economic factors that set migrants flowing in the first place? This is a book that attends to these questions.

In the process of writing *Migrant Aesthetics*, I have returned again and again to Kafka's story, because its formal qualities broaden its scope well beyond the ape's individual experience. Kafka seems to have been inspired by the real-life story of a chimpanzee named Peter, trained in the early twentieth century to assume human habits and brought on tours of Europe and America.[1] For whose benefit is Kafka's ape captured and caged? And did Kafka call his ape Red Peter as a way of highlighting the lasting marks of violence left on the ape's body? Criticism of the tale tends to focus on what it tells us about human/animal relations: the connections between language, humanity, and animality; the potential translatability of experience across species;[2] and how Kafka enlists this and other animal stories to explore the ontology of otherness.[3] Critics also recognize that the story, by implication, deals with the assimilation and conversion of Jews: in the words of Dagmar Lorenz, it "criticizes the contempt that many of Kafka's assimilated Jewish contemporaries, including his own father, had for traditional Jewish life and Eastern European Jews."[4] The story, published three years before the Nazi Party was founded, offered its critique at a moment when "German nationalism and racial anti-Semitism had eclipsed the ideal of cosmopolitanism."[5]

But what should we make of the story's allusions to the brutal history of captivity, displacement, and acculturation of humans from Africa to the West? One possibility is to read the story as Kafka's engagement with the anthropological and modernist focus on primitivism in the early twentieth century, specifically its Jewish instantiations.[6] Another is to examine how the story underscores the historical animalization of millions of human beings through the transatlantic slave trade—the largest forced migration in human history—and the subsequent imposition of so-called civilizing forces in both Africa and the Americas.

The end of Kafka's story leaves us with a haunting image: Red Peter mentions for the first time his female companion, "a small half-trained female chimpanzee" with whom he takes his pleasure at night ("the way apes do") but whom he does not want to see during the day because "she has in her gaze the madness of a bewildered trained animal."[7] Red Peter, "the only one who recognizes" this gaze, "cannot bear it," for it reflects his own wretchedness.[8] The final solitude of Red Peter, as a trained animal alienated both from his past as an ape and from the human community, ironizes the triumphal tone with which he has recounted his acculturation up to that point. The story's brevity and the strategic placement of the female ape at the end make it impossible to look away from or rationalize the pain it represents. Instead, the manifold associations contained within the story—with the real-life chimpanzee Peter, with the slave trade, with the Jewish diaspora, and even with the current migration of refugees the world over—challenge readers to think both granularly and on a sweeping scale of time and place. In *Migrant Aesthetics*, I explore a similar set of formal strategies in contemporary fiction, strategies that allow us to comprehend the broad scale and temporality of forced migration while staying focused on the specificities of particular experiences.

From its beginnings in the late nineteenth century, the genre of immigrant literature has been nearly obsessed with the plot of acculturation. In the American context, this has resulted in countless stories about becoming (or failing to become) American, and about the negotiations that individuals and communities must undertake to become recognizable to society and the state. Often written and marketed as a genre that promotes empathy—and thus works to bridge gaps between foreigners and "natives" (an ironic term in settler colonial societies like the United States)—the tales of Americanization that characterize immigrant literature tend, in fact, to reinforce difference and to keep readers stuck in the realm of feeling: a sentimental terrain wherein feeling bad for immigrants rarely, if ever, leads to questioning one's own assumptions and actions.

While the theme of Americanization has enabled, to some degree, the political and social representation of migrants, it also obfuscates several phenomena. First, it often dovetails with the American dream myth, which celebrates stories of transcendence, of migrants who "make it," while obfuscating the stories of those who do not survive or who struggle continually for basic human rights, living marginal lives.[9] Second, the plot of acculturation focuses on how migrants adapt to their new environment, often without exposing the forces that have led to their migration in the first place. The onus of representing migration has rested on the migrant rather than on the entities (corporations, governments, lawmakers, etc.) that cause and direct migration flows. More broadly, the genre of immigrant literature depends on a model of reading founded on empathy—a model that my book takes to task. Literature promotes empathy, we are told, but empathy can easily slip into a projection of readers' feelings and even into outright condescension. What I call "migrant aesthetics," by contrast, are formal narrative strategies adopted by several contemporary authors that ask readers to *think* rather than just feel, to question the assumptions that they bring to texts about migration, and to examine their own investments in the larger forces that create migration.

My aim, and the aim of the authors I examine, is to shift the focus away from the migrant as a sympathetic creature upon whom feelings can be projected and toward migration as a phenomenon that involves us all, albeit from diverging perspectives. To speak in terms of Kafka's story, this critical shift takes us away from Red Peter and toward the academy (an entity that in the story remains offstage), encouraging us to pursue the links between the two. In historical terms, embracing this shift means reckoning with how European and American geopolitical and economic interests have shaped the entire world, forcing millions of people to migrate. It means adopting the broad vantage point of the history of empire and its complex, far-reaching effects in today's world. To make this perspective vivid for the reader, the writers here included call into question many of the conventions by which immigrant fiction has been traditionally produced and received. They challenge us to read migrant fiction in a historicized and global context.

Dinaw Mengestu's 2010 short story "An Honest Exit" offers a succinct example of this challenge, explicitly riffing on Kafka's story about Red Peter. It opens with an imaginary conversation between its nameless narrator and his estranged father, Yosef, who has recently died. "We had never spoken much during his lifetime," the narrator tells us. He then transitions to a scene in which he is speaking about Yosef to his students at a private high school in Manhattan, a school he calls "the Academy." He tells them how his father escaped Ethiopia as a young man stowed away on a cargo ship, traveling first to Sudan, then to Europe, and eventually to America. Although the narrator was born in the Midwest and teaches American literature, he identifies with Kafka's Red Peter: "I used to wonder if that was how my students and the other teachers, even with all their liberal, cultured learning, saw me—as a monkey trying to teach their language back to them."[10] The allusion to Kafka's story simultaneously frames Mengestu's narrative and suggests echoes of the transatlantic slave trade, as well as its far-reaching legacy in the modern world: the thousands of contemporary refugees leaving Africa for Europe and America, risking human trafficking, inhumane conditions, and death. The narrator enhances these connections by depicting his father as another version of Red Peter. In the tale of his father's escape, a man named Abraham, who helps Yosef to leave Sudan, advises him on how to train for his voyage, which he will endure cramped inside a box: "Stretch all the time," Abraham says, "until your body becomes as loose as a monkey's." Just as Red Peter and his real-life namesake were captured and shipped to Europe as commodities, Abraham refers to Yosef as his "investment," another commodity, since he expects payment for his help once Yosef gets to Europe.

The narrator explains that the story of his father's migration is based on strangled bits that his father had passed on to him and admits to making up "missing details" to create a more complex history. The invented details play on his students' vague knowledge of Africa, which they associate simplistically with war and extreme poverty. Yosef, an Ethiopian engineer fleeing political persecution, makes an arduous trek to a port city in Sudan with the hopes of setting out for Europe or America, "where life was rumored to be better." In Sudan, he struggles, like other refugees, against poverty and flees just as war breaks out. The story seems at first to lessen the narrator's alienation at the Academy: "Huge tides of sympathy were mounting for my dead father and me. Students I had never spoken to now said hello to me." While the attention temporarily buoys the narrator, he knows it is all an illusion. Whether his stories have "any relationship to reality hardly mattered; real or not, it was all imaginary for them." In fact, the students start embellishing and multiplying his tale:

> Soon, stories about my father were circulating freely around the Academy. I heard snippets of my own narrative played back to me in a slightly distorted

form—in these versions, the story might take place in the Congo, amid famine. One version I heard said that my father had been in multiple wars across Africa. Another claimed that he had lived through a forgotten genocide, one in which tens of thousands were killed in a single day. Some wondered whether he had also been in Rwanda—or in Darfur, where such things were commonly known to occur.[11]

Mengestu's wry satire emphasizes the superficiality of the students' sympathy.[12] As the narrator notes, their investment in the tale arises primarily from its foreignness, from the fact that it brings "directly to their door a tragedy that outstripped anything they could personally have hoped to experience."

"An Honest Exit" operates at three distinct levels. First, it is a story about a son mourning his father by imagining his painful migrant past. Second, it is Yosef's migrant story itself. Third, it is a metafiction that exposes the limits of sympathy as a mode of relationality. The tapestry formed by these three narrative threads unfolds to reveal a warning about what happens to stories as they are consumed: the narrator's personal attempt to mourn his father is lost in the distorting echoes and misreadings of his students. In turn, Mengestu makes conspicuous how *his* story could be consumed and misread. Published in the *New Yorker*, the story could be yet another tragedy that, from their positions of relative privilege, the magazine's readers could engage with superficially. By weaving this phenomenon into "An Honest Exit" itself, Mengestu challenges his readers to question the location of truth within the story: Is it to be found in the narrator's grief, mingled with the fabrications he invents for the sake of narrative continuity? Or does it lie in the satire of the students' vague recollections of genocide in Darfur and famine in the Congo? Or perhaps it is contained in some imagined, inaccessible archive that holds the true record of Yosef's struggles? More likely, the story's truth is to be found in fragmented form, scattered within the folds of fact, fiction, satire, and elegy.

"An Honest Exit" deploys metafiction to challenge its readers to become better interpreters than the students at the Academy. For the reader, this means knowing that, whether factual or imagined, Yosef's journey—a journey that extends beyond his sea voyage into scenes of abject suffering in a refugee camp in Italy, followed by survival stints in Europe and America—is rooted in the larger migration flows that arose from the history of colonialism. The narrator's description of Yosef's experience of the ship suggests as much:

> My father stared at the boat for a long time and tried to imagine what it would be like to be buried inside ... There was a square hole just large enough for my father to fit into if he pulled his knees up to his chest. He understood that this was where he was supposed to go and yet naturally he hesitated, sizing up the dimensions ... He arrived in Europe just as Abraham had promised he would, but an important part of him had died during the journey, somewhere in the final three days, when he was reduced to drinking his urine for water and could no longer feel his hands or feet.[13]

These images provide granular details of Yosef's experience, calling attention to the lasting effects of the journey on his psyche while also invoking the impossibly cramped and inhumane conditions of the slave trade.[14] "An Honest Exit" encourages its readers to ask pressing questions: What forces Yosef to make such a brutalizing journey? How are those forces historically constituted?

Mengestu wove "An Honest Exit" into his 2010 novel *How to Read the Air*. There, Yosef's suffering primarily serves as background for the narrator's plight as a second-generation Ethiopian American. The narrator, now known as Jonas, struggles to come to terms both with himself and with his father's silence about his migration and his physical abuse of the narrator's mother.[15] One might even argue that the narrator instrumentalizes Yosef's migration story to explain his own abusive impulses toward his girlfriend. The migration story's historical and geographical connections are buried, therefore, by this instrumentalization and by the account of Jonas's own life, which takes center stage and offers readers the more familiar task of witnessing an individual form an identity. Contrasting Yosef's diminished migration story in *How to Read the Air* with the more multivalent short story version shows us the limits of representing migration through identitarian structures. By embedding Yosef's migration story within Jonas's story of self-discovery in the novel, Mengestu embraces the conventions of immigrant literature as bildungsroman and domestic drama. These conventions, because of their familiarity with life stories and with semi- or pseudo-autobiographical accounts of acculturation, and because they appeal to readers' empathy, obscure more than they illuminate.

By contrast, in his subsequent novel *All Our Names* (2014), Mengestu strategically obscures the story of the protagonist, an Ethiopian refugee known only as "Isaac" (we never know his real name). We are made privy to the poverty and violence that led to his escape from Ethiopia to Uganda and ultimately to the United States in the aftermath of the civil rights movement, but Mengestu does not focus on Isaac's acculturation in America. Instead, in alternating chapters, we follow Helen, a white Midwestern social worker assigned to his case, and see how she perceives him, what she projects onto him, and what she reveals about herself in the process. Even in the sections narrated by Isaac, it is hard to tell (just as it is in "An Honest Exit") how much of his story he is willing or able to reveal. Mengestu's alternating chapters, moreover, keep the reader's focus on the dynamic between the migrant and the social worker, giving the novel a metafictive layer. Helen becomes a negative model for relationality vis-à-vis the migrant, in ways that recall the students of "An Honest Exit" who, with their stereotyping embellishments of Yosef's story, show us how *not* to respond to it. In other words, Helen's narrative helps Mengestu to challenge prevalent assumptions relating both to migrants and to reading immigrant fiction. In chapter 1, I turn to *All Our Names* to expand this analysis.

Migrant Aesthetics challenges the view of migration as a problem of two opposed entities: the migrants, who must beg admission to sites of power, and the powerful, who must figure out how to protect their borders. Instead, my book argues that migration needs to be understood as a global phenomenon, one that, much like global warming, is produced by the actions of institutions that permeate every level of society. How do the habits of readers—their voting and banking choices, their consumption of goods, their reading practices, and their monetary and emotional investments—contribute to a world in which some are forced to migrate while others can claim the luxury of stable homes and identities? To make their readers focus on this question, the writers I examine reject empathy as the main mode of relationality, opting instead for what Hannah Arendt called "representative thinking"; that is, they urge readers to think, as themselves, from the position of another person and thus to call into question their own preconceptions and actions.

INTRODUCTION

"THE BANALITY OF EMPATHY"

In her brilliant 2019 essay "The Banality of Empathy," Namwali Serpell notes that, for Hannah Arendt, the "political function of the storyteller—historian or novelist—is to teach acceptance of things as they are. Out of this acceptance, which can also be called truthfulness, arises the faculty of judgment."[16] But, as Serpell writes, "Arendt does not mean 'acceptance' as a form of political quietism. She means 'truthfulness,' as opposed to propaganda, which is partial—biased, incomplete information."[17] Truthfulness facilitates judgment that can clarify one's relationship to justice. Art that works toward political justice seeks truthfulness. By contrast, art that works to create empathy lets readers off the hook: readers of such works can feel for others without having to interrogate themselves.

The idea that art creates empathy "goes back at least to the eighteenth century," writes Serpell, and "is particularly prevalent when it comes to those works of art described as 'narrative': stories, novels, TV shows, movies, comics. We assume that works that depict characters in action over time must make us empathize with them, or as the saying goes, 'walk a mile in their shoes.' And we assume that this is a good thing."[18] We assume this, in part, because art that creates empathy purportedly allows us to become better people and, by extension, better political subjects. While this idea has had wide purchase, it has also been vigorously contested. Serpell cites Jean-Jacques Rousseau, who argued against the theory in 1758, and Paul Bloom's 2016 book *Against Empathy*, which, as James Dawes notes, argues that "we are hardwired to have empathy for people who exist and, of the people who exist, people we know," but that as our empathy expands beyond these groups, it often morphs into other feelings—pity, "narcissism and even voyeurism"—and becomes selective.[19] For instance, Dawes writes, we "generously donate time and money to the victims of spectacular catastrophes even when more time and money isn't particularly helpful.... Meanwhile, we stingily withhold resources that could make critical differences for the vast population suffering from the invisible, slow tortures of poverty, violence, and disease."[20]

Our empathy, moreover, depends more than we realize on the type of media coverage that an event receives. When the teenager Natalee Holloway went missing in Aruba in 2005, writes Bloom in a *New Yorker* article, "the story of her plight took up far more television time than the concurrent genocide in Darfur."[21] We also have a difficult time experiencing empathy for those we can only imagine abstractly. "Opponents of restrictions on CO_2 emissions are flush with identifiable victims," writes Bloom, "all those who will be harmed by increased costs, by business closures. The millions of people who at some unspecified future date will suffer the consequences of our current inaction are, by contrast, pale statistical abstractions."[22]

The literary critic Deborah Nelson notes that ethical systems dependent on empathy presuppose a "face-to-face encounter with the Other," as can be seen in "trauma studies or the efforts to understand emotional flow in affect studies; or the work on identity and identification across forms of subaltern studies."[23] Yet crucially, as Dawes argues, even at the level of personal relationships, empathy is slippery. "If we don't get close enough to the other, our empathy is thin and superficial. We under-identify. But if we get too close, we over-identify."[24] Dawes concludes, "Our empathy can erase the other; we can find ourselves emotionally standing-in for the other."[25] Even if we were to get the balance just right, argues Dawes, feeling for others does not necessarily lead us to *act* in their stead or on their behalf. Bloom warns us: while empathy "is what makes us human," and "what makes us both subjects and objects of moral concern," it has limits, and these limits come to the fore when we try to make empathy "a moral guide."[26]

Nelson reminds us that the term "empathy" was originally meant to describe a physiological capacity of the nervous system to conduct emotions both through the body and from one body to another. It was not linked to psychology until, in the early twentieth century, aestheticians and psychologists adopted the term to describe the process of projecting oneself and identifying with *objects*, specifically works of art, to understand them. By the late 1940s, the term came to denote the field of interpersonal relations, thanks to the work of Rosalind Dymond Cartwright, an experimental psychologist who, working with her mentor, the sociologist Leonard Cottrell, conducted some of the first measurements of interpersonal empathy. Their work inspired several other studies, the results of which prompted public usage of the term. Susan Lanzoni notes that, by 1955, *Reader's Digest* defined the term ... as the 'ability to appreciate the other person's feelings without yourself becoming so emotionally involved that your judgment is affected.'"[27]

INTRODUCTION

While the usage of the term has steadily increased since then, its meaning has become more and more diffuse. The social psychologist C. Daniel Batson observes that it can now refer to at least "eight different concepts: knowing another's thoughts and feelings; imagining another's thoughts and feelings; adopting the posture of another; actually feeling as another does; imagining how one would feel or think in another's place; feeling distress at another's suffering; feeling for another's suffering, sometimes called pity or compassion; and projecting oneself into another's situation."[28] Despite the term's slippery nature, however, public consensus about empathy's efficacy as a political and moral tool is strong, as is the belief that reading fiction improves individuals' empathetic power.

Nelson attributes the rise in the public usage of the term to the tremendous suffering experienced during and after World War II, and she notes the extensive scholarship on related terms, such as "sympathy." Indeed, a central debate in literary studies of the late twentieth century, inspired by Jane Tompkins and Ann Douglas and including work by Lauren Berlant, Amy Kaplan, and Cindy Weinstein, revolves around the sentimental novel's embrace of feeling over action, and those who defend the purported political power of "feeling." Nelson argues, by contrast, that we ought to explore the power of *un*sentimentality to develop ethical systems that do not rely on empathy and related terms. For Nelson, unsentimental works purposefully seek to make readers uncomfortable, even to the point of causing pain, to disrupt their worldview and force them to alter themselves and their opinions. Such works do not aim for readers' cognitive empathy—the ability to understand how other people feel and what they might be thinking—but instead entail a dual discipline of perception and representation. Readers must be willing to be altered by the facts that writers, through their art, make clear. Nelson borrows the phrases "facing facts" and "facing reality" from Mary McCarthy and Hannah Arendt, respectively, to point to phenomena that have the power to alienate you from yourself and disrupt your worldview. (In McCarthy's wide-ranging use of the term, a "fact" could be anything from a document or a novel to a real or fictional character or event.[29]) Unlike nonsentimental work, Nelson argues, unsentimental writing is marked not by the lack of emotion but by its disciplined mode of representing and perceiving reality, entailing an "uncomfortable sharing of a painful world without the sharing of the pain itself."[30]

In this book, I am concerned with the question of empathy in fiction as it relates to racialized migrants within the history of empire. The racialization and commodification of human beings during the transatlantic slave trade, which is central to the history of migration, has shaped how white people engage with racialized Others in general. It has also shaped how authors who are Othered represent themselves to white audiences. Slave narrators in the nineteenth century, for instance, had to adopt and manipulate conventions designed for white readers. Often, they ironized those conventions, inventing formal strategies to expose racialized violence, but, nonetheless, they had to tame their rage in order not to alienate potential allies. A similar dynamic characterizes today's immigrant fiction, which tends to rely on empathy to represent immigrants as people worthy of allyship.

The idea that art promotes empathy has gained momentum in large part from the strange, often unarticulated pleasures of consuming the lives of people who suffer. Some critics today call this mode of consumption "trauma porn," a phenomenon that, in racialized contexts, discursively reproduces the dynamics of commodifying people. Serpell argues as much:

> The empathy model of art can bleed too easily into the relishing of suffering by those who are safe from it. It's a gateway drug to white saviorism, with its familiar blend of propaganda, pornography, and paternalism. It's an emotional palliative that distracts us from real inequities, on the page and on screen, to say nothing of our actual lives. And it has imposed upon readers and viewers the idea that they can and ought to use art to inhabit others, especially the marginalized.[31]

In this context, empathy entails more than trying to put oneself in "another person's shoes"; it entails one person assimilating "the other into his or her mind" through "a kind of ghostly possession or occupation."[32] This idea echoes Doris Sommer's *Proceed with Caution, When Engaged by Minority Writing in the Americas*, which argues strongly against an assimilationist model of relationality and which I discuss in chapter 1.

The concept also prompts me to ask, here and throughout this book: What formal strategies can migrant writers use to guard against this kind of commodification? I have deliberately chosen to focus on authors who express their consciousness of such commodification explicitly, as opposed to those immigrant writers who either do not tackle the problem directly or collude with conventions reinforcing the idea that addressing migration is a matter of empathy. In other words, I focus on authors who practice migrant aesthetics.

MIGRANT AESTHETICS

My book explores how migration shapes and is shaped by language and narrative, specifically how we write and read fiction, and how the language of migration in turn influences real-life phenomena. As I show, particularly in chapter 3, the predominant language of migration plays a crucial part in producing the political, economic, social, and humanitarian crises at borders, detention camps, and other bureaucratic sites where migrants fight for human rights. In parallel, the terms, genres, perspectives, and plots that dominate narratives about migration tend to treat it as a problem that migrants alone must suffer, while nonmigrants can ignore it or look on from a distance, defending their national borders in pity, fear, or disdain.

The writers I examine in *Migrant Aesthetics*—Teju Cole, Dinaw Mengestu, Aleksandar Hemon, Valeria Luiselli, Julie Otsuka, Junot Díaz, Edwidge Danticat, and Karla Cornejo Villavicencio—offer a paradigm shift in the language of migration. They destabilize the binaries and trajectories of the standard story of migration and expand the temporal and geographic scales in which that story is told. As a practice, their migrant aesthetics forecloses or thwarts empathy by rejecting autobiography in favor of strategic anonymity, choral or collective narration, and shifting vantage points, all of which challenge the idea that representative voices can offer the reader truthful affective links to the text. These formal strategies, in and of themselves, are not specific to the writers I have chosen; other writers have used collective narration, for example, for other purposes. But, in these featured writers' hands, the strategies become a means to reject the empathy model of fictional relations, inviting readers to inhabit positions, not persons. The writers do not purport to give "voice" to the disempowered; rather, they delineate the positions that their subjects take in time and space, and thus guard against the commodification of migrants as racially marked Others.

For these writers, migration is not about national (un)belonging or identity formation; rather, it is a global phenomenon that takes specific and varied shape according to capitalist interests, related global conflicts, and war. While they focus on migration to the United States, they also highlight historical resonances across time and space to vivify the broad scale of migration and its relationship to the slave trade, European colonialism, and global neocolonialism. I've chosen this group of writers because their work allows me to highlight a set of aesthetic practices that, while characteristic of their fiction, is not limited to it. In other words, migrant aesthetics—in addition to being a set of formal strategies—is a perspective, a way of seeing the world, based on the belief that, so long as we treat migration solely in terms of the nation-state, belonging, acculturation, and individual and collective identity formation, we will limit our apprehension of a global phenomenon that constitutes our world to the great suffering of many and the benefit of a few.

This perspective entails paying attention to the lives of those who have been or are outside what historian Mae M. Ngai calls the "telos of immigrant settlement, assimilation, and citizenship," a telos that has had an enduring power in American culture.[33] It entails reckoning with the criminalization of nonwhite immigrants and ethnic minorities, especially during times of global conflict and war. It entails confronting the use of what I call "carceral migration"—the condition of living under "parole," waiting for documents and for permission to enter, remain, or be reunited with family, or, if undocumented, living under the constant possibility of arrest and deportation—as a system of intimidation, discipline, and persecution. And it entails being cognizant of the deep and intertwined roots of racism and xenophobia in America's immigration and citizenship laws. This book analyzes the formal innovations—the migrant aesthetics—of writers who make this perspective and its ramifications brilliantly clear.

What distinguishes the writers featured in *Migrant Aesthetics* from other authors is their preoccupation with the scale of migration and their efforts to contextualize current instances of forced migration within the larger history of colonialism. To this end, they superimpose diverse time periods in a palimpsestic mode, as in Teju Cole's work, or create historical resonances or echoes, as in Aleksandar Hemon's and Valeria Luiselli's novels, or zoom in and out of micro and macro historical frames, as in Junot Díaz's oeuvre. These writers are unwilling to translate difference for their readers' easy consumption, or to represent or cater to specific ethnic groups. Instead, they manipulate one of the primary expectations for the genre of immigrant literature—that it will offer personal, semi-autobiographical testimony of successful or traumatic acculturation for empathetic engagement—by turning our attention to the larger historical, political, and economic conditions that produce migration. Almost all the texts I include employ metafictive structures, akin to the methods deployed in Mengestu's "An Honest Exit," which make conspicuous the process of reading itself, thus encouraging readers to question their own habits and preconceptions of migration. Such habits and preconceptions become ever clearer as we analyze the conventions that have heretofore governed the genre of migrant literature.

CATEGORIZING MIGRANT LITERATURE

I have strategically chosen the term "migrant" over "immigrant"—a word that, as Madelaine Hron notes, was "coined in the early nineteenth century to refer to migrants to the United States"[34]—because it encompasses a broader range of migratory experiences. I also chose it to create what Kenneth Burke called "perspective by incongruity."[35] I couple "migrant" with "aesthetics," two terms that are rarely, if ever, associated with one another, to pull apart common understandings of both. "Migrant" denotes economic precarity and illegality; it is popularly associated with "illegal" workers, even though it simply describes people who move "from one place to another, whether internally within a country, or from one country to another."[36] "Aesthetics," by contrast, refers to the philosophical study of beauty and taste and carries with it associations of elitism via class and cultural privilege; yet the term can also simply mean a set of stylistic conventions.

In this book, I use "migrant aesthetics" to refer both to stylistic innovation and to a method by which writers manipulate literary conventions (such as the trope of the unreliable narrator or collective narration) to "face reality," in Hannah Arendt's sense of the phrase. By coupling the two terms, I challenge simultaneously the idea that literature, as a mode of aesthetic experience, ought not to be instrumentalized for political causes, lest it compromise its integrity as art, and the notion that migration is best represented through (self-)documenting media—media lacking in artistic artifice—to ensure political efficacy. If this challenge recalls the art-versus-propaganda debates best exemplified, to my mind, by the work of W. E. B. Du Bois, Alain Locke, Langston Hughes, and George Schuyler, and later by Richard Wright, Ralph Ellison, and James Baldwin, that connection is a measure of the persistence of questions about the role of literature in social and political life in general, and in the struggle for racial justice specifically. For me, as for all the writers I examine, aesthetics and politics are intricately intertwined.

I am deliberately *not* using the terms "immigrant literature" or "new immigrant literature" to describe the works I consider in *Migrant Aesthetics*, since these categories have been associated almost exclusively with identitarian and nation-bound discourses and have become part of the standard lexicon about migration. How is the genre commonly understood? Immigrant literature in the United States, while present since its earliest colonialist days, flourished in two major periods: one at the end of the nineteenth and the beginning of the twentieth century, the other in the latter half of the twentieth century. In the first of these periods, an assimilationist phase, immigrant literature emphasized the immigrant's transformation from foreigner to American citizen—though, as William Q. Boelhower observes, acculturation is never "pure and simple but rather the presentation of a pluricultural reality depicting minority cultures with specific languages, world views, customs, and memories."[37] In the second period, a multiculturalist phase influenced by the civil rights movement and related ethnic movements, immigrant literature tended to advocate for the subject's negotiation of bi- or multicultural identities. In both periods, a typical narrator, often also the protagonist, seeks to accommodate the reader by translating difference. In assimilationist texts, this migrant acts as a mediator between their ethnic group and a "mainstream" audience by providing access to the group's cultural and linguistic practices (often including glossing or literal glossaries). In multiculturalist texts, writers address two main audiences, creating forms of recognition for the group they represent while instructing outsiders on the cultural differences that the text affirms.

These conventions are contingent on history. Immigrant literature of the late nineteenth and early twentieth centuries tended to focus, as Pankaj Mishra observes, on "the sufferings of the old world, the intellectual and emotional awakening in the new, and the complex negotiation between the claims of the community and the temptations of individualism."[38] These early American migration texts, like Mary Antin's classic autobiography *The Promised Land* (1912), represent the self-transformation that assimilation requires through a typology, established from the Puritans onward, that includes images of exodus and deliverance to a promised land. Antin tapped into this mythos strategically,[39] presenting the self as an entity so malleable that it can be fully transformed, and thus helped "to offset a growing sense of American nativist hostility to immigration by presenting the inwardness of a consciousness that underwent the transformation from foreign immigrant to American citizen successfully," in the words of Werner Sollors.[40] Yet this political goal forced Antin to relegate to the margins the intense suffering that her successful acculturation necessitated. And what about the many migrants for whom even this painful path was not available, those outside the "normative teleology of migration"?[41]

Ngai notes that scholars of immigration have paid particular attention to the period before 1924, "the era of open immigration from Europe," and the one after 1965, when "immigration from the third world increased."[42] Yet the period in-between is also crucial in our understanding of migration and citizenship. Ngai argues that the immigration restrictions imposed in the 1920s, particularly the Johnson-Reed Act, "produced the illegal alien as a *new legal and political subject*, whose inclusion within the nation was simultaneously a social reality and a legal impossibility—a subject barred from citizenship and without rights," and a subject that was also criminalized.[43] The Labor Appropriation Act of 1924, which established the border patrol as a law-enforcement agency, transformed unauthorized entry into a criminal act carrying the risk of deportation, while the Immigration Act of 1929 made unlawful entry a misdemeanor and reentry a felony, both subject to high fines and imprisonment.[44] Ngai argues that these acts, together with restrictive immigration laws, "put European and non-European immigrant groups on different trajectories of racial formation, with different prospects for full membership in the nation," and that "particular ethnoracial groups," such as "Filipinos, Mexicans, Japanese, and Chinese [people]," were now transformed into "illegal aliens, alien citizens, colonial subjects, and foreign contract-workers—all liminal status categories that existed outside the normative teleology of immigration."[45] The so-called new immigration, arriving from third-world countries after 1965, entered this increasingly racialized sociopolitical climate, which was further affected by mass deportations of Mexicans, Mexican Americans, and Filipinos during the Great Depression; the internment of Japanese Americans during World War II; and the extension of "legal traditions that had justified racial discrimination against African Americans" to encompass other ethnoracial groups, most of whom were deemed aliens ineligible for citizenship.[46]

Contemporary immigrant fiction, sometimes referred to as "new immigrant literature,"[47] asks us to read against the grain of classic immigration texts like Antin's, focusing less on the plot of Americanization and more on the hardships of acculturation in an American society rarely willing to integrate new, mostly nonwhite immigrants. Written in the age of the internet and cheap air travel, this literature does not stress the separation from countries of origin or present identity formation in binary or hyphenated terms; instead, it embraces the fluidity of identity, bilingualism, and hybridity more generally. Chimamanda Ngozi Adichie, Gary Shteyngart, Yiyun Li, NoViolet Bulawayo, Laila Lalami, Zia Haider Rahman, Gish Jen, Jhumpa Lahiri, and Chang-Rae Lee, among others, are considered part of this new immigrant literature. These writers are skeptical of the metropole, be it in America or in Europe, and overall, they are less nostalgic about their home countries than concerned with characters who don't survive or can't transcend the obstacles of acculturation—obstacles made more difficult by the rise of nationalism worldwide. Some of the writers in *Migrant Aesthetics*—particularly Dinaw Mengestu, Teju Cole, Junot Díaz, and Edwidge Danticat—also fall under this rubric. But, as I mentioned earlier, they distinguish themselves from their contemporaries in their use of migrant aesthetics to critique empathy and expand the scale for representing migration.

Important as immigrant fiction has been, the conventions of the genre have come to pigeonhole writers of migration so much that, for some artists, "immigrant literature" constitutes a literary "ghetto."[48] One reviewer of *All Our Names*, for instance, argues the following:

> All three of Dinaw Mengestu's novels are about people who, for various reasons, come to this country and fashion new lives. But it would be a huge mistake—it would be an insult, in fact—to call him a novelist of "the immigrant experience" or a chronicler of "life on the hyphen" or any of the other shabby, summary clichés deployed to characterize (and too often diminish and even dismiss) authors whose birth certificates identify them as foreign-born.[49]

Another reviewer announces that *All Our Names* is "not an immigrant story we already know quite well," meaning that it isn't primarily concerned with how migration "upends an immigrant's identity."[50] Immigrant literature, with a few notable exceptions, has been considered by critics in terms either too narrow or too broad—as pertaining only to issues of identity and the ethnic groups it represents, or as treating universal topics and thus becoming a questionably isolated category. "Aren't the themes of immigrant literature—estrangement, homelessness, fractured identities—the stuff of all modern literature, if not life?" Parul Sehgal muses in a 2016 article for the *New York Times*.[51] Sehgal then quotes Jhumpa Lahiri: "I don't know what to make of the term 'immigrant fiction'... If certain books are to be termed immigrant fiction, what do we call the rest? Native fiction? Puritan fiction?"[52] Lahiri, like other contemporary writers on migration, "chafe[s] at being narrowly categorized, consigned to an ethnic beat, their work treated as sociology instead of art."[53]

In literary studies, "migrant literature" refers to "texts about displacement and movement," and it is this more expansive sense of the term "migrant" that I use, in contradistinction to the legal lexicon of migration which, as Madelaine Hron reminds us, enforces false distinctions among several overlapping migratory experiences.[54] For instance, refugees, according to the UN Charter and the Geneva Convention, are people "seeking asylum in a foreign country because of persecution, war, extreme poverty, or natural disasters"; they are defined, Hron explains, as "involuntary migrants 'pushed' by life-threatening and coercive political conditions, while the 'immigrants' are known as voluntary resettlers 'pulled' by expectations of a better future and attractive economic opportunities."[55] Yet "it is not always easy to distinguish forced migration from voluntary resettlement, or between immigrants and refugees," especially—as I argue throughout this book—because the political and financial interests of empire constantly erase the differences between the two groups.[56] Nevertheless, the legal distinctions between immigrants and refugees often dictate the form of their narratives. As Hron notes, "refugees must master the art of [producing or even] inventing an amply heart-wrenching story to be granted asylum on political and humanitarian grounds in foreign countries ... [whereas] applicants for immigrant status must demonstrate that they won't trouble the host society in any way."[57] In other words, one category necessitates narratives that depend on eliciting empathy, while the other requires plots that support the political status quo.

The writers I examine in this book underscore how political terms used to categorize migrants shape both human interaction and literary production. In *How to Read the Air*, for instance, Mengestu's character Jonas works at an agency providing legal representation for refugees; he is tasked with "editing out the less credible or unnecessary parts of some of the narratives" and expanding upon or magnifying the details of others "for greater narrative effect," in much the same way that he does with his father's story. Jonas is even encouraged to mix and match among different refugee accounts, since "it's all really the same story" of suffering and need. He invents details, "based on common assumptions" about "the poor in distant, foreign countries" to make compelling legal cases.[58] Mengestu doesn't probe the ethical ramifications of Jonas's actions, preferring to underscore, in satirical and subtle ways, his creative response to legal categorization. In *All Our Names*, Mengestu employs a different strategy for similar ends, dramatizing how Helen projects "common assumptions" about immigrants onto Isaac, which initially makes a genuine connection with him impossible. All the authors included in *Migrant Aesthetics*, especially Valeria Luiselli (see chapter 3), shatter the political grammar of migration, offering instead a self-reflective alternate lexicon and new modes of narrating migration. While conscious of the fact that documentary and fictional modes of representing migration often intertwine, they reject the method of instrumentalizing pain to make "compelling" cases.

For Madelaine Hron, it is precisely because migrant pain is so often banalized and viewed as "the same story," or made to conform to readymade categories of suffering and transcendence, that migrants have developed sophisticated rhetorical strategies to represent their pain.[59] She shows that, contrary to theories of trauma proposed by scholars such as Cathy Caruth, Shoshana Felman, and Elaine Scarry, who argue that pain is ineffable, migrants successfully translate their pain across cultural and semiotic barriers, whether to elicit empathy, critique a host country, or conduct a form of individual or collective healing. "Adeptly employed," Hron writes, "rhetorics of pain might offer the immigrant subject representation, agency, voice, and even power in social discourse."[60] Hron is well aware that the politics of pain has its limits—she cites Nietzsche's criticism of "power of the weak" and of *ressentiment*, as well as Wendy Brown's critique of wounded attachments and Lauren Berlant's rejection of pain as a reliable basis for justice claims—but ultimately she argues that the rhetorics of pain are useful in creating testimony about experiences of suffering that are too often dismissed or erased.

The problem with her analysis, as with other critical work on migrant literature, is that Hron remains wedded both to the empathy model of reading and to representing migration at the micro level of individual stories. While she offers a comparative study of narratives by Maghrebians in France, Haitians in the United States and Canada, and Czech exiles and émigrés, many of which are not widely accessible (only five out of the forty novelists she examines have been translated into English), the scale at which she views migration remains relatively narrow. She acknowledges that immigrant suffering can be all too easily commodified but still proposes it as a useful topic that allows us to find common ground across a wide variety of cultural contexts. And while she knows that the empathy model has its limits, she still offers this question in her conclusion: "Might a sympathetic reading of immigrant texts provoke greater understanding and compassion for the immigrant condition?"[61]

Despite its limitations, Hron's study, *Translating Pain: Immigrant Suffering in Literature and Culture* (2009), is far more expansive than other scholarship on the subject, which has remained almost exclusively focused on the normative telos of immigration. For decades, scholars have focused on "cultural clashes; hyphenated identities; generational conflict; intermarriage; and competing national, ethnic, or religious loyalties."[62] Important as these topics are, they have overdetermined both the study and the impact of immigrant fiction. Worse yet, as seen in the American context, they can be used to reinforce pernicious myths. For instance, David Cowart in *Trailing Clouds: Immigrant Fiction in Contemporary America* (2006) argues that, while the "autobiographical narratives of isolation, assimilation, and scrambled ethnicity" that characterize immigrant fiction register struggles with "prejudice and homesickness," they ultimately embrace America as a "sanctuary and refuge" and show that the idea of the American dream remains "valid."[63] Immigrants, Cowart argues, "think having to learn English, or work at menial jobs, or deal with petty discrimination and prejudice a small price to pay for deliverance from poverty, tyranny, bloodshed, and political and religious coercion."[64] No doubt refugees who are able to make a life in America feel relieved to some extent, but this does not necessarily mean that they think of America as the promised land. Cowart refuses to acknowledge the critiques of American neocolonialism that are present in much of contemporary immigrant fiction, preferring to focus on the writers' aesthetic choices, as if these choices could be separated from the writers' representation of history and politics. The immigrant authors examined in his book, he argues, "identify themselves as artists first, immigrants second."[65] But, as I show throughout this book, the split between formal innovation and political identity is a false binary; for the artists in *Migrant Aesthetics*, formal experimentation facilitates political engagement, even as their political perspectives shape their aesthetic choices.

Another stubborn methodological approach to the study of immigrant literature is that of either segregating ethnic groups or imposing overused organizing principles, while purporting to provide multicultural coverage. Gilbert H. Muller's *New Strangers in Paradise: The Immigrant Experience and Contemporary American Fiction* (1999) offers five chapters, each dedicated to a specific ethnic group and its distinct features, which are examined alongside common themes of dislocation, marginality, duality of identities, cultural self-representation, and the reconstruction of cultural and national identities. Most anthologies and syllabi on immigrant literature are similarly structured, even though categorizing by groups inevitably leaves out some groups altogether and flattens differences within others—e.g., Asians, Latinx, and African communities.[66]

Werner Sollors, in his seminal book *Beyond Ethnicity: Consent and Descent in American Culture* (1986), shows us how to examine the "cultural interplays and contacts among writers of different backgrounds," to apprehend the cultural merging, the pervasive and inventive syncretism, that has taken place in America as a result of both immigration from other nations and migration within the country.[67] Sollors invites us to go beyond ethnic categorization and challenge notions of cultural authenticity to examine the grammar, codes, and "rites and rituals" of Americanization, especially those inherent in the tension between relations of descent (blood and heritage) and those of consent (law and marriage).[68] Across a wide range of scholarly texts, he demonstrates the central role of migrant literature in creating the multilingual and multinational nature of American literature and culture. Similarly, in *Migrant Sites: America, Place, and Diaspora Literatures* (2009), Dalia Kandiyoti examines how ethnic and immigrant spaces—the immigrant prairie, the Jewish ghetto, the border town, and the barrio—are constituted by the multiple places, languages, and legacies that migrants bring to them. The multiauthored collection of essays *Immigrant Fictions: Contemporary Literature in an Age of Globalization* (2007) also advances an approach like Sollors's, examining novels written by immigrant writers in several different realms of production, circulation, and translation. These essays move away from national and ethnic paradigms and show how globalization and technology have reshaped migration.

Yet, despite the important lessons in these studies, other critics continue to emphasize identity, whether personal or collective, as shaped by acculturation.[69] Sonia Weiner's *American Migrant Fictions: Space, Narrative, Identity* (2018) is an excellent study of form in contemporary migrant fiction, particularly in its analysis of spatial paradigms and linguistic diversity, but it focuses on questions of identity and belonging. Other scholars are concerned, as Susan Stanford Friedman writes, with "identity as it is in a continual process of (re)formation in relation to changing spaces and times" and with developing theories of displacement, diaspora, and exile.[70] Art historian Miguel Á. Hernández-Navarro argues that, under the influence of Gilles Deleuze and Félix Guattari's "ideas on nomadism and the ideas of hybridity and cosmopolitanism by authors such as Homi Bhabha"—concepts much in vogue during the late twentieth century—"a kind of idealization of the migratory universe" has emerged in scholarship, which emphasizes the mobility in migration to the point of fetishizing it.[71] However, as I argue throughout this book, migration often entails not just mobility but indefinite periods of *immobility*, in detention and refugee camps, places of sanctuary, or prisons. Given this focus, my work dovetails with that of Kandiyoti, who argues that "the age of global flows is also the era of fences and walls," and that we must consider the "historical and ongoing immobilizations and containments of our places, interactions, and literatures."[72]

Both Hernández-Navarro and the cultural theorist Mieke Bal have paid close attention to how migration entails "a double, contradictory movement, composed of stagnation and mobility," and how this leads to an "experience of time as multiple and heterogeneous."[73] In collaborative projects and workshops, as well as art shows involving several scholars and artists, Bal and Hernández-Navarro have explored works of art, particularly videos, documentary films, and installations, that "give account to this experience" by "both showing spaces and experiences where multi-temporality occurs and incorporating techniques, processes and modes of narration penetrated by alternative temporalities that bond, integrate, or directly clash and produce conflict."[74] Bal, who is also a video and film artist, introduced the term "migratory aesthetics," an operative concept rather than a generic descriptor, to explore mobility and its contradictions: how migration produces both trauma and aesthetic experiences; how perception is conditioned by migration as both movement and immobility; and how it constitutes loss but also leaves traces of memory and affective connections in material and aesthetic ways.

My own concept of "migrant aesthetics" is partly inspired by Bal and Hernández-Navarro, with their attention to stasis, stagnation, and immobility as constitutive of migration, as well as their exploration of the aesthetic experiences that migration produces across time and space. In this book, however, I steer away from their emphasis on identity and their capacious, nearly all-encompassing definition of what constitutes migratory aesthetics. Hernández-Navarro writes that "migratory aesthetics" refers "to a series of transformations that derive from the migratory experience and today provide an inevitable paradigm for contemporary societies and ways of feeling, of experiencing time, spaces, memory, and subjectivity." It is "not only about migration but also about how those moods are exported to other contexts and can be the key to artistic transformations," and in this way it "does not only refer to migration itself, although it never completely stops referring to it."[75] By contrast, in this book, I stay closely connected to the political and social realities of migration, focusing on the aesthetic forms through which it is represented. To do otherwise would be to risk forgoing the testimonial imperative of the migrant fiction I examine.

Throughout the six chapters that follow, I show how this fiction remembers the migrant dead and pays tribute to those who, instead of finding refuge in a new land, encounter only police brutality and xenophobic violence. Since the writers examined in *Migrant Aesthetics* operate on a broad historical scale, their elegies for the migrant dead are offered in the context of two massive human catastrophes: the transatlantic slave trade, a genocidal system of forced migration that reshaped the world, and the "Great Dying" of the indigenous peoples of the Americas between 1492 and 1600, which, as a recent study shows, killed nearly fifty-six million people from European-brought epidemics and colonialist warfare. It was a reign of death so intense that it "globally lowered surface air temperatures" due to "the large-scale depopulation of the Americas," and has been said to mark the beginning of the Anthropocene epoch in our planet's history.[76] The legacy and effects of these two apocalyptic events, as shown by the writers featured in this book, reverberate in contemporary instances of forced migration.

How have colonial forces directed and how do they continue to direct migration flows? I explore this question with the understanding that the "geopolitical and spatial distribution[s] of inequalities cast across our world today are not simply mimetic versions of earlier imperial incarnations but refashioned and sometimes opaque and oblique reworkings of them," as Ann Laura Stoler argues in *Duress: Imperial Durabilities in Our Time* (2016).[77] Stoler rightly warns against assuming that imperial formations existed only in the past. Instead, they "wrap around contemporary problems," including "toxic dumping in Africa, devastated 'waste lands,' precarious sites of residence, ongoing dispossession, or pockets of ghettoized urban quarters," as well as migration crises the world over. Imperial formations also "adhere in the logics of governance; are plaited through racialized distinctions; and hold tight to the less tangible emotional economies of humiliations, indignities, and resentments that manifest in bold acts of refusal to abide by territorial restrictions."[78] Contemporary imperial formations may not seem imperial on the surface, because they don't always manifest the characteristics of past empires, but the writers in *Migrant Aesthetics* give us the means of apprehending neoimperial machinations. They ask us to face reality, again in Arendt's sense, and to act against what Stoler calls the "occlusion" and "aphasia" that characterize imperial power, meaning its intentional concealment of and silence about its own brutality, failures, and disorderliness, which invariably victimize so many. Colonial powers often produce in their subjects a simultaneous will to know and a strong urge to disavow and ignore colonialism's effects.[79] Against these forces, the writers examined in this book create vital testimony of imperial violence, displacement, and exploitation.

CREATING MIGRANT TESTIMONY

The title of Dinaw Mengestu's novel *All Our Names* refers in part to the countless deaths that its protagonist, Isaac, witnesses in the Ugandan war. When he flees to America, the dead continue to haunt him. Yet, rather than focusing on Isaac's trauma, Mengestu intertwines Isaac's story and his elegy for the dead with a white American social worker's account of meeting him. In my first chapter, I show how, by juxtaposing these strands of the novel, Mengestu challenges the preconceptions and projections that readers are likely to bring to a text about an African migrant. In the same chapter,

I examine Teju Cole's 2011 novel *Open City*, which, like Mengestu's novel, uses its migrant narrator's anonymity to challenge the empathetic model of reading. Cole simulates the intimacy of memoir by seemingly giving readers access to his narrator's interiority, but this is ultimately a ruse to obtain readerly investment, which Cole then redirects to the global history of forced migration and dispossession. Both the Great Dying and the Atlantic slave trade are constant, though inconspicuous, points of reference in the novel, as Cole upends the conventions of migrant fiction and trains our attention on the human cost of empire.

Chapter 2 focuses on Aleksandar Hemon's *The Lazarus Project* (2008), which plays with the notion that migrant fiction is, by definition, autobiographical. Hemon makes his own migrant past fictional, refracting it rather than reflecting it, and transforms it further by intertwining it with other migrant lives, including a fictionalized version of a historical figure, Lazarus Averbuch, who in 1908 was shot and killed by the police after migrating to Chicago to escape a pogrom in Eastern Europe. *The Lazarus Project* is at once an elegy for Averbuch, a representation of migrant precarity, and a meditation on abiding ethnocentric forces in American culture. Hemon keeps our attention on the intensification of xenophobia during times of global conflict by interweaving several different time periods: the anarchist scare of 1908, which led to anti-immigrant violence; the time in which the novel's present evolves (approximately the beginning of the War on Terror); 2008, the year of the novel's publication, which witnessed the intensification of that war; and our own current moment of reading, which, as I write, includes the vilification and persecution of Asians and Asian Americans due to disinformation about the COVID-19 pandemic.

In chapter 3, I explore Valeria Luiselli's migrant aesthetics in her nonfiction book *Tell Me How It Ends: An Essay in Forty Questions* (2017) and her novel *Lost Children Archive* (2019), both of which analyze and take apart the language used to represent the plight of undocumented children seeking asylum at the U.S.-Mexican border. This crisis began in the mid-1980s, intensified through the 2010s (peaking in the four years of Trump's presidency), and continues with renewed intensity in the present. Rather than emphasizing the children's humanity to invoke empathy, Luiselli focuses on the political contexts that have compelled their migration, showing how the children's predicament echoes many other connected histories of dispossession and genocide, all produced in the name of white supremacy and imperial expansion. Both the essay and the novel are preoccupied by how the children's suffering is sensationalized through and commodified as news-cycle material. Each exposes the toxic impact of euphemisms on public discourse about forced migration, while also offering alternate modes of engaging with the children's plight. The essay does so by interrogating the language of immigrant bureaucracy. The novel meanwhile uses a metafictive structure that calls into question how, as a literary artifact, it can represent forced migration. Narratives embedded within the novel—a family road trip and an elegy for the migrant dead—use allusions to other literary works about migration to create a network of diverse but resonant historical timeframes. These echoes (historical, literary, mythical) simultaneously mourn the many migrants who die anonymously at the U.S.-Mexican border and place their struggle within the larger, brutal history of empire. Like Antigone, Luiselli offers burial rights to those condemned to be unburied and unmourned, but she also gives testimony to how the state deliberately uses natural hazards like the desert to make crossing so deadly that the bodies of migrants are pulverized by extreme heat and thus erased from the record.

In chapter 4, I examine how Julie Otsuka represents carceral migration. Her two novels, *When the Emperor Was Divine* (2002) and *The Buddha in the Attic* (2011), are part of a rich literary tradition about the internment of Japanese immigrants and Japanese Americans during World War II. In addition, because of Otsuka's particular migrant aesthetics, the novels speak more generally to the precarity of migrant life and citizenship for ethnic minorities, especially during times of global conflict, when they are often lumped together, criminalized, or otherwise persecuted. In her first novel, Otsuka, like Mengestu and Cole, strategically uses anonymity, withholding the names of all the characters except minor figures. She also rejects narrative plotting that would frame internment as an individual's transcendent or tragic story of survival or loss, instead shifting our attention to the experience of time in carceral migration—the present stretching out in seemingly eternal ways while the past and future become hazy, and obscure, subject to fantasy and distortion. She zooms in on that sense of suspension in time and makes vivid how, when combined with the spatial constraints of detention, it leads to psychological suffering that wounds and scars. Yet, rather than pretending that the reader can identify with her characters in their suffering, Otsuka vivifies the diurnal details of survival while providing a minimalist indexing of historical context; she thus encourages readers to inhabit the positions her characters occupy, instead of their subjectivities. In *The Buddha in the Attic*, Otsuka works with a choral, first-person-plural narrative to highlight the historical anonymity of Japanese internees, especially immigrant women who came to the United States as "picture brides." I read Otsuka's two novels as part of a larger project that rejects the teleology of immigrant settlement, assimilation, and citizenship as the überplot of migrant fiction, instead aiming to show how migration can lead to incarceration and historical oblivion. Pushing against this oblivion, Otsuka urges readers to relate the questions raised by her novels to the post-9/11 context in which her first novel was published, and to the so-called War on Terror that continued through the publication of her second novel.

Chapter 5 shows how Junot Díaz practices migrant aesthetics at a scale that ranges from the intimacy of sexual relationships to the long centuries of New World colonialism. Examining his corpus, which spans over twenty years—from his debut collection of short stories, *Drown* (1996), through his novel *The Brief Wondrous Life of Oscar Wao* (2007), to his second collection of short stories, *This Is How You Lose Her* (2012)—I explore how the intertextual links within his work produce migrant stories that overlap and create something like a choral narrative. Through this self-reflexive intertextuality, Díaz explores how colonial violence reverberates in the lives of people fleeing despotic governments that are backed by the United States. He shows how that violence infiltrates intimate relationships shaped by machismo and other forms of toxic masculinity and how it manifests in the environmental wastelands that so many migrants are forced to inhabit. Both forms of toxicity, Díaz shows, spring from the earth-shattering violence of New World slavery and from the genocide of Native peoples, two apocalyptic historical events that ushered in global warming and a new, pervasive stage of capitalism. Their effects continue to resound in the waves of migration and dispossession left in their wake. The fact that most critics identify Yunior, a recurring character in Díaz's fiction, as a reflection of the author, whose controversial private life has become increasingly public, may seem to present a challenge to the anti-autobiographical stance taken by most of the writers featured in this book. However, since Díaz, like Hemon, operates through refraction rather than reflection, I argue that we should *not* read Yunior as a stand-in for the author. Instead, we should stay attuned to how—with this slippery, shape-shifting character who multiplies throughout the author's oeuvre—Díaz challenges the empathy model of reading, creating migrant fiction that works at both a broad and an intimate scale.

In the last chapter and the epilogue of *Migrant Aesthetics*, I turn to two nonfiction texts, Edwidge Danticat's *Brother, I'm Dying* (2007) and Karla Cornejo Villavicencio's *The Undocumented Americans* (2020), which testify to carceral migration in detention centers and to life under the threat and reality of deportation. Danticat and Cornejo Villavicencio work directly through autobiography, attempting to manipulate the broad appeal of memoir to draw attention to their subjects. Using her status as a well-known writer, Danticat exposes in *Brother, I'm Dying* the inhumane conditions under which her uncle died in a Florida detention center. Yet Danticat, despite her best efforts to contextualize his death in a broader history of colonialism, gives her readers an out by couching his story within her own narrative of successful acculturation. Not surprisingly, many reviewers focused on the transcendence and success of Danticat's own life story, rather than the tragedy of her uncle's. To highlight the testimonial weight of this latter story, I analyze it alongside a selection from the Flores statements of 2019—sworn declarations by migrant children (and by parents on behalf of their children) filed by legal, medical, and mental-health experts who, after witnessing the criminal conditions in which children are detained at the U.S.-Mexican border, filed an amici curiae brief to appeal for justice. In thus reframing Danticat's testimony, I use migrant aesthetics from a critical perspective, aiming to heighten Danticat's political critique of empire, which in *Brother, I'm Dying* was overshadowed by its autobiographical framing.

Karla Cornejo Villavicencio renders the lives of the undocumented across America with razor-sharp clarity, intertwining her own story throughout. She shows us how the undocumented struggle to find work, healthcare, and safety while also maintaining their families, integrity, and sanity. She becomes a medium for immigrant stories that might otherwise remain illegible except as fodder for ideological battles. *The Undocumented Americans* thus offers a telling exception to readers: it retrieves autobiography for migrant aesthetics because it interweaves memoir with choral storytelling and because its language, perspective, and structure work against the conventions of immigrant literature. Nonetheless, the fact that Cornejo Villavicencio was one of the first undocumented immigrants to graduate from Harvard and was a PhD candidate at Yale at the time of her book's publication marks her as an exceptional kind of speaker, and the book's marketing and reviews rarely failed to mention these facts. While Cornejo Villavicencio vehemently rejects the American-dream mythology that would make her life exemplary, the mythology orbits around her book nonetheless, showing how difficult it is to disentangle false themes of transcendence from migrant literature.

Autobiographical accounts of migrants who transcend the odds, even when used to testify to migrant suffering and death, are too often co-opted by those who prefer "comforting myths." I take the phrase from the Lebanese American writer Rabih Alameddine, who argues that books critical of empire are rarely sanctioned by a market that merely simulates critique, while producing "comforting myths"—stories that assuage guilt at the expense of truth. Alameddine cites as examples several American war novels about Vietnam, Afghanistan, and Iraq that are commonly "considered critical of war" and "dangerous to the institution of war," even though "most of them deal [exclusively] with the suffering of the American soldiers":

> The Marines who were forced to massacre a village, the pilots who dropped barrel bombs and came home suffering from PTSD. If anything, this is helpful to the cannibalistic war machine. Such war novels make us feel bad and at the same time allow us to see ourselves as the good guys. We are not all terrible, for we suffer, too. . . . We invade your countries, destroy your economies, demolish your infrastructures, murder hundreds of thousands of your citizens, and a decade or so later we write beautifully restrained novels about how killing you made us cry.[80]

By contrast, books written from the perspective of the invaded, argues Alameddine, rarely if ever evade "imperial censorship," which "is usually masked as the publisher's bottom line. 'This won't sell.'"[81]

Migrant aesthetics, as both an artistic and a critical practice, works against the logic of the literary market (as described by Alameddine) by emphasizing the conventions governing how migrant fiction is produced, marketed, and consumed. It operates in the spirit of Kafka's "A Report for an Academy" in that it targets academics and the mainstream literary industry, which Viet Nguyen rightly identifies as "white, well educated" poets and fiction writers and the "reviewing, publishing and gate-keeping apparatus that is mostly white and privileged."[82] As a critical practice, migrant aesthetics exposes the pressure that the publishing industry exerts upon migrant subjects—pressure to conform to assimilationist literary conventions that, as Kafka's tale makes clear, hide the violence not only of acculturation itself but also of having to account for that acculturation within complicit institutions. The proof of this pressure can be seen in the work of writers from marginalized communities who adopt these mainstream conventions. "So much of immigrant literature," Nguyen writes, "despite bringing attention to the racial, cultural and economic difficulties that immigrants face, also ultimately affirms an American dream that is sometimes lofty and aspirational, and at other times a mask for the structural inequities of a settler colonial state."[83] Nguyen argues that "much of immigrant and multicultural literature fails to rip off that mask." He calls on the publishing industry to stop paying lip service to political change by making empty pleas for "empathy" and "diversity."

Like the other thinkers with whom I have engaged on the subject—Hannah Arendt, Namwali Serpell, Deborah Nelson, Paul Bloom, James Dawes, and others—Nguyen argues that empathy, while being necessary for human connection, cannot be relied upon as the basis of political action because it is selective and unstable; it can easily morph into solipsism and escapism. Empathy has become the "emotional signature" of liberalism and multiculturalism, but it has mostly produced only more comforting myths, occluding the necessary political work of ripping the mask off "the structural inequities of a settler colonial state." As a result, the work of effecting vital change in aesthetic practices has fallen mostly on writers from marginalized communities, "writers of color, queer and trans writers, feminist writers, anticolonial writers," who can write both from within and against the literary mainstream.[84]

The authors I explore in *Migrant Aesthetics* are among these writers. They manipulate the conventions of immigrant literature, make conspicuous our calcified methods of reading it, and invent new ways of apprehending migration's broad scope. They zero in on specific migrant experiences while simultaneously panning out, revealing a historical perspective on how (neo)colonialism produces forced migration. They are conscious that their strategies may not necessarily change a literary industry entrenched within empire, but they write with the confidence that, through their work, they are offering testimony to migrant life and death. *Migrant Aesthetics* gathers and analyzes their testimony to further that work and to explore the rich formal innovations that make it possible.

Chapter One

MIGRANT ANONYMITY
Strategic Opacity in Dinaw Mengestu and Teju Cole

Is "immigrant fiction" a useful category? In the American context, the category has facilitated an understanding of how the country's social, political, and intellectual life has been refreshed and reshaped by immigrants. Moreover, it has provided a challenge to the idea of American culture as primarily white, Anglo-Saxon, and self-contained. But the category has also been used to segregate American literature, suggesting that subcategories such as "Asian American" or "Latinx" works of "immigrant fiction" speak primarily to the ethnic groups they represent and obscuring the fact that immigrant themes such as alienation, homelessness, and fractured identities have far broader import. As I have argued elsewhere, migration exposes the fiction of the self as a cohesive unit attached to one identity, language, family, nation, and so on. Its literary forms intensify and demonstrate the instability of identity, thus exteriorizing the crisis of subjectivity so central to modernist fiction.[1]

The writer Pankaj Mishra sees "immigrant fiction" as a "leaky" category at best, one that isn't always invoked with historical specificity.[2] Comparing writers from the early twentieth century to those in the early twenty-first, he notes how much the context within which the latter have written— the age of the internet and cheap air travel—has shifted the form and content of their fiction. The contrast between Europe and America, the Old and the New World, is no longer the central drama in their work, especially since most contemporary immigrants in America, after the ratification of the 1965 Immigration and Nationality Act (the Hart-Celler Act), arrive from Latin America, the Caribbean, Asia, and Africa. Meanwhile, America is "undergoing massive demographic shifts—those that are projected to make whites a minority by 2043" and which, paradoxically, are one reason for the rise of white nationalism.[3] Historical context, technological advances, geopolitical changes, and trends in the literary marketplace all keep the category of "immigrant fiction" evolving.

Consider the literature coming out of the so-called new African diaspora, the large migration of Africans to the United States, Europe, and Asia that began in the 1960s and has increased exponentially ever since. According to population statistics, more Africans have migrated voluntarily to the United States since the 1990s than were forcibly brought to North America as part of the transatlantic slave trade.[4] While commentators stress the voluntary aspect of this later migration, the fact that it has been fueled by the collapse of social, political, economic, and educational structures in the wake of colonialism suggests a more complex set of circumstances.[5] By exploiting religious and ethnic conflicts to drain Africa's natural resources (and thus support Europe's industrialization programs), and by undermining—or outright destroying—indigenous systems of leadership in favor of political structures that benefited their own empires, colonial powers made it difficult, if not impossible, for postcolonial African countries to flourish. African resources, moreover, "continued to be appropriated by the former colonizers working in corrupt collusion with the indigenous political leadership," leading to military coups, civil wars, and genocidal conflicts in South Africa, the Congo, Nigeria, Rwanda, Liberia, Sierra Leone, and several other countries.[6] As Nigerian novelist Isidore Okpewho writes, "Those who have been lucky enough to escape with their lives, or have simply decided that they need to carry on their careers in less threatening conditions," have left for other continents.[7]

In 2005, the writer and photographer Taiye Selasi identified a particular demographic: highly skilled Africans who had left the continent—a "scattered tribe of pharmacists, physicists, [and] physicians," as well as lawyers, bankers, engineers, and academics—and their children, now "working and living in cities around the globe," claiming "no single geography" but feeling at home in many.[8] This new generation of "Afropolitans," Selasi argues, rejects their parents' traditional careers, working instead in media, fashion, music, design, art, and architecture. Their successes challenge stereotypes of Africa (and Africans) as static—forever war-torn, poor, and victimized—while promoting fluid, transnational African identities that nonetheless honor "the intellectual and spiritual legacy" of their parents' cultures.[9]

The political theorist Achille Mbembe has offered a more nuanced and historicized vision of Afropolitanism, identifying it as both a political and cultural stance and "an aesthetic," a way of being in the world that refuses "on principle any form of victim identity—which does not mean that it is not aware of the injustice and violence inflicted on the continent and its people by the law of the world."[10] He reminds us that precolonial African societies were created by the collision of cultures from all over the world, and that the cultural history of the continent, which "can hardly be understood outside the paradigm of itinerancy, mobility and displacement," has always included ethnic minorities that have made the continent multicultural in nature.[11] Mbembe reminds us also that the forced migrations driven by the slave trade, colonization, and postcolonial violence have, of necessity, produced flexible forms of belonging to and imagining Africa. The transnational aspects of Afropolitanism are thus not new, but, nonetheless, Mbembe identifies in the movement a challenge to the nativism of the politico-intellectual paradigms that have shaped modern Africa (e.g., anticolonial nationalism, African socialism, and Pan-Africanism).[12]

For the literary critic Yogita Goyal, Afropolitanism has been most clearly articulated in fiction. The writers of the new African diaspora, she argues, have moved away from "the concerns of previous generations—anticolonial resistance, the clash of tradition and modernity, alienation and exile"—and focus instead on "migrations other than those occasioned by the Middle Passage or Atlantic return." They navigate "the fraught space of Africa as an overdetermined signifier of trauma on the one hand" and "celebratory narratives of immigrant assimilation or triumphal globalism on the other."[13] Finding a balance between these two poles entails being attuned to how contemporary African migration relates to the diaspora produced by the slave trade, without "collapsing past experiences into the present in a melancholy vein, or conflating a range of geopolitical situations"; it necessitates exploring, rather than simply assuming, correlations between "modern experiences of being a refugee or trafficked person or child soldier" and the "historical experience of Atlantic slavery."[14]

Dinaw Mengestu and, in a more conspicuous way, Teju Cole clearly invoke the aesthetics and ethos commonly associated with Afropolitanism in their fiction. Based in the contemporary United States, both Mengestu and Cole manipulate stereotypes of Africa and African migrants to challenge preconceptions of both while also representing migration in ways that are not bound by concepts of the nation or by identitarian minority discourses. Rather, their fiction emphasizes the shared responsibility of engaging with cultural differences beyond national and ethnic boundaries. In this respect they echo the work of Kwame Anthony Appiah, whose *Cosmopolitanism* (2006) envisions a human community in which individuals can, despite differences in location, class, religion, etc., enter into relationships of mutual respect. Mengestu and Cole also invoke the view of African identity and culture as multiracial, informed by movements both within the continent and all over the globe—a view that forms the core of Afropolitanism. At the same time, they push back against the glossier, consumer-driven versions of Afropolitanism and guard against the commodification of Afropolitan fiction by tracing the limits of *literary* cosmopolitanism,[15] specifically its claim of facilitating intercultural encounters through aesthetic experience, and by refusing victimhood as a starting point for representing African migration.

Cole's and Mengestu's aesthetic practices simulate but ultimately foreclose emotional engagement, instead pushing their readers to question the concepts of progress, aesthetics as a means to mutual understanding, and immigrant characters' function as conduits for empathetic connection resulting in political change. Mengestu shows us the work that readers themselves need to do—as opposed to the immigrant narrator bearing the burden of representation and translation—to approximate Appiah's cosmopolitan ideal. Cole produces a palimpsestic representation of history to expose the multiple and "discordant temporalities" it has masked,[16] to decenter the idea of the nation as a bounded entity encroached upon by migrants, and to bring into view the imperial violence that has powered and continues to power the industrialized West and its peripheries. In this way, Cole contextualizes the new African diaspora within a broad historical scale while also exploring the correlations between it and the diaspora produced by the Atlantic slave trade, specifically their common origins within the history of colonialism.

As I noted in the Introduction, Mengestu's 2014 novel *All Our Names* is structured as two alternating tales, one told by a man known as "Isaac"—his actual name is never revealed—and the other by Helen, a white social worker assigned to Isaac's case when he arrives in America as an immigrant and refugee from Uganda. The Uganda sections begin at a university in Kampala, where "an important gathering of African writers and scholars" took place a "decade earlier" (this is the Conference of African Writers of English Expression, which took place at Makerere University in 1962, though neither is named directly in the novel), and dramatize a failed revolution against a dictator who is never named, although one can surmise it is Idi Amin.[17] The American sections take place in Laurel, a fictional Midwestern town, in the aftermath of the civil rights movement—but, again, there are no direct indices of that historical context. Isaac, the immigrant figure, is forced to flee from a country that, like the rest of the African continent, had been "booming" with "ecstatic promises of a socialist, Pan African dream" but that, by the early 1970s, was being violently consumed by bloody civil wars (3). Helen, by contrast, lives in a small town that seems to have been barely touched by the momentous social changes in American culture during the 1960s.

Mengestu pulls his readers "away from fixed dates and places"[18] to focus instead on the potential for intimacy between two people from opposite ends of the world. This turning away from historical specificity risks perpetuating the stereotypes of Africa that Afropolitan writers reject, since it allows for generalized ideas of Africa (ideas almost exclusively connected with war and suffering).[19] But the strategy also allows Mengestu to explore new ways of narrating migration. Instead of providing us with his personal life story, "Isaac" offers only the barest biographical details about himself, focusing instead on the violent events that he experiences in Uganda. The novel, moreover, eschews the confessional mode of the traditional refugee narrative and rejects the immigrant narrative's conventional acculturation plot. Instead, Isaac's existence in the United States is presented from the point of view of the "host" (Helen), whose limited access to Isaac's inner life is made clear to the reader while, in his sections, Isaac revisits the violence of the revolution not as a means to transcend his own trauma but rather to elegize the nameless dead who were victimized by it.

Cole's *Open City* similarly employs strategic anonymity. It simulates a diary and yet makes an enigma of its narrator, thus frustrating readers' expectations that the novel will be a personal, cosmopolitan account of migration. Julius, the narrator, is a thirty-something psychiatry fellow at Columbia Presbyterian Hospital in New York City. He lives alone and takes long walks, during which he meditates on the history and post-9/11 life of the city, reading its landmarks as if the city were a palimpsest upon which layers of human struggle and suffering have been inscribed. We follow him also when he takes a trip to Brussels where, as in New York, he meets with a series of characters, most of them immigrants, whose stories often take over from his own, with the storyteller assuming the narrative voice. Although we know from the start that Julius is himself an immigrant who arrived in America as a university student, we learn only indirectly that he is Nigerian when, about thirty pages into the novel, he provides brief biographical information about his German-born mother, from whom he is estranged, and his Nigerian father, who died when Julius was fourteen. Julius's narrative makes the reader privy to his immediate thoughts during the events of his life, from the most mundane (walking through a park, meeting his accountant, going to a concert) to the more dramatic, as when he gets mugged or reconnects with an important figure from his past. At the same time, it selectively withholds access to Julius's past and consciousness.

Both Mengestu and Cole manipulate the conventions of life writing to shift away from discourses of assimilation and hyphenated identities. Instead, they challenge the reader to find meaning in partial knowledge and to embrace forms of relationality that respect the limits between the reader and the novels' migrant subjects. Through this dynamic, the authors prompt readers to ask themselves probing questions: What is *my* responsibility to those whose past and place of origin I do not know, and perhaps cannot know? Do the global and historical forces that produce migration also create a common ground between strangers that can foster relations of solidarity—as opposed to those of sentiment, with their attendant slippages into pity and projection?

For those who see the ethics of migration solely in terms of the state, these questions might seem naïve at best. Historically, the "institutional reality" of the modern state—which, at least legally, takes precedence over individual relations—has been defined by its "authority to admit or exclude aliens as it chooses since that authority is widely acknowledged to be one of the essential elements of sovereignty."[20] Mengestu's novel, however, presses us to think beyond the state, to engage with the ethics of migration at an interpersonal level, while Cole's novel combines the two methods by offering a different view of the state in relation to migration. State sovereignty is designed to protect the wealth of some nations while relegating others to mind-boggling poverty, but the wealth of such nations has been historically produced by violently enforcing the migrations of large populations and the colonization of others. Cole's *Open City* allows us to comprehend how contemporary waves of immigration to the United States and Europe are intrinsically connected to this history.

Much like W. G. Sebald's *The Rings of Saturn* (1995), *Open City* presents history as an interconnected web of events, an approach that allows Cole to reshuffle the linear chronology of forced and voluntary migration in the New World and to highlight migration's intimate connection to the rise and maintenance of capital and empire. While Sebald's focus is Europe and the calamities it has inflicted both on people worldwide and on itself, Cole's focus is the New World—the histories of loss and dispossession at its core and the conditions under which people have migrated and continue to migrate to its shores. Like Mengestu, Cole presents a migrant figure who is affectively unavailable and, arguably, ethically compromised. In suggesting but then denying, even making undesirable, identification and intimacy with their characters, these two authors force readers to examine their own assumptions about migrants and the layers of history that have produced migration flows.

Doris Sommer has argued powerfully for the productive potential of creating "impassable" distances "between reader and text," as Mengestu and Cole both do.[21] Texts that purposefully offer only "limited access," she argues, "barricade against the rush of sentimental identification"—the impulse to understand, empathize, assimilate—that our most commonly exercised reading practices encourage, but that usually last for "barely as long as the read."[22] In limiting the potential for readers' identification with their characters, Mengestu and Cole make possible other forms of interaction between reader and text, between native and foreigner, between the state and individuals. In contrast with other contemporary immigrant writers, they refuse to translate difference to ease the reader's consumption of their work, or to represent (or cater to) specific ethnic groups. Instead, they not only create impassable distances but provoke a desire for intimacy that they then frustrate, manipulating the expectation that immigrant literature will provide "emotive transport."[23] Their goal, indeed, is to "produce enough desire for refusal to smart."[24]

Mengestu's novel produces this desire in part through the relationship between Helen and Isaac, which quickly becomes romantic and sexual, and then triangulates it to include the reader. With this relationship, Mengestu dramatizes the dynamic between migrant and so-called native, heightening the assumptions that obfuscate the ethical and political challenges of migration. For the reader, Isaac remains enigmatic, even opaque, but not wholly inaccessible—a willing reader can engage with him, but this intimacy has limits. Ultimately, the novel requires that the reader stand at a respectful distance, paying witness primarily to Isaac's elegy for the dead who perished in the failed revolution in Uganda.

In *Open City*, the narrator slyly seduces his target audience, the urbane and erudite reader. Critics have uniformly identified Julius as a twenty-first-century flaneur, "an aesthete who uniquely manages to engage with the realities of the modern city without fully surrendering to them, and who exemplifies a cosmopolitan ethos that thrives on intercultural curiosity and on the virtues of the aesthetic."[25] This posture, however, turns out to be a ruse to draw the reader into a simulated intimacy. The novel eventually delivers what, to the first-time reader, might feel like a sting: at its end, Julius is accused of rape. (On a second reading, one can find plenty of signs foreshadowing this revelation.) This ending brings home the full import of Julius's unavailability for identification, forcing the reader to reconsider the novel altogether. Cole's strategies for creating impassable distances between reader and text are thus more aggressive than Mengestu's: while the latter seeks to create respectful distances, the former confronts and agitates the reader.

By thwarting empathy with a suffering immigrant figure, both Mengestu and Cole prompt the reader to move restlessly instead—between subject positions, moments in history, and geographic spaces. This process widens the scope of migration from the personal to a vast web of interconnection that entangles us all, albeit from uneven positions of power, within the legacies of colonialism and the ongoing machinations of global capitalism.

These authors' formal strategies are part of what, throughout this book, I identify as *migrant aesthetics*, stylistic techniques the authors employ to enlarge the scale of migration beyond identitarian struggles with acculturation and toward a view of migration as a world-building phenomenon central to the development of human life. Given its scale and temporality, narrativizing this phenomenon is as challenging as representing climate change, which, in its "slow violence," occurring "gradually and out of sight" and "dispersed across time and space," is nearly impossible to represent in toto.[26] The fictions that I examine in this book approach the goal of representing the wide scope of migration by focusing on how European and American imperial histories have created the migration flows that shape our current political landscape. To access this broader perspective, we must contest the conventions by which we write and read fiction on migration.

Like other novels in this study, notably Aleksandar Hemon's *The Lazarus Project*, Valeria Luiselli's *Lost Children Archive*, and Junot Díaz's *The Brief Wondrous Life of Oscar Wao*, both *All Our Names* and *Open City* feature a writer searching for a way to bear witness to the global and historical suffering resulting in and produced through migration. For both Isaac and Julius, that search is intertwined with their own complicity in past crimes, suggesting how enmeshed each of us is in the broad and often brutal story of human migration.

"NOT A GHOST BUT A SKETCH OF A MAN": *ALL OUR NAMES*

In the middle of *All Our Names*, a father tells a story to a child who fears the dark. The story is about a city that "existed as long as one person dreamed of it each night":

> In the beginning, everyone kept some part of the city alive in their dreams—people dreamed of their garden, the flowers they had planted that they hoped would bloom in the spring, or the onions that were still not ripe enough to eat. They dreamed of their neighbor's house, which in most cases they believed was nicer than their own, or the streets they walked to work on every day, or, if they didn't have a job, then of the café where they spent hours drinking tea. (129)

After many years, the people tire of having to dream the same things; they want the freedom to fantasize and to imagine places and communities other than their own. At first, to maintain the city, they depend on a "few people who were willing to take on the extra responsibility" of dreaming about it. But eventually these volunteers tire too, and the people give the full responsibility to one man, who, over time, lets the city disappear. When the people complain, he decides to make them disappear too. And when the rest of the community try to "dream of the city again," they can't; they can only reconstruct it through memory, as it looked years before. They are thus stuck in nostalgia, and "in a world where seeing was power, nostalgia meant nothing" (130–131).

Reminiscent of Italo Calvino's *Invisible Cities* in its play between dream, fantasy, and reality, as well as its focus on civic life, this allegory highlights the conflict between the desire for personal freedom and the responsibilities of living in a collective. As in Calvino's stories, the tale reveals as much about its teller and its listener as it does about its own events. "I'm not inventing this for you," the father says to his son (129). Insofar as it is a cautionary tale about abdicating responsibility in the name of freedom, the story is, indeed, a parable rather than a simple invention. The boy listening becomes the man Helen knows as "Isaac." There are only two scenes with his father, who also remains nameless, and this one, when he tells his story, is the most extensive. His short tale goes a long way toward exposing the central conflict in Isaac's life prior to his first migration.

Later in the novel, we learn that Isaac is not originally from Uganda, having left his native Ethiopia because he felt imprisoned by both his family and his nation. In a rare moment of disclosure, he tells Helen:

> When I was born, I had thirteen names. Each name was from a different generation, beginning with my father and going back from him. I was the first one in our village to have thirteen names. Our family was considered blessed to have such a history. Everyone in our family had been born and died on that land. We fed it with our bodies longer than any other, and it was assumed I would do the same, and so would my children. I knew from a very young age, though, that I would never want that. I felt as if I had been born into a prison ... I was no one when I arrived in Kampala; it was exactly what I wanted. (179)

For Isaac, migration is thus initially a form of escape, stemming from a desire to shed his names. But, as in his father's allegory, this longing for freedom paradoxically brings new forms of imprisonment. In Kampala, Isaac becomes involved in a revolution headed by a man named Joseph Mabira (whose last name Isaac eventually adopts). Mengestu dispenses with historical specificity: we don't learn about the ideological underpinnings of the rebellion; we know only that it starts as a movement to liberate poor people from oppression but soon disintegrates into a series of murderous attacks against those same people. During the revolution, Isaac bears witness not only to his namesake's transformation into a brutal man but also to the acts of mass murder that he leads others to commit. At one point, Isaac is forced to bury Mabira's victims in a mass grave. In another instance, he delivers arms to seven young boys who are forced to fight in Mabira's revolution, and who are ultimately sacrificed in the bloodshed that ensues.

Isaac's dream of escape from his names suggests a vision of cosmopolitanism as detachment, an eschewing of "roots" for a purported freedom, one that turns out to be an illusion. Without consciously choosing a new set of loyalties or new ways of connecting to a collective, Isaac becomes, willy-nilly, a participant in murderous violence. Mengestu has deliberately constructed a character without a broad perspective or clear objectives to underscore contingency. Isaac does not know the political landscape of Uganda, and "he can barely understand what's happening to him" as his namesake and the other rebel leaders "degenerate from liberators to monsters."[27] His narrative produces a "prevailing sense" that he, and even the movement's leaders, "might be shot at any time."[28] Mengestu wants his readers to imagine what it might be like to search—with limited understanding—for freedom, and to find chaos and terror instead.

In the novel's opening pages, we learn that Isaac has vague hopes of becoming a writer and has made a pilgrimage to Uganda that was originally inspired by the 1962 literary conference in Makerere. "I read about it in a week-old newspaper that had finally made its way to our village," he tells us, adding that the "conference gave shape to my adolescent ambitions, which until then consisted solely of leaving" (4). We also learn that the conference occurred ten years before Isaac sets out, and that he "read the same Victorian novels a dozen times" because he had access to nothing else (4). When he finally arrives in Kampala, he takes the nickname "Langston," after Langston Hughes, who was a guest of honor at the conference. But Isaac also confesses that he "never read anything by [Hughes], and wasn't even certain that he was a poet" (41).

Despite this ignorance, the brutality that Isaac witnesses and in which he becomes complicit takes him to the heart of the literary-political debate surrounding Hughes's essay "The Negro Artist and the Racial Mountain." First published in *The Nation* in 1926, the essay argues that an artist has a responsibility to the collective to define, build, and sustain community.[29] The Makerere conference focused on similar issues, staging debates about what criteria should define African literature and what relationship it ought to have to the social and political realms, especially at a time when many African countries were on the cusp of political independence. Ironically, while Isaac is attracted to both Hughes and the conference, he leaves Ethiopia imagining that the enterprise of becoming an author necessitates cutting himself off from the social and political realms. To his naïve mind, authorship means leaving the anonymity of his village for a famous career in which he can be "surrounded by like-minded men in the heart of what had to be the continent's greatest city" (4).

His experiences in Kampala teach him otherwise. Isaac's life there consists of bare survival at the edges of shantytowns and being subjected to unrelenting surveillance, for he is, like all the city's citizens, considered a potential threat to the government. The ground beneath him always seems to shift. While walking through a neighborhood whose "rules and recent history" he does not know, he carries a pro-government paper—which he buys with his last coin, to seem to adhere to the rules of the regime—only to be beaten severely by anti-government men (89). "My memory of what happened after the paper was taken has never returned," he writes, "[and] if parts ever did start to emerge, I would do whatever was necessary to keep them buried. There's a coin-sized circle in the back of my head where no hair will ever grow again, along with three thin, distinct scar lines along the right side of my scalp" (90). Soon after this attack, Isaac flees to the United States with a fake passport that was originally meant to save his namesake but that, in an act of friendship, the latter bequeaths to him.

Because Mengestu intertwines Isaac's narrative with Helen's, we read about the beating just when Helen is beginning to wonder who Isaac might be, beyond the sketch of a man she has been trying to fill in with exotic fantasy. Isaac is initially a mystery to Helen, a folder that contains only "a single loose leaf of paper . . . There was no month or date of birth, only a year. His place of birth was listed only as Africa, with no country or city. The only solid fact was his name, Isaac Mabira, but even that was no longer substantial: any name could have filled that slot, and nothing would have changed" (98). If Isaac is an enigma to Helen—someone "made of almost nothing, not a ghost but a sketch of a man [that she] was trying hard to fill in"—he is only slightly more accessible to the reader, who is privy only to his account of the events that eventually forced him to emigrate to America (21).

All Our Names' split narrative forces the reader to envision the migrant figure in two dramatically different contexts, seeing him both as the immigrant Helen barely knows and as a young man amid a revolution. Initially, Helen embodies a negative model of relationality, as she fills in her sketch of Isaac with racialized fantasies. Through her perspective, we see Isaac as a laconic immigrant with whom she develops a romantic relationship, but we don't know how and why Isaac falls for Helen, for the sections that he narrates focus solely on the past relationship between him and his namesake. Mengestu capitalizes on this dramatic irony: readers see the limits of Helen's vision because they have more access to Isaac's life than she does. Yet readers, too, have only partial access to Isaac. Helen's narrative constantly interrupts the story of Isaac's background, which itself Mengestu delivers only through halting, limited details, and acts as a steady reminder of the perils of overidentification.

Though at first Isaac is simply an exotic enigma for Helen, sexually attractive because of his foreign status and race, over the course of the novel she becomes aware of the naivete and racial arrogance underwriting her desire.[30] At the start of their relationship, she describes her town and the impact she thinks Isaac can make on it:

> We weren't divided like the South and had nothing to do with any of the large cities in the North. We were exactly what geography had made us: middle of the road, never bitterly segregated, but with lines dividing black from white all over town, whether in neighborhoods, churches, schools, or parks. We lived semi-peacefully apart, like a married couple in separate wings of a large house. That was the image I had in mind during breakfast when I decided something different had to be done. Change! It seemed to be everywhere except Laurel. (33)

The "something" Helen has in mind is taking Isaac to a diner that, for all intents and purposes, is still segregated, thus using him to force her community to "change." The plan, unsurprisingly, backfires, even more so since she does not inform Isaac beforehand of her intent. Her failure becomes a watershed moment for Helen, who realizes that her romantic conception of "separate but equal" race relations in America ("like a married couple") is woefully naïve.

If the novel treated only this side of the relationship between the two characters, we would not be wrong to label it trite or, worse, pernicious in its reaffirmation of Helen's privilege, for Isaac would then exist only as the catalyst for her growth. It would mean, too, that Mengestu's innovative decision to narrate migration from the perspective of the "host" would use the immigrant figure simply to focus myopically on American culture. But the sections narrated by Isaac not only literally interrupt Helen's account—they typographically cut her narrative into sections—but also require the reader to form a separate relationship with Isaac, one that differs drastically from Helen's approach. The contrast between the way Helen sees Isaac as an immigrant in her community and the way that Mengestu allows the reader to see him also dramatizes the gap between Isaac's consciousness and the way he is perceived from the outside. Thanks to this gap, we can see, at least partially, past the stereotype that Helen initially projects onto Isaac.[31]

If Helen sees Isaac as a sketch of a man, the reader might, given the violence and grief that pervades his narrative, see him only as a victim of brutality. But Mengestu, when writing the book, knew that Isaac's story would be read against the explosion of child-soldier narratives in the first decade of the twenty-first century. As I showed in the Introduction, he also knew that immigrant suffering is susceptible to being "essentialized, banalized, or relativized" because it has come to be a seminal but little-understood feature of immigrant writing.[32] For these reasons, in *All Our Names* he sets a trap for the reader: he endows Isaac's story with aspects of the child-soldier, refugee, and immigrant narratives, thereby offering familiarity, but then frustrates these narratives' "familiar satisfactions without necessarily offering new ones."[33]

Yogita Goyal has shown how narratives by (ex-)child soldiers tend to present their authors as "both exemplary and exceptional," flattening out the violence experienced and meted out by these figures in the name of emphasizing the (ex-)soldiers' rehabilitation.[34] This emphasis has as its goal "the moral education of the Western reader over the political agency of the victim": it offers the illusory comfort of sentimentality, of "feeling over reason," by casting the child soldier as an "object of sympathy, available for rescue through therapy for a new life in the United States."[35] While Isaac is not a child abducted and forced into war, his narrative features similar war-torn conditions and casts him in the blurry boundary between refugee and immigrant.

Madelaine Hron has argued that, despite the frequent overlap of voluntary and involuntary migration, sociological and legal literature insists on distinguishing between refugees and immigrants by focusing on levels of suffering.[36] Refugees "are compelled to feel grateful" for having been saved from painful situations and are encouraged to amplify their suffering to be granted asylum.[37] By contrast, immigrants are encouraged to minimize the suffering of acculturation because it is presented as a necessary condition of successful integration; this is why "the immigrant narrative risks being conflated with other prototypical narratives of suffering, whether it be the classic American 'rags to riches' story or the Christian narrative of redemption."[38]

All Our Names does not feature Isaac as an exemplary and exceptional figure but rather as one of many bloodstained men, two of whose names he bears. Nor does his narrative focus on acculturation or offer a redemptive telos. Yet, because his story unfolds in conditions similar enough to the child soldier turned refugee, and because Helen frames him as an immigrant, we can find in his tale layers of allusions to those narrative conventions. This is especially the case because Isaac's tale charts the process by which he becomes a writer; in choosing this path for his protagonist, Mengestu wryly revises one of the conventions of child-soldier narratives, which, like the genre of slave narratives, typically present the acquisition of writing as synonymous with freedom.

"Child soldier fictions," argues Yogita Goyal, "mimic the form of the slave narrative" and match their sentimental mode; those fictions move from abduction and torture toward rescue and equate "the acquisition of self with the right to write, to own property, including the property of one's own name and narrative." This equating of freedom with writing, adds Goyal, allows for a substitution: "the white reader for the traumatized slave, immigrant life in the United States as redemption for the slave past."[39] It is precisely this equivalence that Mengestu undermines. Isaac's actualization as a writer does not constitute his transcendence of trauma; if anything, it allows him to continue dwelling in a painful past, a process that is itself riddled with struggle.

All Our Names, in its very title, signals its function as an elegy both for the nameless dead in Uganda and for unknown immigrants like Isaac. In this respect, the moment in which Isaac is forced to bury the victims of the failed revolution is crucial for understanding the novel as a whole:

> The youngest boys were sent to dig the grave while the rest of us formed a chain from the back of the lorry to the ground, where the bodies were stacked one on top of another. I was in the bed with the bodies—the second link in the chain, with a man much older than me whose thin arms were still defined by the muscles of his youth. Like all the other men, he performed his job in silence, without pity . . . He took the legs and I took the arms of each body passed to us, which meant that, whether I wanted to or not, I had to stare into every face . . . After the fifteenth or twentieth, I decided to think of them as a single body named Adam. In my head, I said, "You were a brave soldier, Adam . . . Your mother and father will miss you . . . You should have stayed in your village, Adam . . . You had no reason to come here . . . You could have gone to school . . . Adam." And when I ran out of alternate endings, I simply thought, "Adam, Adam, Adam." (229–230)

Isaac willfully suppresses the most brutal aspects of his experiences in Uganda, yet he provides an elegiac account of the many nameless individuals whom he buries. The American sections of the novel contrast with and heighten the pathos of these memories and make the novel's readers witnesses to Isaac's elegy. In this way, though it is in some respects a refugee story, Isaac's narrative shifts the focus away from his own trauma and toward the dead; though an immigrant story, it is ultimately a memorial rather than an autobiographical account of his acculturation in America.

Unlike the Helen sections of the novel, those narrated by Isaac trace the process of his becoming a writer; the implication, indeed, is that his elegy is the realization of Isaac's artistic aspiration. His narrative, moreover, is both a form of mourning and a means of contrition. During Mabira's revolution, when he is tasked with delivering guns to young boys, he memorizes the map of a section of Kampala to find his way to the house where they wait. In doing so, Isaac invents a "second life" for the city and its streets (168), imagining himself "walking along each one," as if he were living among its people, whom he imagines as characters in a fiction: "There was a street where my girlfriend lived, another that I walked down every Friday afternoon on my way home from work. I had family members—brothers, aunts, grandparents—that I visited regularly, scattered throughout the neighborhood" (168). Isaac here invokes but ironizes the figure of the flaneur as he wanders through a city, detached, using it as fodder for his imagination. If in his father's allegory people must dream their city into being, in Isaac's fiction it is he who gives them a "second life," yet in doing so he is condemning the real people of the town to death. Far from enabling the detachment of the flaneur, Isaac's meanderings serve a bloody purpose. Similarly, though one of the dreams motivating Isaac's first migration was to be a writer, his first act as an author is to make up a world that facilitates his complicity in bloodshed.

After the scene with the child soldiers, he witnesses a village murder a group of refugees, while he is himself hiding among the victims. The villagers kill about a hundred people, "half were children," many of them "men and women [who] were injured," because they are seen as a threat, "both foreign and desperate and twice as dangerous as a result" (219–220). "I had no names," notes Isaac, describing the slaughter, "not even of the village, which was too small to have existed on any map" (222). Afterward, he tries, for the first time, to write something down as a way of marking the killings: "I tried to write down what had happened. I thought of counting the dead, but I was too far away to do so. I tried next to describe one of the bodies, but all I could see was death—no eyes, no face, just a blank emptiness I didn't have the stomach to look at closely" (221). In the end, he makes a sketch of his escape route from the village, even though he knows it is "far from poetry, less than a journal, and worthless as history" (222). As a refugee and immigrant, Isaac knows what it feels like to be looked on as "both foreign and desperate and twice as dangerous as a result." He knows, too, that his own escape route from death's grip is lined with the bodies of the dead; and he knows his hands are not clean.

Helen's account of Isaac's life as an immigrant strikes ironic notes in conjunction with Isaac's narrative of his past. She muses that "being occasionally called 'boy' or 'nigger,' as he was, didn't compare to having no one who knew him before he had come here, who could remind him, simply by being there, that he was someone else entirely" (22). But the reader knows that Isaac cannot simply use his anonymity to run away from his guilt both for his participation in Mabira's crimes and for having survived, unlike the countless dead. Helen's naïve sense that being racialized in America does not compare to being reminded of his past only reveals her own shortcomings. She does not know the first thing about either experience and yet has the arrogance to compare them. But Mengestu gives her character an arc of growth.

Eventually, she learns to respect her limited access to Isaac's interior life, and he begins to share some of his past with her. Intimacy between strangers in this novel is not produced through the forms of recognition often thought to be facilitated by fiction but, rather, becomes a possibility predicated on mutual respect. Nor does the novel offer a neat and happy conclusion. Instead, it leaves open the question of whether the intimacy will develop into a full-fledged relationship; the novel ends with the future of the couple in suspense. The alternating narratives in the novel never connect fully, just as the characters never know enough about each other to fully bridge the gaps between them.

While *All Our Names* presents forms of relationality between strangers that have the potential to reframe the ethics of migration, the novel's power is limited by its historical vagueness. The novel operates in a fabulist mode, best exemplified by Isaac's father's allegory. Yet this approach, which limits how specifically Mengestu can represent Africa, also gives its readers an out: they can choose to ignore the novel's referentiality altogether and thus decline the responsibility of fully engaging with the interpersonal ethics of migration that the novel exemplifies. In contemplating their personal responsibility to people whose pasts and places of origin they do not know, the novel's readers, guided by the novel's allegorical style, can entertain answers at an abstract level, leaving aside the political struggles that have shaped both Isaac's and Helen's lives and, by extension, the novel's readers themselves. But those political struggles are specific to the history of New World slavery and European colonialism in Africa and are part and parcel of how the novel's central question—the extent of our responsibility to each other—needs to be considered.

Cole's *Open City*, by contrast, does not give either its characters or its readers an out.

ILLUMINATED SHADOW: *OPEN CITY*

Julius, the narrator of *Open City*, offers a "combination of confession and reticence" that makes him, as James Wood puts it, an "enigma of an illuminated shadow."[40] This phrase captures much of what is immediately alluring about the novel. Julius may not reveal much about himself, but since he has a keen eye and an erudite and sensitive mind, the reader is likely to follow his migrations with interest and pleasure. Julius, in Wood's words, "has a well-stocked mind: he thinks about social and critical theory, about art (Chardin, Velázquez, John Brewster), and about music (Mahler, Peter Maxwell Davies, Judith Weir), and he has interesting books within easy reach—Roland Barthes's 'Camera Lucida,' Peter Altenberg's 'Telegrams of the Soul,' Tahar Ben Jelloun's 'The Last Friend,' Kwame Anthony Appiah's 'Cosmopolitanism.' "[41] In this respect he is excellent company, especially for readers who share his intellectual and aesthetic sensibility.

Though he may be an enigma, Julius draws the reader into what, borrowing a term he offhandedly provides, we can call "twinned solitude."[42] That is, he is a solitary and opaque figure, while the reader in turn (by necessity) is anonymous to him and occupied with the solitary experience of reading. Yet the two share the references and narratives that Julius's peregrinations make available. He introduces the phrase while crossing a park: "I walked under the arbor of elms, passing by rows of concrete chess tables, which were oases of order and invitations to a twinned solitude."[43] Sitting across a chess table from one another, two people, taking pleasure in private thought, can accomplish the paradoxical: sharing solitude while engaged in a common endeavor. Since the novel simulates a diary, it serves as a bridge connecting Julius's reflective moments of writing with the reader's silent moments of reading.

But what are we to make of the fact that most of the fragments of history and experience in Julius's narrative involve the dispossession and persecution of racialized peoples? At one point, Julius goes to listen to a Polish poet, who opens by saying, "I don't want to talk about poetry tonight. I want to talk about persecution, if you will permit a poet this license." Then he asks, "What can we understand about the roots of persecution, particularly when the target of this persecution is a tribe or race or cultural group?" (43). The discrete narratives and allusions in the novel orbit around histories of persecution and stand strikingly at odds with the civility implied by Julius's posture of a cosmopolitan flaneur. A visit to one of his old professors allows Julius to record the professor's account of his life in Japanese internment camps; mention of a patient's book on Cornelis van Tienhoven, the secretary of the Dutch East India Company and a ruthless murderer of the Canarsie Indians of Long Island, leads to a contemplation of Native American genocide; a casual spotting of Octavia Butler's *Kindred* (1979) in the subway next to someone reading the *Wall Street Journal* places together two very different indices of slavery—a (neo)slave narrative written by a black woman and a symbol of economic power built on slave labor (as well as a reference to the place where New York's slave market once stood). These are but a few examples of the historical citations embedded in Julius's meditations on art, from the classical music he listens to at home and at concerts, to the paintings and photography he sees in museums and galleries, to the literature he reflects upon as he writes about his restless ventures in New York and Brussels.

For critic Pieter Vermeulen, the problem with viewing Julius as a flaneur is that he fails to be even minimally transformed by either the intense aesthetic experiences that he relates or the accounts of suffering that he transmits to the reader. While the flaneur posture entails a "productive alienation" (i.e., a detachment that produces perspective),[44] it also calls for an aesthetic and/or empathetic engagement with the world being observed. Julius, however, only appears to be so engaged, for he remains fundamentally unchanged throughout the novel. Cole has created his protagonist in this way with an acute awareness of the limits of literary cosmopolitanism. Indeed, as Vermeulen writes, the novel "time and again conveys its concern that the aesthetic does not have the power to initiate significant, empathetic encounters with the diverse experiences it recounts for its readers."[45] *Open City* "insistently denies its readers the illusion that imaginative transports can stand in for real global change."[46] Vermeulen reads Julius's disassociation as the principal means through which Cole critiques literary cosmopolitanism: the character's detachment reproduces how readers consume stories about other people's suffering without being profoundly affected by what they read, thus showing, by negative example, the limits of relying on either aesthetic or empathetic forms of engagement.

The novel achieves this result most forcefully through a counterintuitive tactic: it spins the reader away from the character through whom those narratives are conveyed. The penultimate chapter of the novel offers an astonishing twist, when Moji, a friend's sister whom Julius knew back in Nigeria, accuses him of having raped her. This is when, as Vermeulen rightly notes, Julius conclusively loses any potential for "readerly empathy."[47] In fact, it constitutes a moment that I would characterize, following Doris Sommer via Toni Morrison, as a slap to the reader.[48] With this accusation, the twinned solitude that the reader has shared with Julius ruptures dramatically.

The revelation comes filtered through Julius, who reports Moji's account but grants her minimal narrative voice and omits his own response. Even more disturbingly, the novel then goes on for another chapter with no mention of the accusation or of Moji herself, making the incident more conspicuous while denying the reader a resolution to the glaring ethical problem that the novel has raised at the last minute: who is this narrator with whom the reader has been communing about art?

If Julius embodies the "enigma of an illuminated shadow" for most of the novel, in that moment of accusation and thereafter he becomes a threatening shadow, the ultimate unreliable narrator. Julius has betrayed the novel's readers, seducing them through his flaneur sophistication and purported sensitivity to human suffering—implying that the reader and the narrator mirror each other—and then revealing not only a deep chasm between them but, even more alarming, the potential for a complicity between them. Moji's accusation also raises the specter of xenophobia and racism, as Julius in this new guise, despite his erudition and social standing, seems to represent the immigrant figure as a (potential) criminal, invoking a centuries-old racist stereotype of black men as rapacious sexual deviants. Cole raises this specter not to affirm it but to agitate the audience into self-examination, forcing them to reevaluate their reading experience. In effect, Cole sends the reader back to the beginning of the novel, which, given the twist at the end, becomes a narrative that demands a second reading.

What significance does this late twist have for the fragments of history and accounts of suffering that the novel presents? Moji's accusation and its repercussions deny readers an empathetic protagonist through which they might be able to process the stories of suffering embedded in the novel. At the same time, the accusation makes deeply problematic the detached attitude that Julius exhibits toward those who suffer; indeed, like Helen's initially sentimental way of reading Isaac in *All Our Names*, Julius's attitude becomes a negative model for the reader. By the end of *Open City*, tasked with reading so many accounts of suffering but deprived of Julius as a trustworthy guide, readers *must* make their own meaning out of the fragments and stories, factoring in the fact that Julius, the medium through which readers have accessed them, is not only deeply flawed but also potentially both a victim and a perpetrator of violence.

Recall the Polish poet whose lecture Julius attends. The glare of the stage lights bounces off his glasses, "making it appear as though he had a large white patch over each eye" (43). Cole here invokes the classical trope of the blind poet going back to Homer. A few pages earlier, Julius stands in front of works by the early American painter John Brewster Jr., who was deaf. While references to disabled people appear sporadically throughout the novel (in ways that suggest analogies between disability and social liminality), the two invocations of the figure of the artist as either blind or deaf imply that Julius, while presenting a collage of others' loss and dispossession, is figuratively blind and deaf to his own crime.

More precisely, he does not remember his crime. Julius first re-encounters Moji halfway through the novel, but he does not recognize her and has trouble remembering her. "She appeared (apparition was precisely what came to mind) to me in a grocery store . . . It was clear that she expected me to remember her. I didn't" (156). Julius tellingly frames the encounter as an instance in which an "irruptive sense of things past" cuts into his "solidified" account of who he has been (156). The scene following this event shows Julius suffering a seemingly banal crisis of memory: he forgets his checkbook for a meeting with his accountant, as well as his PIN at an ATM (161). He also feels "subject to a nervous condition" that he later links, in the form of a haunting nightmare, to losing his memory altogether: "I imagined I had forgotten not just that number but all numbers, as well as all names, and why I was even there on Wall Street in the first place. I got up from the bed and checked the oven" (166). As other evidence in the novel reveals, this nightmare—with its macabre reference to the oven—turns out to be representative of Julius's experience of personal memory: he pathologically blocks out memories of his past.

But the novel makes it impossible for the reader to trace the source of his pathology, since we know so little about Julius. Vermeulen argues that Julius ought to be seen not as a flaneur but as a *fugueur*, a "shadowy figure from the history of psychiatry, who emerged in the late nineteenth century as a direct counterfigure to the *flâneur*." The *fugueur* "was a traumatised, compulsive walker whose journey was 'less a voyage of self-discovery than an attempt to eliminate self.'"[49] *Open City* undeniably presents Julius as a traumatized figure, yet it would be wrong to dismiss Julius's accounts of human suffering solely as screens to hide his own experiences. Rather, in making Julius an unreliable medium for readers to use when processing the novel's narratives of suffering, Cole demands that readers employ their own analytical capabilities to situate those narratives in a broader historical context, within which they attain meaning but are not explained away. Unable to trust Julius's guidance, readers must trace the patterns, juxtapositions, and contexts, both literary and extraliterary, of the accounts that Julius makes available.

Cole creates a weblike set of stories that intersect across a broad range of historical timeframes, threaded together by the narrative structure of the novel. A palimpsest, when viewed from afar, appears as layers superimposed upon one another. As a narrative, however, at least in Cole's novel—and in Sebald's *The Rings of Saturn*—those layers are connected instead in what one might call a hyperlink mode, which ultimately produces a web. Cole has clearly taken his cue from Sebald's novel, which is organized as "a series of concentric narrative circles that move around a gravitational center formed by the first-person narrator."[50] As Paul Sheehan argues, these circles "reshuffle linear chronology" and offer history "as palimpsest, or as a montage of match-cuts, in which heterogeneous elements cross paths to produce new affiliations, reformatting the causal logic of narrative history into a constellation of incongruous, semi-surreal image-relationships."[51] Cole similarly, and self-consciously, invokes the palimpsest as the mode through which Julius views his surroundings, reshuffling the linear chronology of forced and voluntary migration.

While the focus of *Open City* is primarily New York and, by extension, the United States, and its connection to other countries via neoimperialism and immigration, five of the novel's twenty-one chapters take place in Brussels, which Julius visits with a vague plan to reconnect with his maternal grandmother, who is purportedly living there. The Brussels chapters place *Open City*'s focus on immigration within a broader context, for Julius reveals Brussels to be, like other European cities, a city of immigrants suffering from xenophobia and outright racism in the aftermath of the early twenty-first-century terrorist attacks in the United States and Europe (97). The choice of Brussels is also deliberate, one assumes, in light of the intricate intertextual connections between Cole's novel and Sebald's *The Rings of Saturn*, which highlights Brussels's deep connections to one of the darkest chapters in European colonialism.

Sebald turns to Brussels in the context of discussing Joseph Conrad's life and work, in particular his experiences in the Congo, from which *Heart of Darkness* sprang. As Sebald notes, Belgium ruthlessly exploited the Congo's "inexhaustible wealth" through trading companies that drew "legendary profits" via a "system of slave labour" that decimated the indigenous population; "those who were taken there from other parts of Africa or from overseas died in droves" from disease and "physical exhaustion."[52] Conrad visited Brussels after witnessing the horrors of the Congo, and Sebald imagines him seeing the capital of the "Kingdom of Belgium, with its ever more bombastic buildings, as a sepulchral monument erected over a hecatomb of black bodies" (122). Even now, writes Sebald in 1995, "one sees in Belgium a distinctive ugliness, dating from the time when the Congo colony was exploited without restraint and manifested in the macabre atmosphere" of parts of the city (122).

Nearly two decades later, Julius in *Open City* notes that it is "easy to have the wrong idea about Brussels": given its centrality "to the formation of the European Union," one might assume that it is "a new city, built, or at least expanded, expressly for that purpose," and yet "Brussels is old—a peculiar European oldness, which is manifested in stone" (97). While Julius does not ponder the history inscribed in that old stone,[53] as he does when visiting sites in New York, the intertextual links between Sebald, Conrad, and Cole contextualize Julius's peregrinations in an expanded web that joins together migration, race, and empire. This web challenges myopic and presentist emphases on immigration "crises," revealing the intimate, ongoing connection of immigration to the rise and maintenance of capital and empire.

Earlier, visiting Ground Zero in New York, Julius notes that before the Twin Towers "had gone up, there had been a bustling network of little streets . . . [which] had been obliterated in the 1960s . . . and all were forgotten now":

> Gone, too, was the old Washington Market, the active piers, the fishwives, the Christian Syrian enclave that was established here in the late 1800s. The Syrians, the Lebanese, and other people from the Levant had been pushed across the river to Brooklyn, where they'd set down roots on Atlantic Avenue and in Brooklyn Heights. And, before that? What Lenape paths lay buried beneath the rubble? The site was a palimpsest, as was all the city, written, erased, rewritten. There had been communities here before Columbus ever

set sail, before Verrazano anchored his ships in the narrows, or the black Portuguese slave trader Esteban Gómez sailed up the Hudson; human beings had lived here, built homes, and quarreled with their neighbors long before the Dutch ever saw a business opportunity in the rich furs and timber of the island and its calm bay. (59)

Before detailing the layers of history inscribed upon the site, Julius notes how much it has become "a metonym of its disaster," seen only in terms of its uppermost layer: "a tourist who once asked me how he could get to 9/11: not the site of the events of 9/11 but to 9/11 itself, the date petrified into broken stones" (52). He suggests, too, how the location has become one of the "various tourist sites in lower Manhattan," which together create a circus of the city's histories, indexed by its landmarks (58). By contrast, Julius's view of the city as a palimpsest, his readings of the layers inscribed on its sites, brings into both his and the reader's consciousness not only its long, multicultural history of migration but also its precolonial life. "What Lenape paths lay buried beneath the rubble?" he asks, moving our attention back to a time before Native Americans were forced from the island, and before Africans were forced to the New World in chains. At the same time, he underscores New York's role in the War on Terror by choosing Ground Zero as the site of focus, highlighting how central forced migration and genocide have been in the history of empire.

At the beginning of *Open City*, Julius describes his habit of watching bird migrations, slowing down the narrative pace by detailing the species of birds he watches, and wonders if his own peregrinations might be connected to them. And they are, insofar as Julius's "aimless wandering" facilitates his reading of the city as a palimpsest of history and provides occasion for myriad casual observations, many of which are of immigrant figures who appear peripherally (3). Walking through Bowling Green Park, he notes that it was used in the "seventeenth century for the execution of paupers and slaves," while across Battery Park he sees a group of Chinese women practicing Tai Chi, two *erhu* players, and a singer, all performances that he describes with the air of someone taking a video (164). Soon afterward, he sits on a bench next to a man who is "dressed in a linen suit, with carefully polished shoes, and a straw hat: summer clothes on a winter's day. His shirt was yellow and his tie dark brown ... His mustache was white and neatly trimmed. The man read *El Diario*, seriously and slowly" (164–166). Like the descriptions of the Chinese performers, this snapshot description of someone we know nothing about except what we can infer (a Caribbean soul insisting through the cold on the warmth of other suns?) is part of a series of images that accrue as Julius creates a collage of New York's immigrant life. This collage makes immigration a constant, if sometimes understated, refrain that Julius subtly links to the loss and dispossession at the core of the history of the United States.

Sitting next to the man in the linen suit, Julius thinks of one of his patients, a Native American woman who wrote a book on Cornelis van Tienhoven and who becomes so depressed from writing about genocide—"I can't pretend it isn't about my life," she tells Julius—that she commits suicide (27). Julius has a sudden urge to tell the man next to him about his patient, but he does not. Instead, he sits in silence, looking "across the water" and "southward, toward the Statue of Liberty" (166). The "glimmering green figurine of the Statue of Liberty" emerges while Julius's thoughts are engrossed in instances of the greedy accumulation of capital at the expense of human rights during slavery (163). He describes the massive profit that merchants and bankers in nineteenth-century New York accumulated from the slave trade by "outfitting, insuring, and launching" slave ships, and—as in the case of Moses Taylor, a banker who "helped fund the war effort in the Union side"—by "brokering the sale of Cuban sugar in the port of New York, investing the profits of the sugar planters, facilitating the processing of the cargo at the New York City Customs House, and helping finance the acquisition of a 'labor force'" (163). This juxtaposition of the Statue of Liberty with the Custom House highlights the fact that New York City, and by extension the United States, has amassed the economic power to serve as a beacon for "the tired, the poor" by exploiting slave labor, a fact that makes deeply ironic the freedom supposedly symbolized by the "Mother of Exiles." Julius earlier describes the statue as a "fluorescent green fleck," a phrase that anticipates the "glimmering green" in his vision while he thinks about the green dollar notes that bankers and merchants bled out of the slave trade. Julius also muses on Ellis Island, "the focus of so many myths," and notes dryly that "it had been built too late for those early Africans—who weren't immigrants in any case—and it had been closed too soon to mean anything to the later Africans" like him and the other immigrants with whom he interacts (54–55).

In the closing passage of the novel, Cole again invokes the Statue of Liberty, presenting two apparently incongruent images. One is of Julius in what seems to be a classic scene from an immigrant narrative, though placed at the end and not, per convention, at the start of the tale. He is on a boat in New York's harbor approaching the statue, seeing her as millions of immigrants might have, first as a "faint green in the mist, then very quickly massive and towering" (258). He notes that, although the statue had "symbolic value right from the beginning, until 1902, it was a working lighthouse, the biggest in the country," with a burning flame that fatally disoriented large numbers of birds. Julius then, as he has done before, provides details of these birds—their kind and number, the use that was made of their carcasses (at first for profit, then for science)—slowing the reading experience once again with this image of mass death. The novel is thus bookended by images of avian and human migration, invoking an analogy that is well established. But the sacrifice of the birds further recalls the moments in the novel where Julius contemplates the Statue of Liberty while thinking about the forced migration of enslaved Africans. The novel ends, therefore, with an "incongruous, semi-surreal" image that is oddly but tellingly linked to the millions who were sacrificed for the "glimmering green" that made New York rich.[54]

Throughout the novel, Cole is careful to place those countless sacrifices within a larger historical and temporal context. Earlier in the book, Julius walks by the U.S. Citizen and Immigration Services building in downtown New York and observes the long line of immigrants: he perceives their "nervous anticipation," notes the "unusual number of interracial couples," and marvels at their many different backgrounds—Bangladeshi, Vietnamese, Hispanic. Soon he gravitates toward a patch of grass nearby, drawn by a "curious shape" that turns out to be a monument for an African burial ground, now marked by a "tiny plot," though in the seventeenth and eighteenth centuries the ground had spread over "some six acres" (219–220). Again, Julius draws the reader's attention to the deep layers of history inscribed upon the city, and to the "bodies of some fifteen to twenty thousand blacks, most of them slaves," that had been interred in an area once on the outskirts of the city (220). The city was built over the dead, but, as Julius puts it, the "dead returned when, in 1991, construction of a building ... brought human remains to the surface," remains that bore "traces of suffering:

blunt trauma, grievous bodily harm" and also of burial traditions "perhaps retained from the Congo, or from along the West African coast, from which so many people had been captured and sold into slavery" (220–221).

Two subtle details in this description connect the suffering of the enslaved to that of immigrants in subsequent eras: the monument at the burial ground "was designed by a Haitian artist," and the uniforms of the security guards at the nearby immigration bureau bear the name of a private company that controls immigrants at a detention center visited by Julius earlier in the novel. The first detail signals back to Pierre Toussaint, a nineteenth-century former slave turned philanthropist, originally from Haiti, whom Julius earlier encounters in a supernatural moment among "the underground catacombs of Penn Station" (70). The second detail links back to the story of Saidu, an undocumented immigrant from Liberia whose plight Julius hears about just before he introduces Pierre Toussaint. Cole thus interlaces multiple timeframes and geographies that share the history of slavery as a common denominator, connecting the forced migration of Africans with the struggles of contemporary black immigrants.

Such connections, many of which depend on the reader's extraliterary knowledge, are fluid and suggestive rather than narrowly drawn; Cole's priority is to maintain the integrity of each historical referent while suggesting links within a larger network. Toussaint, for instance, is never mentioned by his full name, though he delivers an account of his life that begins as a tale of immigration but slowly becomes a slave narrative. Julius encounters him at a shoeshine store in the arcade of shops in Penn Station, and his reference to "Pierre from Haiti" makes it easy to miss the fact that he is a historical figure. Yet, as Pierre takes over the narrative voice, we learn that he was brought to New York by a Mr. and Mrs. Bérard to escape the terror of Dutty Boukman, that he sought his freedom only after his masters died, and that he eventually married a woman named Juliette (also a historical figure), with whom he later founded an orphanage for black children. Cole's intertwining of Pierre's narratives of migration and enslavement is so subtle, the historical allusions so delicately placed (and also strategically omitted: Toussaint, for example, named himself after the famous Haitian leader, but his avatar in *Open City* does not mention this fact), that it is possible to miss—as at least one reviewer has—the fact that Pierre is a ghost, who appears to Julius one afternoon when he feels time becoming "elastic" and hears "voices cut out of the past into the present" (74).

Julius describes this apparition without commentary, immediately after a segment devoted to the story of Saidu, who has spent over two years at a detention center after making an arduous journey from Liberia to Morocco, then to Spain and Portugal, and eventually to New York, where he is apprehended while using a fake passport. Again, the reader must provide the extraliterary context through which Saidu's story resonates with the ghostly appearance of Pierre Toussaint. Unlike Toussaint, Saidu is a fictional character whose story touches upon both the Liberian Civil Wars and the American Colonization Society, which founded Liberia to "repatriate" free African Americans. Saidu is a refugee from a war that displaced over half a million people, in a country founded to solve the "problem" that free blacks posed to American slaveholders, for their presence served as "a standing perpetual excitement" to the enslaved.[55] Supported by both pro- and anti-abolitionists, who shared the belief that "free blacks could not be integrated into white America,"[56] the American Colonization Society was fiercely criticized by black leaders, Frederick Douglass among them, who saw the Liberian colonization plan as "tantamount to exile in a foreign country" and who "resented being deprived of free U.S. citizenship and the rewards of their own toil in their homeland."[57]

Saidu dreamed of America even before the Liberian Civil Wars, which lasted twelve years (1989–1997, 1999–2003) and rendered him without home or family. At "school and at home," he was taught "about the special relationship between Liberia and America, which was like the relationship between an uncle and a favorite nephew" (64). The darkly comical distortion of facts in Saidu's account serves to underscore the euphemisms through which a thorny history can be rendered innocuous. Told from within a detention facility, a consequence of the attacks of 9/11 and the xenophobia they produced, Saidu's immigrant narrative, like Pierre Toussaint's, references American slavery and, at the same time, highlights new forms of subjection. Julius describes the place where the detention facility is located as a "wasteland," its waiting room as "purgatorial," its buildings as long, flat, gray metal boxes with no windows (63). "I have only been outside three times," says Saidu, "on the days when I went to court" (69). Considered a threat to security—in ways that echo the threat free blacks seemed to pose to slaveholders—Saidu will soon be deported.

The order and mode in which Saidu's and Toussaint's narratives are presented in *Open City* demonstrate the strategic way in which Cole weaves diverse narratives of migration into a network. He places them just after Julius's reading of Ground Zero as a palimpsest, offering first Saidu's tale and then Toussaint's, as if he, too, were reading the layers of migrant experience embedded in New York. The two narratives take up the entire middle chapter of the novel, which closes with a startling image: walking down a street, Julius gets caught up in what seems to be a "commotion from an earlier time"—he sees a "huddled knot of men," a brawl, and beyond them "the body of a lynched man dangling from a tree" (75). The slender figure, "dressed from head to toe in black, reflecting no light," turns out to be a mirage, a trick of the eye played on "dark canvas sheeting on a construction scaffold," but it creates an ominous atmosphere as the lingering final image of the chapter (75).

Both Saidu's and Toussaint's narratives invoke black liberation struggles. Saidu's does so in an ironic mode: on the one hand, it alludes to the troubled founding of Liberia (which makes the country's very name sardonic, derived as it is from the Latin word *liber*, meaning "free"); on the other hand, it points to that country's later first civil war, led by Charles Taylor, who was aided by both the CIA and Muammar al-Qaddafi in his rise to power, and who became one of the most prominent warlords in Africa, one infamous for his brutality and use of child soldiers. Pierre Toussaint's narrative invokes both the Haitian Revolution and the struggle for black freedom in antebellum America. Julius's subsequent, startling vision of the lynched figure raises the specter of violence as a macabre conclusion to these narratives.

Cole does not let his readers rest in the face of such accounts. Throughout the novel, he intersperses metafictive elements that emphasize both the instability of his narrative—dependent as it is on an unreliable narrator—and the fact that, unlike a historical narrative, his novel conjoins disparate events, figures, and facts in anachronistic ways. The experience of reading within this weblike set of relations among historical allusions and citations is akin to being suspended in time, in an almost dreamlike state not unlike Julius's when he "sees" Pierre Toussaint in Penn Station. We too "see" fictional and historical characters interact as if they were on the same plane, in a trancelike condition that allows us to view several layers of history's palimpsest simultaneously. By thus representing the web of social, political, and historical forces producing migration, alongside its profound influence on the world of both his characters and his readers, Cole portrays migration as the fundamentally global and shifting phenomenon that it is.

At the same time, the narrative stays grounded in Julius's perspective, which is biased at best. The precision with which Julius describes the people he meets and the scenes he observes—in language that has both the economy and the partiality of photographic snapshots—calls attention to the novel's status as fiction: the reader is hyperaware of Julius's and, by extension, Cole's narrative style. These metafictive interventions ultimately underscore the fact that the novel cannot substitute for a critical examination of the historical citations it deploys. As fiction, it allows us to rethink the assumptions we might hold about history and the historical production of subjects; it can even flout historical narrative conventions to invoke the simultaneity of different times and to explore history's palimpsest inscriptions upon a particular space. But it cannot process history's consequences and implications, nor can its readers depend on it to provide something more personal: an emotive transport into the personal experience of the immigrant narrating the tale.

The novel's metafictive signposts, which come frequently and unexpectedly, keep the reader in check. For instance, though Julius is so absorbed in Saidu's narrative that a sudden knock from a detention-center guard startles him, he pauses to wonder "whether it wasn't more likely that [Saidu] had been a [child] soldier" and whether Saidu had embellished details to "perfect his claim of being an innocent refugee" (67). The thought not only interrupts Saidu's story but suggests Julius's own unreliability: by calling into question the account of the narrator in front of him, Julius undermines his own storytelling. A second reading of the novel, when the reader knows about Moji's upcoming accusation, makes these signposts more evident.

Julius's relationship to Nadège, a girlfriend whom we learn about mostly through his references to their breakup, also becomes more conspicuous. Julius notes how Nadège's slight limp reminds him of a "girl who had been hidden in [his] memory for more than twenty-five years" (60). He adds, "To suddenly remember her, and instantly tie her to Nadège, was a shock" (60). Is this half-hidden girl Moji? No. The girl, whose name Julius has forgotten, "whose face had blurred in memory," turns out to be someone who suffered from polio (Moji did not) and whom Julius knew only briefly as a child. Nevertheless, the irruption of memory here, connected to a woman with whom Julius is romantically involved, raises the specter (at least on a second reading) of the rape accusation. It also prompts this question: If there is a woman other than Moji that has remained hidden in Julius's memory, what and who else remains hidden?

This moment comes at the start of the chapter in which Julius listens to Pierre Toussaint's slave-immigrant narrative and Saidu's account of his life in the detention center. Cole thus creates and maintains a productive tension between the unreliability of Julius's memory—making the reader question just what kind of narrative they have in their hands—and his capacity to be a medium for verifiable historical citations and biographical scenarios. Julius's blocked memory is, therefore, not simply a pathology that the reader can observe but a catalyst that mobilizes the reader to engage with what *is* more stable than Julius's memory—the design of Cole's novel. That formal structure reaches for the colossal scope of migration in time and space, while also calling into being the temporal, temporary, and tempered consciousness of a particular migrant. The scale of the novel ranges wide but remains focused closely on Julius, whose personal perspective is revelatory only insofar as it is clearly flawed.

By blocking Julius's memory, Cole challenges the American convention of representing immigration as an experience leading to self-reinvention, through (semi)autobiographical narratives that testify not only to transformation but to the memories of what is lost in the process—the selves, worlds, and languages that must give way to the new life created through migration. Cole's novel, by contrast, suggests that migration may also be "an act of forgetting" and self-erasure (140).

Julius makes the point explicit in a scene in a Brussels church, where he recalls a recent moment at a club in which he observed a group of young Africans dancing. The music, he writes, "was American hip-hop, and the average age was twenty-five or thirty. It was a scene such as one would see in any city in Africa, or in the West: a Friday night, young people, music, liquor" (139). Then he discovers that the dancers, who he assumed were Congolese given Brussels's colonial relationship to that African country, are instead Rwandans. He thinks:

> What losses, I wondered, lay behind their laughter and flirting? Most of those there would have been teenagers during the genocide. Who, among those

present, I asked myself, had killed, or witnessed killing? . . . The innocence on view was inscrutable and unremarkable. They were exactly like young people everywhere. And I felt some of that mental constriction—imperceptible sometimes, but always there—that came whenever I was introduced to young men from Serbia or Croatia, from Sierra Leone or Liberia. That doubt that said, these, too, could have killed and killed and only later learned how to look innocent. (139)

This thought echoes what Julius thinks about Saidu and his Liberian past and raises, once again, the specter of suspicion vis-á-vis the immigrant figure. Julius goes on to wonder if an African immigrant woman he observes in the church might not also be "in Belgium as an act of forgetting. Her presence in the church might doubly be a means of escape: a refuge from the demands of family life and a hiding place from what she might have seen in the Cameroons or in the Congo, or maybe even in Rwanda. And perhaps her escape was not from anything she had done, but from what she had seen" (140).

Julius's words uncannily recall Isaac's condition in Mengestu's *All Our Names*. Think of Isaac's original wish to flee, and the violence from which he flees. Might we then think of migration as escape? As a refuge from world conflicts that fuel migration? These are certainly not new propositions, for exile and migration have long, intersecting histories. But in Cole's and Mengestu's fiction there is an intensified turn to forgetting (both willed and enforced) as an intricate part of migration.

Yet, though both novels present migrants as traumatized figures, neither suggests that this trauma should be transcended through the process of acculturation or invites engagement with migrant suffering through empathy. Instead, *All Our Names* and *Open City* ask us to consider the conditions that produce such trauma and, furthermore, to determine our own subject positions in relation to those conditions. The opacity and the potential for violent complicity characterizing the narrators of both novels demand that the reader step outside the narrow parameters of the self to engage—not with individual stories of struggle that are representative of the so-called immigrant experience, but with the material forces that imbricate the world of the reader with that of the text. Through the alternating structure of *All Our Names*, Mengestu stages the difficulties of doing so even under conditions of need and desire. Cole's nonlinear, anti-progressive, discontinuous account of dispossession and persecution in *Open City* makes the effort an ethical imperative.

Julius describes his lapse in memory at the ATM as a "nervous condition." Nasia Anam rightly notes that the phrase "conjures the specter of the traumatized colonized subject," even though Julius is hardly representative of people "subjugated under an oppressive imperial regime," since he is "a free, mobile, and moneyed individual [who is] fully cosmopolitan"—he is, in short, Taiye Selasi's version of an Afropolitan.[58] Anam notes that the "'nervous condition' Julius alludes to is Cole's explicit nod to Jean-Paul Sartre's introduction of Frantz Fanon's seminal text, *The Wretched of the Earth*," in which Sartre, summarizing Fanon, writes that "the status of the 'native' is a nervous condition introduced and maintained by the settler among colonized people *with their consent*."[59] But, as Anam argues, Julius's crisis—his nervous condition—is not the predicament described by Sartre but rather "the predicament of identifying either as a member of the historically oppressed or the historically triumphant": he "does not know whether he has more in common with those captured and enslaved on the West coast of Africa or with the profiteers of slavery who laid out the groundwork for American capitalism."[60]

Even this, however, is not quite right: for Julius, the West is already entangled with Africa; they are no longer two discrete entities. His nervous condition is a result not of his indecision about which group to identify with but of the fact that he is both victim and perpetrator, witness and culprit. The novel does not dwell on Julius's nervous condition in a psychopathological sense; instead, it is one of the formal strategies by which Cole challenges the idea that the violence of history and the material realities it has produced are external conditions from which we can be removed or absolved. Rather than represent this challenge as his character's psychological predicament as an immigrant—a predicament that the reader can safely observe from a remove—Cole makes it constitutive of the form his novel takes and the reading experience it demands. *Open City* requires that we reframe our relationship to the history and contemporary conditions of migration to the United States and Europe. Like Julius, we cannot claim to be detached and absolved from history.

The chapters to come explore the migrant aesthetics of a variety of authors who, like Cole, highlight historical resonances across time and space to render legible the far-reaching relationship between migration and the slave trade, European colonialism, and global neocolonialism. From this vantage point, the authors allow us to see what Mengestu stages at an intimate level: that forced migration is a problem we *all* need to confront, not one that the migrant alone must embody and suffer while putatively stable subjects look on with pity, fear, scorn, or brazen indifference.

Chapter Two

MIGRANT REFRACTION
Aleksandar Hemon's Anti-Autobiography

In his 2008 novel *The Lazarus Project*, Aleksandar Hemon intertwines two narratives. One is a fictionalized account of the life of a historical figure, Lazarus Averbuch—a young man who survived the 1903 Kishinev pogrom in what is now Moldova only to be shot and killed by the police in Chicago five years later. The other is the account of a fictional character named Vladimir Brik, who writes Lazarus's story. Vladimir, like his subject, is an immigrant; he first arrives in Chicago on a writer's fellowship but is stranded when the ethnoreligious war in Bosnia (1992–1995) breaks out in his native Sarajevo. Having been spared the bloodshed of the war, which displaced over two million people and was the most devastating conflict in Europe since the end of World War II, with estimates of 100,000 casualties of genocide and ethnic cleansing, Vladimir feels the need to create something beyond his own story of acculturation, something that can attest to the broader, human story of migration of which his trajectory is part. He is drawn to Lazarus's story because it resonates with the America he inhabits, a post-9/11 country swept up by patriotic ardor, paranoia about "foreign terrorists," and anti-Muslim and anti-immigrant fervor.[1]

Averbuch (whose first name might have been Harry, Jeremiah, or Lazar, though he appears in historical records generally as Lazarus), was just "shy of his 19th birthday" when he was shot and killed.[2] The circumstances surrounding his death are buried in what Vladimir calls a "haze of history and pain."³ What we know for certain is that Averbuch visited the home of George Shippy, Chicago's chief of police, on March 2, 1908 and that, within three minutes of entering the residence, he was dead. According to Shippy, Averbuch appeared in his entryway armed with a knife and a gun and wounded Shippy, his son Harry, and his bodyguard, James Foley, before being shot repeatedly by Foley and Shippy. The Jewish press in Chicago claimed that Averbuch carried only a piece of paper with Shippy's name and address on it, and that he was seeking only a letter of good character to travel or obtain work outside of Chicago.⁴ Lazarus's sister, Olga Averbuch, who was interrogated for seventy-two hours by the police, testified that Lazarus could not have afforded a gun and did not know how to use one.

Moved by Olga's grief and the injustice of the case, the activist Jane Addams, whose Hull House had assisted many Eastern European Jewish immigrants since its establishment in 1889, arranged for an independent investigation into Averbuch's death. She hired a lawyer, Harold LeClair Ickes, who ordered Averbuch's body exhumed and had an independent autopsy performed. This autopsy showed that Averbuch had been fatally wounded by a shot from behind, and that he had also been shot at least once from above. Though the evidence of this autopsy, as well as testimony from Olga and from Lazarus's boss (who provided Averbuch with an alibi for the time during which he had supposedly bought the gun), was presented at the coroner's inquest on March 24, 1908, the jury still decided that the shooting was justified, and Shippy and Foley were exonerated.⁵

In the aftermath of the murder, local newspapers portrayed Averbuch as an "anarchistic assassin." Chicago residents still "vividly recalled the violent Haymarket incident," the bombing that had taken place during a labor demonstration on May 4, 1886, at Haymarket Square, supposedly at the hands of eight anarchists, five of whom were immigrants. The portrayal of Averbuch as another anarchist "raised the specter of a vast, foreign-born conspiracy intent on toppling law and order across the country."⁶ The *Chicago Tribune*, for instance, not only corroborated Shippy's account but added xenophobic flourishes, describing Averbuch as a young man "with a foreign cast of features [that] would send a shiver of distrust into any man's heart."⁷ Averbuch was thus woven into the larger anarchist scare of the early twentieth century, which resulted in anti-immigrant violence, deportation laws, and racialized views of immigrants' purported threat. Fear of foreign radicalism was not new; it can be traced back at least to the Alien and

Sedition Acts hysteria of 1798. But the fear of anarchism erupted with new fervor in 1901, when an American-born son of Polish immigrants, a self-proclaimed anarchist, assassinated President William McKinley, which led directly to the Anarchist Exclusion Act.[8]

No evidence has ever emerged that links Averbuch to anarchism, though Shippy claimed that he knew Averbuch was an anarchist "because he looked 'Armenian or Jewish.'"[9] Instead, the independent investigation discovered that the police records were riddled with inconsistencies and lies: the police, for example, added the knife and gun to the list of what had been in Averbuch's possession. Most stunning of all were the revelations that Averbuch's body had been taken from the potter's field where he had been originally buried by the police. When investigators recovered the body three days later, it was discovered that his brain had been removed, possibly "because some scientist wanted to study the mind of a proven anarchist."[10] Averbuch's body had been exhumed in the first place because Olga wanted to give her brother a proper Jewish burial and because Ickes, the lawyer, wanted to gather evidence to exonerate Averbuch. In the end, only Olga achieved her goal.

In Hemon's novel, Vladimir strives to bear testament to the sacrilege and slander inflicted on Averbuch's body and name. He wants to testify to the tragedy of his flight from religious persecution, which ended with violent death in America. We see Vladimir traveling to Eastern Europe to retrace Lazarus's steps, accompanied by his friend Rora, a veteran of the Bosnian war who photographs the journey. Rora's pictures become part of the novel, along with reproductions of photographs from the Chicago Historical Society related to Averbuch's case; Hemon intersperses these images so that they cut across the two intertwined narratives.

Published one hundred years after Lazarus's death, the novel superimposes two distinct timeframes and encompasses Vladimir's return to Sarajevo, his reflections on life as an immigrant in the United States, Rora's stories about the war, and the latter's murder during their trip. It ends with Vladimir's decision to stay in Sarajevo "for a while" as he writes Lazarus's story and grieves for Rora, whose murder reflects Lazarus's in reverse: he survived the war and fled to America, only to be killed on a trip back "home" (29).

Vladimir's story seems to reflect Hemon's own, since the author, too, is a native of Sarajevo who was stranded in America when the war broke out in Bosnia; he also made a life for himself in Chicago and traveled to Eastern Europe—accompanied by his friend Velibor Božović, who took the photographs attributed to Rora—to do research for *The Lazarus Project*. Hemon thus constructs a world that doubles on itself, mixing fact and fiction while multiplying connections across diverse geographies and temporalities through immigrant and return narratives, which in turn spin from and define one another. Hemon's approach may seem out of step with those of the other writers I consider in this book, who eschew the autobiographical altogether. But Hemon's relationship to genre is complicated. The critic Wendy Ward has noted that, in the course of his career (and *The Lazarus Project* is no exception), "Hemon has perfected protagonists that cling closely to his own life trajectory while, at the same time, jettison off into their own fictional spheres, leaving the reader all the more anxious to somehow certify that identification bind."[11] But the short-circuiting of that bind is one of Hemon's aims.

We've seen how Mengestu and Cole use strategic anonymity to disabuse readers of two expectations: that the migrants in their novels will be representative figures, and that those migrants will offer points of empathetic connection. In this chapter, I explore how Hemon manipulates aspects of life writing, including both details from his own autobiography and elements of Lazarus's biography, to achieve a similar goal. Hemon has explicitly refused the self-ethnographic, identitarian trappings of autobiography, arguing that his fiction springs from what he calls an "antibiographical" impulse. As he told an interviewer, he "compulsively" imagines "scenarios alternative to what happens to [him]." "To my mind," he added, "my stories are not autobiographical; they are *antibiographical*, they are the antimatter to the matter of my life. They contain what did not happen to me."[12] Thus, while his fiction seems to reflect his personal trajectory—his life in Sarajevo and, later, his experiences as an immigrant in Chicago—it does not reproduce the trajectory of Hemon's successful acculturation and triumph as an immigrant writer publishing in English to critical acclaim. "I like to think that what happens in my books and in my life," Hemon stated in another interview, "is that those two spaces overlap. They overlap through the experience of immigration and diaspora, and they also overlap because I want them to overlap."[13]

While Hemon emphasizes the concept of "overlapping," the more precise term, at least for *The Lazarus Project*, is *refraction*. I take the term from

Vladimir Nabokov, a writer whose influence on Hemon is well known and after whom Vladimir Brik is probably named.[14] Nabokov, himself a refugee of various historical upheavals, fled revolutionary Russia in 1919 and later escaped Hitler's Germany by fleeing to France in 1937. In 1940, just weeks before Paris fell to the Nazis, he boarded a French ocean liner for its last voyage to New York, accompanied by his Jewish wife and son. In his fiction, Nabokov's lived experiences appear only as refracted through the prism of his art. Nabokov was adamant about protecting his private life from the prying eyes of readers and, like his beloved butterflies, he excelled in the art of camouflage. He guarded his own memories, which held stories of the worlds he had lost to history, with the intricate formal patterns of his novels. Nabokov believed that reality cannot be apprehended directly, that it is necessarily subjective. Even in his autobiography, *Speak, Memory*, he writes that literary creation involves a preliminary refraction of reality, through what he calls the "tremulous prism" of the artist's mind.[15] He objected to reading novels in terms of autobiography, politics, and history because he believed that artists do not represent the world through mimesis but rather create worlds that, while connected to ours, aren't its copies.

Hemon has a similar sensibility.[16] He shares Nabokov's conviction that aesthetic play is at the center of artistic production, and that it is an effective way to narrate loss and suffering. Play and suffering may seem, at first glance, like contradictory terms. But Nabokov and Hemon both offer versions of tragicomedy within metafictive "play"—meaning the use of formal experimentation with a comic sensibility that includes dark, even gallows humor; satire aiming to pillory societal structures and agents of injustice; and parody designed to challenge ossified narratives. Used in this way, play preempts pity as a response to suffering.

The Lazarus Project is a prism through which a network of stories, both factual and fictional, from the past and the present, from America and Eastern Europe, refract; they bend and disperse into fragments, twist around and verge toward each other. In this prism, Hemon's life, which refracts and is refracted in Vladimir's, undergoes a transformation: it becomes fictional, as does Lazarus's life, even while Hemon maintains and underscores the testimonial weight of the narratives' historical anchoring. The metafictive aspects of the novel keep us attuned to the fact that Hemon is building a world in which this kind of aesthetic play is happening consciously, to prevent a narrow understanding of how a migrant writer's life story informs his art.

By the same token, this aesthetic play highlights the "haze of history and pain" under which the historical Lazarus is still shrouded. Hemon fictionalizes aspects of this historical figure not to make up for what is missing in the archive or to provoke empathy for a particular individual, but instead to underscore the "haze" surrounding that individual's life. This emphasis reveals how, for the state, Lazarus's life was inconsequential—just another migrant shot and killed, to be displayed as evidence of the need to enforce brutality against a purported foreign threat. Hemon uses his novel to refract several fictional and historical lives—including Lazarus's—as testament to the long-standing fracturing of human life by state powers bent on vilifying migration.

The critic Sonia Weiner reads the multiple strands of the novel as emanating from the rupture of migration, working off Salman Rushdie's metaphor of the "broken mirror" of the migrant writer's "fragmented consciousness"—the result of dislocation and discontinuity, and of the loss they trigger. "In evoking the mirror as his central metaphor," Weiner writes, "Rushdie conjures a sense of reflection, doubling, and fracturing, themes taken up by Hemon in his work" and embodied in the formal qualities of his novel.[17] Yet Weiner sees Hemon as principally preoccupied with how Vladimir deals with "issues seminal to the migratory consciousness, such as memory, loss, dislocation, and the ever elusive question of what constitutes home."[18] By contrast, I see Hemon reaching beyond these identitarian and melancholic concerns. For one thing, the novel is by turns witty, satirical, and tragicomic, all tones that resist the stereotype of the mournful immigrant psyche. In this chapter, accordingly, I will focus less on how Vladimir experiences his fragmented consciousness and more on the experimental, humorous, and metafictional novel he narrates, to explore Hemon's migrant aesthetic.

Through the various stories that refract and overlap throughout the novel, Hemon expands the scale of migration, offering something like Cole's palimpsests and (as we shall see in the next chapter) Valeria Luiselli's echoes of forced migration across time. Like the other writers examined in this book, Hemon not only dramatizes a migrant writer's wariness of identitarian discourses and the conventions of assimilationist narratives, but he also develops formal strategies to offer an alternative: stories, both historical and fictional, that refract upon one another within a broad temporal and spatial scale to create a wide-angle perspective on migration as a world-building phenomenon. This formal experimentation also allows for what Hemon calls "immigrant solidarity," a form of affiliation that isn't based on national belonging. Rather, it is a community constructed through literature that heightens—through analogies, echoes, and refractions—connections among migrants across time, space, nations, and ethnic and racial differences.

Hemon used the term "immigrant solidarity" in an interview when he was asked why he focused on Lazarus Averbuch's story even though he himself is not Jewish and does not share the same national point of origin.[19] Pushing back against the all-too-prevalent idea that an artist's identity ought to match that of his subjects, Hemon declared his wish to write for and about an immigrant community broadly speaking, in the name of building solidarity around social and political issues. Here I revise his phrase, preferring "migrant solidarity" because it invokes a more expansive set of migratory experiences. The literature of "migrant solidarity" created by Hemon and the other writers featured in this book shares the breadth and scope of literary cosmopolitanism, but it is more specifically rooted in history and politics—in particular the history of people displaced by (neo)colonialism and the persecution of migrants. As a genre, it seeks not the transcendence of identity but its deconstruction. More importantly, it seeks to expand the scale of migration well beyond identitarian and nation-bound concerns.

A WRITER IN SEARCH OF A FORM; A MIGRANT DOUBLE BURIAL

When Vladimir first tries to write about Lazarus Averbuch, he fails. He attempts in vain to immerse himself in the world of 1908 through research. He even riffs on the Biblical Lazarus, whose story comes to signify the death and resurrection that immigrants undergo as they transform through acculturation. But the acculturation plot stunts his creative energy:

> I had to admit that I identified easily with [Lazarus and Olga's] travails: lousy jobs, lousier tenements, the acquisition of language, the logistics of survival, the ennoblement of self-fashioning. It seemed to me I knew what constituted

that world, what mattered in it. But when I wrote about it, however, all I could produce was a costumed parade of paper cutouts performing acts of high symbolic value: tearing up at the sight of the Statue of Liberty, throwing the lice-infested Old County clothes on the sacrificial pyre of a new identity, coughing consumptive blood in large, poignant clots. I kept those pages but shuddered at the thought of reading through them. (41)

At this point, Vladimir has been teaching English as a second language and writing a newspaper column about his students' struggles, which are "not at all unlike [his] own: looking for a job, getting the Social Security number, finding an apartment, becoming a citizen, meeting Americans, dealing with nostalgia, that sort of thing" (31). The column "did pretty well, though it paid very little," but Vladimir senses that there is something patronizing behind its mitigated success; people liked the column not only "because it was honest and personal" but also because they "found the quirky immigrant language endearing" (32). And he knows that such columns are read by benefactors who are far more likely to support "cultural diversity, ethnic tolerance" if they are convinced that ethnic cultures are "nothing like theirs" (13).

Vladimir seeks a new form, one that can resolve what he calls his "moral waddling," the guilt and emptiness he feels as an immigrant whose life seems—but only superficially—to have followed the neat narrative trajectory featured in assimilationist texts: "displacement, travails, redemption, success" (133, 32). In fact, Vladimir's "success" is a running gag in the novel: on the one hand, he has become a citizen (through marriage) and mastered English well enough to teach it to others; on the other, he has trouble keeping his job as a journalist because writing about acculturation blocks his creativity, and therefore he relies on his wife's handsome income as a doctor, becoming a kept man. Vladimir knows that the "displacement, redemption, success" trajectory does not accurately represent what is so blandly called "the immigrant experience," and he recognizes, moreover, that it could never do justice to either his own experience or the testimony he needs to create.

In the sections of the novel devoted to Vladimir, we watch him searching for an alternate form, but with the opening of *The Lazarus Project*, we have already seen that form fully realized. The novel starts when Lazarus is shot and killed, and his decaying body haunts that narrative strand.

Because Lazarus's body is buried, exhumed, scattered, and recovered, his corpse becomes an extended part of the plot, especially when his bereaved sister, Olga, insists on retrieving it for a proper burial. Unable to produce the entire body, since parts of it have been stolen, the police dig up the body of another immigrant, Isaac, who was beaten to death because he was suspected of being Lazarus's accomplice. When Olga finds out about the disappearance of her brother's body, she is outraged and distraught, but she then uses the tragedy to help Isador, another immigrant and friend of Lazarus who is being hunted on similar charges and must escape both the police and the anarchist circles that want to make him a cause célèbre. Vladimir thus replaces the acculturation plot with the story of Lazarus's murder, which in turn refracts stories of other immigrant victims, creating testimony and elegy in aggregate.

While the details concerning Isaac and Isador are fictitious additions, the Chicago police's search for a "curly-haired man," someone believed to have been with Averbuch before the shooting, is a matter of historical record.[20] The search's object is so ridiculously vague that at first I thought Hemon had made it up in a fit of exaggeration, a miscalculation of wit. But Hemon, as it turns out, had to do very little to satirize not only the police but also the journalists covering the case. The Chicago police, using that bogus physical description, "quickly started rounding up reputed anarchists, those resembling anarchists, as well as random foreigners who could one day turn into anarchists."[21] In the novel, Hemon focuses on the police force's violence against Isaac and Isador, using a form of gallows humor. Isador's escape becomes a way for Hemon to make visceral the deadly absurdity of the police's xenophobic persecution. At the same time, his absurdist humor works as a distancing mechanism, allowing us to imagine Isador's struggle without the trappings of sentimentality.

We meet Isador when he is in the shit—literally. As "the most wanted anarchist in Chicago," he is forced to hide and ends up in the shithole of an outhouse, where Olga finds him (93). She hauls him up out of the hole, but then must leave him in the outhouse until she can formulate a plan, so he is left "beshitten on the absurd throne, wrapped in a flimsy blanket, thinking up free worlds in which everybody has indoor plumbing" (95). "I just hope I don't have to relieve myself," he tells Olga, "but she [doesn't] laugh" (95). Olga eventually strikes a deal with the police: they will help Isador escape to Canada in exchange for her silence about their crimes against her brother. To carry out this plan, they hide Isador under Isaac's corpse, which is serving as a replacement for Lazarus's now-fragmented body in a ceremony meant to quell protests against police brutality in the city of Chicago. When Isador is freed from the coffin (shortly after the ceremony but just before the full burial), Isaac's corpse is lifted off Isador's body, and he asks, "Am I dead?" Those nearby "laugh at him, then help him hatch out" (271).[22]

Hemon invented the double burial, the substitution of bodies, and the story of Isador's near-interment and escape, using these absurd conditions to make vivid the threat of death to the immigrants who knew Lazarus, and the precarity of migrant life more generally. At the same time, he balances his intense focus on the abject—shit and corpses; the physicality of Isador's live body as it literally rubs shoulders with death; Lazarus's decaying, cut-up corpse—with literary play: doubling (in Isaac's and Isador's echoing names), substitution (Isaac for Lazarus), and simulation (Isaac must act like a corpse when he is alive). This playfulness, while affording distance from the suffering represented, paradoxically vivifies it too, in that Hemon imbues the materiality of death and dying, of being persecuted and threatened by murder, with the lively spark of humor.

Even Lazarus plays this game, for he looks eerily alive in the photographs of his corpse displayed by the police. He is dressed in a suit without a shirt or tie, his eyes are closed, and his body is seated on a chair, simulating a formal pose; his head is propped up by one Captain Evans of the Chicago Police Department. There are two such photographs, one reproduced early in the novel and the other toward the end.

Hemon has identified the photographs of the dead Lazarus as "the heart" of the novel because they testify both to Lazarus's brief life and to his violent death in America.[23] The images also testify gruesomely to the sacrilege of his body, to how the police made a spectacle of him in his death. His corpse was exposed to the public and examined because his "violent nature was supposed to be manifest in his face and the shape of his head: The public marveled over his 'low forehead,' 'large mouth,' and 'simian ears,' all presumably markers of his anarchist proclivities."[24]

In the novel, the photographs accompany the moment when Olga first sees her dead brother in the flesh, a moment witnessed by a voyeuristic crowd made up of "common citizens . . . scruffy idlers and pomaded socialites, weeping churchwomen, off-duty firemen and mail carriers . . . [and] policemen of every rank," some of whom angrily strike the body and spit

FIGURE 2.1. A photograph of Lazarus Averbuch, an immigrant killed by the Chicago police in 1908. *Source*: DN-0005898, *Chicago Daily News* collection, Chicago History Museum.

on it. Several citizens bribe the morgue attendant to "take a look at the Jew's member" (57). Olga briefly believes Lazarus to be alive, given the fact that he is dressed and seated. But, stepping toward him, she sees that his head is being held up and that his "eyes are closed, his face ashen." Her heart stops, frozen. When she finally takes a few more reluctant steps to "touch his lifeless cheek," she collapses, and "the crowd gasps" (57). Of the "common citizens" that have gathered to gawk at Lazarus, Vladimir writes that "many are still there," as if suspended in cultural memory, still gawking (57).

Hemon has Vladimir narrate these scenes (Isaac's murder, Isador's plight, and the display of Lazarus's corpse) in the present tense, emphasizing the fact that, at some level, their violence continues. Indeed, the display of Lazarus's corpse will go on for as long as the photographs survive—as they must to preserve memory. Yet, to be useful and not simply egregious, the photographs need a context—here provided by Vladimir's account—so that, when they are displayed, that act of sacrilege is framed.[25] Hemon does so by making the crowd itself the central spectacle of the scene, contrasting its behavior with Olga's grief, which becomes even more notable because it stands out so markedly from the callous brutality around her.

We are intermittently privy to that grief in a few other scenes that focus on Olga. In brief drafts of a letter, she attempts to write to her mother, relaying the news of Lazarus's death, though she cannot find the words to tell it. As she returns to the apartment she shared with her brother, Olga reviews a series of mental images of him ("Lazarus in his silly boy-sailor suit . . . Lazarus teaching a stray dog to fetch in the refugee camp in Czernowitz") and looks around her. The place "is hollow without Lazarus, the objects in it stand excluded from her world, uninvolved in her woe" (89–90). While in the outhouse, holding an English-Russian dictionary that Lazarus liked to take there, she loses all control and weeps ("My little brother. All the lives he could have lived") (91). Suddenly she hears a voice calling her name. "The voice is sourceless and hoarse, coming from the darkness around her . . . With unbearable relief she considers the possibility that she has lost her mind" (92). Instead, it's Isador, speaking from the bowels of the shithole. This jolting shift in mode is endemic of Hemon's tragicomedy, which allows us to linger in Olga's grief only briefly before we are pulled out. The effect recalls Nabokov's method in *Lolita*, which offers us only glimpses of the child's pain through the tangle of thorns that Humbert Humbert's fancy prose creates.

In Hemon's novel, Olga's grief is obscured not only by Isador's appearance but by the darkly comic antics of the police. The gawking crowd surrounding Lazarus's body includes two detectives, Fitzgerald and Fitzpatrick. Known as the Fitzes, they carry out the orders of Assistant Police Chief Herman Shuettler in beating Isaac to death, hunting Isador down, ransacking Olga and Lazarus's home, and persecuting anyone they think might be an anarchist. Hemon depicts them and their actions in an exaggerated mode that calls comic books to mind, ironically invoking their association with the assimilation of immigrants in America and their early glorification of vigilantes who act as adjuncts to law enforcement.[26] Hemon borrows specifically from superhero comics, which conventionally rely on surface and action; he casts the Fitzes as thugs who prey on the weak and innocent: "Fitzgerald begins interrogating [Isaac] *vigorously*, throwing him to the floor, pounding the man in the face, kneeing him in the kidneys ... Fitzpatrick flings the door across the hallway open and startles a woman setting the table for supper" (54; emphasis in original). In superhero comics, physical action is often amplified to provide entertainment, thus diminishing "the *emotional* impact of the violence."[27] In Hemon's novel, the exaggeration of violence has the opposite effect: the Fitzes' shocking brutality and their victims' pain are emphasized by the contrast between the narrative's tone and its content.

The Fitzes are accompanied by William P. Miller, a journalist who turns the story into an opportunity to rev up anti-anarchist hysteria. His reportage appears in the novel mixed in with Vladimir's narration, marked by italics: "The detectives ransack the place *with the passion of soldiers fighting a just war*"; "*Bitter tears are streaming down the Jewess's cheeks*, William P. Miller writes, and underlines *bitter tears*, twice" (55, 56). The readers are thus privy to how Miller deliberately turns the Fitzes into heroes while debasing Olga's grief into melodrama.[28] Critic Geoffrey Johnson has pointed out that the Miller character was inspired by "Judith Miller, the former *New York Times* reporter criticized for her coverage of the lead-up to the U.S. invasion of Iraq," who writes in "florid, xenophobic prose ... not that far removed from the stories printed by the [*Chicago*] *Tribune* " after Lazarus was murdered.[29] The allusion to Judith Miller, who was also criticized by Edward Said for her anti-Islamic views, is one way that Hemon connects the hysteria about anarchists in 1908 with the hysteria about terrorists in the aftermath of 9/11. At other times, he is more explicit: Vladimir notes that the "immigration laws were changed" in 1908, after "patriotic preachers" raved against "the sinful perils of unbridled immigration" and editorials bemoaned "the weak laws that allowed the foreign anarchist pestilence to breed parasitically on the American body politic"; he concludes: "The war against anarchism was much like the current war on terror" (42).

Hemon further deepens the connections between the two time periods through his aesthetic choices. For instance, Rora's stories about the Bosnian war orbit around his escapades with a Bosnian criminal known as Rambo and an American journalist named Miller. The latter raises the specters of both William P. Miller and Judith Miller, causing them and the xenophobia they inspired to hover over the places Vladimir and Rora revisit. Meanwhile, Bosnian Rambo invokes a figure who, in the twentieth century, "was practically synonymous with American military might," the name "valorizing the soldiers who were carrying out the United States' increasingly interventionist foreign adventures" while embodying Americans' purported moral and physical dominance.[30]

The first time that Rora speaks of the war in earnest, he and Vladimir are on a flight from Chicago to Frankfurt, observing some of their fellow passengers:

> [A] herd of visibly virginal young women, part of a Christian group on its way to missionary work and guilt-inflicting deflowerment somewhere in the East. They sang songs of Jesus and eternal life . . . There were also American soldiers, presumably on their way to Iraq via a base in Germany . . . They were checking out the virgins, relishing their last hours before returning to a life of manual self-abuse, trigger-happiness, and a possible limb-by-limb entry intro eternity. (65–66)

Rora's stories describe a world in which Americans are involved in ethnoracial and political warfare, creating more migrants and refugees, whether through missionary colonialism (embodied here by the nuns) or through an anti-Muslim war. While Lazarus's story dramatizes the irony of seeking religious refuge in America, Rora's stories keep in view contemporary American conflicts abroad. And, since Hemon facilitates these parallel narratives' refraction and mutual interference throughout the novel, readers gain a long view of the myths of America clashing against political realities.

In another example of such refracting clashes, Vladimir and his American wife, Mary, fight over their conflicting interpretations of the photographs and videos taken by American soldiers at the Abu Ghraib prison to record their torture and humiliation of Iraqi prisoners. Those contemporary images, while not reproduced in the novel, hang like a scrim over the photographs of Lazarus's corpse:

> What she saw was essentially decent American kids acting upon a misguided belief they were protecting freedom, their good intentions going astray. What I saw was young Americans expressing their unlimited joy of the unlimited power over someone else's life and death. They loved being alive and righteous by virtue of having good American intentions; indeed, it turned them on; they liked looking at pictures of themselves sticking a baton up some Arab ass. Eventually, I flipped and turned crazy . . . I told her she was no different from any of those angelic American kids who plug curly-haired people into an electric current after a relaxing waterboarding session. (188–189)

Vladimir's use of the term "curly-haired" connects these images of humiliation and terror to those of Lazarus's corpse—recall the red-herring hunt for the "curly-haired" suspect. For the reader the images are vivid: Hemon does not need to reproduce the Abu Ghraib photographs in his novel because he can draw, in Sonia Weiner's words, "upon a charged event stored in the collective memory of his readers, relying on it to connect the past and the present, to make a clear and direct connection between the dynamics that produced" instances of abuse.[31] The Abu Ghraib photographs intermingle in the reader's mind with the images of dead Lazarus, highlighting their common denominator: the "unlimited joy of the unlimited power over someone else's life and death," exercised against "foreign" bodies deemed both threatening and pliable.

Weiner argues that the images of dead Lazarus, "taken by a photographer of the *Chicago Daily News*, plainly grants the perspective of the perpetrator, framing Lazarus as a dangerous anarchist. The triumphant pose of the dignified police officer, holding the victim like his trophy for the world to see, was meant to humiliate, degrade, and violate the privacy of Lazarus, and to demonize him in the eyes of the viewers."[32] Similarly, the Abu Ghraib photographs, several of which were broadcast on CBS's *60 Minutes II* in 2004, "show leering G.I.s taunting naked Iraqi prisoners who are forced to assume humiliating poses," including masturbating with a hood over the face and forming naked human piles with U.S. military agents "grinning and giving the thumbs-up behind."[33] The photographs also included images of two dead Iraqi men: "the battered face of prisoner No. 153399, and the bloodied body of another prisoner, wrapped in cellophane and packed in ice," both shown with G.I.s grinning and giving the thumbs-up.[34] These photographs, implicitly refracted in *The Lazarus Project* by the images of Lazarus's corpse and by the fight they provoke between Vladimir and Mary, contribute to Vladimir's questioning of his life in America. His crisis is emblematic of the ambivalence experienced by many migrants: How can one choose the United States as an adopted country, knowing its horrifically violent history and its ongoing practices of brutality?[35]

THE CONSTANT VANISHING OF THE WORLD

Given that Vladimir is a refugee of the Bosnian war, adopting America as his new homeland was not originally a question of choice.[36] But, after the war, he decides to become a U.S. citizen, even though he is suspicious of the Americanization process—or, more precisely, of how some Americans understand it. Vladimir's father-in-law, George, insists that Vladimir remain grateful "to American greatness"; he sees Vladimir's country of origin as a "remote, mythical place ... a remnant of the world from before America, a land of obsolescence whose people could arrive at humanity only in the United States, and belatedly" (162). Worse yet, George confuses his own deep investment in Catholicism with his political views, seeing religious and secular salvation wrapped up together in a vision of America that he has bequeathed to his daughter. As Vladimir confesses, "I could recognize George in her" (163).

Religious persecution sent the Averbuch siblings to America, though neither found refuge there.[37] Vladimir knows that they met with violence and death because, despite purporting to be an enlightened nation founded on the separation of church and state, America has been and remains entrenched in a quasi-religious belief in its own exceptionalism. That is what Vladimir hears in his father-in-law's devotion to American greatness: the belief that, as Donald Pease puts it, "the United States and its citizens are divinely ordained to lead the world to betterment," that the country "differs politically, socially, and morally from the Old World of Europe," and that it is "exempt from the 'laws of history' that lead to the decline and downfall of other great nations."[38] While historical realities have proven otherwise countless times, this myth and its rhetoric have persisted for centuries, even as they adapt to differing historical circumstances.

Sacvan Bercovitch, who has traced this myth to Puritan political theology, tells us that "America's foundational story," which presents the Puritans' journey as "a flight from tyranny, a 'great migration' to a new site of redemption," also "sanctified ideology as religion, banning as heresy all social and economic alternatives to capitalism, and making utopia itself captive to its beliefs."[39] For Vladimir, the sanctification of ideology as religion is what makes America betray its higher impulses, its history as "a nation of immigrants." Thus, in addition to laying bare the links between "two poles of European racial and ethnic conflict in the twentieth century (Kishinev Pogrom and war in former Yugoslavia)," and examining them in "the xenophobic atmosphere" of early twentieth-century Chicago and the post-9/11 War on Terror, *The Lazarus Project* also suggests analogies between European and American religious and racial persecution as twin sources of endless migrations.[40]

Retracing Lazarus's steps in the "dusty streets of Chernivtsi," where Jewish refugees fled from the "many pogroms" before the Shoah, Vladimir underscores the disassociation from history that allows people to survive the persistence of persecution (154, 157). This dissociation, however, also keeps injustice turning in an endless loop. When he visits the Jewish Center to ask after Lazarus's life in the refugee camp, he is told, "that was so long ago, a whole horrible century ago" (155). Vladimir realizes that the people he meets are "sleep-talking" through the historical events that set so many fleeing (229), that the elders who survived wish only to forget, and that the traces of those who perished are now gathering dust in musty museums or lying under the ruins of places "bombed and burned in the Second World War" (228). This disassociation from history is what Vladimir calls the "constant vanishing of the world" and what causes an endless repetition of suffering (229). As Vladimir and Rora make their way across a "post-soviet [sic] wasteland,"[41] they see disturbing signs that the immediate future holds more of the same: they meet a "decrepit man in Cossack attire, with an acrid, corpsy smell, selling fresh-off-the-press copies of *The*

Protocols of the Elders of Zion"; a homophobic and anti-Muslim man who drives them to Chernivtsi; and another driver whose real job is human trafficking (72, 109, 259).

While Rora's photographs do not reflect the bleakness of Vladimir's account of Eastern Europe, they reiterate visually both what he conveys about the inability to access a vital past and "the uncanny connections between past and present."[42] Rora's photographs are ambiguous, sometimes even indecipherable (they include, for instance, a stray dog, a car passing at high speed, and a sunflower field seen from a moving vehicle), and interact with the text in oblique ways. They invoke a combination of "randomness, arbitrariness or historicity," reflecting the shifting ways in which Vladimir and Rora experience time, while also generating an indeterminacy of interpretation; readers reach for meaning but must also, in Wendy Ward's words, "readjust their expectations of how image matches (or does not) with the text."[43] While Vladimir dreams of the Bosnian war criminals "Milošević, Mladić, Karadžić, and, lately, [of] Bush, Rumsfeld, and Rambo," keeping the analogies between Bosnia and America in play, Rora's photographs continue the novel's exploration of contingency and its endemic role in migrant life (257). This can be seen vividly when, after Vladimir and Rora have recognized the futility of tracing Lazarus's steps and are headed on to Sarajevo, Rora is killed—not by Rambo or anyone from his life during the war, but by a random "boy with a gun" who is "high as a balloon" (291).

Repetition becomes uncanny only when it is seen outside of historical time, isolated by the willful erasure of historical connections; within the context of history, it can be viewed as a phenomenon produced by contingency. Hemon instantiates, with the dual narratives of *The Lazarus Project*, how it feels to experience repetition, without advocating for historical determinism—contingency, after all, is what allows Isador to be saved over Isaac, as well as what characterizes Rora's death. The novel's two main narratives, Lazarus's and Vladimir's, are not neatly divided into alternating sections; instead, the Vladimir sections allude to and narrate parts of Lazarus's story as if, once refracted through the novel, the parallel plot lines not only bend and twist around each other but even blur into one another. As they do, short narratives within them radiate outward, increasing the instances of repetition. For example, when Vladimir tells Rora the plot of his Lazarus project, Rora responds by sharing the story of "a Bosnian who had recently been killed by the San Francisco police" because he refused to leave "the patio of a nonsmoking Starbucks" before he finished his cigarette (43). When the police arrived, the Bosnian told the police in "polite, restrained Bosnian" that he would leave as soon as he was done, but the police "couldn't understand him, and they wouldn't wait for someone to interpret. Ever in a hurry to enforce law and order—for law and order never have time to spare—they choked him to death in front of a disinterested choir of healthy grand latte guzzlers" (43).

This story never comes up again, but the Bosnian's name, "Ismet," the fact that he had "been in a Serbian camp," and Rora's acquaintance with his sister all point to the Lazarus story: the name Ismet recalls Isador and Isaac through alliteration, while the sister's presence in the story invokes Olga and anticipates the fact that Rora's sister will also become part of the novel's plot. (Adding yet another layer, Hemon dedicated the novel to *his* sister.) These implied analogies are like waves of light from a single source—persecution and migration—which, radiating outward, form kaleidoscopic patterns. Rora's description of Ismet surviving a Serbian camp only to "snap" after the war makes Vladimir wonder what "horrible things" Lazarus saw during the pogrom of 1903. He was fourteen at the time. "Was he a survivor who resurrected in America? Did he have nightmares about [the pogrom]? Did he read books that promised better, new worlds?" (43). These repetitions, which seem uncanny within the context of the story, are, in effect, historically constituted by the persistence of religious persecution.

Hemon's doubling of characters' names throughout the novel enhances the theme of repetition while pushing readers to make temporal distinctions. When Vladimir decides to reconstruct Lazarus's past, he receives a grant from a donor named Susie Schuettler to go to Ukraine and Moldova.[44] Vladimir generally refers to the grant as the "Susie money," but her last name echoes that of Assistant Police Chief Shuettler, who directed the Fitzes to go after Isador, Isaac, and Olga. The name of Vladimir's father-in-law, George, recalls George Shippy, while Miller is not only the name of the journalist from the *Chicago Tribune* and a covert allusion to Judith Miller but also the name of another American journalist who figures in Rora's tales about the Bosnian war. These echoing names—another Nabokovian game—keep the two main story lines intertwined, even as Vladimir's story moves forward in his search for the best aesthetic form for his Lazarus project, while Lazarus's story moves backward, from the time of his death to his life in the refugee camp after the pogrom. These intertwining but opposite-bending arcs are interspersed with scenes of Olga's grief as she buries Lazarus in Chicago and Isador's madcap escape, along with the photographs from the Chicago Historical Society and those taken by Rora/Božović. Reading *The Lazarus Project* entails keeping track of its numerous different plotlines even as they seem to blur, while recognizing the intricacy of Hemon's design—the echoing names, while simulating contingency, emphasize the historical connections among several distinct timeframes.

Repetition in Hemon's novel works against the "constant vanishing of the world," insofar as it creates migrant solidarity: the repeated images and stories underline the common threads in migrant lives and how they are historically constituted: the precarity of survival, the constant fact and threat of death (both physical and spiritual), the equally constant need for testimony for the nameless dead and the desecrated. The novel's scope is thus vaster than critics usually claim. Weiner, for instance, reads the twenty-two photographs in the novel as part of Hemon's preoccupation with authenticity and identity: while the Lazarus photographs create a "sense of a life lived" within the "Chicago Lazarus lived in, a space and place that existed physically, yet is lost in the mists of time," the images of post-Soviet Eastern Europe "capture absence and transience, reflecting the migrant predicament and probing connections between representation, authenticity, and 'reality.'"[45] But the photographs from the two main narratives also mirror each other, in a visual correlative to the intertwining plot lines, because they are presented in the same manner: they are all black-and-white, with blurry margins, and emerge from the center of pages that are ink-black on both sides, the photographs printed on the verso page. The result is that the novel's sections, with only a few exceptions, are broken up by deep black, empty pages. In the print book, their presence produces the feel of mourning drapes.

This effect also links the intertwining plotlines by emphasizing a common trend that operates at different levels within the novel: Vladimir mourns Lazarus's tragic death even as he brings Lazarus's world to life; he also mourns his friend Rora while celebrating him by making his stories of the Bosnian war a significant part of the plot. More precisely, it is Rora's way of telling stories, his gift for world building, that lives through Vladimir. In this way, even as Vladimir both accepts that "before-the-war

Sarajevo" is unattainable and becomes unmoored from his American experiences, he creates an imaginary homeland for himself, and for us, migrants, and refugees (20). Destruction feeds creation as Vladimir and Hemon build a world from grief and loss.[46]

MIGRANT SOLIDARITY

In the prismatic richness of *The Lazarus Project*, there is yet another subplot running parallel to and informing the two main narratives: Vladimir's breakup with his wife, Mary, which develops slowly during his trip to Eastern Europe and allegorizes his split from America. This breakup plot inverts a long literary tradition of using marriage or love relationships across considerable social boundaries and Old World antagonisms to establish new American identities.[47] *The Melting Pot* (1909), by British-born playwright Israel Zangwill, is a prime example.[48] One of the most successful productions in the history of Broadway, and a play that gave us an enduring if problematic metaphor for acculturation in America, *The Melting Pot* involves two star-crossed lovers: Jewish David Quixano, a survivor of the 1903 Kishinev pogrom, and Christian Vera Revendal, daughter of the Russian officer responsible for the pogrom. Quixano, whose name invokes his quixotic aspirations, writes a great symphony called "The Crucible" that expresses his hope for a world in which ethnic hatred can be melted away. At the end of the play, Vera's father repents, while David and Vera decide to wed. In the words of Werner Sollors, "The past may be anchored in old-world hardness, but the future in America is identified with the melting pot," where "the severe wounds of the past" can be overcome to forge a new life.[49]

In *The Lazarus Project*, the breakup between Vladimir and Mary suggests the opposite: rather than promoting a marriage of nations or a melting pot of cultures, this plotline refuses interpersonal sentimentality in favor of migrant solidarity. In the Kishinev Jewish Center, where he goes seeking Lazarus's roots, Vladimir meets Iuliana, a beautiful woman who recounts the long history of Jewish persecution with unwavering sorrow in her eyes but also, due to constant repetition, the air of being able to list the atrocities "by heart" (230). Vladimir has a brief, ephemeral fantasy of kissing her; his desire for her is entangled in a wish to reclaim a sense of belonging to the Old World. Shortly afterward, while looking for traces of Lazarus's ancestors in a cemetery, Vladimir realizes that he can no longer remember how long ago he left Chicago and his wife; he cannot "recall her face ... [or] what it was we called our life" (234). "Some part of my life ended there," he writes, "among those empty graves; it was then that I started mourning. I can tell you that now, now that there is little but mourning" (235). A truth crashes in on Vladimir at that moment: there is no place where ethnic hatred can be melted away, no promised land where a brave new world can be made manifest, except in the imagination.

Vladimir's trip to Eastern Europe, as Weiner argues, "unhinges him from his American grounding and casts him as the perpetual migrant, the eternal transient, always adrift, never 'at home.'"[50] But rather than remain in this state, where he risks "falling into what Eva Hoffman terms the 'new nomadism,' which emerges in a 'decentered world,' devoid of 'any one symbolic locus of meaning,'" Vladimir produces *The Lazarus Project*.[51] His answer to the question of where to make one's home in the absence of a native land and the rejection of an adopted one is to create a novel as an alternate locus of recognition and belonging. *The Lazarus Project* is both a testimony to the sacrilege inflicted on Lazarus and a place where we can imagine his life and those countless migrants like him.

The novel is thus akin to Salman Rushdie's well-known concept of an "imaginary homeland," a locus of meaning for all those refugees and migrants who share a history of migration and dispossession across different timeframes, races, ethnicities, nationalities, and sociopolitical registers. "It may be," wrote Rushdie in 1982, addressing Indian writers in particular, that "exiles or emigrants or expatriates, are haunted by some sense of loss, some urge to reclaim, to look back ... but if we do look back, we must also do so in the knowledge... that our physical alienation from India almost inevitably means that we will not be capable of reclaiming precisely the thing that was lost; that we will, in short, create fictions ... imaginary homelands, Indias of the mind."[52] Rushdie conceives of an "imaginary" home being produced through literary traditions that are not nation bound. He urges Indian writers not to confine themselves to a particular national canon in creating their "imaginary homelands" but instead to make use of a "second tradition, quite apart from their own racial history," in a cultural and "political history of the phenomenon of migration, [and] displacement": "We can quite legitimately claim as our ancestors the Huguenots, the Irish, the Jews; the past to which we belong is an English past, the history of immigrant Britain. Swift, Conrad, Marx are as much our literary forebears as Tagore or Ram Mohan Roy."[53]

Hemon's/Vladimir's version of an imaginary homeland employs Rushdie's expansive sense of literary heritage at an even broader scale. Included in that homeland are literary forebears not only from the global history of migration and displacement but also from the histories of the novelist, his characters, and his readers. For critics Weiner and Ward, who concentrate primarily on Vladimir's struggle to resolve his question of home, his imaginary homeland helps him to resolve his sense of being both American and Bosnian, to embrace his double citizenship while not feeling entirely at home in either place. But the novel's scope extends well beyond Vladimir's personal identity struggle—which, after all, results in a breakup rather than an embrace. As an expression of Hemon's "migrant solidarity," the novel refracts a condition of homelessness in which the categories of migrant, refugee, and exile overlap, a condition shared by all those who cannot make their place of birth a home—because it has been either destroyed or rendered unlivable, due to war or persecution—and whose lives elsewhere are plagued by xenophobia and injustice. If Lazarus's story represents this condition, Vladimir's is that of an ally whose trajectory renders him capable of thinking and imagining the world from that condition of homelessness—a condition that he also experiences. Far from signifying a retreat into fantasy, this turn to the imaginary makes possible forms of belonging that do not depend on religion, ethnicity, race, nation, or other markers of difference. As an "imaginary homeland" that does not depend on concepts of nationhood, *The Lazarus Project* elicits migrant solidarity—an affiliation among all people who have had to migrate. Vladimir mutually refracts his life with that of Lazarus across time, space, ethnicity, and religion, thus enacting a form of fictive belonging.

At another level, the novel aims toward a broader human solidarity in ways that recall the work of Richard Rorty. Rorty recognized that "our sense of solidarity is strongest when those with whom solidarity is expressed are thought of as 'one of us,' where 'us' means something smaller and more local than the human race," such as a city, nation, religion, ethnicity, and so on.[54] But, as part of Rorty's vision of a liberal utopia (characterized by a belief that cruelty is incontestably evil), he proposed a form of solidarity that would aim for a higher connection, one based on "shared conceptions of what constitutes suffering."[55] This solidarity is achieved not by "clearing away 'prejudice' or burrowing down to previously hidden depths," but through "the imaginative ability to see strange people as fellow sufferers."[56] Rorty singled out the novel as a genre uniquely suited to facilitating solidarity (although he also included "ethnography, the journalist's report, the comic book, the docudrama") because it can provide a "description of what unfamiliar people are like and of redescription of what we ourselves are like,"[57] while also helping us "recognize cruelty suffered and inflicted" and challenging the binary of "us and them."[58] Traditional differences of perceived race, religion, and culture matter in this scenario, but should not supersede the shared human capacity to feel pain and humiliation.

Rorty's emphasis on suffering and on "what unfamiliar people are like" might seem to echo the empathy model of literature, which promotes the idea that "there are those who suffer, and those who do not and thus have the leisure to be convinced—via novels and films that produce empathy—that the sufferers matter."[59] We also know that descriptions of "what unfamiliar people are like" can take the shape of Vladimir's articles about the quaint differences between immigrant and American life, or the callous journalistic reports on suffering produced by the various Millers in the novel. Description as such often pretends to clear away prejudice, by offering a look into "how the other half lives," while in fact asserting difference all along.[60] Sometimes, as in the case of yellow journalism, it does not even pretend but actively seeks to reinscribe an "us/them" dynamic. Rorty, however, preferred to think of sensitivity rather than empathy, and his aspirational view was that literature can facilitate human solidarity based on *mutual recognition* of suffering. A novel like *The Lazarus Project*, by employing migrant aesthetics, represents migration as a historically constituted drama of *shared* suffering and can thus facilitate solidarity across national divides.

To fully apprehend how this works, it's helpful to employ Hannah Arendt's concept of "representative thinking" and the role that literature plays in producing it. As Namwali Serpell notes, for Arendt "literature's special talent" lies in facilitating access to as many perspectives on a given issue as possible, in order to enlarge one's views of the issue and to clarify what political action should be taken.[61] "The more people's standpoints I have present in my mind while I am pondering a given issue," Arendt wrote, "the better I can imagine how I would feel and think if I were in their place, the stronger will be my capacity for representative thinking." But Arendt qualified this statement: "This process of representation does not blindly adopt the actual views of those who stand somewhere else, and hence look upon the world from a different perspective; this is a question neither of empathy, as though I tried to be or to feel like somebody else, nor of counting noses and joining a majority but of being and thinking in my own identity where actually I am not."[62] As Serpell notes, "Arendt derived her theory of 'representative thinking' from Kant's aesthetic theory in *The Critique of Judgment*," specifically his concept of enlarging one's mentality to arrive at judgment.[63] Representative thinking requires both an enlarging of perspective *and* a detachment from our own idiosyncrasies.

For Arendt, storytelling is a critical tool of cognition that allows us "to see things in their proper perspective, to be strong enough to put that which is too close at a certain distance so that we can see and understand it without bias and prejudice, to be generous enough to bridge abysses of remoteness until we can see and understand everything that is too far away from us as though it were our own affair."[64] Given the enormous scope of migration as a human phenomenon, narrative can be useful in providing "proper perspective" on it—one that is neither "too close," as in the much fetishized U.S./Mexico immigrant crisis, nor "too far," such that the *longue durée* of migration can be ascertained only in fragmentary instances. With Rorty and Arendt in mind, we can see that narratives of migration, specifically those that employ migrant aesthetics, allow us to comprehend specific figures and events (Lazarus Averbuch in 1908, Vladimir Brik as a refraction of Aleksandar Hemon in 2008, and so on) within a broader canvas (the mass migrations produced by persecution the world over) without depending on empathy.

There are limits to Arendt's model of representative thinking, and to narrative's role in facilitating it, and that is why the metanarrative distancing produced by migrant aesthetics is crucial. First, there is the question of whether, in "being and thinking in my own identity where actually I am not," one can ever see and understand any given condition "without bias and prejudice." Following Kant, Arendt argued that an enlarged mentality could facilitate the formation of "disinterested" judgments, or a kind of impartiality. But is true impartiality possible? In her controversial essay "Reflections on Little Rock" (1959), for instance, Arendt argued against the integration of public schools, concluding that "oppressed minorities [are] never the best judges on the order of priorities."[65] As Franco Palazzi notes, she argued further "that African-Americans should have fought first of all for the abolition of segregationist marriage laws, instead of being 'almost exclusively concerned with discrimination in employment, housing and education.'"[66] Palazzi calls this stance an "infelicitous application of representative thinking," where "Arendt pretended to be a better advocate for African-Americans' rights than African-Americans themselves." Palazzi also notes a second limitation to Arendt's notion of representative thinking, namely that, in depending on inhabiting the perspective of others, Arendt presumed that she could understand the existence and relevance of the most marginalized, of "the points of view of those who are constantly deleted from the field of social intelligibility, let alone the public sphere—i.e. precisely those marginal positions from which the most insightful criticisms of a given system of values are likely to emerge."[67]

Palazzi emphasizes that noting the limits of Arendt's representative thinking does not preclude us from "trying to imagine viable ways to overcome them."[68] The writers examined in this book, each in their individual ways, give shape precisely to the "marginal positions" that Palazzi invokes by exploring the lives of migrants, whether they are the figures who orbit around Julius in Cole's *Open City*, Mengestu's anonymous refugees and the nameless dead they leave behind, Hemon's religious refugees, or, as we will see in subsequent chapters, Valeria Luiselli's lost children and Julie Otsuka's anonymous camp internees. These writers do not seek to "give voice" to marginal migrant subjects or to elicit our empathy for their suffering. Rather, they take on and mark the positions of those subjectivities, while showing how the machinations of empire entangle the histories of people worldwide, resulting in mass migrations that obviate the rhetoric of state sovereignty and borders.

They also call for migrant solidarity. To make this solidarity possible, we need to refine Arendt's idea of how an enlarged mentality might facilitate the formation of "disinterested" judgments. Serpell suggests that one way to do this is to return to Bertolt Brecht's "estrangement effect"—the highlighting of the props through which art is created—thus keeping audiences alert to the differences between representation and experience. Similarly, the metafictive qualities of migrant aesthetics, evinced in Hemon's prismatic design, playful refractions, and contingent plots, allow us to consider the positions of migrants while preempting the projection of our biases by constantly reminding us of the boundaries between representation and lived experience. Hemon and the other writers featured in this book call on us to think, as ourselves, from the position of migrants, and thus develop an enlarged view of the world, but *not* to make a judgment on how marginal lives should be lived (as Arendt did with respect to African Americans); instead, they prompt us to examine how *our own* political choices implicate us in making lives marginal and invisible to the public sphere.

Among these choices is the question of what kind of solidarities, if any, we are part of and why. Hemon refracts the lives of several figures, both fictive and historical, to allow us to imagine forms of migrant solidarity across time and space, on a broad scale. While the interconnections that he projects are expansive, they remain mostly abstract because they are contained within a fictive world. In the next chapter, we will explore how Valeria Luiselli, more so than Hemon, projects migrant solidarity at a wide scale that is also deep, because it operates not only through fiction but also through literary history and the history of empire.

Chapter Three

MIGRANT SOLIDARITY
Valeria Luiselli's Echo Canyon

> Writers have to bear witness, it's their vocation. Some would say the writer *has* no higher calling than to bear witness to injustice and suffering.
>
> —SIGRID NUNEZ, *THE FRIEND*

Valeria Luiselli's *Tell Me How It Ends: An Essay in Forty Questions* (2017) and her novel *Lost Children Archive* (2019) center on the plight of undocumented children seeking asylum at the United States–Mexico border or caught in the immigration bureaucracy at detention centers, of which the United States has the highest number in the world. As Gaiutra Bahadur notes, Luiselli's work forms part of the "visceral, and full-throated" outcry against the U.S. government's separation of "thousands of migrant children from their parents," detaining them far from their families or losing track of them altogether.[1] Since the crisis intensified in the summer of 2018, "there seemed to be an imperative, both professional and moral, to pay particular attention to the experiences of the children," which produced a veritable "stampede of storytelling," with several accounts that "immerse us in the internal and external" struggles of unaccompanied child migrants seeking asylum.[2] "There was a duty to humanize [the children] to counter political language such as 'illegal alien,'" notes Bahadur, who argues that "what such stories really hope to do is humanize their readers, listeners, spectators: the desensitized consumers of news."[3] Luiselli, however, is invested not so much in humanizing the asylum-seeking children and the consumers of news—though she does this too—as in showing that the humanitarian crisis of migration is, at its core, a problem of language and narration. Luiselli does not simply seek to counter the political language that distorts the humanity of refugees; rather, she shows the extent to which the language of migration *produces* the political, economic, social, and humanitarian crisis of unaccompanied children at the border.

The normative terms, genres, perspectives, and plots for representing immigration allow American citizens to think of all refugees and migrants as "a foreign problem."[4] Such citizens thus skirt the responsibility that they themselves bear for electing governments that created the need to migrate in the first place. "No one," writes Luiselli in *Lost Children Archive*, "thinks of the children arriving" at the U.S.-Mexican border as "refugees of a hemispheric war that extends" from the border itself down across "the Mexican sierras, forests, and southern rain forests into Guatemala, into El Salvador, and all the way to the Celaque Mountains in Honduras." No one thinks of the children as "consequences of a historical war that goes back decades. Everyone keeps asking: Which war, where? Why are they here? Why did they come to the United States? What will we do with them? No one is asking: Why did they flee their homes?" (*LCA*, 51).

Luiselli isn't entirely right here. Very few people ask, "Which war, where?" More likely for most American citizens is a focus on what to do with the children or, more to the point, how to get rid of them. As for "Why did they flee?," if the question is ever asked, the assumed answers always involve the corruption and violence of the children's home countries, without the crucial (neo)colonial context that would truly answer the questions Luiselli lists. As Dinaw Mengestu notes in his review of *Tell Me How It Ends*, the "general arc and the often brutal details of these children's narratives have been reported" since at least 2014, "when more than 68,000 children surrendered themselves at the border," with stories pointing to the "havoc wreaked across Central America by gangs like Mara Salvatrucha [commonly known as MS-13] and Barrio 18" and the "brutal treatment of migrants by coyotes, police officers and cartels."[5] Missing from these stories is the history of the "United States military's involvement in Central America in the 1980s" and its immigration policies in the 1990s, which together produced the political and economic conditions that forced the children and their families to seek asylum.[6] Luiselli's books rightly insist that we take these elements of history into account.

The best reporting on the subject highlights the fact that the gangs blamed for the refugee crisis "originated," as Luiselli writes in *Tell Me How It Ends*, "in Los Angeles in the 1980s, a time when [gangs such as] the Bloods,

Crips, Nazi Low Riders, and Aryan Brotherhood, among many others, were already well established in the United States."[7] Luiselli then goes a step further, linking the gangs' rise to American foreign policy, specifically actions taken by the Reagan administration, including the military and financial funding of repressive governments throughout Latin America—governments that massacred thousands of people and made life impossible for countless others.[8] Approximately "one-fifth of the population of El Salvador fled" to the United States during that era, with nearly 300,000 landing in Los Angeles as political exiles (*TM*, 46). But when, in the 1990s, "anti-immigration policies and programs in the U.S. led to massive deportations of Central Americans," the plot became maddeningly circular (*TM*, 46): among the thousands that were deported were many MS-13 members. Their deportation, far from eradicating the gang, facilitated its transformation from an LA phenomenon to a "transnational army, with more than seventy thousand members spread across the United States, Mexico, and the Northern triangle" of Guatemala, El Salvador, and Honduras (*TM*, 46).

In *Tell Me How It Ends*, Luiselli writes: "The problem with trying to tell [the children's] story is that it has no beginning, no middle, and no end" (7). She is in part referring to the fact that, as Mengestu notes, human lives, "real or imagined, rarely follow the clearly delineated start-stop borders that stories impose."[9] More urgently, she is indexing American domestic and transnational policies, which obscure the reasons why migrants flee their countries in the first place. Like others, Luiselli sees those policies as embedded in a long, circular history of colonialism and neocolonialism.

In *This Land Is Our Land: An Immigrant's Manifesto*, the writer Suketu Mehta cites the case of Haiti which, after wresting its independence from France through the first successful slave rebellion in the Americas, had to pay France. France did not hesitate to use its military might as a threat while demanding ninety million gold francs (around forty billion dollars today) in so-called reparations for the property that France claimed to have lost, including both lands and enslaved people. The United States at this time, fearing that its own slaves would be encouraged to revolt, refused to recognize Haiti as an independent nation and issued a crippling economic embargo against the island that lasted until 1863. The following year, it began to lend Haiti money to help with its "reparations" to France. Haiti finally finished paying France in 1947, thanks to a major U.S. bank loan. In addition to being thus indebted to a neocolonial power, Haiti had to suffer nineteen years of occupation from that same nation: from 1915 to 1934, the United States controlled Haiti's customs, collected its taxes, and ran many of its governmental institutions. Then, from 1957 to 1986, Haiti was forced to live under the U.S.-backed dictators "Papa Doc" and "Baby Doc" Duvalier. This brutal sequence of events was instrumental in making Haiti the poorest country in the Western Hemisphere and has sent its people migrating all over the world. It is entirely fitting that the United States is home to the largest Haitian migrant population.

Haiti is but one of several examples of the chaos wreaked by European and American imperialism, which has devastated whole continents through looting, war, political and military intervention, and forced labor. Mehta notes that "40 percent of all the national borders in the entire world today were made by just two countries: Britain and France," a fact that has led to political instability and internal wars worldwide, and transformed millions of people into migrants.[10] At present, neocolonial practices are more clandestine, operating through transnational corporations that are protected by powerful governments, their interests invariably prioritized over those of poor people in so-called developing countries. We need to look at the history of the United Fruit Company and its ties to CIA interventions in Latin America to understand the history of migration from that area. Drug wars, and the related arms trade, offer additional origin points. As Mehta writes, "Americans sell their neighbors the weapons of mass destruction" required to operate drug cartels "and buy the main crop their farmers have left to sell, their coca leaves and marijuana plants," and both of these exchanges render countries "ungovernable."[11] The problem is too often attributed solely to Mexico and the countries of the Northern Triangle. This is not to say that corruption in those countries is not a factor; as Luiselli argues, if there is to be an end to the crisis at the Mexico–United States border, it will come only when "all the governments involved—the American, Mexican, Salvadoran, Honduran, and Guatemalan governments, at least—acknowledge their shared accountability in the roots and causes of the children's exodus" (*TM*, 46). But the history of (neo)colonialism cannot be discounted.

I have not touched on what will be the biggest factor for migration in the twenty-first century: climate change, which is being caused in great part by American and European practices. "Americans are only 4 percent of the world's population but are responsible for one-third of the excess carbon dioxide in the atmosphere," writes Mehta; the European Union is a close second, but "America creates a third of the world's solid waste and consumes a fifth of the world's energy. The average American uses as much energy as 35 Indians, or 185 Ethiopians, and consumes as many goods and services as 53 Chinese."[12]

Far from exposing the deeper causes and consequences of migration, which are more complicated than my brief summary could hope to cover, most literature on the crisis at the border, especially news coverage, focuses on the "problem" that the children pose to the U.S. Department of Homeland Security: what it should do with them and, most persistently, how it should dissuade the children and all migrants from coming to America (*TM*, 44). By contrast, *Tell Me How It Ends*, a work of narrative nonfiction based on Luiselli's experiences as a volunteer court translator for undocumented migrant children, insists that we ask harder questions: most pressingly, what responsibility do we bear for the children's plight?

She also turns her questions back on herself: Who is her audience, and what illusions does she have about what her books can do about the refugee crisis? Luiselli knows well that she is writing to a limited audience. The well-traveled daughter of a diplomat, she earned a PhD from Columbia University and arguably writes for her highly educated peers, though she aims to reach a broader public. She published *Tell Me How It Ends* with Coffee House Press, a nonprofit independent press whose mission is to expand "the definition of what literature is, what it can do," and to whom "it belongs."[13] Luiselli is also keenly aware of the sentimental trappings that often come with using literature as a political tool. A character in *Lost Children Archive* reflects on the perils of turning the children, "their lives, into material for media consumption": "Why? What for? So that others can listen to them and feel—pity? Feel—rage? And then do what? No one decides to not go to work and start a hunger strike after listening to the radio in the morning" (*LCA*, 96).

Like Sigrid Nunez, whose words open this chapter, Luiselli believes that writers must bear witness, that they must offer testimony to the world's injustice and suffering. But there is a tension between "document and fabrication," between the urge to document in a journalistic fashion, as Luiselli does in *Tell Me How It Ends*, and the need to testify and mourn through fiction, as she does in *Lost Children Archive* (*LCA*, 42). These two aims are not mutually exclusive—they both facilitate bearing witness to injustice and involve capturing reality as much as shaping it—but they have different end points and face different ethical dilemmas. Journalistic accounts of suffering seem to escape the ethical question that nags the artist: Can or should one "make art with someone else's suffering"? Yet journalistic accounts can also be co-opted by politics, especially since so many politicized issues no longer call urgently for "committed debate in the public arena" but instead become bargaining chips "that parties use frivolously in order to move their own agendas forward" (*LCA*, 79).

These tensions contributed to the gestation period of Luiselli's novel. As she reported in an interview:

> I started writing *Lost Children* before I wrote *Tell Me*, which was an appendix that grew out of writing *Lost Children*. I stopped writing *Lost Children* for about six months when I realized I was using the novel as a vehicle for my political frustration and rage, which is not what fiction does best. So I stopped and wrote this essay instead. Once I had been able to do that, I could go back and continue writing something as porous and ambivalent as a novel.[14]

In the essay, Luiselli bears witness by pulling apart the language with which refugee children are screened in the immigration process. In the novel, she does so by creating a set of haunting literary echoes that contextualize the children's suffering within a broader history of forced migration. Additionally, to balance her creation of that more "porous and ambivalent" medium, a novel, she includes metafictive reflections. Luiselli believes, whether in journalism or in a novel, that the writer must ask, "Who am I to tell this story ... am I too angry, am I mentally colonized by Western-Saxon-white categories?" (*LCA*, 79).

FROM LANGUAGE TO ECHO

Tell Me How It Ends is composed of four parts: "Border," "Court," "Home," and "Community," titles suggesting a narrative of survival that only some of the children live out. "Border" introduces a family—Luiselli, her husband, and their two children. While applying for permanent residency in the United States, they travel by car from New York to Cochise County, Arizona, near the U.S.-Mexican border. As Luiselli recounts their travels, she reflects on the vast differences between a green-card application and the intake questionnaire for undocumented minors. The contrast between the two processes—one is mildly absurd, the other cynically brutal[15]—establishes the relative privilege from which Luiselli dissects the screening questionnaire and makes clear that she constitutes an added frame through which the children's responses are filtered.

Aside from this opening, *Tell Me How It Ends* is not autobiographical; it is devoted almost entirely to the political contexts that compel the migration of children and their families. Luiselli focuses on two sisters from Guatemala, aged five and seven, who are hoping to be reunited with their mother, and an adolescent named "Manu" (his real name must be concealed), who escaped from Honduras under the threat of death from MS-13. Luiselli does not make the children's lives the objects of consumption; rather, she employs their stories to expose how the American government uses the questionnaire not only to select whom to deport but also to mask the violence that produces migration.

The questionnaire consists of forty questions, most of them absurd in the context of the children's lives: "How do you like where you're living now?," "Are you happy here?," "Are you safe?"

> It's hard to imagine that these children, considered a hindrance to institutions and unwanted intruders by a large part of the society to which they've just arrived, soon to face a judge and defend themselves against a removal order, indeed "like where they are living." In the media and much of the official political discourse, the word "illegal" prevails over "undocumented" and the term "immigrant" over "refugee." How would anyone who is stigmatized as an "illegal immigrant" feel "safe" and "happy"? But the children usually respond yes to those three questions. (*TM*, 44–45)

The problem of language in this process is quite literal, as most of the children speak only Spanish and need translators to help them understand the questions and answer them in English. Sometimes the children are not native Spanish speakers either (their mother tongues belonging to the twenty-four Native American linguistic groups in Mexico and Central America) and need translators to help them across at least two language barriers. The absurd ideological gaps, cynical euphemisms, and cruel ironies inherent in the questionnaire present even harder challenges, especially as these include many bureaucratic obscurities and adult-oriented assumptions. More than anything, the questionnaire obfuscates—its design purposely avoids "any attention to detail" or complexity, rendering the children's stories only in "generalized, distorted" terms (*TM*, 11).

Yet the answers the children give can mean the difference between life and death. Luiselli explains that, in "court and in detention centers, people who volunteer for different positions conduct interviews that either prepare a person for an asylum interview or a credible fear interview."[16] The former determines whether you are qualified for asylum, while the latter stops deportation from the United States until your asylum case is processed. The interviews that Luiselli translates for the children "give lawyers a sense of a case, so they can decide whether to take it on or not," and are "ultimately meant to prepare a child to stand in front of a judge and contest a deportation order."[17] A wrong set of answers, which more often than not are the product of the obfuscating questionnaire rather than the child's actual situation, can send the child back to a country where they will face death threats from gangs, rape, physical and emotional abuse, and/or economic destitution.

The questionnaire also has consequences reaching far beyond the immediate context of the children, for it shapes American public opinion about the children and why they flee, ultimately determining the fate of other refugees to come. In *Tell Me How It Ends*, instead of attempting to overcome the limits imposed by the questionnaire or to devise another one, Luiselli uses its forty questions as opportunities to dissect the euphemisms of migration and the political and economic history that they obscure. We may not stop what we are doing to riot, she implies, but we can, at the very least, provide clear testimony to the crimes committed against refugees, both now and historically.

"Euphemisms hide, erase, coat. Euphemisms lead us to tolerate the unacceptable. And, eventually, to forget," reads a note included in *Lost Children Archive*. "Against a euphemism, remembrance. In order to not repeat. Remember terms and meanings. Their absurd disjointedness":

> Term: *Our Peculiar Institution*. Meaning: slavery. (Epitome of all euphemisms.)
> Term: *Removal*. Meaning: expulsion and dispossession of people from their lands.

Term: *Placing Out*. Meaning: expulsion of abandoned children from the East Coast.
Term: *Relocation*. Meaning: confining people in reservations.
Term: *Reservation*. Meaning: a wasteland, a sentence to perpetual poverty.
Term: *Removal*. Meaning: expulsion of people seeking refuge.
Term: *Undocumented*. Meaning: people who will be removed. (*LCA*, 255–256)

Both Luiselli's essay and her novel expose the toxic impact of euphemisms on the public discourse about forced migration and its history. Whereas her essay dissects the language of the immigration questionnaire, her novel intertwines texts, sounds, and images to create an alternate way of narrating migration. One of the novel's primary raisons d'être is to mourn the migrant dead, especially those who leave no trace. "Numbers and maps tell horror stories," Luiselli writes in *Tell Me How It Ends*, "but the stories of deepest horror are perhaps those for which there are no numbers, no maps, no possible accountability, no words ever written or spoken. And perhaps the only way to grant any justice—were that even possible—is by hearing and recording those stories over and over again so that they come back, always, to haunt and shame us" (*TM*, 30). Thus, in the essay, Luiselli imagines creating a haunting echo of the nameless victims of migration and, in the novel, she enacts it.

For Luiselli, the humanitarian crisis at the United States–Mexico border echoes the many connected histories of dispossession and genocide produced in the name of white supremacy and imperial expansion. The repetition of violence—in the form of expulsion, confinement, and indentured servitude—in each of the historical instances Luiselli invokes highlights their similarities, though it does not erase their stark differences. The third line in the quotation about euphemisms refers to the Orphan Train Movement, a program that "placed out" approximately 250,000 orphaned, abandoned, and homeless children, mainly from New York and Boston to places throughout the United States and Canada between 1854 and 1929. The children, many of whom were immigrants, were sometimes adopted but often taken in as indentured servants; they traveled by train, mostly to the Western United States. Luiselli invokes their history alongside New World slavery, Native American expulsion, and the movement of "undocumented" refugees to vivify the broad scale of forced migration and, further, to create solidarity among its victims across time.

Each instance, from the relatively contained events of the Orphan Train Movement to the vast, far-reaching phenomenon of New World slavery, echoes the others in Luiselli's novel, through carefully chosen recurring images. The network of freight trains known as La Bestia (The Beast), which carries migrants across the United States–Mexico border, echoes the Orphan Train Movement. Similarly, the history of Native American forced migration surfaces in the image of Apaches being forced into train cars, which in turn invokes both the Orphan Train Movement and the children crossing the U.S.-Mexican border, who are one of the novel's foci. Rather than resolve the tension between "document and fabrication," which preoccupies one of the main characters in the early part of the novel, Luiselli creates meaning from that tension, imagining the plight of children at the border while also placing their suffering in a broader perspective that looks back to the history of Native American dispossession and the forced migration of millions through the transatlantic slave trade. Through a text-within-a-text that I will discuss later, Luiselli also projects the children into other regions of conflict and forced migration across the globe, thus preventing the fetishization of the U.S.-Mexican border.

The echoes—from the past to the future—interlink over a broad span of time, as in Teju Cole's *Open City*. Recall that in Cole's novel, Julius's "aimless wandering" throughout New York facilitates his reading of the city's sites as if they were palimpsests of the history of migration. I called this reading-in-motion Julius's "migrant aesthetics," referring to his method of threading together diverse temporal and spatial frames as he meditates on the history of New York and its residents. Luiselli's novel enacts its own migrant aesthetics: it moves across a vast portion of the country in an inverted use of "a grand American trope—the road novel."[18] Fictionalizing the first part of *Tell Me How It Ends*, Luiselli presents to us in *Lost Children Archive* a nuclear family that also travels by car from New York to Cochise County, Arizona. The echo between fiction and lived experience is deliberate and part of a more elaborate, allusive, and interrelated structure connecting the two texts—Luiselli's version of Aleksandar Hemon's prismatic refraction.[19]

The use of echoes is made literal in the novel. The character of the father (all the characters remain nameless) feels inspired by the work of Raymond

Murray Schafer (composer, writer, music educator, and environmentalist) and Steven Feld (ethnomusicologist, anthropologist, linguist) to create an "inventory of echoes"—a collection of "sounds that did not exist anymore but that people would still be able to hear" through recordings of the reverberant sounds of natural and human sounds, echoes of the past in the present (*LCA*, 203). Specifically, he hopes to record the soundscape of the Apaches in Apacheria,[20] the place where "the last free peoples on the entire American continent" lived before the surrender of their leader Geronimo to white Americans in 1886, a surrender that marked the end of open resistance by Native Americans in the West (*LCA*, 26).

Soundscapes are acoustic environments "as perceived or experienced and/or understood" by a person or a people in a particular context, and acoustic environments are composed of "all sound sources," be they "actual or simulated, outdoor or indoor, as experienced or in memory."[21] Building on Schafer's work in the field of soundscape studies, Feld conducted an ethnography of sound, using a symbol system, in Papua New Guinea, among the Kaluli people of Bosavi. From the Kaluli people, he learned that their songs "become what Kaluli call a 'path,' namely a series of place-names that link the cartography of the rainforest to the movement of its past and present inhabitants. These song paths are also linked to the spirit world of birds, whose flight patterns weave through trails and water courses, connecting a spirit cosmology above to local histories on the ground."[22] The songs thus connect spirits and living beings in both the past and the present, within a specific locale. Schafer and Feld argue that, just as light waves travel through time, so do sound waves, bringing with them the echoes of soundscapes across time—and these echoes in the landscape contain memory.[23]

The concept resembles one that Toni Morrison's character Sethe uses in *Beloved* (1987) to explain to her child Denver how memory may outlive perspective: "If a house burns down, it's gone, but the place—the picture of it—stays, and not just in my rememory, but out there, in the world. What I remember is a picture floating around out there outside my head. I mean, even if I don't think it, even if I die, the picture of what I did, or knew, or saw is still out there. Right in the place where it happened."[24] Whereas Morrison uses visual imagery, Luiselli focuses on sound. In her novel, she does so both thematically and formally. The father tells part of the history of the Apaches to his family, narrating stories that reverberate as refrains during the rest of the road trip. The mother also reflects on archives in sonic terms:

"You whisper intuitions and thoughts into the emptiness," she writes, "hoping to hear something back. And sometimes, just sometimes, an echo does indeed return, a real reverberation of something, bouncing back with clarity when you've finally hit the right pitch and found the right surface" (*LCA*, 42). The reverberating echoes of memory and history also structure *Lost Children Archive* as a whole, working in tune with intermedial links to visual and sonic documents to spin radically outward from the migrant crisis at the United States–Mexico border, connecting it to historical, literary, and mythical narratives of migration while simultaneously highlighting its roots in the machinations of capital and empire.

To see how this method works, we need to examine the main strands of the novel and analyze how they work together.

A NETWORK OF GENRES: *LOST CHILDREN ARCHIVE*

In *Lost Children Archive*, Luiselli expands the road-trip frame of *Tell Me How It Ends* to structure the entire novel, while also setting the road-trip genre "sideways," as Claire Messud observes. The family travels "not between coasts but away from the city, from the center to the margins—their progress, if it can be called that, recalls *The Sheltering Sky* more than *On the Road*."[25]

From one vantage point, the road-trip narrative is the quintessential genre of self-realization and American mythmaking, and Jack Kerouac's *On the Road* (1957) is its exemplar. In this definition of the genre, the road is "perceived as a mythic space of possibility," affording and reaffirming purportedly foundational aspects of American identity: "freedom, rebellion, or reinvention."[26] This myth of the road has "taken shape in a century's worth of road films, novels, and nonfiction" and is part of an older Euro-American literary tradition of male escape from domesticity (think of Huckleberry Finn lighting out for the territory).[27] *On the Road* epitomizes the form by acting out "the fantasy of a borderless world, which reincorporates and rescales white masculinity as a figure of expansion that obliterates or subsumes" other identities.[28] When one puts pressure on this myth, however, what emerges is another story: mobility as freedom sitting side by side with mobility as "shiftlessness, as deviance, and as resistance," embodied by figures such as tramps, gypsies, fugitives, and migrants who signify threats to national cohesion.[29] Road narratives thus enact the tensions between these two opposing visions of mobility and between their competing definitions of American identity.

In framing *Lost Children Archive* as a road-trip narrative, Luiselli capitalizes on these tensions, ironizing Kerouac's vision of the road by placing it at odds with the forced mobility of refugees and migrants. Like the family in *Tell Me How It Ends*, the mother and children in the novel have the complex privilege of choosing to apply for residency in the United States and are thus not like the refugees whose plight they helplessly witness. Their account of their adopted country as they travel its roads follows another tradition—the observations of an outsider of relative privilege, whose account of America tries to take in its great contradictions. The mother writes:

> I know, as we drive through the long, lonely roads of this country—a landscape that I am seeing for the first time—that what I see is not quite what I see. What I see is what others have already documented: Ilf and Petrov, Robert Frank, Robert Adams, Walker Evans, Stephen Shore—the first road photographers and their pictures of road signs, stretches of vacant land, cars, motels, diners, industrial repetition, all the ruins of early capitalism now engulfed by future ruins of later capitalism. (*LCA*, 102)

Kerouac is invoked mostly as a point of contrast ("Kerouac's America is nothing like this America, bony, so desolate, and factual") or of critique ("My sister, who teaches literature in Chicago, always says that Kerouac is like an enormous penis, pissing all over the USA") (*LCA*, 77). By contrast, the photographers that the mother lists do not depict mythic America; instead, they capture the America of outsiders, of refugees, of the forces that set off waves of migrants on the road, and of surges of movement into and within the United States. By invoking these photographers' contexts and images, the mother expands the scale of forced migration beyond the crisis at the border and contextualizes the children's plight historically.

The photo-essay of the Soviets Ilya Ilf and Yevgeni Petrov, *American Photographs* (1936), like Walker Evans's book of the same name (1938), depicts America during the Great Depression. It casts an eye toward the internal contradictions that made the United States both a haven for refugees in the decade that Hitler assumed power and a country that set its own citizens "flowing" within its borders—to borrow a term from Jean Toomer's *Cane*

(1923) and the title of Farah Griffin's 1995 book on the Great Migration.[30] Escaping the threat of Nazism, Robert Frank was at first taken by its myth of freedom: "Leaving Switzerland and coming to America, we felt like the door opened. We were free. And I liked it. I liked it a lot. It was another world, where you could move, where you could take the train somewhere. Travel."[31] But as he crisscrossed the country to create his masterpiece, *The Americans* (1958), he discovered the myth's underside: "I looked at poor people, how they tried to survive, what a lonely time it can be in America, and what a tough country it is, and also I saw for the first time the way the blacks were treated. It was surprising."[32] The other photographers Luiselli invokes, Robert Adams and Stephen Shore, reveal an American landscape made barren and bleak from overdevelopment. Adams's books—*The New West* (1974), *Denver* (1977), *Summer Nights* (1985), and *What We Bought* (1995)—focus on the environmental damage caused by suburbanization along Colorado's Front Range. Shore's *Uncommon Places* (1982), like the road photography of Evans and Frank, focuses on "the American landscape, and its transformation at the hands of twentieth-century consumer culture."[33] The mother in *Lost Children Archive* writes, "The deeper we drive into this land, the more I feel like I'm looking at remains and ruins" (51).

Like Teju Cole's Julius, the mother is an intellectually agile narrator who intertwines many texts, sounds, and images as she reflects on the history inscribed in the American Southwest. She and her children, her five-year-old daughter from a previous relationship and the father's ten-year-old boy, also from a previous relationship, head south in support of the father's documentary project. His plan, to "record the sounds that now, in the present, travel through some of the same spaces where Geronimo and his people, in the past, once moved, walked, spoke, sang" (*LCA*, 141), conspicuously rehearses aspects of the Vanishing Indian trope. The novel underscores the father's ideological limits, but also enacts a version of his documentary by including the history of the Apache people through the stories the father tells the children. The mother, meanwhile, has her own project: she hopes to document the plight of children at deportation centers, the thousands of children locked up at the border in "Galveston, Brownsville, Los Fresnos, El Paso, Nixon, Canutillo, Conroe, Harlingen, Houston, and Corpus Christi" (*LCA*, 25). When Manuela, a woman she met in New York, asks for help—her two daughters from Guatemala, who have crossed the border, have gone missing (echoing another strand from *Tell Me How It Ends*)—the family vainly tries to track them down. During their search, they witness another group of children being deported from New Mexico (*LCA*, 182).

The form of the novel resembles that of contemporary autofiction, as defined by James Wood: its "plot is relaxed into essay, with room for authorial digression, political and theoretical commentary, and reports on what the author has been reading, along with just enough storytelling to keep the novel moving forward."[34] But the intensely metafictive and intertextual nature of the novel, which creates a network of allusions to diverse historical timeframes, gives *Lost Children Archive* a political urgency lacking in much of contemporary autofiction. The mother, like Luiselli in *Tell Me How It Ends*, thinks long and hard about the perils of speaking for the children at the border, as she plans a documentary about the crisis, a project she calls "Lost Children Archive." (Like her husband, she documents soundscapes; in New York, they were both part of a group trying to document the myriad sounds of the city.) Eventually, because of her thoughts and experiences, she changes the scope of her project, producing the novel itself.

The change in structure also signals a shift in perspective: the mother cedes control of the narrative to her stepson in the second of the novel's four parts. The boy addresses his younger sister, narrating his account of the road trip and sharing his growing understanding that soon their family will be fragmented by their parents' impending breakup. He depicts how he sets off with his sister, searching for the missing girls at the border, and their subsequent struggles when they get lost in the desert. Part 3 mixes the mother's account of the parents' search for their missing children with that of the boy, while part 4 returns to the boy alone, addressing his sister as their family breaks apart.

Interwoven throughout the novel are different textual, audio, and visual media, each doing its part to shape the novel aesthetically and thematically. The family listens to an audio version of William Golding's *Lord of the Flies* (though, due to a technical error, the opening lines of Cormac McCarthy's *The Road* keep playing: "When he woke in the woods in the dark and the cold of the night he'd reach out to touch the child sleeping beside him"), to music (David Bowie's "Space Oddity" becomes the children's favorite, an anthem for displacement), and to news of the border crisis. Seven bankers boxes, containing a host of visual and textual documents—photographs, maps, postcards, stereographs, brochures from park services, books, notebooks—serve as archives for each family member. Four boxes belong to the father, while the mother, son, and daughter have one each. These archives appear interspersed throughout the novel in boxlike framed lists, simulating for the reader the process of digging through the boxes themselves. The mother's box contains

> a few photos, some legal papers, intake questionnaires used for court screenings, maps of migrant deaths in the southern deserts, and a folder with dozens of "Migrant Mortality Reports" printed from online search engines that locate the missing, which listed bodies found in those deserts, the possible cause of death, and their exact location. At the very top of the box, I placed a few books I'd read and thought could help me think about the whole project from a certain narrative distance: *The Gates of Paradise*, by Jerzy Andrzejewski; *The Children's Crusade*, by Marcel Schwob; *Belladonna*, by Daša Drndić; *Le goût de l'archive*, by Arlette Farge; and a little red book I hadn't yet read, called *Elegies for Lost Children*, by Ella Camposanto. (*LCA*, 24)

The book by Camposanto, "who probably wrote it over a span of several decades, and is loosely based on the historical Children's Crusade, which involved tens of thousands of children who traveled alone across, and possibly beyond, Europe, and which took place in the year 1212 (though historians disagree about most of this crusade's fundamental details)" (*LCA*, 139).

While the Children's Crusade is a historical event, *Elegies for Lost Children* is a fictional book that Luiselli embeds in her novel, presenting the elegies individually and in groups (there are sixteen) as cutaways from the main narrative strands.[35] "In Camposanto's version, the 'crusade' takes place in what seems like a not-so-distant future in a region that can possibly be mapped back to North Africa, the Middle East, and southern Europe, or to Central and North America (the children ride atop 'gondolas,' for example, a word used in Central America to refer to the wagons or cars of freight trains)" (*LCA*, 139). Through these elegies, Luiselli melds history, fiction, and myth to mourn the children who die as they try to cross the United States–Mexico border. They also enable her to place their deaths in the context of global migration flows.

As Camposanto, Luiselli writes *Elegies for Lost Children* as a set of allusions to "literary works that are about voyages, journeying, migrating, etc." "Embedded and paraphrased but not quoted or cited" are works by Conrad (*The Heart of Darkness*), Eliot ("The Waste Land"), the first two texts listed in the quotation above (Schwob's and Andrzejewski's, which serve, respectively, as thematic and aesthetic models), Juan Rulfo (*Pedro Páramo*), and Rainer Maria Rilke (*Duino Elegies*) (*LCA*, 358). In the first elegy, Luiselli alludes to "Ezra Pound's 'Canto I,' which is itself an 'allusion' to Homer's Book XI of the *Odyssey*," both of which are "about journeying/descending into the underworld" and thus "establish an analogy between migrating and descending into the underworld" (*LCA*, 358).[36] In this richly intertextual novel, some texts play more prominent roles than others. As Wood observes, the "troika of patron texts, guiding and drawing this novel onward," are represented by "lost children (Golding), a last child (McCarthy), and the ghosts of the dead (Rulfo)."[37] Implicit in Luiselli's intertwining of *Elegies for Lost Children* with the son and daughter's own experience of getting lost in the desert is the suggestion that, within the context of the novel, allusion and reenactment bear an analogous relationship; the reenactment that the children carry out is an embodied form of allusion.

The analogy isn't without problems, and Luiselli is well aware of this fact. The second half of the novel explores the tension between the plight of the refugee children at the border and that of the couple's children, who, from the vantage point of their relative privilege, go on a misguided adventure, one that shows the perils of overidentification. Sitting in the back of the car, the children start pretending that they are "lost and walking in the endless desert" like the refugee children; they reenact scenes based on the stories they've heard from their parents and in the news. The mother thinks of reprimanding them—"I want to tell them to stop playing this game," this reenactment game that "is silly and frivolous . . . [W]hat do they know about . . . hardship or hopelessness or getting lost in deserts?"—but in the end she does not (*LCA*, 155). Maybe, she thinks, "any understanding, especially historical understanding, requires some kind of reenactment of the past, in its small, outward-branching, and often terrifying possibilities" (*LCA*, 155–156). Still, the mother's opposition to the children's game frames part 2 (appropriately titled "Reenactment"), in which her children get lost in the desert. We are left to wonder more deeply about the role of reenactments in historical understanding. Are they, as the mother suggests earlier in the novel, a way of registering "the soundmarks, traces, and echoes" that the refugee children "leave behind"? (*LCA*, 144). Or are such performances a sign of overidentification? Who, moreover, is entitled to perform reenactments?

These questions characterize the metafictive mode of part 1, while parts 2, 3, and 4, focused on reenactment and elegy, constitute the realization of the mother's project. In these parts, as described above, she sometimes gives away her narrative power to her stepson, who recounts his and his stepsister's reenactment of the plight of the children, with *Elegies for Lost Children* interspersed throughout his tale. When the mother comes to understand that her project is not to document the lives of children at detention centers but, rather, to tell the story of children "who are missing, those whose voices can no longer be heard because they are, possibly forever, lost," she at first does not know what form that story will take (*LCA*, 146). The finished novel, of course, is her eventual solution.

Luiselli creates the haunting echoes of *Lost Children Archive* through historical, intertextual, and intermedial allusions and thoroughly considered metafictive and historiographic meditations. Her aim is to represent the crisis at the U.S.-Mexican border on a scale and in a timeframe that acknowledges the long history of migration, specifically the history of forced migration to and within the United States and its deep connections to empire and capital. In so doing, she creates the possibility for migrant solidarity across time, space, and ethnic and racial categories.

To delve deeper into how this works, I will now examine two of the novel's central elements: the elegies for the lost and the dead and the reproduction of the family's (and the novel's) archives.

ELEGIES FOR LOST CHILDREN

"Whenever the boy and girl talk about child refugees, I realize now," writes the mother, "they call them 'the lost children.' I suppose the word 'refugee' is more difficult to remember" (*LCA*, 75). When the girl asks what "refugee" means, the mother thinks of all the waiting that a refugee must endure in bureaucratic mazes, in shelters, prisons, and camps, on roads and at ports, for family and papers and dignity. The mother almost says that a refugee is a person who waits but opts instead to tell her daughter that a refugee is a person who "has to find a new home" (*LCA*, 47–48). She then reflects: "Even if the term 'lost' is not precise, in our intimate family lexicon, the refugees become known to us as 'the lost children.' And in a way, I guess, they are lost children. They are children who have lost the right to a childhood" (*LCA*, 75).

MIGRANT SOLIDARITY

The book-within-a-book, *Elegies for Lost Children*, follows seven figures of diverse ages (the youngest is three, the oldest about ten) as they travel by foot and then by train toward and across a border. Four survive; the seventh and oldest is murdered, though Luiselli does not directly represent his death; and two others die of exhaustion. As they move through space, they seem suspended in time. "Time, in the desert, was an ongoing present tense" (*LCA*, 312). When they are not walking the desert—described as a valley of dry bones, where they hear echoes of the "impetuous, impotent dead" (an allusion to Ezra Pound) and where the "incandescent light" seems to bend the sky and time itself (*LCA*, 166, 312)—they are caught inside trains, which, in a direct reference to the Mexican-U.S. border, are portrayed as beasts.

Elegies for Lost Children echoes the novel in which it is contained. "Mouths open to the sun, they sleep" is the novel's first sentence, which, in modified form, becomes the first sentence of the first elegy ("Mouths open to the sky, they sleep") (*LCA*, 5, 142); another variation of the line appears as the beginning of Elegy 15, and others are embedded within other elegies (e.g., in Elegy 14). Similarly, references in the mother's section of *Lost Children Archive* are echoed in those narrated by the stepson. The mother sometimes reads the elegies aloud (once to the children) and records her reading (the boy does this too), suggesting a polyphonic version of what we ourselves are reading. The experiences and voices of the lost children thus become a choral, haunting echo—our experience of reading the main narrative is repeatedly interrupted by it—even if they are conjured from fragments of the literary canon, from the stories Luiselli heard in detention centers (which also inform *Tell Me How It Ends*), and from her imagination.

Created through a version of intertextuality that Luiselli views as "a method or procedure of composition" rather than as "an outward, performative gesture" (*LCA*, 357), *Elegies* embeds and paraphrases the work of many authors from a variety of literary traditions.[38] Luiselli as Camposanto not only intertwines these texts, because they are about "journeying/descending into the underworld," she also reappropriates "certain rhythmic cadences as well as imagery and lexicon" from these works; she repurposes and recombines specific words and word pairings that derive from lines in "Canto I" (*LCA*, 358).[39] These references operate as "echoes" of past literary works that, as in a soundscape, bring with them traces of past histories, contextualizing both *Elegies* and *Lost Children Archive* itself in a broad literary and historical "ecology." Just as soundscape ecology is "based on the causes and consequences of biological (biophony), geophysical (geophony), and human-produced (anthrophony) sounds," Luiselli's intertextuality connects the living realities of the child refugees at the border, within the specific context of the American Southwest, to the region's many other organisms and inanimate features (the deserts and their plants, rocks, sand), as well as to the experiences of refugees across time and space.[40]

Nearly all the literary allusions in the early sections of *Elegies* come from Conrad (parts 2 and 3 of *Heart of Darkness*), Pound (Cantos I–III), and Eliot ("The Burial of the Dead"). Luiselli's intertextuality emulates and extends Pound's and Eliot's collage-like methods of composition. Both poets borrowed extensively from the Western literary tradition (in Pound's case also from Greek and Latin classics and from Chinese and Japanese poetry); both mixed literary and historical allusions and made extensive use of myth to suggest comparisons between different historical periods; and both used this kind of intertextuality to demonstrate how "language contains the past."[41]

Eliot, with Conrad, also figures in *Lost Children Archive* as a writer who represented the West in crisis. Eliot's "The Waste Land" has been widely read as an epic expression of post–World War I desolation in Europe—in the words of I. A. Richards, "of uncertainty, of futility, of the groundlessness of aspirations, of the vanity of endeavour, and a thirst for a life-giving water which seems suddenly to have failed."[42] Composed of vignettes loosely linked by the legend of the Holy Grail, "The Waste Land" culminates with allusions to Buddhism and Hinduism, as if in search of images of redemption from outside the Western tradition. Conrad's *Heart of Darkness*—which, as we have seen, is also important to Teju Cole's *Open City*—describes a journey to central Africa and can be read as a political critique of imperialism and race. The book stinks of the rot of colonialism that was eating Europe from within and spreading death and violence in other parts of the world. Luiselli invokes these texts in *Elegies* to root the suffering of the lost children in that same long, cruel history.

As *Elegies* incorporates other sources, especially Schwob's *The Children's Crusade* and Andrzejewski's *The Gates of Paradise*, colonialism's long history becomes ever more prominent. Already, with its allusions to "The Waste Land," Luiselli has invoked the Crusades (through the Holy Grail motif), the church-sanctioned religious wars that enabled European territorial expansion outside the continent and were later used to justify colonialism, warfare, and terrorism. While the link between European colonialism and migration patterns from ex-colonies is not often made explicit in general accounts of migration, Luiselli's *Elegies*, set in a region that can be "mapped back" to parts of the world that were either colonized or shaped by colonialism, emphasize that connection.

Schwob and Andrzejewski both fictionalized the Children's Crusade, a tale that itself blends fact and myth. According to traditional accounts, in 1212, bands of children from France and Germany marched for the Holy Land in an attempt to peacefully convert Muslims to Christianity. They never reached their destination, since most either died on the march or were sold into slavery when they reached Marseilles, where adults tricked them into boarding ships purportedly taking them to Jerusalem. While this crusade never received official recognition from the pope and might have included poor people of all ages, not just children, in later centuries it has inspired writers as different as Voltaire, Brecht, Agatha Christie, and Kurt Vonnegut. The history and myths surrounding it revolve around the poignance of youthful self-sacrifice through innocence or foolish ignorance, or both.[43] The story of the Children's Crusade presents an opportunity for writers to manipulate the symbolic meaning of children, often as figures of purity that pull at our heartstrings.

Luiselli, however, paraphrases Schwob's and Andrzejewski's accounts because, while they portray children as pawns of the protocolonialism of the Crusades, they do not sentimentalize them or capitalize on their victimization. Both *Elegies* and *Lost Children Archive* also reject such instrumentality and idealization. The children in Luiselli's novel, both those in the frame story (the ten- and five-year-olds) and those who are refugees are imagined with the full range of their humanity. The recurrent allusions to *Lord of the Flies*—which plays as an audiobook in the car as the family drives—reminds us of the brutality that children, as human beings, are capable of. Luiselli uses the story of the Children's Crusade to highlight the suffering of child refugees, but she does so by underscoring colonialism's instrumentalization of children as figures that can mobilize sentiment. She also transforms specific aesthetic representations of the Children's Crusade into literary echoes in her own text.[44] These self-conscious allusions prevent sentimental readings of *Elegies for Lost Children* and shield it from easy consumption.

While Luiselli never quotes directly from Schwob's novella *The Children's Crusade* (*Le Croisade des Enfants*, 1896), the basic story and polyphonic quality of that book—the fact that the plight of the children is told from multiple perspectives—clearly structure not only *Elegies* but *Lost Children Archive* as a whole. More importantly, in naming Schwob as one of her sources, she leads us to an astonishingly prescient text, one that consistently associates the protocolonialist crusades with whiteness as an ideology of domination. Eight tales make up Schwob's book: one by a wandering cleric, another by a leper, two by pilgrim children, two by popes (Innocent III and Gregory IX), another by a cleric in Marseilles, and one by a Muslim holy man. In each of these tales, whiteness is associated not only with purity but also with the force that leads the children to Jerusalem—the belief in a Christian God who is explicitly identified as white.

When the leper meets one of the children, they have the following exchange:

> "Where are you going?" I said again.
> And he answered: "To Jerusalem, to conquer the Holy Land."
> Then I began to laugh, and I asked him: "Where is Jerusalem?"
> And he answered: "I do not know."
> And I said again: "How will you get there?"
> And he said to me: "I do not know."
> And I said again: "What is Jerusalem?"
> And he answered: "It is Our Lord."
> And so I began to laugh again and I asked: "What is Your Lord?"
> And he said unto me: "I do not know; He is white."[45]

Jesus and the crusading children are constantly referred to as white or associated with whiteness: "Lord Jesus is lily white"; "let all these white children who bear the cross"; "the Lord Jesus is white, in a white land"; "they filled the roads like a swarm of white bees"; "they were dressed in white." The representatives of the church are also associated with whiteness: "Lord, I am very old, and here I am dressed in white before you, and my name is Innocent"; "I kneel, white, in this white, gilded cell."[46] All of the adults in Schwob's novella are moved by the purity of the children—the only one who sees them as "a foreign turbulence" is the cleric at Marseilles, and this is because he sees them as needy and poor. At the end of the book, however, whiteness ultimately signifies death. The children hear "white voices," which are likened to those of "birds dead in the winter" as they walk long distances; their "great voyage's white end" is in a country where "all is white"; the sea where many of them drown is "hemmed with white"; the children's "little white bones" constitute the text's closing image.[47]

In Luiselli's novel, both associations remain. Whiteness is associated with imperialism and with death, in a cause-and-effect relationship: whiteness, as the ideology that supports imperialism, begets death. The children at the border are not considered pure because they are phenotypically not white. Imagine the outrage, Luiselli asks, if the refugee children at the border were white: "Would they be treated more like people? More like children?" (*TM*, 15). Xenophobic rhetoric about the border crisis frames the children as an "illegal alien" mass that carries "viruses," echoing a long American tradition of associating immigrants with disease (*LCA*, 124).[48] "I suppose," the mother writes, "that the convenient narrative has always been to portray the nations that are systematically abused by more powerful nations as a no-man's land, as a barbaric periphery whose chaos and brownness threaten civilized white peace" (*LCA*, 124). *Elegies for Lost Children*, by contrast, turns our attention to the refugee children themselves as they migrate, insisting on their humanity without making them symbols of purity.

Whereas Schwob provides only a few details about the children's journey in his novella, Luiselli as Camposanto follows the children closely. In *Elegies*, we see children as they march, their feet aching, their "lips chapped, cheeks cracked," their bellies empty (*LCA*, 142). We see them frozen in silent terror, listening to the "metallic intestines of the train [that emit] a sound like a thousand souls shrieking"; they wonder, as they cross a river, when they will arrive, knowing that they are "cut off forever from everything they'd once known, that they were really going nowhere" (*LCA*, 144, 165). We see one vomit at the sight of his own "blood-drenched socks and peeling skin"; we see them wait among throngs of refugees in fear and confusion, listening with dread to the threats and orders of the "man in charge," while others are overcome with exhaustion and lay down their lives on the desert sand (*LCA*, 167, 169). We sometimes see them play (with a broken cell phone, for instance) and laugh. In Elegy 14, a girl begins to hit the roof of the train, and others slowly follow, "hitting the beast with all their accumulated strength, fear, hatred, vigor, and hope" (*LCA*, 313). This produces an "almost feral sound, which begins in a howl, travels around the group of children contagiously, and ends in roaring laughter" (*LCA*, 313). The scene presages the recently published story of refugee children at a detention center in Texas (a sprawling ex-Walmart store) who periodically make animal noises that echo around the vast space, setting the children laughing contagiously despite their dire conditions.[49]

As we read *Elegies*, we regularly cut back to the nuclear family in the car and contrast the refugee children's march with the lives of a ten- and a five-year-old enjoying a relatively carefree childhood. Sitting in the back seat, they are utterly "alive," writes James Wood, "hurling questions (What is a refugee?) and mangling adult signals." As Wood notes, the daughter keeps asking, "[who] is this 'Jesus Fucking Christ' her parents invoke so often? When they stop at Graceland, at the Elvis Presley Boulevard Inn, she looks at a portrait of Elvis: 'Is that Jesus Fucking Christ, Mama?'"[50] The boy learns how to take photographs as the family travels, placing his Polaroid pictures in-between the pages of *Elegies* (the little red book) to dry. Once he throws a wild tantrum, frustrated by the long hours in the car; his sister asks if they will "live in the car forever" (*LCA*, 64–65, 209). We watch them as they sense the tension between their parents, fight with each other, care for one another, learn the history of Apacheria, and tire of their parents' obsessions. And we watch the love, tenderness, and frustration with which their parents treat them. Wood writes, "The book offers a beautiful and patiently loving portrait of children and of the task of looking after them."[51] The contrast between these children and the child refugees makes palpable the latter's lost childhood, as well as the cruel fragmentation of migrant families. It is their sheltered innocence that sets the brother and sister in search of the lost Guatemalan girls; the boy thinks that by rescuing the girls he and his sister will finally gain their mother's full attention. But their search, like that of the children of the crusade, is doomed, for the girls are later found dead in the desert (perhaps a reference to two Guatemalan girls who died in Border Patrol custody in December 2018).

Luiselli mourns lost children and lost childhoods but does not follow the "traditional elegy's basic triad of lamentation-confrontation-consolation"; rather, like other modern prose elegies, her book shifts the focus away from both the "formalized frenzy of grief" and the emphasis on consolation toward an epic account of the children's struggle—an extended confrontation.[52] In this respect, *Elegies for Lost Children* is like Daša Drndić's

Belladonna (2012), which is also included in the mother's archival box. Drndić's novel, "like a modern-day Homeric narrative of wars that are anything but glorious," recalls the "invisible dead" of Europe's Holocaust (particularly 2,061 Jewish children from The Hague, aged between six months and eighteen years), the Balkan genocides, and other victims of neocolonialism.[53] Occasionally, Luiselli as Camposanto describes the child refugees from a vantage point high above, thus giving their stories the grand scale of the epic: "If someone were to map them, the six of them, but also the dozens like them and the hundreds and tens of thousands that have come and will follow on other trains like this one, the map would plot a single line—a thin crack, a long fissure slicing the wide continent in two" (*LCA*, 143).

Luiselli sustains the epic scale by making the voices of the brother and sister, of the lost children from *Elegies*, and of the child refugees crossing the United States–Mexico border all intersect. This happens in a section of *Lost Children Archive* titled "Echo Canyon," which follows and extends the elegiac effect of *Elegies*. Named after a place at the heart of the Chiricahua mountains that the family visits on their pilgrimage to honor Geronimo and other Apache warriors, "Echo Canyon" is also the culmination of Luiselli's polyphonic virtuosity. The literary echoes within the novel fuse in this section to create one intense and haunting sentence that is twenty pages long. Luiselli models this section after Andrzejewski's *The Gates of Paradise* (1960),[54] a novel of 40,000 words written in one long sentence, followed by a short one containing only five words (four in its original Polish). Like Schwob's novella, *The Gates of Paradise* focuses on the Children's Crusade, but Andrzejewski uses the myths about that obscure historical event to explore how teenagers fall prey to the corruption of the adult world, how faith and fanaticism can blur together, and how challenging it is to narrate these phenomena.[55] Luiselli borrows some of Andrzejewski's novella's most persistent imagery (for instance, that of young people walking in the desert "scorched by the sun") and its use of punctuation (colons, dashes, commas) to sustain one long sentence encompassing multiple points of view (*LCA*, 29). She also emulates the sentence's effect. The length of Andrzejewski's sentence and "the length of the never-to-be-completed journey to Jerusalem" are correlated, instantiating the struggle of the journey in the challenge of reading one breathless sentence, an effect that Andrzejewski reinforces through his "varied use of repetition" of particular words, phrases, and imagery, which "extend our sense of time and space."[56]

Luiselli's long sentence begins with the ten-year-old boy addressing his sister as they walk in the desert, lost in its blinding light, but soon switches almost imperceptibly to the perspective of the lost children (those from *Elegies* and those attempting to cross the border), before switching back and looping out again. By making the section a soundscape, Luiselli registers the voices of migrants "begging for water before fading into silence with a final whimper, then darker sounds, like cadavers diminishing into skeletons snapping bones, skeletons, skeletons snapping into bones, bones eroding and disappearing into the sand"; these sounds are "carried eternally across empty valleys, sounds unregistered, unheard" (*LCA*, 323–324). But Luiselli makes the inaudible perceptible. At the same time, she anchors the lost children's journey in a specific political context. A brief mention of Lynne Cheney's novel *Sisters* (1981), for instance, leads to Dick Cheney and his Operation Jump Start, which sent the National Guard to build a twenty-foot wall along the border in 2006—an obstacle that pushed migrants toward more dangerous places to cross.

The long sentence of "Echo Canyon" creates a sense of cross-temporal simultaneity, so that the different lost children all seem to be walking in the same desert at the same time. Like Andrzejewski, Luiselli reinforces this effect through repetition—the different sets of children echo each other's words and phrases, such as "it must be hard to be dead" (*LCA*, 327). She also uses a technique borrowed from Virginia Woolf's *Mrs. Dalloway*, having the different children's gazes converge on the same objects in the sky: "airplane, eagles, thunderclouds, or lightning" (*LCA*, 357–358). While Luiselli employs this technique throughout the novel, she does so most intensely in "Echo Canyon," where the predominance of the eagle motif recalls a myth that the brother and sister heard earlier from their father about the Eagle Warriors, Native American children who "had learned the power to control the weather" and were so "swift and fast they looked like eagles" (*LCA*, 209). Echoing the road-trip parts of the novel, the eagles in "Echo Canyon" also invoke this other legion of Native American children, albeit in mythical form—children whose migration history recalls those of the child refugees. All the lost children in the novel thus join in a single sentence, a polyphony of voices at once elegiac and haunting, for they include the voices not only of the living but of the recent and long dead.

But Luiselli also wants her readers to "face facts," in Hannah Arendt's use of the phrase; she does not want them to simply witness tragedy from a remove. She wants them to experience discomfort and examine their own positionality. At the end of "Echo Canyon," the brother and sister meet a group of child refugees who are taking shelter from a storm in an abandoned train car. Out of desperate hunger, they all eat the eggs from an eagles' nest that they find there. The image is striking—is it a kind of cannibalistic ritual?—suggesting the commemoration of a wound or the consumption of a ghost. The interconnected images of migration in *Lost Children Archive* suggest that the forced migration of Native Americans, represented by the Eagle Warriors, constituted a seminal trauma in the region. The crisis at the United States–Mexico border takes place over a geographical space marked, in myriad ways, by the dispossession of Native Americans. Their loss was one of the first ways in which the border was marked (another frequently mentioned loss in the novel was the Mexican loss of territory to the United States through the Treaty of Guadalupe). To seek refuge in the United States, therefore, is to seek refuge in a place forever bloodied by persecution.

A phrase that Luiselli borrows from Andrzejewski further layers the associations to be found in the image of the children eating eagle eggs. The title of Andrzejewski's novella refers to a horrific vision of Jerusalem, metaphorically known as the "gates of paradise," that appears to one of his characters, a priest who joins the youths as their spiritual confessor. In his nightmare, the priest hears a voice telling him that the gates of paradise exist only in the desert: there, under the scorching sun, the Jerusalem of the "thirsty and the hungry" exists, in the desert where they are sepulchered and where the immense gates of paradise open up to gather them: "las puertas del paraíso existen en verdad sólo en el desierto inanimando, calcinado por el sol . . . el desierto es el sepulcro de los sedientos y hambrientos . . . en el desierto yerguen los santos muros y torres de Jerusalén, y en él, inanimado y calcinado por el sol, se abren ante los sedientos y hambrientos las imensas puertas del paraíso."[57] In classic texts of migration to the United States, the country often figures mythically as a promised land, a Jerusalem. But the image of the children eating eagle eggs, alongside the incorporation of Andrzejewski's language—Luiselli replicates it almost verbatim—points us not to the myth of America but to the border and its deserts, where the nation's foundations were really laid and where the meaning of what America is and what it could be is still being fought. Readers are left with the task of examining what part, if any, they take in this fight.

ARCHIVE FEVER

"Stories are a way of subtracting the future from the past, the only way of finding clarity in hindsight" (*LCA*, 186). The mother in *Lost Children Archive* writes these words right before she gives narrative control to her stepson, thus expressing faith in his agency while underscoring her relatively modest view of storytelling. Yet the novel's self-consciousness about its own status as a set of documents for posterity—an archive—tempers this modesty. Luiselli knows that the novel may have little to no impact on the political machinations driving the ongoing crisis at the border. But she also knows that the book constitutes testimony for the future, even when that future (and future readers) cannot be depended upon.

Creating archives of her work is part of Luiselli's artistic process: "I usually collect a lot of material things—scraps, pieces, cutouts, and photos—while I write a book . . . [E]ach book drives its own archival process."[58] But she confesses that, with *Lost Children Archive*, the "collection process went overboard." She "recreated the archive of the family in the book"[59]—all seven boxes, including the Polaroid pictures that the mother takes, as well as a number of photographs (of Geronimo and his fellow prisoners traveling to Florida by train in 1886, and of the Orphan Train), accompanied by notes from books about enslaved children and objects "found on migrant trails in the desert" (*LCA*, 250). This visual material—Polaroids, maps, posters—is not meant simply to illustrate the novel's content; rather, the fiction directed the documentation.[60] In the same vein, the book's many sonic references, reaching far beyond the work of Feld and Schafer on soundscapes, manifest the novel's almost obsessive drive to create its own archive and to gesture to other archives; these references include musical scores, compact discs, notes, clippings, facsimiles of "sound maps," audiobooks (which are also included in the novel proper), and references to music inspired by and inclusive of soundscapes (such as James Newton's 1984 album *Echo Canyon*). The archives embedded in the novel are part of its self-awareness as a testimonial force, a time capsule that Luiselli is leaving for posterity.

The novel's intertextuality, intermediality, and polyphonic echoes show that, while Luiselli places faith in the lasting power of literary texts—Homer, for example, lives on in her novel via Pound, just as Pound lives on in her use of his *Cantos*—she does not fetishize textuality. The textual allusions index key historical moments that created the political context for her novel, their echoes situating the border crisis in the broader history of capital and empire. But Luiselli knows that there are many ways to tell a story, and that to tell a story through multiple aesthetic forms is itself a political act. Luiselli creates her own intertextual and extraliterary "Echo Canyon" to make palpable what poet and critic Nathaniel Mackey once wrote: "The world... inhabits while extending beyond what meets the eye, resides in but rises above what's apprehensible to the senses."[61] Luiselli goes beyond textuality to hear and record the echoes of the dead, especially because, too often, the migrant dead leave no mark of their own and have not been otherwise remembered by others.

Luiselli also registers a gnawing doubt of what documentation means in the present time. When the ten-year-old boy asks his stepmother what it means to "document stuff," the mother responds that it "just means to collect the present for posterity." Characteristically for a child his age, the boy follows up by asking what "posterity" means. "I mean—for later," she says, but then she thinks:

> I'm not sure, though, what "for later" means anymore. Something changed in the world. Not too long ago, it changed, and we know it... We feel time differently. No one has quite been able to capture what is happening or say why. Perhaps it's just that we sense an absence of future, because the present has become too overwhelming, so the future has become unimaginable. And without future, time feels like only an accumulation. An accumulation of months, days, natural disasters, television series, terrorist attacks, divorces, mass migrations, birthdays, photographs, sunrises. (*LCA*, 103)

Time on social media can certainly feel this way: like a collage of experiences that vary in depth and impact but get flattened by the medium into one plane. The passage also recalls Harry Harootunian's 2007 essay "Remembering the Historical Present," which tracks moments in history since 9/11 and portrays an "absence of periodicity," citing claims "of a new temporal tectonics, shifting time plates to set the present [and the future] adrift."[62] He argues that, "if any axial event marked the turn in time it was undoubtedly the collapse of the Berlin Wall and the subsequent end of the cold war [*sic*], even though this episode was the culmination of a process long in the making."[63] The fall of the wall, he continues, "and the disappearance of the communist idea lived by actually existing socialism and conveyed by the future of revolution" assaulted the temporal order; together they entailed "the withdrawal of a foreseeable future as a perspective for figuring the aspirations of the present." And it isn't just the idea of futurity within a linear conception of time that came to a crisis. The idea of progress itself, whether through capitalism and the concept of "developing" countries or through communist revolutions, "had managed to veil . . . a collision of temporalities":

> An exported world-standard time demanded by capital and its overseas expansion—a new imperialization of time—clashed with diverse local times and modes of existence as it established a world market and instigated colonial expropriation. This is not to say that the spectacle of divided or mixed temporalities did not already exist in the industrial heartlands of Euro-America but only that expansion provided the occasion to map the instance of unevenness, as denoted in classifications of "delay" and "arrest," onto the hinterlands.[64]

Thus, Harootunian argues that the biggest impact of the fall of the Berlin Wall was its unveiling of uneven and colliding temporalities, which had long existed both in centers of power and in their colonies.

The mother in *Lost Children Archive* registers the shifts that Harootunian highlights and offers a suggestion: "Perhaps if we found a new way to document [the present]," she writes, "we might begin to understand this new way we experience space and time . . . [O]ur ways of documenting the world have fallen short" (*LCA*, 103). Claire Messud notes that, while Luiselli's meditations on how shifts in world politics necessitate new literary forms are not new, they are particularly pertinent now. Further, she argues that "Luiselli's novel itself endeavors to find a new way to 'document' the present,"[65] by creating a sense of temporal circularity.

Luiselli's novel repeatedly invokes temporal return, even as it registers evolving changes, especially to the environment. At times, such invocations come directly. For instance, when the father tells the children about Geronimo, Andrew Jackson, and the Indian Removal Act, the mother thinks, "The more I listen to the stories he tells about this country's past, the more it seems like he's talking about the present" (*LCA*, 133). Later, in a moment of despair, she writes, "All I see in hindsight is the chaos of history repeated, over and over, reenacted, reinterpreted ... And in the middle of it all, tribes, families, people, all beautiful things falling apart, debris, dust, erasure" (*LCA*, 146). It is only when she realizes her project, intertwining the different stories and voices that make up *Lost Children Archive*, that she finds "clarity" rather than chaos. In the novel, Luiselli does not represent history as a chaotic repetition of suffering; rather, through the polyphony and echoes she creates, she represents distinct historical events as reverberations from a common source: empire, with its attendant cycles of racial persecution and dispossession. This insight, her work implies, can form the basis of a migrant solidarity, one which both the mother and Luiselli herself enact in their relationship with the children at the border. At the same time, Luiselli contrasts the cyclical nature of forced migration with the road-narrative trope, ironizing the latter's white masculinist expression of mobility as rebellion, reinvention, and freedom. She thus puts at odds two concepts of time: the teleology of the road and the cyclical repetition of violence.

In *Tell Me How It Ends*, Luiselli makes clear that the clandestine modes of neocolonialism require the obfuscation of the reasons behind forced migration. She argues that we need non-euphemistic language and new narrative forms to understand migration in its proper scale, to represent accurately the wide and historically deep networks of violence that create refugees and migrants. And such narrative forms must portray the echoing repetition to be found in the history of empire. Recall Ann Stoler's argument that older imperial formations "wrap around contemporary problems," and the "occlusion" and "aphasia" that characterize imperial power, meaning its intentional concealment of and silence about its own brutality, failures, and disorderliness.[66] I have argued here that Luiselli's novel works against this occlusion and aphasia through both its intertextuality and its polyphony. These are set in tension with the novel's metafictive concerns, which evince an acceptance of literature's limits to instigate political change. One might argue that, at least for writers of color (itself a euphemism for a polyphonic multitude), there was a time when faith in literature's power was higher. Making literature a medium for change without becoming propaganda was the aim of once-communist writers such as Richard Wright. Is Luiselli's more sober sense of literature's potential impact an effect of the fall of the Berlin Wall? In other words, without a belief in a revolutionary future where literature can play its part, are writers confined simply to bearing witness, as Sigrid Nunez has suggested? Is it true, in Nunez's words, that "the writer *has* no higher calling than to bear witness to injustice and suffering"?

Luiselli's archive fever is fueled by a conviction that, even if literature's power to effect change is limited, even if the future is uncertain, she *must* create testimony, *must* leave her mark with a network of signs that both point to and zoom out from the crisis at the border. Like any archive, hers is full of gaps and silences. Conspicuous among these is the missing Elegy 10 (which might focus on the murder of the seventh boy) and the death of a migrant woman who rolls off La Bestia and tears "open her stomach on a broken branch," an event that receives only a passing mention in the novel (*LCA*, 225). There is no one to bury or mourn this woman, and probably no one to register her death. Instead, the "first living thing to notice her, the next morning, was a porcupine . . . It sniffed one of her feet . . . uninterested" (*LCA*, 225). As we know from the work of anthropologist Jason De León and others, bodies like this woman's often disintegrate without leaving any trace in the unforgiving conditions of the desert; more interested animals soon devour them, and the heat pulverizes the remains, erasing both the bodies and, with them, all evidence of the crimes committed against people denied human and constitutional rights.[67] Like the previously mentioned Operation Jump Start, the Clinton-era Border Patrol strategy called Prevention Through Deterrence has forced migrants to cross the border in remote, hazardous areas, like the Arizona desert, essentially weaponizing the environment to kill migrants.[68] Bodies disappear without a trace as these conditions effectively do the state's bidding, expunging incriminating evidence of the state's brutality. Luiselli signals this history of erasure with the nameless woman who falls to her death from La Bestia, but she does not attempt to use fiction to rectify the record. She has no illusions that fiction can do so, or that her testimony could ever be comprehensive—and so, instead, she highlights its limits and gaps.

As careful as Luiselli is, she takes risks with her method. Her intertextuality as a practice involves moving to an imperial scale to show how migrant experiences resonate across time, space, and a range of media (textual, sonic, visual). Imagining at this scale shows the limits of narrower accounts of migration, with their unidirectionality and closure—think of the assimilationist plot in immigrant fiction—but it also comes, as Luiselli knows, with the danger of commensurating widely varied experiences of mobility and loss. Intertextuality is a middle ground for her, between singularity and homogeneity, allowing her to attend to resonances and echoes without falling into the trap of creating easily digestible and commodifiable migratory aesthetics. Her political and aesthetic practice moves beyond simply bearing witness, for it also entails creating fictive planes of possibility beyond those dictated by the brute force of the world. As I have suggested throughout this chapter, Luiselli's testimony brings to light the historical basis of migrant solidarity, which, like the solidarity envisioned by Hemon, extends over vast temporal and spatial frames, and has the added power of calling on history to deepen its roots.

Chapter Four

CARCERAL MIGRATION
Julie Otsuka's Internment Novels

> The girl looked out the window and saw hundreds of tar-paper barracks sitting beneath the hot sun. She saw telephone poles and barbed-wire fences. She saw soldiers. And everything she saw she saw through a cloud of fine white dust that had once been the bed of an ancient salt lake. The boy began to cough and the girl untied her scarf and shoved it into his hand and told him to hold it over his nose and mouth. He pressed the scarf to his face and took the girl's hand and together they stepped out of the bus and into the blinding white glare of the desert.
>
> —JULIE OTSUKA, *WHEN THE EMPEROR WAS DIVINE*

Two unnamed children hold hands as they walk into the "blinding white glare of the desert"; they see barracks, barbed-wire fences, soldiers. This passage, from Julie Otsuka's first novel, *When the Emperor Was Divine* (2002),[1] could easily be from Valeria Luiselli's *Lost Children Archive* or from any account of the thousands of children currently arriving at immigrant detention centers in the United States. The novel, which Otsuka finished in June 2001, is about the internment of a Japanese American family during World War II. Yet, when it was published in 2002, it became "a significant text for illuminating the persecution of Americans in the wake of the attacks," especially the persecution of Muslim Americans.[2] Though the contexts of Japanese American internment and post-9/11 persecution are distinct, they are linked by a shared history: the criminalization of nonwhite immigrants and ethnic minorities, especially during times of global conflict and war. This shared history underwrites Otsuka's first novel (hereafter shortened to *Emperor*), whose migrant aesthetics afford simultaneously a focus on Japanese internment and a scaling out to other, similar instances of migrant and ethnic persecution.

Emperor is part of a rich artistic tradition of representing the forced removal during World War II of roughly 120,000 men, women, and children—legal immigrants as well as American-born citizens, mostly from the Pacific coast—to so-called relocation centers and incarceration camps in Utah, Arizona, New Mexico, North Dakota, and Montana. What distinguishes *Emperor* within this tradition is Otsuka's style, her minimalist, unsentimental, but "incantatory" prose,[3] and her strategic narrative decisions in representing a family suspended in time and space. Their time of waiting in internment feels eternal, their future is obscure at best, and their past provides unreliable comfort, becoming mirage-like under spatial constraints. Otsuka strategically withholds all the characters' names, except those of minor figures, and rejects any plotting that would frame internment as a transcendent or tragic story of survival or loss. She thus short-circuits the kind of empathic engagement with literary migrant figures that I have discussed earlier—one that, in Namwali Serpell's words, "perpetuates an assumed imbalance in the world: there are those who suffer, and those who do not and thus have the leisure to be convinced—via novels and films that produce empathy—that the sufferers matter."[4]

Otsuka also shifts among multiple points of view throughout the novel and uses elements of the short-story form in each chapter. Just as short stories can distill a moment of potential change and hold it up for analysis without following its natural arc to realization or disappointment, Otsuka's chapters afford only glimpses into how each family member experiences separation, dislocation, and internment. Because she does not provide much character development, she forecloses readers' empathic identification with her subjects. Instead, she focuses our attention on each character's perception of time and space, so that, rather than inhabiting the fictionalized lives of sufferers, we must dwell on the time and space of internment itself.

Otsuka marshals narrative strategies that, while common to other writers, become particularly effective tools in her fiction for training readerly focus on the experience of time in what I call "carceral migration." Scholarship on immigrant literature has emphasized mobility to the point of fetishizing it, yet migration can also involve intervals of living under "parole": waiting for documents; hoping for permission to enter, to remain, or to be reunited with family; and, if undocumented, living under the constant possibility of arrest. This is carceral migration. As seen not only in the World War II internment camps but, more recently, in detention centers, it can involve imprisonment for an indefinite span of time. Detention upends linearity, suspending migrants in clashing temporalities that Otsuka, like the other writers examined in this book, vivifies and invites readers to occupy. By imagining themselves in this confinement and temporal suspension, readers engage in migrant aesthetics, which both provide a visceral understanding of specific conditions and broaden the scope of particular historical experiences (e.g., Japanese internment) to connect them with other, analogous experiences both in the past and in contemporary life (e.g., immigrant detention).

Social scientists are increasingly focusing on the intersection of prison and detention regimes, studying that intersection against the "complex history of immobilizing, isolating, and forcefully removing black, Indigenous, and, later, migrant bodies within and from the nation."[5] In this pursuit, they are like Luiselli, Otsuka, and other writers featured in this book, focusing on the "linkages and correlations, as well as critical disjunctures, between these two carceral states."[6] While migrant detention does not entail official prison sentences or laboring in prison industries, immigrant detainees can still be "easily conflated with the criminally imprisoned through racist stereotypes and the multifaceted force of criminalizing technologies"; they are "often counted among incarcerated persons in the U.S. prison industrial complex—accounting for infrastructural growth and body count."[7] Detainees also share with other incarcerated people the experience of clashing temporalities, albeit at different intensities, within spatial constraints. The "embodied experience of time in carceral space" and "the overlapping temporalities" of "doing time" are two of Otsuka's main preoccupations in *Emperor*.[8]

Otsuka's second novel, *The Buddha in the Attic* (2011, hereafter shortened to *Buddha*), also deals with internment but is, in a sense, a prelude to *Emperor*, since it is about the generation of immigrants to which the mother and father from the earlier novel belong. Using a first-person-plural perspective, *Buddha* renders the lives of Japanese women who arrive in California as "picture brides," only to become farm laborers and maids, laundry workers, and shop clerks, before ultimately being sent to internment camps along with their families. Both *Buddha* and *Emperor* reject the telos of immigrant settlement, assimilation, and citizenship that is too often viewed as the überplot of migrant fiction. Instead, they make vivid the precarity of migration and citizenship for ethnic minorities, while highlighting the deep investment that migrants make in the land and the societies where they work.

In both novels, Otsuka denies the reader entry into subjectivities, refusing to narrate her characters' life stories in the conventional fictionalized autobiographical form so prevalent in immigrant literature. In *Buddha*, the narrative's choral point of view allows us to see the women's lives in the context of their labor, both physical and emotional, and to discover how that labor lays claims to place, a deliberately marked Californian geography. Yet the novel ends with internment, thus turning what at first appears to be a narrative of acculturation into one that underscores the precarity of the women's lives. Again, these narrative strategies—character anonymization and choral storytelling—are not particular to Otsuka (think of the first-person plural of workplace fiction by Joshua Ferris, for instance), but Otsuka deploys them to underscore the historical erasure of personhood through the criminalization of migrants and ethnic minorities.

In this chapter, I argue that Otsuka forestalls empathy as a relational mode of connecting with her subjects to preempt the commodification of suffering and to expand the scale of migration beyond particular instances. Otsuka employs her own version of migrant aesthetics—a strategic use of unsentimentality, a focus on surfaces and diurnal details, and a minimalist indexing of historical context. Her shifting points of view and calculated use of anonymous characterization force her readers to think, as opposed to feel, from the positions of her characters. Otsuka wants us to perceive the specific conditions of internment and to question not only our own relationship to that history but also how that same history is manifesting again in the present. In *Buddha*, Otsuka expands her reach through plural narration to underscore the historical anonymity of the internees, especially immigrant women. Thus, while she, like Teju Cole and Dinaw Mengestu, uses anonymity as a narrative strategy in her first novel, in *Buddha* she focuses on anonymity as an effect of carceral migration. Rather than attempting to rectify historical erasure through her fiction, she highlights it, while also creating testimony for those subsumed in its violence.

WAITING IN *WHEN THE EMPEROR WAS DIVINE*

> Mostly, though, they waited. For the mail. For the news. For the bells. For breakfast and lunch and dinner. For one day to be over and the next day to begin.
>
> —*WHEN THE EMPEROR WAS DIVINE*

Julie Otsuka's grandfather was "arrested by the FBI the day after Pearl Harbor was bombed," and then incarcerated in camps in Montana, Texas, and

New Mexico, while her mother, uncle, and grandmother were sent to an internment camp in Topaz, Utah.[9] To write *Emperor*, Otsuka read histories, memoirs, newspaper accounts, family letters, her grandfather's FBI file, and collections of oral history. But, while she includes details from these texts, she does not attempt to recreate historical lives or to model her characters after historical figures. As she has made clear, the "characters in the novel don't resemble anyone in [her] own family."[10] And, rather than rely on the pathos that might be generated through character development or dramatic scenes, she creates and sustains tension between surface and depth. At unexpected moments, she allows for brief, calculated glimpses of her characters' internal lives. But, like Mengestu and Cole, she strategically denies entry, thus recalling the Morrisonian slaps and embraces invoked by Doris Sommer. At the same time, she conjures the specific contours of time under carceral migration. If, as Mieke Bal writes, migration is "the experience of time—as multiple, heterogenous," under carceral conditions, these aspects of migration intensify. Otsuka depicts the "time of haste and waiting" of the family's evacuation, "the time of movement and stagnation" of their trek by train to the desert, and the endless waiting in the "unsettling present" of internment, a time full of memory that is not "sustained by a predictable future."[11] These strategies work to block facile consumption of the suffering she invokes.

Emperor is part of what is generally known as post-redress internment literature; that is, literary works published after the passing of the 1988 Civil Liberties Act, a federal law that granted reparations to Japanese American citizens who had been interned, after decades of grassroots activism. Otsuka's formal experiment was made possible because earlier generations responded to the need to document an injustice that was under threat of distortion or even erasure. While incarcerated, Issei (first-generation Japanese immigrants) and Nisei (American-born children of Japanese immigrants) created literary magazines in which they wrote about their lives in confinement. Visual artists in the camps, despite limited resources, offered classes and produced a rich record of life behind barbed wire. Texts such as Miné Okubo's illustrated memoir *Citizen 13660* (1946), which Otsuka lists in her "Notes on Sources" at the end of *Emperor*, document how Japanese and Japanese Americans withstood internment, detailing the lives they sustained while incarcerated and the generational conflicts that arose among incarcerated families because of the state's required loyalty questionnaires and the recruitment of Nisei soldiers for the war.

Yet, because the War Relocation Authority (WRA) kept the prisoners under surveillance, they were necessarily confined in how they portrayed camp life. Moreover, the state's use of euphemistic rhetoric to mask its racist violence and the trauma it caused skewed public opinion, which was already poisoned by xenophobia. As a result, both during and after the war, those who were incarcerated often did not want to talk about or otherwise represent their experiences.[12] In consequence, most of the published literature on internment from that period was written by non-Japanese authors. African American novelist Chester Himes, for example, published a story "purporting to be extracts from the prewar diary of a Nisei" in the Los Angeles magazine the *War Worker* in 1943. Karon Kehoe's novel *City in the Sun* (1946) grew out of her experiences as a secretary to the chief of internal security at the Gila River Camp.[13] The historian Greg Robinson explains the early wave of white authors writing about internment—that is, during the war and its immediate aftermath—in this way: "White Americans seem to have enjoyed more access to contacts with publishers, and they could not be dismissed as engaging in special pleading when they wrote in defense of Japanese Americans." He adds, "Since they had not personally faced the trauma of mass arbitrary confinement, they had greater emotional distance from the subject, which may have aided them in writing about it."[14] This interpretation seems one-sided at best. Is it not just as likely that, because they were not emotionally attached to the subject, those white authors felt free to trade in the pathos of internment for profit?

In 1946, Miné Okubo and Karon Kehoe followed different paths to publishing precisely because the former was a Japanese American ex-prisoner while the latter was a white internment-camp employee. Okubo had to take a "documentary" approach to her subject in *Citizen 13660*, while Kehoe could be openly adamant in her protest against internment in *City in the Sun*.[15] After the war, with a few exceptions—notably John Okada's *No-No Boy* (1957), a novel about a Nisei draft resister—few Japanese American literary works on internment appeared. But, in the 1970s, energized by the redress and civil rights movements, Japanese American writers began to break the silence surrounding the most traumatic aspects of incarceration. A profusion of literary works by Japanese Americans followed in the late twentieth century. For instance, Yoshiko Uschida's autobiography, *Desert Exile: The Uprooting of a Japanese American Family* (1982), which is also listed in Otsuka's "Notes on Sources," not only details the humiliation and losses that her family suffered during internment but also "illustrates the lasting impact that the U.S. government policies had on Japanese Americans' economic, cultural, physical, and psychological well-being."[16]

Perhaps inevitably, a new wave of internment literature by white authors also followed. Robinson attributes this latter development to the "absorption of the internment as an accepted piece of the mainstream American past, sufficiently distant to count as history or metaphor but not humiliating as a subject of mass reflection."[17] Yet the pushback against that mainstreaming—as exemplified by the controversy surrounding the mass market success of David Guterson's novel *Snow Falling on Cedars* (1994) and Scott Hicks's 1999 film adaptation, which Robinson himself mentions—suggests that his interpretation is inaccurate. Criticized for perpetuating stereotypes, particularly that of the white hero-savior and the purportedly passive character of Asian women, both *Snow Falling on Cedars* and its film adaptation were profitable, one could argue, precisely because they trade in fantasies facilitated by racial and gender stereotypes.[18] Similarly profiting from such fantasies were Danielle Steel, with her novel *Silent Honor* (1996), and Sophie Littlefield, whose Harlequin romance *Garden of Stones* (2013) took "dramatic liberties" in portraying "widespread sexual abuse of inmates by white guards."[19] Given the stereotypes perpetuated in these books, one could argue that internment has become not so much an "accepted piece of the mainstream American past" as an event distant enough to be commodified by those whose understanding of that past is superficial at best.

It was and still is the case that white writers enjoy greater access to publishing, although Asian Americans and other minorities have made some gains.[20] Indeed, it is perhaps due to these gains that Otsuka's novels have been published. Her strategic use of unsentimentality and other aspects of migrant aesthetics shows us that representing a traumatic past does not necessarily entail the commodification of pain. Critic Deborah Nelson has argued that the unsentimental work of writers Simone Weil, Hannah Arendt, Mary McCarthy, Susan Sontag, Diane Arbus, and Joan Didion purposefully seeks to make readers uncomfortable, even to the point of causing pain, to disrupt the readers' worldviews and force them to alter their opinions.[21] Otsuka operates through a less intense but nonetheless effective unsentimentality. She has said, "I didn't write this book with an angry screed, and I didn't want it to be a moralizing book. I just wanted it to be a book about people and what they had gone through. I hope it's an experience that the reader can enter."[22] At the same time, her stylistic restraint short-circuits both empathy and simplification.

"Evacuation Order No. 19," the first chapter, is told from the perspective of a mother, who packs the few things her family will be allowed to take to the internment camp while her children are at school. We enter the novel after the father has already been arrested on suspicion of espionage—he will be held at camps in Montana, Texas, and New Mexico—and thus we have no direct knowledge of either his arrest or his imprisonment. We also cannot immediately identify any of the characters as Japanese, since in the first few pages Otsuka does not make overt references to the family's ethnicity. Instead, she makes the time and place explicit: we are in Berkeley, California, in 1942, moving through scenes that are recognizably, almost generically, associated with middle-class American families of the mid-twentieth century (references to music and books serve as the main anchors here). Lush descriptions of sensory experience are sprinkled throughout: "The Radio Symphony was performing the last movement of Tchaikovsky's *1812 Overture*. Cymbals were crashing. Cannons boomed" while the boy eats a snack; "hundreds of jays were twittering madly in the Greers' magnolia tree next door" as the family eats dinner (14, 16).

Then, at the center of the chapter, the mother kills the family dog: "Pets were not allowed. That was what the sign had said ... It was the fourth week of the fifth month of the war and the woman, who did not always follow the rules, followed the rules" (9). The disconnect between her action and the matter-of-fact style of the sentence exemplifies the tension that Otsuka is building between a calm exterior and a turbulent, even violent interior drama. The mother gives their cat away to the neighbors but snaps the neck of the "chicken that had been running wild in the yard" (9). Her killing of the dog—a small, elderly, and nearly blind creature named White Dog—is chilling not only because of the unexpected violence (the woman feeds it a delicious meal, rubs its belly, asks it to "play dead," then hits it with a shovel) but also because it breaks the mood of the first half of the chapter, only for the chapter to return to that mood immediately afterward. The children come home from school just as the mother finishes digging a grave for

White Dog, and the business of the family resumes. When the children go to sleep, the mother frees the girl's adored pet macaw, but this time, in a fit of absurdist laughter, the mother begins to cry. It is thus, in Amanda Geller's words, that the "mood of the novel tensely reflects the protagonists' emotional state: calm surfaces above, turmoil just beneath."[23] Otsuka sustains this tension throughout the chapter, letting it explode only briefly to suggest the grief and fury underlying the mother's methodical actions. The combination, as in the unsentimental work of the writers in Deborah Nelson's study, deliberately creates readerly discomfort.

Otsuka focuses on her characters' quotidian life, allowing her readers full access to their sensory experiences but giving only limited entry into their interiority. In the rest of the novel, she shows how space becomes alien and alienating due to evacuation and forced migration, and how time is distorted by incarceration, by focusing on "mundane objects, places, and people"[24] and de-emphasizing character development in favor of episodic, vignette-like scenes. Similarly, she situates her subjects in a specific historical context but takes a minimalist approach, inviting readers to "inhabit the position, not the person," that her characters signify. Again, here, one should consult the work of Namwali Serpell, who writes of Hannah Arendt's "representative thinking": "[This] way of relating to others is not just tourism. Nor is it total occupation—there is no 'assimilation' of self and other. Rather, you make an active, imaginative effort to travel outside of your circumstances and to stay a while."[25] It entails a way of thinking—still as yourself—from the position of another.

Critics have taken Otsuka's minimalist approach to historical context and her decision to make the family nameless as part of her wish to reach for a so-called universality. Otsuka has explicitly supported this view, stating that she "didn't want to weigh down the novel with historical details" because it "was always the characters that interested [her] most, as well as the landscape, and the psychology of the situation," adding, "lives interrupted by war, populations sent into exile, these are timeless and universal themes."[26] A more precise way to understand the effect of Otsuka's formal strategies is to see them as facilitating representative thinking via analogy, or—to use Valeria Luiselli's terms—to understand them as modes for creating echoes that travel across time and even across texts. For instance, in "Train," *Emperor*'s second chapter, Otsuka juxtaposes mythical images of the West with the family's forced migration, in much the same way that

Luiselli contrasts the myth of the open road with the struggles of refugee children walking the desert and riding La Bestia (another train). As many recent historians have argued, the West is often imagined as the site of "noble savages and noble pioneers struggling quaintly in the wilderness" or rugged cowboys claiming a vast frontier, but it also signifies the "legacy of conquest."[27] It has been the site of "systematic oppression of indigenous peoples and the exploitation of raced bodies for labor."[28] By juxtaposing the family's forced migration and incarceration with the myth of the West and its history, Otsuka creates her own version of an "echo canyon"; she places the family's story in a specific historical context while allowing space for analogies with other instances of forced migration, incarceration, and dispossession. This opens the possibility of creating cross-ethnic solidarity against the brutal legacies of empire.

In keeping with the episodic quality of *Emperor*, chapter 2 opens when the family has already spent four and a half months at a temporary detention camp at the Tanforan racetrack, south of San Francisco.[29] The chapter also shifts its perspective to the daughter's, thus emphasizing the dislocation of time and space in form as well as content. The reader is dropped both in medias res and into the mind of a child, as the family is forced to move west by train. The girl dreams of her earlier childhood, when White Dog "was still a noisy white dog" and she could read comics in the kitchen while "drinking large glasses of steaming hot cocoa" (44). Now, on the train, hot and thirsty, she and the other evacuees travel in "crowded compartments [that] smelled of vomit and sweat," since many of the prisoners get sick from the "uneven rocking" of the train, which is "old and slow and had not been used in years" (25). They must keep the shades drawn from "sunset until sunrise" and while passing through towns (43).

These historical details vivify the violent xenophobia that Japanese and Japanese Americans endured after Pearl Harbor. The U.S. government really did require the drawing of shades on the trains, "for wartime security and to hide the movement of the imprisoned population."[30] By 1942, the government was building its military-industrial complex in the Southwest; they would begin atomic testing there three years later. This plan, combined with conspiracy theories about the Japanese and Japanese Americans as alien enemies, made the military wary of letting the evacuees see either the industrial sections of cities or the soon-to-be-developed desert areas. But the government presented the requirement to draw the shades as an effort to protect evacuees from xenophobic attacks, thus hiding their own motivations of secrecy and distrust.

In Otsuka's novel, despite the drawn shades, someone throws a rock at the train one night that crashes through a window. The girl wakes up from her dreams sweating, thirsty, and feeling as if she is suspended in a kind of surreal time; she cannot "remember where she [is]" (43). The intense contrast between her dreams of home and her current conditions constitutes a sudden rupture, like that of the rock through the window, rendering her unable to find her bearings. Again, Otsuka makes palpable the disruption of time and space for her characters, instantiating it through both the form and the content of her novel.

At the same time, she shows us how the girl, a spirited force, engages her imagination to survive psychologically. When the shades aren't drawn, the girl dreams up fantasies of the West that she derives from maps, magazines, and the books she has read at school, as well as from photographs and postcards sent by her father after his arrest. The chapter opens with her looking out, somewhere "along the western edge of upper Nevada":

> [She saw] a lone white house with a lawn and two tall cottonwood trees with a hammock between them gently swaying in the breeze. A small dog lay sleeping on its side in the shade of the trees. A man in a straw hat was trimming hedges. The hedges were very round. They were perfect green spheres. Someone—maybe that same man or maybe that same man's gardener—had planted flowers inside of a red wagon next to the mailbox. In front of a wooden picket fence was a victory garden and a hand-painted sign that said FOR SALE. Behind the house was the dry bed of a lake and beyond the lake there was nothing but the scorched white earth of the desert stretching all the way to the edge of the horizon. (23)

As Stephen Hong Sohn has argued, the girl "attempts to mold the desert region by reducing it to narratives of romance, domesticity, and quaint communities," a visual approach that Otsuka persistently destabilizes.[31] While the girl sees tall trees, a hammock, a sleeping dog, and a red wagon with flowers, Otsuka also registers the precarity of the landscape with the "FOR SALE" sign, replicated in capital letters, and the emptiness and dryness just beyond this lush scene.

Otsuka similarly presents and undercuts the daughter's fantasies in other passages, not out of disdain for the girl's inability to see through the myth of the West (she is only eleven), but out of tenderness for a mind searching for order amid uncertainty and violence. Her father's postcards, sent to the family in Tanforan, distract the girl from the grim reality of her family's separation and incarceration, though they are ominously marked by censored omissions. Perusing them on the train, the girl sees "the pictures of the Indian pueblos and the ancient cliff dwellings" (42). This all-too-familiar "Vanishing Indian" motif, commodified for tourism, encourages the girl's romantic vision of the West even as she herself becomes a victim of a new form of violent deracination therein.

We see this contrast again when her brother asks her if they will see horses:

[She remembered] the mustangs she had read about in *National Geographic*. The Spaniards had brought them over hundreds of years ago and now there were thousands of horses just roaming around, wild. Every autumn they came down from the hills to graze on the high desert plains. If a cowboy needed a new horse all he had to do was go out into the desert and get himself one. It was as simple as that. She imagined a cowboy snapping his fingers and a horse, a wild white stallion, galloping up to him in a cloud of hot swirling dust. (29)

Hong Sohn argues that, here, the girl turns the horse "into a symbol for an unadulterated American West, one that fails to elucidate how horses enabled Spanish colonists to subdue indigenous populations in the Americas."[32] More precisely, Otsuka relies on the contrast between the child's naïve view of the West and the reader's historical awareness. Just as we know that the Vanishing Indian motif has been mobilized to erase a history of genocide, we also know that horses were not just "brought over" by the Spaniards; in fact, colonialism "directly altered ecosystems and communities, often violently, as animals and humans moved across oceans and from one continent to another."[33] Similarly, we recognize the image of the cowboy "snapping his fingers" for a horse as a romantic euphemism. The reader's knowledge of the history of conquest can fill in what the novel only gestures toward; the history of colonialism hangs as a kind of scrim over the scene, making its violence more potent for being invoked and then flattened into postcards and magazines.[34]

Otsuka ensures that this strategy will function—even if the reader has only limited knowledge of the violence of that history—by including pointed details within the novel. On the night when the rock smashes the train window, the girl sees real horses, a "herd of wild mustangs galloping across the desert," their "dark bodies" against the moonlight leaving "great billowing clouds of dust as proof of their passage" (45). Only later, when she, her mother, and her brother are at a camp in Utah, does she realize that they are being fed horse meat, perhaps from the very horses she saw, the proof of their demise being the "horse skull bleached white by the sun" that her brother finds (52). Throughout the novel, Otsuka's repeated allusions to Spanish colonialism and white violence widen the historical scope in which the forced internment of Japanese immigrants and Japanese Americans takes place, encouraging analogies across diverse instances of dispossession, while the details themselves (e.g., the horses turned into meat for consumption) materialize the historical linkages among those instances.

Once the family reaches the camp, Otsuka shifts her focus to their experience of time, which becomes by turns empty, distorted, and unmoored because of the endless waiting and uncertainty. The reader doesn't know exactly where the family is, for Otsuka never names the camp where they are incarcerated. Instead she suggests its location via details borrowed from archival sources, details having to do with the weather, "the invasive dust and dust storms, the extreme hot and cold," and the "plant-based street names" of the forty-two blocks that constituted the camp at Topaz, Utah.[35] She also includes an incident in which a guard shoots and kills an elderly man. While not named in the novel, this character is a reference to James Hatsuaki Wakasa, who was killed at age sixty-three on April 11, 1943.[36] The man's death within the novel dramatizes the constant precarity in which the Issei and Nisei must live in the camp, surrounded by violence both physical and psychological.

Otsuka outlines that life but concentrates mostly on rendering the feeling of time for the internees, particularly the depression to which the mother succumbs in the "dead time" of waiting, not knowing if or when her family will be reunited, or what kind of lives they will be able to rebuild, if any (89). In the camp there is seldom recourse to fantasy; instead, the characters rely on rumors:

CARCERAL MIGRATION

EVERY WEEK they heard new rumors.
The men and women would be put into separate camps. They would be sterilized. They would be stripped of their citizenship. They would be taken out onto the high seas and then shot. They would be sent to a desert island and left there to die. They would all be deported to Japan. They would never be allowed to leave America. They would be held hostage until every last American POW got home safely. (70)

There are three constants in this section of *Emperor*, which is narrated from the boy's perspective: waiting, uncertainty, and absence. These three experiences fuse, creating a surreal state of being that echoes and intensifies tropes introduced in the first two chapters. No one in the family can keep track of time, which seems both forever stuck (the girl's watch reads "six o'clock for weeks") and confusingly various, since the future could look like any of the rumors they hear (65). Otsuka's use of subjunctive repetition here gives the family's uncertainty palpable weight ("They would . . ."). Always, in addition, there is the father's absence, which leads the boy to "see" him everywhere: "Outside the latrines. Underneath the showers. Leaning against barrack doorways. Playing *go* with the other men" (49). Fighting the psychological pressure of internment, the boy finds a tortoise and takes it for a pet, making a home for it in a "wooden box filled with sand" (60). "He had not given the tortoise a name but he had scratched his family's identification number into its shell with the tip of his mother's nail file. At night he covered the box with a lid and on top of the lid he placed a flat white stone so the tortoise could not escape" (60). The animal scrabbles against the side of the box to no avail, and eventually dies in captivity. Like his sister on the train, the boy often wakes up suddenly, not knowing where he is: "Sometimes he heard the wind blowing through the sagebrush and he remembered he was in the desert but could not remember how long he had been there, or why. Sometimes he worried he was there because he'd done something horribly, terribly wrong . . . Sometimes he thought he was dreaming, and he was sure that when he woke up his father would be downstairs in the kitchen whistling" (57). At other times the family's old life "seemed far away and remote to him . . . like a dream he could not quite remember" (93).

The mother, too, stops "keeping track of the days. She no longer read the paper or listened to the bulletins on the radio"; most "days she did not leave the room at all." Her depression is rendered from the point of view of her son, a perspective that amplifies the long-lasting effects of incarceration (93). When his mother loses her appetite, he brings "food for her from the mess hall," but Otsuka leaves it up to the reader to imagine what the boy might have thought or felt when he sees his mother get a "faraway look in her eyes" and then decide that "she couldn't bear it anymore. The wind. The dust. The endless waiting. The couple next door constantly fighting. She hung a white sheet from a rope and called it a curtain and behind the white curtain she lay down on her cot and she closed her eyes and she slept" (94). Otsuka's words here strongly hint at suicide ("hung," "rope," "sleep") but veer just enough to imply a more internal, less final, psychological lying down.

As I noted earlier, Otsuka's focus on the heterogenous time of carceral migration resonates with the work of prison sociologists and time geographers, who highlight the "overlapping temporalities which exist within carceral space":

> the externally imposed clock time which measures sentences in days, weeks, months and years, and the experiential time as experienced by individual prisoners, who variously sense stasis (with time seeming to stand still while they are incarcerated through the daily repetition of penal routines), who perceive time to flow more quickly outside the prison than inside (as events in the lives of others seemingly pass them by), or who observe the passage of time biologically (through their own embodied processes of ageing and attendant deterioration).[37]

While social scientists have concentrated on how "prisoners seek to wrest some form of control over time, through the deployment of various resources and tactics," Otsuka makes us dwell in the strain of temporal suspension itself.[38] The family does not know how long it will remain separated and incarcerated. Under this strain, and also because, as criminologists and prison sociologists argue, "age [and] gender . . . change the way in which prisoners experience time," each family member becomes isolated from the others.[39] Otsuka suggests that both the boy and the girl share the mother's despair and shame, and that they all suffer similarly from their father's absence and the weight of time, but only up to a point. Ultimately, each family member experiences the dislocation of time according to their own biological clock and gender.

For all, "every day seemed to pass more slowly than the day before," but the boy alone "spent hours pacing back and forth across the floor of his room," thinking of his father: "He counted his steps. He closed his eyes and recited the names of his old classmates whenever a dark ugly thought—*he's sick, he's dead, he's been sent back to Japan*—tried to push its way into his head" (102). Josephine Park has eloquently traced how the boy's relationship to his father transforms under the pressure of incarceration, particularly under the compulsory acts of loyalty to America that were demanded of the incarcerated community through "daily tasks as mundane as the pledge of allegiance and in crises as painful as a 1943 loyalty questionnaire that roiled the camps. Refusal to comply with WRA orders resulted in reprimands, banishment to another facility, and even death."[40] The boy at first remembers his father as a "small handsome man" who "knew the answers to everything," but he ends by wondering if his father is indeed the enemy alien, the "little yellow man," "unknowable," "inscrutable," that the WRA wants to banish or even murder (62, 49). Park argues that the transformation of the absent father "sets a pattern for the changes that await the rest of the family." The boy's appearance changes so dramatically that he hardly knows himself, especially once he puts on a U.S. Army surplus coat: "His hair was long and uncombed and his face was dark brown from the sun. The coat hung down past his knees. He narrowed his eyes and stuck out his two front teeth. *I predge arregiance to the frag . . . Whatsamalla, Shorty? Solly. So so solly*" (87). Park writes, "The halting pledge of allegiance skewers the possibility of an American allegiance, and the unfamiliar reflection utters an all-too-familiar apology: 'So so solly.' Like his father, the boy sees himself melded into the yellow horde."[41]

The girl, meanwhile, undergoes puberty while incarcerated. She looks into a "cracked mirror" antagonistically, saying "What? What? What?" feeling alienated both by her body and by the identity imposed upon her as an "alien enemy" (88). With both children, Otsuka focuses on surfaces—the racial minstrelsy that the boy performs, the implied multiplicity of the girl's image—to allow her readers only brief entry into her characters' interiority as they are forced to develop a double consciousness. But their feelings are only implied, not stated or evoked directly, and in this way, Otsuka preempts pity, sadistic interest, or facile empathy.

As I have argued, throughout *Emperor* Otsuka roots the family's suffering in a specific Japanese American context while also making their internment resonate with other instances of carceral migration. Park argues that Otsuka uses "exemplarity," making each family member a type and showing how each one becomes marked irreversibly as a "hypervisible" alien enemy within a domestic polity.[42] This same "enemy subjectivity," Park continues, was "all too evident" in the post-9/11 context in which the novel was published—and indeed, as I noted earlier, the novel ultimately became a "significant text for illuminating" the racial profiling and persecution of Muslims in the aftermath of the attacks.[43] Emily Hiramatsu Morishima argues that, "by narrowing the focus to family dynamics and depicting their emotions through psychological realism," Otsuka forfeits "the opportunity to illustrate the diversity of Japanese American experiences."[44] But Otsuka's emphasis on the distortion of time in carceral migration further connects the family's experiences to other instances of carceral migration across ethnic and migrant communities. Otsuka shows us how different temporalities clash for the incarcerated, suspending them in a temporal vortex that feels all the more surreal because they are spatially confined. As we will see explicitly in this book's epilogue, this distorted experience of time is also common among the children and other migrants now being detained at the U.S.-Mexican border.

The novel's title, *When the Emperor Was Divine*, which is also the title of the chapter narrated from the boy's point of view, refers in part to what Emiko Ohnuki-Tierney calls "an outrageous misunderstanding, with an undercurrent of Orientalism": the idea propagated by Westerners that the Japanese as having "perceived and 'worshiped'" their emperors as God.[45] The novel's title thus describes a time that never existed except in the Western mind. Yet, at the end of World War II, the United States forced the then-emperor, commonly known by his personal name, Hirohito, to abdicate his purported divinity. Moreover, the United States forced the incarcerated Japanese Americans to swear off their allegiance to Hirohito, even if, like the boy and the girl, they had never been to Japan and never believed in the emperor's divinity.[46] The title also echoes another phrase—"*When the war is over*"—which the mother and children repeatedly tell each other as an invocation of a future that ought to bring resolution and repair, though it never materializes as such (112). Even the novel's name, therefore, calls into being the mythical aspect that time comes to have for the internees. They exist suspended between a time that never was (*When the Emperor Was Divine*) and a time that never comes to be ("*When the war is over*").

At the camp, the present feels eternal and empty even though it is marked by the seasons ("the winter seemed to last forever"; "summer was a long hot dream"), by the mother's aging, and by the children's physical growth (92, 103). The past becomes as insubstantial as dreams, fantasies, and memories, so much so that all of these seem to blend. The children try to remember their life in Berkeley, but it slips away from them. "His father used to call him Little Guy. He called him Gum Drop, and Peanut, and Plum. 'You're my absolute numero uno'" (64). And yet: "Do you know what bothers me most?" the girl asks the boy. "I can't remember his face sometimes" (72). Meanwhile, the future can be thought of only as an ambiguous hope ("when the war is over") or in a conditional form, marked as both future and memory. "Always, he would remember the dust . . . It made your eyes sting. It took your voice away." It got into "your mouth. Your bed. Your dreams" (64). To find solace in the present, the characters retreat into deeper memories (under her white sheet, the mother dreams of her own father and her childhood in Japan); the boy sometimes fantasizes that his father is a hero returning in a "cowboy hat" or wearing a "halo" (104). Sometimes they reimagine the space they are in, placing it in a different temporality altogether; the girl tells the boy about an "ancient salt lake that had once covered all of Utah and parts of Nevada":

> This was thousands of years ago, she said, during the Ice Age. There were no fences then. And no names. No Utah. No Nevada. Just lots and lots of water. "And where we are now?"
> "Yes?"
> "Six hundred feet under." (58–59)

The salt lake and the cowboy recall the girl's naivete in the previous chapter, but now it is she who utters the disillusioned phrase: "Six hundred feet under."

The clashing temporalities of internment do not find resolution when the family finally returns to Berkeley and reunites. Their return, in fact, forms a circle that cannot close. The father is a broken man, psychologically destroyed by imprisonment; the children suffer from racial persecution and paranoia; the mother becomes the breadwinner, aging even more rapidly under the toil of physical labor than she did during evacuation and internment. By the end of the novel, the phrase "six hundred feet under" eerily suggests that the transformation experienced by the family is a kind of death.

The novel's penultimate chapter, "In a Stranger's Backyard," is narrated by both the girl and the boy and details the surreality of their return—surreal both because their home was vandalized in their absence and because no one in the family can go back to their prewar selves. Yet they know they are "lucky to be home," for many "of the people who had come back with [them] on the train had no homes to return to at all" (109). Then there are those who come back only to suffer more persecution: "One man's house had been doused with gasoline and set on fire while his family lay sleeping inside. Another man's shed had been dynamited. There had been shootings in the valley, and gravestone defacings" (112). Under such conditions, the children reflect on the phrase they all thought and uttered so often at the camp: "*When the war is over*" (112). The fantasy of return is shattered, and their once-hopeful statement comes to signify the ever-receding horizon of the war's end, which bleeds into postwar trauma and persecution, while the "hypervisible" enemy alien morphs, as Josephine Parks argues, from the "'Jap' into the Chinese Communist, the 'Vietcong,'" the Arab and Muslim, "and beyond."[47]

Despite the fact that the children are American born, they, like their parents, are "impossible subjects," alien citizens whose rights are effaced because they are born to legal aliens who are barred, by law and practice, from citizenship and thus from the normative telos of migration.[48] Their shared categorization as alien enemies underscores not only the precarity of the children's citizenship but also the fact that citizenship itself is not, despite the myth of "immigrant America," a choice that migrants can freely make. Rather, it is a status selectively bestowed upon certain individuals, by an empire that purports to be a nation, the borders of which must be protected even as it consistently violates the integrity of other nations. The plot of assimilation is thus wholly incompatible with the family's experiences. In its stead, Otsuka's migrant aesthetics gives form to the liminality of the family's status as "impossible subjects," while undercutting the empathetic model of reading that would render them merely objects of pity or sorrow. The narrative of the unclosed circle formed by the family's internment offers neither transcendence nor tragedy. At the end of the novel, the narrative abruptly cuts off, barring us from learning the full arc of each character's story and denying us a catharsis of emotion. In its place, Otsuka offers an unsentimental reckoning with the reality of internment and of carceral migration more generally.

In an interview conducted when *Emperor* was first published, in 2002, Otsuka spoke of being "surprised that there [had] not been more of an outcry against the Bush administration's recent assault on civil liberties: the secret arrests and indefinite detention of more than 1,200 Middle Eastern men, the suspension of habeas corpus and of the right to trial by jury, the electronic monitoring of lawyer-client conversations, the use of military tribunals." Then again, "in February of 1942, there were very few who protested or even questioned the president's order to intern over 120,000 Japanese in this country. (Many people, in fact, actually seemed relieved to see the Japanese go.)"[49] As if to make up for this scarcity of resistance, "Confession," the last chapter of *Emperor*, is a tour de force of sly protest. Narrated by the father and comprising little more than three paragraphs, the chapter performs the fantasy of the "enemy alien" admitting his "crimes": "You were always right. It was me. I did it. I poisoned your reservoirs. I sprinkled your food with insecticide ... I pulled out the nails from your white picket fence and sold them to the enemy to melt down and make into bullets. I gave that same enemy your defense maps for free ... I went out into the yard ... to make sure he knew where to find you. *Drop that bomb right here, right here where I am standing!*" (140–141). Reviewing the novel, Michiko Kakutani argued that this "ill-conceived" and "didactic" final chapter mars an otherwise fine literary accomplishment."[50] I would argue, by contrast, that the chapter offers a "slap" to the reader, like the one that Teju Cole delivers at the end of *Open City*. It is a final sting that guards the characters' emotions, preventing readerly catharsis and continuing Otsuka's strategy of allowing only brief, though sometimes aggressive expressions of the family's grief, anger, despair, and longing.

The absence of the father throughout the novel, along with the fact that his voice is only reported secondhand until its final outburst at the end, suggests a long buildup culminating in an explosion. Yet, because the "confession" is so clearly a satire of the paranoid, xenophobic mind, it isn't a direct expression of the character's feeling. The anger is palpable only through, or as, a mask. "Who am I? You know who I am. Or you think you do. I'm your florist. I'm your grocer. I'm your porter. I'm your waiter ... I'm the saboteur in the shrubs . . . I'm the traitor in your own backyard" (142–143). In the previous chapter, the children depict their father as becoming paranoid himself, quick to anger and convinced that he is being tracked by the state ("He was suspicious of everyone . . . Little things . . . could send him into a rage") (134). Readers might expect the first-person "Confession" to reveal, finally, what is really in the father's mind, but Otsuka refuses to give that satisfaction; she still does not allow entry into his interiority. Instead, the father voices the assumptions of those profiling him, confirming their fears in a forceful rejection of readerly empathy. It is a threatening version of the boy's minstrel performance—the "alien enemy" grown up—and the connection is reinforced by the fact that the father's confession ends with similar statements: "I'm sorry. There. That's it. I've said it. Now can I go?" (144). The boy's "*So so solly*" echoes here, but the father's words are spoken from under a different mask and with a different tone. Adding further resonance, Otsuka's minimal inclusion of context-specific details in the "confession" allows it to also be read as a statement from any of the "1,200 Middle Eastern men" she later invoked in an interview.

In the same interview, Otsuka said: "It is actually possible, today, for a long-term U.S. resident suspected of terrorist activity to be arrested and sentenced to death in a secret military trial based on hearsay evidence."[51] In her second novel, *The Buddha in the Attic*, Otsuka depicts how, in the 1940s, longtime Japanese residents of the United States—people who had worked its fields, raised children there, cleaned other people's homes, set up businesses—all ended up in internment camps. As I noted earlier, this second novel is a kind of prequel to *Emperor*, showing on a larger time scale the constant precarity of being an immigrant like the mother and father of *Emperor*, both of whom were residents in the United States for more than two decades and yet, like Issei in real life, were prohibited by law from becoming citizens.[52] In this country—or, more precisely, this empire—the war against racialized enemy aliens does not end; it only morphs.

"AND SOME THERE BE, WHICH HAVE NO MEMORIAL": *THE BUDDHA IN THE ATTIC*

In *Emperor*, Otsuka used the anonymity of her characters strategically, to guard against commodification and to strike a fine balance between historical specificity and analogical possibility. As her second novel demonstrates, Otsuka also knows that anonymity is a product of historical erasure. The protagonists in *The Buddha in the Attic* are "picture brides," fictionalized versions of the many women essentially purchased from Japan by Japanese men living in the United States in the early decades of the twentieth century.[53] These women traveled thousands of miles from their homeland and entered into lives with men whom they had become acquainted with only through photographs and letters, most of which turned out to be forged, fake, or written by others. As Otsuka describes, they would wake up lying next to strange men "in a strange land," in hot crowded sheds "filled with the grunts and sighs of others," and wonder, "*Does anyone even know I am here?*"[54] By some standards, these women went on to lead unremarkable lives—they toiled as field hands, maids, prostitutes, cooks, and nannies, raising their own children and taking care of their husbands. They left little trace behind. Most of them entered history only as inmates of the internment camps, where each bore a state-generated number.

Otsuka uses the first-person plural to tell these women's stories; the protagonists of her novel address the reader as a collective "we." Names and individual voices, marked by italics, wind in and out of the collective voice. This aesthetic choice seems at first to reinforce the historical obscurity to which such women have been relegated since, in the words of critic Ron Charles, "no story in the conventional sense ever develops, and no individuals emerge for more than a paragraph."[55] But Otsuka also chips away at that anonymity, starting with the first two lines of the novel: "On the boat we were mostly virgins. We had long black hair and flat wide feet and we were not very tall" (3). As Mako Yoshikawa notes: "The second line suggests that the group is uniform, but the teasing phrase 'mostly virgins' cues us that these women resist easy categorization, and in the lines that follow, the 'we' becomes increasingly diverse":[56] "Some of us had eaten nothing but rice gruel as young girls and had slightly bowed legs, and some of us were only fourteen years old and were still young girls ourselves. Some of us came from the city, and wore stylish city clothes, but many more of us came from the country and on the boat we wore the same old kimonos we'd been wearing for years" (3). "The diversity," Yoshikawa points out, "is regional as well as economic and generational."[57]

The novel starts on a deceptively traditional note, with immigrants arriving by boat to a new life in the United States. Yet its end point, as in *Emperor*, is in the internment camps. Otsuka also hints at losses that have shadowed the women's lives before migration:[58] "Perhaps we had lost a brother or father to the sea, or a fiancé, or perhaps someone we loved had jumped into the water one unhappy morning and simply swum away, and now it was time for us, too, to move on" (3). As Yoshikawa argues, the "word 'too' in the last phrase, which equates the women's journey to America with a death or suicide at sea, hints at how ghostly and insubstantial these characters are, foreshadowing how their voices will blur together in the narrative as well as how they will eventually vanish into the camps." She concludes: "After all, even though we do hear the words of individual women here and there, their full stories remain untold. Otsuka achieves a rare and paradoxical double feat: she gives these oppressed and silenced women voice and at the same time illuminates how their voices have been lost to history."[59]

This analysis, however, is not quite right. Otsuka does achieve a dual feat: she invokes lost subjectivities even as she marks their absence. Yet she does not "give the women voice," for this would presume that an author, god-like, can give (or take away) "voice" and, moreover, can decide what those "voices" have to say. Instead, Otsuka marks the women's absence in the historical record by imagining what kind of lives they might have led. In the first five chapters of the novel, Otsuka offers a collage of the characters' acts of creation, how they labor, give birth, and raise children, and how they come to know a particular space, the geography of northern California, through work. The last three chapters turn to evacuation and its aftermath. As in *Emperor*, each chapter consists of short, episodic narratives linked thematically and formally, which offer a "great variety" of the women's experiences "blended, often sentence by sentence."[60] Here, for instance, the choral "we" describe their "homes" in America:

> Home was a cot in one of their bunkhouses at the Fair Ranch in Yolo... Home was a wooden shanty in Camp No. 7 on the Barnhart Tract out in Lodi. *Nothing but rows of onions as far as the eye can see.* Home was a bed of straw in John Lyman's barn alongside his prize horses and cows. Home was a corner of the washhouse at Stockton's Cannery Ranch. Home was a bunk in a rusty boxcar in Lompoc. Home was an old chicken coop in Willows

that the Chinese had lived in before us. Home was a flea-ridden mattress in a corner of a packing shed in Dixon. Home was a bed of hay atop three apple crates beneath an apple tree. (24)

Ron Charles argues that lists like this one, of which there are many, though "often lovely, harrowing or surprising . . . will have limited appeal to readers pining for more extended narratives and more emotional investment in individual characters."[61] I would argue that Otsuka planned it just so. She does not want readers' "emotional investment" in individual characters as much as engagement with how the women collectively worked California's land—in Yolo, Lodi, Stockton, Lompoc, Dixon, and many other sites mentioned throughout the novel. Otsuka highlights the conditions under which the women worked, the homes they cleaned in Berkeley and its hills, the restaurants where they washed dishes and served food, the clothing they scrubbed in the laundromats of J-towns (Japantowns, or Nihonmachi) "in San Francisco, Sacramento, Santa Barbara, L.A.," where they also shopped and built communities (50). These communities, which would largely be destroyed by internment, formed the social and geographical landscapes in which Otsuka positions the women, and become contexts in which readers can understand the brutal impact of the evacuation orders and forced migration described in the last three chapters.

Given the precision with which Otsuka places her characters in these social and geographical landscapes, it is a surprise to read Yoshikawa's claim that the women's voices ("snappy, down to earth, wry, and often very funny") "demonstrate how little historical and cultural differences matter: we feel as if we know these women." Yoshikawa offers the following as evidence:

Here's a picture bride from a region without many eligible men speaking of the husband she has yet to meet: "*I took one look at his photograph and told the matchmaker, 'He'll do.'*" Another, who lost one husband to flu and a second to a younger woman, says of her third: "*He's healthy, he doesn't drink, he doesn't gamble, that's all I needed to know.*" Discussing how laboring in the fields has made her forego make-up, one woman complains, "*Whenever I powder my nose it just looks like frost on a mountain,*" and we hear the following about Tommy Takayama's mother, who is known as a whore: "*She has six different children by five different men. And two of them are twins.*"[62]

Though it may have sparked a feeling of connection in Yoshikawa, this collection of "voices" does not grant access to interiority. Otsuka's migrant aesthetics in this novel—the plural narration and the specificity of place, her focus on surfaces and day-to-day details—creates a distancing effect that is designed not only to preempt commodification but also to emphasize the historical anonymity of the women. The sentences in italics invite us to imagine only what such women in real life might have thought and said and provide a balance to the more collective form of narration by showing variation from within.

As with *Emperor*, Otsuka conducted extensive research to write *Buddha*: the section "Notes on Sources" that she provides at the end is even longer than the one for her first book. "This novel was inspired by the life stories of Japanese immigrants," she writes, before listing thirty-four selected titles.[63] She thus works with the available historical evidence but also acknowledges the impossibility of recovering the true perspectives of the countless women who did not leave a record of their lives.[64] Yoshikawa's misreading reveals a fantasy, by no means only hers, of what fiction about liminal subjects can do: deliver unto us restored, ahistorical subjectivities that we can fully know, assimilate, own, and consume. How did this fantasy arise?

Charles's review suggests an answer. He argues that Otsuka's stylistic choices, specifically her use of lists to aggregate the women's experience and the plural narration, clash with the "novel's theme." Such women, he writes, "were cruelly stripped of their individuality and regarded as a monolithic peril in the heightened anxiety of the war years," and Otsuka's style serves only to reduce her subjects once again, this time to lists of "fragmented concerns, manners and moments" that do not allow the reader to know them. Charles claims correctly that the "plural voice is necessarily blurring and distancing," but he posits that it can only "make us feel appropriately sad about how these Americans were treated," without ever challenging "the prejudice that made their internment possible." He argues that, historically, "[had] we known them as full individuals—as real and diverse and distinct—we couldn't have whisked them away to concentration camps in the desert. A great novel should shatter our preconceptions, not just lacquer them with sorrow."[65] Because Charles misunderstands Otsuka's objective as that of inspiring sorrow for her subjects, he thinks she has failed to restitute the women's subjectivity. Had she succeeded, he suggests, Otsuka would have taught us a lesson: to see migrants, like these women, as individuals and thus to avoid reproducing the injustices of the past.

The presumptive "we" in Charles's argument signifies his imagined readership, who, unlike the suffering victims of history, need to be taught how to feel for the unfortunate. It recalls the presumption that Serpell highlights in her argument against empathy, which I quoted earlier: that "there are those who suffer, and those who do not and thus have the leisure to be convinced—via novels and films that produce empathy—that the sufferers matter."[66] In the context of migrant fiction, the implication is also that those who migrate and those who read fiction about migrants are two distinct groups, when in fact migration flows, produced globally by empire and war, connect us all. And this interconnectedness, crucially, depends not on sentiment but on a shared but obfuscated imperial web of power.

Charles's argument also ignores a central chapter of *Buddha*, titled "Whites," which shows how the women see their bosses. These bosses, unlike the novel's current readers, did have plenty of occasions to know the women as individuals, yet they still collaborated in sending the women to the camps. "Most of them took little notice of us at all," the narrators tell us. "We were there when they needed us and when they did not, poof, we were gone. We stayed in the background, quietly mopping their floors, waxing their furniture, bathing their children, cleaning the parts of their houses that nobody but us could see" (44). Even though the women get to know their bosses intimately, the relationship is not reciprocated. White women give the Japanese women "new names. They called us Helen and Lily. They called us Margaret. They called us Pearl ... When they were unhappy and had no one to talk to they told us their deep, darkest secrets ... When their husbands went away on business they asked us to sleep with them in their bedrooms in case they got lonely" (40–41). Some of the white men, all too predictably, see the women as sexual objects, seducing them into relationships that always remain clandestine. But the "whites" do not want the women and their families "as neighbors in their valleys. They did not want us as friends" (35).

The "whites" see the women almost always through a lens of stereotypes, as an undifferentiated group:

> They admired us for our strong backs and nimble hands. Our stamina. Our discipline. Our docile dispositions. Our unusual ability to tolerate the heat,

which on summer days in the melon fields of Brawley could reach 120 degrees. They said that our short stature made us ideally suited for work that required stooping low to the ground . . . We were faster than the Filipinos and less arrogant than the Hindus. We were more disciplined than the Koreans. We were soberer than the Mexicans. We were cheaper to feed than the Okies and Arkies, both the light and the dark. (29)

This kind of "admiration," if one can call it that, also has a paranoid side, characterized by disgust and fear:

> We lived in unsightly shacks and could not speak plain English. We cared only about money. Our farming methods were poor. We used too much water. We did not plow deeply enough. Our husbands worked us like slaves. *They import those girls from Japan as free labor* . . . We were taking over their cauliflower industry. We had taken over their spinach industry. We had a monopoly on their strawberry industry and had cornered their market on beans. We were an unbeatable, unstoppable economic machine and if our progress was not checked the entire western United States would soon become the next Asiatic outpost and colony. (35)

The only reciprocity between these two groups is in their categorical thinking: the women refer to their bosses as a monolithic group of "whites": "We loved them. We hated them. We wanted to *be* them" (39). Yet, because Otsuka's lists include variations on themes, we get glimpses of how the women sometimes see their bosses as individuals, as they "soothe their children . . . bathe their elderly . . . keep their secrets . . . tell their lies" (54). Ultimately, what the women admire most about the "whites" is their appearance of being "at home in the world" and "at ease"—a state of being which is arguably a matter of power and position rather than subjectivity (39).

One might claim that this chapter offers a negative model of relationality, dramatizing how, even when physical proximity and intimacy are possible, empathy remains elusive. Real intimacy, which would entail the white bosses seeing the women as fellow humans rather than stereotypical figures, might lead to empathic relationality, but even then it would not guarantee action. Most of the bosses described in "Whites" do not get to know their servants even when they have every possibility; and if they had, there's no evidence that they would have tried to stop the internment of 120,000 people. A sure way to prevent even the possibility of such resistance, however, is to behave as the bosses do in the chapter. Given the trouble with empathy at both the individual and the aggregate level, it seems naïve to expect fiction to facilitate the "right" kind of empathic engagement with others. A recognition of how empire and capital intertwine, by contrast, could guide us toward collective political justice. Charles is right that readers of *Buddha* do not get to know the Japanese women who narrate the novel, but this is not because Otsuka lacquers "our preconceptions . . . with sorrow." It is because she opts to facilitate another kind of engagement with her subjects, one built upon reason in the pursuit of truthfulness and justice. This does not mean that the novel is devoid of affective power—far from it. The choral narration is often poetic and elegiac, but it maintains the boundaries between reader and subject so that we can focus our attention on truth, not emotion.

Two late chapters, "Traitors" and "Last Day," dwell on themes also laid out in the first chapter of *Emperor*: they depict the experiences of the women as they hear the first rumors about evacuation lists and men being "put on trains and sent far away" (82), and then about "entire communities" disappearing (98). As in *Emperor*, the women experience evacuation as a surreal distortion of reality. In "the first night after her husband's arrest," one of the women wakes up "in a panic, unable to remember why she was alone. She had reached out and felt the empty bed beside her and thought, *I'm dreaming, this is a nightmare*, but it wasn't, it was real" (95). In "Last Day," the women list what they leave behind: one of them leaves "a tiny laughing brass Buddha up high, in a corner of the attic, where he is still laughing to this day" (109). The Buddha's laughter seems to mock the women's forced removal, but in a tragicomic mode. Its "tiny" size emphasizes the small traces that the women leave behind, but its continuing laughter suggests a kind of life-affirming persistence that, nevertheless, has no audience. Otsuka only hints, in this novel, at the women's experience of surreality in the camps—the onset of that clash of temporalities that characterizes carceral migration. Instead, she moves our attention to how others see them, in the chapter "Traitors," and to what they leave behind. This shift keeps our attention on the event itself, on the details of arrests and deracination, rather than on the feelings of the characters and the readers' purported ability to share in them.

The last chapter, "A Disappearance," recalls Dinaw Mengestu's strategy of narrating migration from the point of view of the "native" in *All Our*

Names since it is told from the perspective of white Americans who witness the evacuation of the Issei and Nisei from their communities; it tracks how ill-informed citizens can be about a social injustice happening right in front of them. The chapter's opening reads like an episode of *The Twilight Zone*: "[The] Japanese have disappeared from our town. Their houses are boarded up and empty now . . . Abandoned cars sit in their driveways. Thick knotty weeds are sprouting up through their lawns . . . [T]he Japanese are gone" (115–116). The citizens remember seeing the evacuation orders but admit that they never got close enough to know what the lists were about: "we passed by the notices every day on our way into town, [but] it never occurred to us to stop and read one. 'They weren't for us.' " (117). They recognize the euphemisms that the state uses to refer to evacuation and internment ("The Japanese are in a safe place") and formulate paranoid theories about why the Japanese had to "disappear": "we would like to believe that most, if not all, of the Japanese here in our own town were good, trustworthy citizens," say the white neighbors; "[but] of their absolute loyalty we could not be sure" (116, 119). Though, eventually, some citizens "begin to demand answers" about the disappearance of the Japanese ("Why were we not informed of their departure in advance? Who, if anyone, will intervene on their behalf? Are they innocent?"), after a while the community comes to accept it as fact. More cynically still, some citizens loot Japanese homes, while others move in and take full possession (123).

  Otsuka marks the passing of time in this chapter by focusing on nature: "Morning glories begin to grow wild in their gardens. Honeysuckle vines spread from one yard to the next. Beneath untended hedges, forgotten shovels rust. A lilac bush blossoms deep purple beneath the Oteros' front window and then disappears the next day. A lemon tree is dug up over at the Sawadas'. Locks are jimmied off of front and back doors. Cars are stripped. Attics raided. Stovepipes pried loose" (121) This list literalizes how the political gets "naturalized" while juxtaposing natural and human action: the language shifts from expansive, lush sentences in which nature blossoms and vanishes to curt sentences describing human theft. The contrast suggests that nothing and no one remains to bear witness, for nature itself is indifferent and subject to theft (a lemon tree is "dug up"). Elsewhere Otsuka achieves a similar effect, using the seasons to mark the process by which the community learns the truth only to forget it: "At the end of summer the first rumors of the trains begin to reach us from afar"; "by the first frost their faces begin to blend and blur in our minds" (126, 128). Reading this chapter in the 2020s adds a layer of dystopic eeriness. How much do communities in America know about the current mass deportations and the extended detentions of migrants? How much would they care if they did know? And how long will it be before, like the white Americans in Otsuka's novel, they learn some truths and then conveniently forget them?

Otsuka's novels, in the context of our current crisis, offer more than mere examples of carceral migration.[67] Her formal choices, her migrant aesthetics, allow us to imagine a particular historical instance of carceral migration while also keeping a broader scale in view. Her novels make us attentive to the *time* of carceral migration—the surreal way in which memory and fantasy mix in the face of a seemingly endless, empty present and a future that fractures into multiple negative possibilities under the pressure of uncertainty. *Emperor* shows us the precarity of belonging, as experienced by a family of mixed citizenship status, while making vivid how each member of that family struggles to cope with the temporal and spatial alienation of incarceration. *Buddha* expands that canvas through choral narration, depicting how many migrants, specifically women, created a sense of belonging through various forms of work, only to be uprooted and incarcerated. That trajectory, the novel shows, is as accurate as the conventional assimilation narrative in describing what it means to migrate to the United States.

The refugee children that I discuss in the Epilogue of this book are not citizens or even migrants in the way that the Issei of Otsuka's novels are. But keeping Otsuka's aesthetics in mind while reading the accounts of children currently held in detention centers allows us to imagine their surreal position in space and time. As Nicole Waller observes, unlike "the dwellers of the borderland, who are theorized as upsetting the categories of self and other, and who are frequently seen as retaining at least the potential for mobility and enunciation, the inmates of detention centers are suspended in time and place, 'disappeared' into a void."[68] This disappearance shows us how the "impossible subjects" that historian Mae M. Ngai examines—"illegal aliens"—exist in limbo, suspended in territories and jurisdictions that are "neither fully charted in national nor [situated] in international" parameters. "In cartographic terms," Waller writes, these spaces "constitute the blank spaces of *terra incognita*, placed outside the legal and social structures of the known world and yet inscribed as markers of political power on the standard map."[69] Otsuka's novels give shape to the blank spaces of the Japanese American internment camps, while vivifying the experience of being "suspended in time and place" that is characteristic of carceral migration more generally. Her fiction asks us to imagine, from our own positions, what it might mean to be "'disappeared' into a void." Perhaps most powerfully, it asks us to examine our own actions, or lack thereof, as we witness the effacement of migrants at detention centers all over the world in our own time.

Chapter Five

APOCALYPSE AND TOXICITY
Junot Díaz's Migrant Aesthetics

During a 2016 public interview that Hilton Als conducted with Junot Díaz, an audience member asked Díaz how, given his "childhood of deprivation, and [his] experience of growing up with crazy role models," he had "succeeded so beautifully," how he had managed not to follow the "dysfunctional paths" set before him. Díaz quickly fired back, "But who says I haven't? I'm not just being tendentious," he added. "This is the mythography of America . . . where you have this idea that everything moves upward, and people are always on this journey to improvement."[1] In many respects, Díaz's answer was not surprising. His fiction rejects the myth of transcendence, interrogating the idea that migrant life ought to affirm this myth and follow what Aleksandar Hemon calls the "displacement, travails, redemption, success" überplot. Yet, a couple of years after this interview, Díaz was accused of forcibly kissing the writer Zinzi Clemmons, of being verbally abusive to the writers Carmen Maria Machado and Monica Byrne, and of being emotionally manipulative while in a long-term relationship with the poet Shreerekha.[2] His comments quoted above thus took on a new resonance, seeming to point to his personal struggle with the toxic masculinity that his fiction continually offers up for critique.

In his novel and short stories, Díaz traces such sexist toxicity to colonial violence and its afterlives in the political oppression exerted by Rafael

Trujillo's dictatorship in the Dominican Republic and others like it. Díaz's work focuses on how people can introject (post)colonial violence, redeploying its misogynist, masculinist, and sometimes violently hypersexual and racialized dynamics in their most intimate relationships. More personally, in a *New Yorker* essay published shortly before the accusations against him came out, Díaz connects his own struggle with toxic masculinity to the trauma of having been raped as an eight-year-old child.

Later some saw this essay as his preemptive self-defense,[3] while others argued that Díaz's "brutish behavior, his emotional manipulation, his machista nonsense" had little to do with his experience of abuse and more with "how men can use their designation as literary geniuses to attempt to dominate vulnerable women, and how some men of color use racial solidarity as a tool to politically coerce these women into silence."[4] The debate over his case has been robust on both sides. There are those who argue that his fiction affirms misogyny under the guise of critiquing it, and that the serious damaging effects of his behavior ought to result in a boycott of his work. Others advocate not banning the reading or teaching of his fiction but empathizing with Díaz for the trauma he suffered while still holding him to account for his destructive and misogynistic behavior.[5]

I cite this debate here not to defend or criticize Díaz but because it presents a challenge to the anti-autobiographical stance that I see in all the authors I've included in this study. As I argue in the previous chapters, writers who practice migrant aesthetics use strategic anonymity, choral or collective narration, and shifting vantage points to foreclose empathy, due to its limitations as a mode of relationality and its inadequacy as the basis for solidarity against injustice to migrants. These authors guard against the commodification of migrants as racially marked Others by inviting readers to inhabit positions, not persons. To that end, they develop formal strategies for preempting assimilationist reading practices, even when their narratives simulate the intimacy of first-person narration and allude to the author's autobiography. Like Hemon, Díaz works through authorial alter egos that refract but do not reproduce his life trajectory. Yet, because this refraction *seems* closer to direct reflection—in part because Díaz is less obviously metafictive than Hemon and in part because Díaz's life story has been made public—it is harder to see that Díaz also resists autobiographical readings of his work.

Díaz's main literary alter ego is Yunior, a Dominican immigrant and aspiring writer whose full name is Ramón de las Casas Jr. (Yunior being a Spanglish version of "junior"). Yunior's identity shifts across Díaz's oeuvre; the character shares a name not only with his father but also with an American-born brother by the same father but a different mother. Yunior is both victim and perpetrator of the toxic masculinity into which he is socialized. He is made witness to his father's affairs, one of which results in his namesake brother; he is bullied by another brother, Rafa, who embodies hypermasculinity; and he is sexually abused. Throughout these experiences, he remains only half-aware of how they are affecting his own intimate relationships. The critic José David Saldívar has noted that Yunior's simultaneous "blindness and insights" about his behavior "allow us to see how his culture's heteronormativity and his masculinist ideas about women so often leave him feeling utterly disconnected or alienated from his lovers, family, and community," and how, moreover, though he rages against "his own oppressive chains ... he is unable to break free from them."[6] His lack of awareness also limits him as an artist. As a writer, we are told, Yunior struggles to imagine women characters beyond his masculinist perspective.

In his various actions, Yunior refracts Díaz's self-disclosed experiences, yet it would be reductive to equate character and author; doing so would, indeed, amount to adopting the all-too-prevalent critical penchant for reading migrant fiction through a strictly autobiographical lens. It would also ignore the fact that Díaz creates, as he told me, "deceptive, very manipulative, very seductive characters that get enormous good will from readers."[7] Yunior himself describes authors and dictators alike as figures who control versions of reality;[8] he sees how both are "fabulous inventors" who "control subjects and exercise their authority through words to dictate their subjects' or characters' actions and thoughts."[9] "One of the things about Yunior," Díaz has said, "is that he loves to destabilize a reader's sense of who he is and who his family is, and he loves breaking up any kind of authoritative narrative about his family or himself."[10] Yunior's—and Díaz's—trickiness preempts both easy assumptions regarding author-to-character mimesis and empathic engagement with his struggle with toxic masculinity.

Díaz has explicitly stated his wish *not* to make his own life the subject of his art. "I use the authority the reader grants me in order to disappear," he said. "Me, Junot Díaz, I mean. I want my characters to appear and I want in turn to disappear. I am not much interested in anyone's scrutiny of me, personally. I'd rather people pay attention to the work, which is where all the good stuff is."[11] One might argue that these statements show Díaz's wish to escape scrutiny by hiding behind his fiction. But paying attention to the work on its own, without interpreting it through a strictly biographical lens, allows us to see the interconnected structures of violence that Díaz depicts.

In this chapter, I argue that in his corpus—his debut collection of short stories, *Drown* (1996); his novel, *The Brief Wondrous Life of Oscar Wao* (2007); and his second collection of short stories, *This Is How You Lose Her* (2012)—Díaz practices migrant aesthetics on a vast scale, ranging from the intimacy of sexual relationships to the long centuries of New World colonialism, and that he is able to do so precisely because he sees all of the events in this vast range as interrelated. Díaz joins the smallest scale of the bedroom to the largest scale of the Anthropocene epoch in earth's history at a nexus of "toxicity," a migrant aesthetics keyed to infection, complicity, and duplicity as modes of violent connection—modes that arguably infect all of us, at different registers, since we are all shaped by interconnected historical and geographical structures of violence. Like the other writers I consider, Díaz highlights historical resonances across time and space, as well as across genres, in order to render perceptible the expansive scale of migration and its relationship to empire and capital. Díaz's migrant aesthetics centers the earth-shattering violence of New World slavery and the genocide of Native peoples as apocalyptic historical events that ushered in a new stage of capitalism and exploitation, the effects of which are still reverberating within the various waves of migration and dispossession left in their wake.

The now well-known opening lines of Díaz's novel establish his wide-angle frame: "They say it came first from Africa, carried in the screams of the enslaved; that it was the death bane of the Tainos, uttered just as one world perished and another began" (*OW*, 1). The "it" is the "Curse and the Doom of the New World," brought into being with the establishment of a capitalist order that uprooted and commodified human beings, tethering that commodification to phenotype and ultimately reshaping human relations the world over (*OW*, 1). Díaz embeds personal narratives of contemporary migration—involving love, sex, infidelity, heartbreak, and breakups—within this monumental history of forced migration. But migration in his fiction is not only a personal upheaval—he does not focus solely on how migrants struggle to remake their lives—it is also part of a series of intertwined catastrophic events, beginning with the arrival of Europeans to the New World, continuing with the climate devastation that their arrival set in motion, and extending through the political dictatorships of figures such as Trujillo and "Papa Doc" Duvalier in Haiti.

Díaz creates an intertextual world in his fiction that achieves something like a choral narrative. In his novel, the two collections of short stories, and versions of those stories that were published independently (mostly in the *New Yorker*), one finds multiple variations of the same story and different characters sharing the same name, suggesting similar yet divergent plots. Yunior's migration story, for instance, is part of *The Brief Wondrous Life of Oscar Wao*, but only as a subplot that Díaz interweaves in subtle ways. Yunior's story first took shape before the novel was published, in *Drown*, and afterward shifted further in *This Is How You Lose Her*, published sixteen years later. The latter collection offers further iterations of Yunior's migrant story by extending plot lines and introducing new characters whose paths refract Yunior's.[12] This multiplicity creates an array of narrative echoes that increase the number of personae, creating an aggregate set of protagonists who share similar paths. The links also alert us to Yunior's slipperiness as a narrator: the stories intertwine but also follow different arcs.[13]

Díaz capitalizes on the fact that short fiction generally de-emphasizes character development in favor of vignettes to provide what appear like fragments of broader stories; the strategy allows him to destabilize Yunior's migrant narrative, which also expands over time. Ever since *Drown*, Díaz has planned on writing a series of books about Yunior, "six or seven" that "would form one big novel." As he told an interviewer, "connect *This Is How You Lose Her* to *Drown* to *The Brief Wondrous Life of Oscar Wao*, and you can read this thing."[14] Yet this cross-genre "novel" does not make "one thing" of Yunior's migrant story. Rather, its development over time creates ever-increasing layers of interpretive possibilities with each shifting context. And since Díaz is not done with the series, we have yet to see if and how that "novel" will evolve.[15]

The diffusion and proliferation of Yunior's migrant story, though viewed by some as an elaborate scheme to mask the author's trauma, in fact works to expand our sense of scale. Díaz prompts us to gather the pieces of this story as we read his short and long fiction, following Yunior's various avatars as they refract each other. And what we discover, as we jump back and forth in time and across literary formats (short to long fiction and back), is how the proliferation of Yuniors expands the personal toxicity reflected in the character's life—and in Díaz's own life—to a larger-scale toxicity, not only of colonial violence but of centuries of human violence to the environment. In Díaz's hands we become enmeshed in several stories simultaneously, connected narratives that spin out of concentric historical spheres. Like the other works I've examined in this book, Díaz's migration fiction, through its aesthetic shape, thus preempts assimilationist and empathic reading practices while broadening the scale at which we can imagine migration.

On a more granular level, stories such as "Negocios," "Otravida, Otravez," and "Invierno," like many other pieces in Díaz's oeuvre, go well beyond the immigrant fiction that parodies the myth of America as the land of milk and honey. These stories represent the parts of the United States where poor migrants arrive as on par with the so-called Third World, especially regarding environmental blight. They capture what it is like to live in a "climate caste system."[16] Moreover, rather than focusing only on the personal effects of global warming, Díaz contextualizes climate injustice within the apocalypse triggered by the "discovery" of the New Word and the chain of other catastrophic events that the arrival of Europeans set in motion. Yunior's sly narrative voice connects all the works in Díaz's oeuvre, encouraging us to see intertextual links that situate migration in a broad historical context, so that we can consider environmental injustice, as well as migration itself, as part of colonial history.

To see how Díaz lays out this historical and intertextual context, I will turn first to his novel, where he most effectively dramatizes the connections between the imperial forces that cause migration and the singular life stories of the standard immigrant novel.

"BEFORE THERE WAS AN AMERICAN STORY..."

The Brief Wondrous Life of Oscar Wao, in the words of Richard Patteson, is "at least three novels in one: the story of Oscar; a tale of immigration to America against a backdrop of tyranny (which Díaz invites readers to see as a manifestation of the mythic trauma experienced by the New World since 1492); and a novel about writing and its power to construct and shape an alternative reality."[17] The book begins by introducing the Curse and then, from this wide-angle frame, zeroes in on Oscar's early life, before his sister, Lola, who twice takes over the role of narrator, facilitates a transition to the core of the novel: the story of their mother, Belicia, known as Beli. Through her story, we can see how Díaz's migrant aesthetics expands character, time, and space to draw a specific life into connection with the much larger history of imperial violence. "Before there was an American Story," Yunior writes, "before Paterson spread before Oscar and Lola like a dream, or the trumpets from the Island of our eviction had even sounded, there was their mother, Hypatía Belicia Cabral . . . a girl so tall your leg bones ached just looking at her . . . so dark it was as if the Creatrix had, in her making, blinked" (OW, 77). Beli is the last surviving member of a family that was light-skinned enough to be considered white, but she is born unquestionably black, and "not just any kind of black. But *black* black—kongoblack, shangoblack, kaliblack, zapoteblack, rekhablack" (248). Beli is, in other words, the embodiment of all that the Curse seeks to destroy.

Yunior's hyperbolic and promiscuous narrative style—mixing everything from Dominican Spanish to African American slang to "tropical magic realism . . . hip-hop machismo, [and] post-postmodern pyrotechnics"—yields a certain interpretative flexibility in defining the Curse.[18] What remains always clear, however, is that the Curse is anti-black. And Trujillo, a "pig-eyed mulato [sic] who bleached his skin," was its "high priest"; he ruled the Dominican Republic (from 1930 to 1961) "like it was a plantation and he was the master," waging a "genocide against the Haitian and Haitian-Dominican community," giving free reign to his hatred for black people in a country already suffering from anti-blackness despite its deep African roots (OW, 2, 3). "No one knows," adds Yunior, "whether Trujillo was the Curse's servant or its master, its agent or its principal, but it was clear that he and it had an understanding, that them two was *tight*" (OW, 2–3).

Note Yunior's depiction of Beli's blackness, which rejects the practice of essentializing race while broadening the geographic scale of the Curse. The first two compound words—"kongoblack, shangoblack"—clearly invoke Africa, but the next three extend the allusion, including references to Kali, the Dark Mother of Hindu mythology whose jet-black body is meant to symbolize her all-embracing and transcendental nature, and Rekha, a 1980s Bollywood diva and Indian sex symbol. Then, with a reference to the Zapotec, a pre-Columbian indigenous people from Oaxaca in Central

Mexico, Díaz playful invokes another "Indian" people, whose dark skin is rarely attributed to the African presence in Mexican culture. This combination of references suggests the mixture of cultures that make up the Caribbean, including people from Southeast Asia (brought to the region through indentured servitude) and native peoples, like the Zapotec, who mixed with African captives. Yunior's wordplay thus allows him to zoom out from Beli's specific geographical position and place her in a cultural context far wider than just the Dominican Republic, while also pointing the reader's attention toward the larger migration forces (the African diaspora, indentured servitude) that preceded Beli's migration to the United States and that, as a Caribbean woman, she embodies in her cultural makeup.

When she migrates, Beli is followed by a particular manifestation of the Curse, which was unleashed by "the arrival of the Europeans on Hispaniola" and has since spread to the whole world: "we've all been in the shit ever since" because the Curse has taken on vast structural economic, political, and social forms (OW, 1). Yunior alerts us to the fact that the Curse "doesn't always strike like lightning" (OW, 4); for Beli and her children, it manifests as a thwarted desire for love, specifically what Díaz calls "decolonial love," "the only kind of love that could liberate them from that horrible legacy of colonial violence"—and yet they cannot achieve it.[19] For Díaz, the Curse, which he also calls the "Fukú Americanus," is not only anti-black, it is born out of the "rape culture of the European colonization of the New World—which becomes the rape culture of the Trujillato (Trujillo just took that very old record and remixed it)." And it is this "rape culture that stops [Beli and her] family from achieving decolonial intimacy, from achieving decolonial love."[20]

Beli is the youngest of Abelard Cabral's three daughters and miraculously survives after Abelard ignites Trujillo's wrath by refusing to sacrifice his eldest daughter to the dictator's sexual voracity. When Abelard is sent to rot in prison and his wife and other two daughters die (in circumstances that clearly point to Trujillo as the perpetrator), Beli is sent to live with distant relatives, who soon sell her as an indentured servant to another family. She is ultimately rescued by Abelard's sister, La Inca, a name that invokes another native people of the Americas. But Beli's aunt-turned-surrogate-mother is unable to prevent her from falling in love with Dionisio, aka the Gangster, who turns out to be married to Trujillo's sister. The affair, which nearly kills Beli—she barely survives rape and a brutal beating in a cane field, orchestrated by Trujillo's sister as revenge—shows the Curse's power to suck its victims into its violent realm; even though La Inca rescues her, Beli is relentlessly pulled back into Trujillo's orbit. In the coming years, Beli's children, Oscar and Lola, become victims to the Curse as well. They are born in the United States, after their mother's escape and marriage to a man who ultimately abandons them all. But Oscar is eventually drawn back to the Dominican Republic to chase his love interest, Ybón, whose jealous boyfriend sends Oscar—like his mother—to a cane field to be beaten to death.

The cane field, a symbol of colonialism the world over, serves in this way as a stage for an intergenerational struggle against the Curse, which Yunior hopes to break by creating a counterspell. He explains that, while the Curse has yet to be beaten, its more local manifestations have sometimes been contained by a "simple word": "Zafa," defined as a "surefire counterspell" (*OW*, 7). The invocation of the Fukú—a word that phonetically calls to mind the mundane curse "fuck you" (as Oscar discovers when he rolls the word "experimentally" around his mouth)—and the "Zafa," probably derived from the Spanish word *zafar* ("to release from"),[21] flaunts Yunior's pleasure in storytelling and keeps the concepts that Díaz employs from becoming rigid (*OW*, 304).[22]

The Brief Wondrous Life of Oscar Wao itself is, as Yunior explains, a "zafa of sorts," meant to short-circuit a fukú "that's got its fingers around [his] throat" (*OW*, 6–7). But why does his zafa take the form of a narrative that traces the Curse against Oscar's family, as opposed to Yunior's? What is Yunior's own curse, and how is it connected to the larger Curse in all its anti-blackness and sexual violence? As we know from the short stories in *Drown* and in *This Is How You Lose Her*, Yunior is both a victim and a perpetrator of toxic masculinity. The strain of it that he inherits from his father and his older brother, Rafa, involves an almost pathological sexual promiscuity that, combined with Yunior's scars from having been sexually molested, render him unable to love and be loved. In *Oscar Wao*, his failed relationship with Lola is the prime example. Oscar, who is perennially open to love but always rejected, seems at first to be Yunior's polar opposite, but, as several critics have noted, Yunior is much more like Oscar than he tends to acknowledge, and "on numerous occasions he lets down the veil."[23] Beyond his distinctive style, then, Yunior's specific features as both narrator and character are key to the migrant aesthetics that Díaz uses to underscore the expansive scale and complexity of colonial violence. Moreover, Yunior's particular curse as the victim-perpetrator of toxicity connects the small scale of the bedroom, where this toxicity manifests as sexual violence to the self and others, to the largest scale of the Anthropocene, where we experience it as violence to the planet and to ourselves as a species.

Toxicity is the nexus at which Díaz connects Yunior's emotional and sexual violence to the historical and economic forces that are laying waste to the planet and our lives on it. But Díaz does not use this context to excuse Yunior's behavior. If anything, he highlights Yunior's complicity in facilitating the Curse even as he tries to counter it with his "zafa." This complicity can be seen most vividly in Yunior's predatory relationship with Oscar. As a narrator, Yunior cannibalizes Oscar's story and uses it as a screen upon which to project not only his own condition under the Curse but also "elements of his own intellectual and artistic development."[24] Worse yet, the novel raises the specter of Yunior's complicity in Oscar's downfall, since it is implied that, had Yunior revealed his commonalities with Oscar instead of mocking him, he might have prevented his death. Combined with Yunior's dictatorial tendencies—recall that he openly recognizes the links between "authorship, authority, and authoritarianism"[25] as he reshapes, controls, and orders other people's stories—this narrative element works to preempt the empathy model of reading. Yunior is not only unreliable but also, like Teju Cole's Julius in *Open City*, ethically suspect and therefore unavailable as an object of readerly identification.

He is also like Julius in that he seduces his readers; indeed, he goes one step further. In chapter 1, I explored how Julius's well-stocked mind and urbane interests encourage a false intimacy between Julius and the novel's readers, who may find those attributes attractive and see themselves (at least initially) reflected in him. The rape accusation at the end of *Open City* comes as a jolt to these readers, forcing them to question both Julius's ethics and their own identification with him. In *Oscar Wao*, Yunior's seduction of the reader works more like that of the narrator in Nabokov's *Pnin* (1957), in that he uses his narrative style and disarming humor to entice the unsuspecting reader into a complicity in his own toxicity. In *Pnin*, the initially nameless narrator—who, like the eponymous figure, is an immigrant—mocks Pnin as an unglamorous, unassimilated version of himself. But he makes that mockery enjoyable to the reader, who, when the narrator finally reveals his identity, has already partaken in the "fun" of the mocking (like Humbert Humbert, *Pnin*'s narrator can churn out "fancy prose"). The mockery gains additional complexity because it is combined with a tenderness toward Pnin, arising from the fact that Pnin represents aspects of the narrator's painful past. Even more so than Yunior in *Oscar Wao*, the narrator of *Pnin* resists disclosing his identity, never clearly explaining his reasons for narrating Pnin's life, although he provides a clue when he takes over Pnin's job and we witness Pnin driving off the fiction that the narrator has created about him.[26]

In *Oscar Wao*, Yunior's ridicule of Oscar is also mixed with tenderness, and for similar reasons. Yunior dictates how we see Oscar—a lovable "Ghetto-Nerd" whose own writing, though frequently referred to, is never shared. The fact that Lola twice takes over the narration reduces "the totality of Yunior's control over the text" and over Oscar's representation, yet at times "her narrative seems to be taken directly from her journal," raising further questions about Yunior's ethics.[27] In these ways, Díaz does not just reject the autobiographical impulse that surrounds myths of immigration; he turns it against itself in Nabokovian fashion. Díaz's migrant aesthetics' refusal to enable readerly empathy here becomes an invitation for the reader to meditate on complicity—Yunior's and the reader's own.

At the same time, Yunior's investment in telling Oscar's story is clearly fueled by his commitment to testifying to the broad implications of Trujillo's violence. As part of the Curse, that violence has infiltrated the lives of the many people he oppressed, and its legacy has been passed down across generations and nations. Yunior is thus both deeply flawed—even contagious—in his toxicity and, simultaneously, committed to justice. He lays out the historical details of Trujillo's terror, using elaborate footnotes that connect that dictatorship to U.S. imperialism and the exodus of Dominicans to the United States.[28] We may not feel empathy for him, we may even resent his dictatorial ways, but we are invited to *think* with him about both the structural and the granular impact of the Curse, especially as it pertains to migration. Moreover, by making his main narrator ethically suspect and potentially seductive, as Cole does in *Open City*, Díaz forces his readers to contend with how testimony is created in the first place and prevents them from taking that testimony at face value. The model of infection through seduction works thematically as well as stylistically. Throughout the novel, Yunior shows that, except for La Inca, everyone around Oscar, including his otherwise loving sister, Lola, pressures him to conform to a version of masculinity that depends on sexual conquest. By exposing his own and Lola's roles in pressuring Oscar to conform to this standard, Yunior shows how deeply Dominicans and their children, even those born in diaspora, have introjected Trujillo's violence.

Trujillo supposedly embodied what Dominicans call a tíguere—a hustler who, in Danny Méndez's definition, "through his wits and *cojones* (testicles), understands the art of social mobility." "This was the image of Trujillo that was projected by his propagandists," writes Méndez, "who in this way made even his vices—his corruption, his brutality, his lechery and sexism—into virtues."[29] Just as Trujillo gave license to an anti-blackness already rooted in the Dominican Republic through chattel slavery, he also promoted a version of masculinity that flaunted his vices and, over the decades of his rule, hardened into an ideology. Yunior, his brother Rafa, and their father Ramón all embody aspects of the tíguere, a fact that limits their ability to relate both to women and to each other. Oscar, in contrast—a sweet, sensitive nerd—tries to commit suicide because he cannot conform either to Dominican expectations or to those that he confronts as a black man in the United States.

The male characters in *Oscar Wao* are not the only ones interpellated by this ideology. Beli's attraction to the Gangster begins innocently on her part; she doesn't know he is an arm of Trujillo. But she takes up with him after a denigrating relationship with Jack Pujols, a cocky loudmouth from an ultrarich white family with ties to Trujillo, whom she meets at a school that she briefly attends on a scholarship. Pujols treats her in a way typical of his class and race: "the fucking of poor prietas was considered standard operating procedure for elites just as long as it was kept on the do-lo, what is elsewhere called the Strom Thurmond Maneuver" (*OW*, 100). Beli, an otherwise strong woman—a "femme-matador," as Yunior describes her—is nevertheless attracted to men cut from the same cloth as Trujillo (*OW*, 101). She continues this pattern on her journey to the United States, meeting Lola and Oscar's dysfunctional father on the plane. He soon abandons her and the children, leaving only his last name (de León) as a trace. Beli's daughter, Lola, is a strong woman like her mother, yet she falls for Yunior. The fact that she leaves him, however, suggests that she might be the first who can break the intergenerational curse.

Becoming and falling for Trujillo-like goons are sure signs of the Curse for Dominicans, and Díaz leaves no doubt about its range—Ana, for instance, a Dominican girl from New Jersey whom Oscar briefly befriends, has an abusive boyfriend who in his testosterone-driven aggression foreshadows Ybón's boyfriend, the one who later kills Oscar out of jealousy. Díaz also highlights the Curse's links with larger narratives of persecution: Yunior's reference to Strom Thurmond in his characterization of Pujols is one of many references to the sexual legacy of slavery in the United States. Thus, using intertextual links and allusions, Díaz suggests the Curse's culture-specific materializations within its broad range. One particularly vivid example is the terrible burn scar on Beli's back, which recalls a similar scar on Sethe's back in Toni Morrison's *Beloved*, as well as the scar on the back of a slave dubbed "Peter" whose image was widely used by the abolitionist press in the nineteenth century.[30] "A monsterglove of festering ruination," Beli's scar extends "from the back of her neck to the base of her spine" (*OW*, 257).[31] In this lingering wound and in countless other elements of Díaz's work, historical intersections combine with literary intertextuality: anti-black and misogynistic violence appear as entangled phenomena, a historical fukú that can be countered only by a literary zafa as broad in scope, as culturally intertwined, and as inescapably complex.

The Brief Wondrous Life of Oscar Wao provides a wide-ranging backdrop for the theme of toxic masculinity also explored in Díaz's short fiction. In effect, the novel offers two contexts for understanding the short stories in *Drown* and *This Is How You Lose Her*: the arrival of Europeans to the "New World" and Trujillo's dictatorship. What difference do these historical frames make to how we interpret these stories, particularly the ones concerning romantic relationships? The recurrence of breakups in Díaz's short fiction recalls the fact that, in American immigrant literature, marriage, infidelity, and divorce have long served as tropes for the ruptures and new beginnings of migrant life. Specifically, in Werner Sollors's words, they have signaled the tension between "contractual and hereditary, self-made and ancestral, definitions of American identity."[32] Díaz, whose focus is *not* American identity but rather the afterlives of (neo)colonialism in contemporary migration, uses the breakup plot to dramatize how migrants lose but still crave the fiction of a stable identity, of belonging to one nation. In his short fiction, Díaz engages intimately with desire, longing, and infidelity as parallel states of migrant (un)belonging. But he applies pressure on the analogy he raises between romantic love and love of the nation through a recurrence of toxic gender dynamics, in which sexual violence replicates historically constituted oppression and breakup plots evince the intimate repercussions of that oppression.

In "Homecoming, with Turtle" (*New Yorker*, 2004), for example, a nameless young man goes back to visit the Dominican Republic for the first time in twenty years; he and his family migrated to New Jersey when he was six. As a return narrative, the story describes the difficulties that the young man encounters because he no longer fits into Dominican culture: his "busted-up Spanish" gives him away, so that people call him "americano" to his face and overcharge him.[33] The story also includes a plotline about the narrator's impending breakup with his girlfriend, who finds out that he has been cheating on her shortly before the trip. "How did I feel?" he asks rhetorically of his trip back to the Dominican Republic. "All I will say is that if you fused the instant when heartbreak occurs to the instant when one falls in love and shot that concoction straight into your brain stem you might have a sense of what it felt like for me to be back 'home.'" His twin desires to be forgiven for his infidelity and to be recognized as Dominican fuse in his language of romantic longing and loss. "What I wanted more than anything," he writes, "was to be recognized as the long-lost son I was, but that wasn't going to happen. Not after nearly twenty years. Nobody believed I was Dominican!"[34] His girlfriend, meanwhile, does not believe he can ever be faithful. Unsurprisingly, the couple break up soon after the trip, but the narrator, who is recounting the split eleven years later, identifies the trip with a beginning as well as an ending—the start of his reconciliation with his native land. After that first trip back, he returns often, improves his Spanish, and receives at least partial recognition from his countrymen that he is—at least partly—Dominican.

The first story in *This Is How You Lose Her*, "The Sun, the Moon, the Stars," which is an extended revision of "Homecoming, with Turtle," identifies Yunior as the narrator and elaborates the analogy between romantic desire and rupture on the one hand and the Dominican migrant experience on the other. "Let me confess: I love Santo Domingo," Yunior writes, like a man admitting to a love affair.[35] This version of the story, however, does not pursue the equation between inauthenticity and infidelity. Instead, it begins with a loaded declaration: "I'm not a bad guy. I know how that sounds—defensive, unscrupulous—but it's true." This statement is prompted by the cheated-on girlfriend's view of Yunior as a "typical Dominican man: a sucio, an asshole" (*TH*, 3). "Sucio" literally means dirty; in Dominican slang, it refers to someone whose promiscuous sexual nature renders them filthy, unclean. Díaz's revision of "Homecoming, with Turtle" shows him moving away from equating infidelity with inauthenticity and toward the use of infidelity as a trope connecting sexual violence to broader histories of colonial violence. This change not only invokes Yunior's trauma but also suggests that he is projecting his desire to regain the fiction of national belonging onto his romantic relationships. So, in "The Sun, the Moon, the Stars," Yunior's attraction to his soon-to-be ex-girlfriend Magda is overloaded with his vision of her embodying the Caribbean, his site of desire.[36] If we read the story in the context of Díaz's novel, we can see that Yunior identifies his Dominicanness with his experience of the Curse, and that his compulsive promiscuity is a legacy of a long history of colonial misogyny and violence. *Oscar Wao* thus gives us a trajectory that we can trace through the whole of *This Is How You Lose Her*, which culminates with the story "A Cheater's Guide to Love."

Yunior's colonial-sexual trauma places Díaz in dialogue with other Afro-diasporic texts that have explored the long legacy of slavery in sexual relations, including Gayl Jones's brilliant 1975 novel *Corregidora*. Díaz's migrant aesthetics—his style and genre hybridity, his narratorial slipperiness and complicit characters, his intertextuality, and his metafictional structures—does not constitute a zafa that can counteract the fukú on Díaz's actions in real life. But it does suggest that, regardless of how we hold that person to account, we must always attend to the larger structures of historical violence in which we are all enmeshed. Examining Díaz's short fiction with his novel's wide-angle frame in mind—an analytical practice encouraged by the intertextuality within his oeuvre—we can contextualize the toxic behaviors that he both depicts and represents, while also focusing on how environmental injustice and migration intertwine.

THE GREAT DYING: "INVIERNO" AND "AGUANTANDO"

"The Central Jersey I grew up in," Díaz told me, "has a lot to teach us about the past, the present, the future of our country and others it is connected to."[37] In the stories in *Drown* and *This Is How You Lose Her*, he refracts his own experience of "growing up super poor in a crumbling fucking neighborhood near a burning landfill where people just seemed to appear and disappear without reason," because it left him with a nagging question: "I felt that I was in a dress rehearsal for the apocalypse. Or perhaps the apocalypse had already happened. This was a question that haunted me and still haunts me."[38] The temporal suspension produced by toxic wastelands is, for Díaz, analogous to the distortion of time of migration, and the analogy hinges on the word "apocalypse." "In the classic apocalyptic pattern," Díaz told me, "there is the pre-apocalypse, which is the pre-apocalyptic world; there is the eschaton, which destroys the world; and there is the post-apocalypse, or the New World . . . The eschaton, of course, [for me] was immigration." Both experiences entail suspension of time, but in the apocalyptic scenario this leads to a transposition of frames: the present looks like both the past and a foreshadowing of the future. In migration, too, the suspension of time has to do with destruction and creation—the past has been transformed by the present time of migration while the future, if it is to come, has yet to arise. For Díaz, the two experiences are connected through history. He depicts the arrival of Europeans in the New World in apocalyptic terms: one world perishes in the screams of the enslaved and the "death bane" of native people, as another world begins What this perishing engenders is nothing less than the beginning of the Anthropocene and the environmental disasters in places like the Dominican Republic and what Díaz calls the "tedious, unromantic corridors" of central New Jersey, a state that currently has the most Superfund sites in the United States (locations requiring a long-term response to clean up hazardous-material contaminations).[39]

For Díaz, the Curse, or Fukú Americanus, brought on what climate scientists call the Great Dying, a phrase most often used to describe the Permian-Triassic extinction event, "a series of extinction pulses" that occurred over fifteen million years and "contributed to the greatest mass extinction in Earth's history."[40] The phrase is also used to denote the mass extinction that followed the arrival of Europeans in 1492 to the New World. According to recent research, 90 percent of the native population (fifty-six million people) died, not only from the waves of diseases that Europeans brought across the Atlantic but also from war, famine, and enslavement.[41] Some argue that this Great Dying was "the largest human mortality event in proportion to the global population."[42] The devastation resulted in the collapse of farming in the Americas, which in turn cooled the global climate. Meanwhile, the networks of trade resulting from the arrival of Europeans to the New World "led to a rapid, repeated, cross-ocean exchange of species, which [was] without precedent in Earth's history" and resulted in a significant loss of biodiversity and the acceleration of species extinction rates.[43]

Climate scientists Simon Lewis and Mark Maslin identify 1610, when the collision of the New World and the Old World a century earlier was first felt globally, as the beginning of the Anthropocene (though the epoch has yet to be officially dated by the International Committee on Stratigraphy). Most scientists and environmental historians identify either the Industrial Revolution or the middle of the twentieth century as its start, since the latter marks the beginning of the Great Acceleration (referring to the increasing pace of energy use, greenhouse-gas emissions, and population growth after World War II) and atomic testing. In an essay published in *Nature* in 2015, however, Lewis and Maslin argue for 1610 as a more accurate date: while the nuclear-age Anthropocene highlights an "elite-driven technological development that threatens planet-wide destruction," the expansion of "colonialism, global trade and coal"[44] marked a turn when the negative impacts of human activity became global and set earth on a new trajectory.[45]

The Atlantic slave trade, which took place concurrently with the Great Dying, was itself another "great dying," as millions of people perished in the Middle Passage—the largest forced movement of people in history—and millions more fell to the brutality of plantation slavery. Geographic and ecological researchers have argued that chattel slavery and the genocide of native peoples constituted the twin epicenters of the Anthropocene's origin, and have traced the legacy of that colonial violence through the Industrial Revolution and the Atomic Age to the current, catastrophic climate change.[46] Some, including geographer Kathryn Yusoff, have gone further, arguing that the grammar used by most geologists to identify and describe the Anthropocene is itself embedded in anti-blackness and the willful ignorance of indigenous dispossession. In *A Billion Black Anthropocenes or None* (2018), Yusoff writes: "The Anthropocene might seem to offer a dystopic future that laments the end of the world, but imperialism and ongoing (settler) colonialisms have been ending worlds for as long as they have been in existence."[47]

Dating the onset of the Anthropocene to the collision between the Old and New Worlds asserts the connections between colonialism and migration and resonates with Díaz's apocalyptic vision. Díaz implicitly identifies 1492 as the beginning of the Anthropocene, and in this he agrees with the Jamaican writer and cultural theorist Sylvia Wynter. As Dana Luciano explains, in her essay "1492: A New World View" (1995), Wynter argues that 1492 marks the start of a "cognitive process that parallels, in some ways, the homogenizing effect on planetary life that Lewis and Maslin note":

> It is, [Wynter] contends, the beginning of the global dissemination of a specifically Western idea of humanism that posits itself as universal but endlessly defers the truly universal distribution of the benefits it confers, one that legitimates and covers over the violence, racial, colonial and otherwise, done in its name. The aftermath of 1492, Wynter shows, is the spread of a humanism that has failed much of humanity, a failure to which even the Arctic ice cores can bear witness, and that in doing so has deeply damaged the planet as well: an inhuman humanism.[48]

Luciano rightly argues that debates about dating the Anthropocene really center on "what kind of story can and should be told about human impact on the planet." She adds: "The claim is often made that climate change is simply too big to see . . . something that cannot be realized in any specific instance. The Anthropocene offers climate change not just periodicity but narrativity. And like any well-told story, it relies upon conscious plotting and the manipulation of feeling."[49] Díaz's and Wynter's identification of 1492 as the beginning of the Anthropocene amplifies the temporality of migration, connecting it to empire and capital. They show how the "inhuman humanism" brought on by the European so-called discovery of the Americas also set in motion the migrant and climate crises we are now experiencing. Díaz's migrant aesthetics radically expand the scale of migration, approximating a global perspective, yet he does not seek the "manipulation of feeling" that Luciano describes. Rather, like the other writers I discuss in this book, he wants us not simply to feel but to think collectively about how migration has built our world and how, like climate change, it is already shaping our future.

In his essay "Apocalypse: What Disasters Reveal" (2011), about the earthquake that struck Haiti in 2010, Díaz makes explicit the connections between colonialism, climate change, and migration as they are playing out in our contemporary world. Again, he dissects the concept of apocalypse and reminds us that the term comes from the "Greek *apocalypsis*, meaning to uncover and unveil," implying "a disruptive event that provokes revelation." Taking his cue from James Berger's book *After the End: Representations of Post-Apocalypse* (1999), Díaz further defines apocalypse as both "the actual imagined end of the world, whether in Revelations or in Hollywood blockbusters" and as "catastrophes, personal or historical, that are said to resemble that imagined final ending—the Chernobyl meltdown or the Holocaust or the [March 11, 2011] earthquake and tsunami in Japan."[50] Focusing on the 2010 earthquake in Haiti, Díaz demonstrates how these categories bleed into each other at a sociopolitical level.

As I have discussed earlier in this book, Haiti has the largest immigrant population in the United States for reasons that can be directly linked to (neo)colonialism. As Díaz reminds us, Haiti was politically and economically punished for decades for being "the first and only nation in the world to overthrow Western chattel slavery, for which it was blockaded (read, further impoverished) by Western powers" and subjugated under "diabolical despots who [drove] Haiti into ruin and who often ruled with foreign assistance."[51] In short, (neo)colonialism has relegated Haiti to desperate poverty— the country has the Western Hemisphere's lowest gross domestic product (GDP) per capita—and that poverty has made it infinitely more vulnerable to ecological disaster, while straining its natural resources to the breaking point. "Deforestation," Díaz writes, "has rendered vast stretches of the Haitian landscape almost lunar in their desolation. Haiti is eating itself."[52] Political and economic catastrophes beget environmental disasters and injustice, but, as Díaz argues, "Haiti's problem is not that it is poor and vulnerable—Haiti's problem is that it is poor and vulnerable at a time in [which] our capitalist experiment," along with globalization, has created abysmal inequality, widening the wealth gap astronomically and leaving billions of people to bear the brunt of every new catastrophe produced by anthropogenic global warming.[53]

Ecological disasters are apocalyptic insofar as they reveal the layers of history that produce them. "Katrina revealed America's third world," Díaz writes, while the earthquake in Haiti disclosed that country as "the third world's third world."[54] Díaz argues that this tendency of catastrophes to include revelations of human impoverishment is no accident of nature.

Katrina was a disaster produced not only by the "ruthless economic marginalization of poor African Americans and in the outright abandonment of the same during the crisis," but also by the fact that the Bush administration decided "to sell hundreds of square miles of wetlands to developers, destroying New Orleans's natural defenses."[55] America, the mythical beacon of hope for immigrants fleeing economic and ecological disasters, in fact relegates the poor, the migrant, and the disenfranchised to the bottom rung of a climate caste system in which they suffer the worst impacts of global warming.

To demonstrate these impacts, Díaz grounds large-scale stories of migrations and environmental disasters in contemporary, local landscapes, namely the Dominican Republic and central New Jersey. The latter landscape recalls Robert Smithson's photo-essay "A Tour of the Monuments of Passaic, New Jersey," in its focus on a neighborhood under construction that looks, even before it is finished, like a ruined metropolis. By analyzing Smithson's influence on Díaz—which Díaz has explicitly acknowledged[56]—we can perceive an abiding if subtle focus in his fiction on environmental toxicity within the lived environment, a phenomenon that relates to his vision of our common future.

Originally published in *Artforum* in 1967, Smithson's essay details the artist's trip to the banks of the Passaic River, where he encounters a number of industrial objects and notices how much they look like "monuments" from a different time.[57] He photographs a bridge connecting Bergen and Passaic counties—"concrete abutments that supported the shoulders of a new highway in the process of being built," an "artificial crater" out of which protruded "six large pipes"—as well as the machines used to build it:

> Since it was Saturday, many machines were not working, and this caused them to resemble prehistoric creatures trapped in the mud, or, better, extinct machines—mechanical dinosaurs stripped of their skin . . . That zero panorama seemed to contain *ruins in reverse*, that is—all the new construction that would eventually be built. This is the opposite of the "romantic ruin" because the buildings don't *fall* into ruin *after* they are built but rather *rise* as ruins before they are built.[58]

Smithson's essay is a rejection of what Andrew Menard describes as "a nostalgic trend that arose both in American studies and American environmentalism during the 1950s and 1960s" for nineteenth-century pastoralism, the premise of which was that the idyllic nature of the American landscape "had been subverted by a trajectory of industrialization that began with the Civil War and accelerated as the frontier 'withered and lost its redemptive power.'"[59] Against the background of a twentieth-century landscape that seemed "poisoned by the ill effects of progress and often criticized as ugly and soulless," an idea began to be recycled that the American landscape before industrialization was part of what made the country exceptional in the world, the Eden sought after by Europeans.[60] Smithson, among others, argues that this pastoral and exceptionalist view of America was illusionary for, as Andrew Menard puts it, "even those nineteenth-century Americans who looked most assiduously to the landscape for their identity *as* Americans were aware that it existed as a *juxtaposition* of artifice and nature, wilderness and cultivation, progress and despoliation."[61]

In his essay, Smithson disrupts the nostalgia for nineteenth-century pastoralism by playing upon the visual and rhetorical conventions of picturesque travel narratives, conventions that helped to create the pastoralist myth in the first place.[62] Menard argues that, since Smithson understands pastoralist nostalgia as evidence that "the nation's *future* was still being idealized," he rejects the idea of the future as "progress, except as a form of obsolescence."[63] Walking among the "monuments" of Passaic, Smithson writes: "Noon-day sunshine cinema-ized the site, turning the bridge and the river into an over-exposed picture. Photographing it with my Instamatic 400 was like photographing a photograph."[64] The simile calls attention to the fact that ideas of landscape, nature, and nature's relationship to culture are always filtered and shaped by other representations. It also draws out the links that Smithson sees between past, present, and future. According to Menard, Smithson perceives "nature and culture" as forces that constantly "displaced each other," always remaining "out of balance," and time as "an endless and *transparent* negotiation between nature and culture in which each became a reflection of the other."[65] It is in this sense that he sees the future—even while "industry, reckless urbanization, or nature's own devastation" increase—as a version of both the present and the past.[66]

Díaz's attention to the environmental toxicity and apocalyptic landscape of Yunior's first home in America affirms Smithson's influence on his work, as does his emphasis on clashing timeframes. By zooming out from the specificity of contemporary New Jersey to the broader history of the African diaspora and the history of the Dominican Republic, as well as the even larger timescale of ecological disaster, Díaz encourages us to connect timeframes and geographies and recreates the suspension in time produced by both toxic landscapes and migration, as one world collapses and another has yet to be born. In Díaz's short story "Negocios," for instance, Ramón, Yunior's father, goes to "a small town outside of Perth Amboy" in New Jersey, to see the London Terrace apartment complex "under construction" there; he hopes that he can eventually buy an apartment in the complex and then bring Yunior and the rest of his family from the Dominican Republic.[67] "Huge craters had been gouged in the earth and towering ziggurats of tan bricks stood ready to be organized into buildings . . . pipes were being laid by the mile and the air was tart with the smell of chemicals" (*Drown*, 195). Ziggurats are ancient Mesopotamian towers, and Díaz's reference to them here gives the unfinished buildings an aura of ruins from an earlier age. Later in the story, we learn that the construction of the London Terrace complex—the name recalls a city famed for its nineteenth-century industrial pollution—was "delayed because of a rumor that it had been built on a chemical dump site" (*Drown*, 205).

In the short story "Invierno," from *This Is How You Lose Her*, we see Yunior arriving with his mother and brother in New Jersey in the early 1980s, a time when the state was only beginning to contend with its brutal legacy from the Industrial Revolution.[68] Yunior tells us that, when they arrive, London Terrace is still a "mess; half the buildings still needed their wiring and in the evening light these structures sprawled about like ships of brick that had run aground. Mud followed gravel everywhere and the grass, planted late in fall, poked out of the snow in dead tufts" (*TH*, 121). There is a landfill "two miles out," and Yunior can hear "bulldozers spreading the garbage out in thick, putrid layers" and see the "gulls attending the mound, thousands of them, wheeling" (*TH*, 134). Yunior and his family thus become part of a painful reality: immigrants, many of whom belong to racial and ethnic low-income communities, are "disproportionately exposed to environmental hazards relative to the rest of the U.S. population."[69] In the story, Yunior plays in the snow with two white children; in less than a year, these playmates "would be gone. All the white people would be. All that would be left would be us colored folks" (*TH*, 137–138). And "each day the trucks would roll into [his] neighborhood with the garbage," the odors of which reach his family "undiluted" (*TH*, 134). While Yunior does not draw a direct line between this exposure and later events, his account of his brother's death to leukemia in "The Pura Principle" (also in *This Is How You Lose Her*) suggests the role of such pollution in spreading disease. The fact that Beli, who lives in a similar community in *Oscar Wao*, also dies from cancer reinforces the connections between environmental toxicity, immigrant life in America, and the rampant health disparities between the country's rich and poor.

"Invierno," as its title suggests, describes Yunior's first encounter with winter, all its desolation and privations, and with the bareness and boredom of his initial life in the United States. His father keeps him, Rafa, and his mother confined to their apartment, and while Yunior makes brief escapes to play in the snow with the white kids, he and his brother spend most of every day watching television, either to numb themselves or to learn English from *Sesame Street*. Their mother, who is even more isolated than they are—she has no "friends, no neighbors," and rightly suspects that her husband is cheating on her—quietly begins to unravel (*TH*, 132). The suspended time in which these characters live is reminiscent of Julie Otsuka's descriptions of time in *When the Emperor Was Divine*, especially in Díaz's use of diurnal details to suggest the psychological effects of waiting in a seemingly endless present for an uncertain future.

Díaz cites Samuel R. Delany's *Dhalgren* (1974) as another source of inspiration, noting how that novel's setting, a postapocalyptic, bombed-out Midwestern metropolis, helped Delany "capture what it was like living in the burnt-out-core" of black American cities in the late sixties.[70] In a similar fashion, Díaz dramatizes contemporary migrant life in America's toxic wastelands, analyzing what those toxic ruins can tell us about the systemic injustice and corruption that created them. In his essay on Haiti's earthquake, he calls this form of analytical narrative "ruin-reading," a method he also uses to imagine our future. His fiction serves as testimony to migrant life in places like London Terrace, while also exposing the historical events that set poverty-stricken migrants flowing. In Díaz's fiction, migrants move in a world created by one apocalypse (European "conquest") and its consequences (global warming), and from so-called Third World countries to another Third World within the imperial power of the United States.

The world Yunior enters in "Invierno" is "frozen solid" in more than one sense, since his new life has yet to take shape (*TH*, 121). The rubbish fires that burn constantly, leaving the earth marked "with sores," suggest that he has somehow traveled temporally, both to a distant past—the fires invoke the devastation of the New World—and to the future of eco-destruction (*TH*, 145). In his new world, the ocean, once a constant in Yunior's life in the Dominican Republic, appears differently, "like the blade of a long, curved knife" cresting "the horizon to the east" (*TH*, 145, 121). This simile, which bookends "Invierno," depicts the sea—and by extension Yunior's homeland—as a distant and receding image. But the Dominican Republic is not, in Díaz's fiction, romanticized as a paradisiacal home in contrast to postindustrial America. "Aguantando," a story in *Drown*, opens with an image of Yunior's Dominican home: everything seems to be under water, for Yunior's family suffers such an intense poverty that it subjects them to the forces of nature. "Since our zinc roof leaked," Yunior tells us, "almost everything we owned was water-stained: our clothes, Mami's Bible, her makeup, whatever food we had, Abuelo's tools, our cheap wooden furniture"—in fact, everything except for some photographs of his father, which his mother keeps in "a plastic sandwich bag" (*Drown*, 69). The story's title in Spanish means to endure, to hold on, to tolerate, but it also includes the word *agua*, or "water," which plays off the title of the collection to suggest the opposite of holding on.

At this point in his life story, Yunior knows his father only through those photographs, one of which was taken just "days before the U.S. invasion" in 1965 (*Drown*, 69). Yunior makes another allusion to the U.S. invasion a few paragraphs later, noting that his mother bears a scar on her stomach from "the rocket attack she'd survived in 1965" (*Drown*, 71). These references to the invasion, especially when read within the wide-angle frame established in *Oscar Wao*, contextualize the poverty that Yunior and his family suffer within the centuries of dispossession created by empire, colonialism, and related dictatorial rule. The invasion of 1965 was not the first: in 1916, the United States invaded the Dominican Republic, annexing it along with Haiti, which it had invaded in 1915, and occupying the island for eight years. As Edwidge Danticat explains:

> In what has become a famous mea culpa by one of the architects of the joint occupation of Haiti and the Dominican Republic, the Marine Corps General Smedley Butler confessed . . . that he spent thirty-three years as a "high class muscle man for Big Business" and as "a gangster for capitalism." "I helped make Haiti . . . a decent place for the National City Bank Boys,"

he wrote. "I brought light to the Dominican Republic for American sugar interests in 1916."[71]

The political analyst Michele Wucker writes that "American multinationals laid out vast new sugar plantations, which needed more workers than Santo Domingo could provide . . . Haiti, with the same population but half the land, was a natural source, so the companies moved thousands of people across the border, establishing a steady flow from west to east."[71] This migratory structure, in Lorgia García Peña's words, "became the basis of an exploitative labor system that relied on undocumented Haitian workers and, to this day, continues to foster race-based economic inequality of ethnic Haitians in the Dominican Republic."[72]

The 1965 invasion, which was fueled by anti-communist hysteria, ensured the end of the first democratically elected government since Trujillo's assassination, in favor of one led by Joaquín Balaguer, who had served as Trujillo's vice president and who ruled the country for twenty-four years, perpetuating Trujillo's violent legacy. "Upon taking power," writes historian Rory Fanning, "Balaguer began funneling nearly all of Dominican Republic's minerals and sugar into the warehouses of US businesses. His three-decade rule was marked by corruption and fraud. Wages plummeted, unions were dismantled, inflation soared."[73] By 1986, a quarter of all Dominicans lived below the government's absolute poverty line; by 1989, that number had risen to half of the entire population, prompting tens of thousands to leave, mostly for the United States. Yunior's family becomes part of this exodus. "We were poor," Yunior states simply. "The only way we could have been poorer was to have lived in the campo," where he and his brother are forced to go when his mother cannot support them, "or to have been Haitian immigrants" (*Drown*, 70). His family's experience of this widespread poverty contains at least two layers of meaning: at the macro level, it points to the long history of colonialism and neocolonialism that the island of Hispaniola has endured, while, at the micro level, "Aguantando" depicts Yunior's particular experience of the consequences of that history.

In contrast to his confinement in "Invierno," "Aguantando" shows Yunior with the freedom to roam his neighborhood. There "wasn't a tree in the barrio I couldn't climb," he tells us, "and on some days I spent entire afternoons in our trees, watching the barrio in motion and when Abuelo was around (and awake) he talked to me about the good old days, when a man could still make a living from his finca, when the United States wasn't something folks planned on" (*Drown*, 72–73). Though he is free to roam, however, he also suffers from dire poverty. When he and his brother get worms, his mother can afford their treatment only by skimping on their meals. "I can't remember how many times I crouched over our latrine, my teeth clenched, watching long gray parasites slide out from between my legs" (*Drown*, 71). Although he attends school, he and his brother do not have books and must share one pencil; at nine, Yunior cannot write his own name. And, though he is not conscious of it until his feelings erupt in a rage, he can hardly endure the absence of his father.

Two years after leaving for the United States, the father writes that he plans to return for the family and bring them to the United States. Then he fails to show up. Yunior demands to see the photographs of his father in the plastic bag and, when he is denied, throws himself around as if he "was on fire" (*Drown*, 83). Yunior is so inconsolable that he is locked in a room for punishment and, in this confinement, he takes his fury out on his clothes, ripping them apart with his hands and with a nail that he rips out of the wall. Later he blocks all memory of this interlude; he recounts it in the story by using the words of others. Yunior's rage, his thwarted desire that turns into fury, dramatizes his family's urgent need to be saved from drowning in poverty; their only possible savior is an absent father who comes to represent the United States, pretending to offer salvation while in fact being complicit in creating their poverty in the first place.[74]

Beli's migration story echoes Yunior's. The campo where she grows up before La Inca saves her is in "Outer Azua," one of the "poorest areas in the DR; it is a wasteland . . . [like] the irradiated terrains from those end-of-the-world scenarios that Oscar loved so much—Outer Azua was the Outland, the Badlands, the Cursed Earth, the Forbidden Zone, the Great Wastes" (*OW*, 256). As we know, though La Inca saves her from that Cursed Earth, Beli is eventually forced to leave for the United States under the threat of death from Trujillo's sister. Unlike the young Yunior and his family, La Inca holds no romantic notions about that destination: "Who knows what might happen to the girl among the yanquis? In her mind the U.S. was nothing more and nothing less than a país overrun by gangsters, putas, and no-accounts. Its cities swarmed with machines and industry, as thick with sinvergüencería as Santo Domingo was with heat, a cuco shod in iron, exhaling fumes, with the glittering promise of coin deep in the cold lightless shaft of its eyes" (*OW*, 158).

The cuco, a shape-shifting mythical monster whose origins can be traced to Spain, often figures in Dominican folklore as a faceless man with a big sack looking for children to steal; the image recalls the faceless man who appears throughout Díaz's work to signify death or its threat. In using the cuco to depict America as a monster of "machines and industry . . . exhaling fumes," Yunior implies the shape-shifting forms of capitalism and colonialism, from Europe to America. Since the cuco is usually "more felt than seen," he also suggests the work of ideology and the pervasive influence of the Curse as it finds its ways into the most intimate layers of personhood.[75] Indirectly, the image even invokes the Statue of Liberty (the iron, the shaft of its eyes), not in its traditional role as the mother of exiles, a symbol of immigration and opportunity, but as a false beacon that promises coin and issues death.

We never see how Beli confronts life as an immigrant, for neither her nor Yunior's migration story follows a traditional narrative arc in Díaz's fiction. Beli's story is embedded as a flashback within Oscar's search for love, focusing on the conditions that lead to her migration and ending as she boards the plane for New York. All we know of Beli's story in America is that she has a fraught relationship with her daughter, works two jobs, and battles breast cancer. Tellingly, the two characters in "Otravida, Otravez" mirror this path in its essentials: both figures work hard, one at a bread factory, where a fellow migrant falls from the rafters to his death, the other washing out the stains of the "sick and dying" in a hospital laundry (*TH*, 55). While Beli eventually returns to the Dominican Republic with her children, having proudly risen above "mind-boggling poverty," she loses Oscar there to the same kind of violence that almost killed her as a young woman (*OW*, 277). Yunior's father, depicted in both *Drown* and *This Is How You Lose Her*, fares slightly better up to the point when his tale abruptly ends, though there are hints that his story never finds resolution: he returns to fetch Yunior and his family in "Invierno," but we learn in another story that he ultimately leaves them again. And while Yunior ostensibly escapes, attending college and becoming a writer, he is also haunted by the Curse: *This Is How You Lose Her* is a testament to his continuing struggle to break free from his nearly pathological sexual promiscuity.

Throughout his oeuvre, Díaz's migration stories lack a plot of transcendence (recall Hemon's identification of "displacement, travails, redemption, success" as the conventional migration narrative's überplot). They are also almost always filtered through Yunior's own story, which, as we've seen, is spread out over multiple texts, published over a twenty-year span and with a promise of more to come. By thus writing a multi-work "novel" about Yunior, Díaz has rendered Yunior's story nonsequential and fragmented, and this formal technique in his migrant aesthetics allows him to expand his portrayal of migration not only across space but across time, from the very depths of the past to the near future. Indeed, as I have suggested throughout this chapter—and particularly if we take the narrator of Díaz's Afrofuturist story "Monstro" to be Yunior—Díaz's multi-text "novel" makes possible a reading of migration fiction against the vast historical context of colonialism, neocolonialism, and the Anthropocene itself.

"MONSTRO"

The future is already here—it's just not evenly distributed.
WILLIAM GIBSON, QUOTED BY JUNOT DÍAZ

Migration, like climate change, is too big to see in its full, centuries-old, globe-encompassing history and variety. It is, in one sense, *the* human story. Just as climate scientists have only recently begun to consider the colonial collision between the Old and New Worlds as the origin of the Anthropocene epoch, so paleogeneticists are just beginning to illuminate the long history of human migration. In 2010, new data extracted from ancient DNA challenged the idea that our ancestors migrated out of Africa and then remained fixed in their respective continents due to the impossibility of geographical borders and the lack of modern navigational technology. As science journalist Sonia Shah argues, this common worldview, which emerged in the eighteenth century, has sustained the understanding of human migration as a disruptive and irregular force that presages ecological doom and disrupts "the natural order" by bringing together "biologically distinct people."[76] Influencing both eugenic and xenophobic policies and practices worldwide, this view of migration persists in current anti-immigrant political crusades, even as new DNA evidence shows that migration has been a constant part of human history. Our ancestors roved and intermixed "to such an extent that even the most seemingly homogenous of their descendants—modern western Europeans, say—could not claim any long period of isolation and differentiation."[77] The idea that early humans were migrants only in the distant past and then enjoyed a long, defining period of stillness, broken only in the modern era, is a powerful illusion. The truth is that humans have "been migrants all along."[78]

In the 1960s, when scientists began to worry about the steep rise in human population that was part of the Great Acceleration, the view of migration as aberrant and ecologically dangerous gained momentum, especially after the publication of Paul and Anne Ehrlich's bestseller *The Population Bomb* (1968), a book that predicted worldwide famine in the 1970s and 1980s unless the world's population was drastically limited. While the authors did not make explicit connections to migration, others who followed them did. In particular, the ophthalmologist John Tanton, citing the Ehrlichs' book as a major influence, founded such anti-immigration organizations as the Federation for American Immigration Reform (FAIR) and persuaded anti-immigrant activists within the Sierra Club, including David Brower, to join him in shifting the focus from overpopulation worldwide to its purported effects within the United States. Immigration restriction, they argued, would save the nation from ecological doom.

When the apocalypse predicted by the Ehrlichs did not come to pass, and global and national populations started to stabilize—thanks to "people working together to develop and share new technology, improve education, and modernize societies," in Shah's words—Tanton and his followers broke from mainstream environmental movements.[79] They moved "deeper into other circles," calling to their ranks eco-nativists who were "worried about the impact of foreign peoples on the environment ... social nativists worried about the degrading effect of foreign cultures, eugenicists concerned about foreigners' impact on the gene pool, and white supremacists worried about the diminishment of their political power."[80] Tanton's influence grew exponentially, and in recent years he gained solid support from the Trump administration, which hired top figures from FAIR and other organizations founded by Tanton (including the Center for Immigration Studies, the Immigration Reform Law Institute, and the English-only group U.S. English). Tanton also founded a publishing company that issued a dystopian novel by the French author Jean Raspail called *The Camp of the Saints* (1973), which depicts Indian migrants as "swarthy hordes ...

who eat feces, invade France, force white women to work in brothels, and engage in orgies involving men, women, and children."[81] Some current political figures believe in this novel's power, despite its ridiculous premise: Marine Le Pen "kept a dedicated copy on her desk... Steve Bannon considered the novel prescient and visionary."[82]

Díaz's 2012 short story "Monstro" strategically exaggerates the fears propelling anti-immigrant groups and manipulates centuries-old associations between disease and foreigners,[83] especially as these are heightened by global warming. He also expands the scale of migration from the United States—where Tanton and his followers obsess, like Raspail in France, over invading "swarthy hordes"—to the migration conflict between Haiti and the Dominican Republic, a conflict that seems disconnected from America only if you don't know the latter's imperial history. Díaz makes Haiti central to his Afrofuturist vision, underscoring the importance of the colonial and neocolonial history of Hispaniola.

In his essay "Apocalypse: What Disasters Reveal," Díaz notes that, for most people, "Haiti has never been more than a blip on a map, a faint disturbance in the force so far removed that what happened there [the 2010 earthquake] might as well have been happening on another planet."[84] Díaz identifies Haiti as both "victim and symbol" of the present "rapacious stage of capitalism," which has resulted in income "'discrepancies in livelihoods across the world [that] are so large that they are without historical precedent and without conceivable justification—economic, moral, or otherwise.'"[85] He adds that capitalism is now in a "cannibal stage":

> In order to power the explosion of the super-rich and the ultra-rich, middle classes are being forced to fail, working classes are being reproletarianized, and the poorest are being pushed beyond the grim limits of subsistence, into a kind of sepulchral half-life, perfect targets for any "natural disaster" that just happens to wander by. It is, I suspect, not simply an accident of history that the island that gave us the plantation big bang that put our world on the road to this moment in the capitalist project would also be the first to warn us of this zombie stage of capitalism, where entire nations are being rendered through economic alchemy into not-quite alive. In the old days, a zombie was a figure whose life and work had been captured by magical means. Old zombies were expected to work around the clock with no relief.

The new zombie cannot expect work of any kind—the new zombie just waits around to die.[86]

Díaz's incisive reflections on this cannibal stage of capitalism find their way into his fiction too, in "Monstro" especially. As Díaz once told an interviewer, that story, which at the time of its publication was "turning into something like a novel," takes place in the 2030s, in a world "on the cusp of a catastrophic ecological collapse, a year or so before things really go down the chute for humanity." He chose Hispaniola as the setting because so "many apocalypses have already taken place on that island, including the one that gave rise to the modern world," and because he wanted to focus on a vulnerable place that is too often ignored.[87]

With its futuristic, Caribbean setting, "Monstro" might seem safely distant from the world of its *New Yorker* readership, but this distance is soon revealed to be an illusion. The story's nameless narrator, a young Dominican visiting from the United States, recounts the onset of a disease that "makes Haitians blacker"—"La Negrura they called it. The Darkness."[88] Initially the disease seems to be a "black mold-fungus-blast that came on like a splotch and then gradually started taking you over, tunnelling right through you—though as it turned out it wasn't a mold-fungus-blast at all. It was something else. Something new." The epidemic starts in one of the "relocation camps outside Port-au-Prince," a place that recalls the camps used to house people displaced by the 2010 earthquake. There the "víktims," while suffering from the black "rotting rugose masses fruiting out of bodies," go silent and even comatose, but most do not perish "outright." Instead, they "linger on and on," like the "new zombie" Díaz invokes in his essay. Eventually they begin to emit a collective shriek that, while lasting only "twenty, thirty seconds," is so disturbing that "no uninfected could stand to hear it." Witnesses begin to call the victims "the Possessed." With their shrieks, which they emit "two, three times a day," the victims call to their ranks people who do not initially show any symptoms other than fluctuating temperatures. Thus the "new zombies" morph into an army that turns cannibalistic, in retaliation for having been forced "beyond the grim limits of subsistence, into a kind of sepulchral half-life." The dispossessed become "the Possessed," and they rise to eat the rich, literally. Though its route of transmission remains unclear, the disease spreads rapidly, turning all its "viktims" into murderous, zombielike creatures who are drawn to each other like magnets. When their violence can't be contained, the "Joint Chiefs of Staff" (of a nation that appears to be America) bombs Haiti, in what comes to be called "the Detonation Event." This action, however, only worsens the situation: after the blast, the "viktims" turn into "forty-foot-tall cannibal motherfuckers running loose on the Island."

As I have suggested, in his voice and predilections, the narrator of "Monstro" recalls Yunior. When La Negrura starts, he is busy chasing a girl and avoiding his sick mother, who is also on the island, having come to receive medical attention that is too expensive in the United States. Even in the Dominican Republic, the new disease at first seems distant; the narrator wryly notes that for "six, seven months it was just a horrible Haitian disease—who fucking cared, right?" He eventually witnesses the disease turn apocalyptic from the plush home of a wealthy friend, Alex, a fellow Dominican and an Ivy League student: With "the planet cooking like a chimi and down to its last five trees—something berserk was bound to happen. All sorts of bizarre outbreaks already in play: diseases no one had names for, zoonotics by the pound. This one didn't cause too much panic because it seemed to hit only the sickest of the sick, viktims who had nine kinds of ill already in them. You literally had to be falling to pieces for it to grab you."

"Monstro" switches back and forth between the story of La Negrura and that of the narrator, who watches it unfold while he continues to pursue his latest girl, Mysty: "I don't think I ever heard her voice an opinion about art or politics or say anything remotely philosophical," our narrator writes, "she wasn't anything close to humane." But he is obsessed with her, possibly because she embodies the wealth and race privilege that he does not have. An interloper in Alex's entourage, the narrator is "un morenito from Villa Con whose mother had made it big selling hair-straightening products to the africanos"; he thus navigates between two staggeringly different worlds. At the same time, the dual plotlines join the smallest scale of sexual conquest to the largest scale of (neo)colonial violence at the nexus of "toxicity."

Alex's house is in a neighborhood called Zona Colonial, a not-so-subtle reminder of the differences in wealth between Haiti and the Dominican Republic, despite the vast percentage of Dominicans living in poverty. Hispaniola was colonized first by the French and Spanish, who divided up the island—the French to make a fortune using slaves to grow sugar cane in

APOCALYPSE AND TOXICITY

Haiti, the Spaniards to cultivate the first European colony in the Americas, in Santo Domingo. They were then replaced by the Americans, who, in the early twentieth century—as I have described above—used Haitian workers as de facto slaves on their sugar plantations in the Dominican Republic. Today, Haitians still work in Dominican sugar plantations under slave-like conditions. The U.S. occupation also "left a legacy of anti-blackness" in a country already suffering from its own version of the Curse: "Marines who served during the occupation of the DR frequently expanded white supremacist ideologies in the hemisphere through imperial policy and force."[89]

Throughout his oeuvre, Díaz notes the casual racism with which Dominicans view Haitians. Even though Beli is "kongoblack" (and she will knock people out if they note it), she is quick on the draw with derisive jokes about Haitians, specifically about their poverty and phenotype. Díaz draws frequently on the history of Dominican racist practices against Haitians, from Trujillo's 1937 massacre of Haitian Dominicans to the contemporary, "widespread belief that Haiti is a failed state, and that the world is conspiring against the Dominican Republic to force it to deal with its neighbor's problems."[90] Many Dominicans have expressed a fear that Haiti is somehow contaminating their country with its ills. And—as Alami argues—like Trumpists, "certain Dominican politicians have successfully manipulated anti-Haitian feeling for political gain, tapping into the racist discourse that has plagued much of the public conversation in the DR for years," while the media "over-report crimes perpetrated by Haitians, portraying them as a threat, always highlighting their ethnicity. Radio shows hype the Haitian 'invasion' that must be stopped at all costs."[91]

Díaz's invention of "forty-foot-tall cannibal motherfuckers running loose on the Island" satirizes such fears by aggrandizing them, and not only within the context of Dominican-Haitian relations. In "Monstro," the world is finally made to pay attention to Haiti—and the United States responds to the crisis by dropping a bomb, according to its usual imperializing logic. For a few seconds, the bomb, which is dropped at night, "turned the entire world white"—an image that recalls Hiroshima and Nagasaki—but that all-too-symbolic whiteness is quickly followed by total darkness, for the bomb short-circuits all electricity "within a six-hundred-square-mile radius." The cannibals—a type of people prominent in the European imagination ever since Europeans encountered the native peoples of the New World—use the darkness to cause havoc, and, crucially, they do so *in solidarity*. Sarah

Quesada notes that, in acting together as a community united in both their pain and their strength, the infected "viktims" recall the marooned societies that developed among "different ethnic populations of slaves" in the New World, uniting to fight against the white planters and create new modes of belonging. They also recall the vanquished, those who perished in the Great Dyings, reappearing in the story as the "colonialists' worst nightmare."[92]

"Monstro," however, is not merely Díaz's indulgence in a revenge fantasy. Instead, it is a "planetary warning"[93]—not about what migrants will do to our planet but what the rapacious pace of capitalism has done and continues to do to both the planet and the people who suffer the brunt of climate change. According to the United Nations, there will be "200 million climate refugees by 2050."[94] Díaz's giant cannibals become an army united by a voracious retributive power, forming a solidarity far more aggressive than the migrant solidarity I envisioned in chapter 2. There I argued that migrant aesthetics can facilitate networks of affiliation based not on national belonging but on the sharing of a literature that uses analogies, echoes, and refractions to heighten connections among migrants across time, space, nations, and ethnic and racial differences. "They call those of us who made it through 'time witnesses,'" notes the narrator at the start of "Monstro." And that is an excellent description of the writers featured in this book: Teju Cole, Dinaw Mengestu, Valeria Luiselli, Julie Otsuka, Aleksandar Hemon, Junot Díaz, Edwidge Danticat, and Karla Cornejo Villavicencio are all witnesses to migrant life as part of the "slow violence" of global warming and the dramatic catastrophes that punctuate it,[95] and they call on their readers to become witnesses too.

As I have been arguing, this call to bear witness is no passive stance. The creation of testimony is a forceful act. As I noted earlier, for Díaz, it entails what he calls "ruin-reading," or peering into the truths revealed by apocalyptic events, both big and small. Through his fiction, he "reads" the ruins left in the aftermath of the collision between the Old and New Worlds, showing us how individual migrant stories, like Yunior's, Beli's, and Ramón's, reverberate within the legacy of that apocalypse: "We must stare into the ruins—bravely, resolutely—and we must see. And then we must act. Our very lives depend on it."[96]

Like Valeria Luiselli, I have nagging doubts about fiction's power to create political action, but I do believe that fiction can produce shifts in perspective and even consciousness. Migrant aesthetics can make us see migration as a story that we, as humans, all share, from our multiple and unequal positions. I've often thought of W. E. B. Du Bois's refusal to answer the question "How does it feel to be a problem?" as the seed for an analogy: Du Bois refused to answer the question because race is not solely the problem of those racialized as Other; instead, it is a phenomenon that affects us all, unevenly, unjustly. Likewise, migration, especially forced migration, is not solely the problem and provenance of the migrant. Migration springs from and shapes processes that constitute us all, unevenly and unjustly. And migrant aesthetics grant us the large-scale perspective needed to see this truth. What we do with that perspective—how we decide to act—is another matter. "Will it happen?" Díaz asks in his "Apocalypse" essay. "Will we, despite all our limitations and cruelties, really heed our ruins and pull ourselves out of our descent into apocalypse?"[97]

"Monstro" ends as the narrator, Alex, and Mysty foolishly take off for the Haitian/Dominican border to get closer to the chaos. We may never know their fate or that of the world created in the story, for the novel-in-progress of which "Monstro" is a part will probably not be finished: Díaz, in the aftermath of the allegations made against him, has abandoned the project. All we know is that he planned for "someone else" to be "at the heart of [the] tale, a poor sixteen-year-old-girl by the name of Isis, who finds herself standing alone between the world and its destruction."[98] Isis is the name of Lola's daughter in *The Brief Wondrous Life of Oscar Wao* and is probably the same character, given Díaz's penchant for intertextuality within his own oeuvre. She appears in the novel's halting conclusion as a little girl, signifying hope (as evinced by her name, which is also the name of the Egyptian goddess of healing and magic). Because it begins with the arrival of the Curse, an event still tragically in process, *Oscar Wao* seems to struggle toward resolution. Its last chapter, "The End of the Story," has several final notes—"On A Super Final Note," followed by "It's almost done. Almost over . . ." followed by "The Final Letter." Among these notes is a scene in which Yunior imagines Isis appearing at his doorstep sometime in the future, "dark and blindingly fast," whereupon he gives her all of Oscar's writings, which he saved after Oscar's murder and to which we are never made privy. In his fantasy, which Yunior admits that he indulges in whenever he is feeling hopeful, Isis takes "all we've done and all we've learned"—the "we" meaning both the characters in the novel and the "we" of humanity—"add[s] her own insights and put[s] an end to it" (*OW*, 329–331). We can only speculate what the final "it" refers to: the de León curse? *the* Curse?

Yunior's fantasy ends with an implied warning. Flipping through Oscar's copy of Alan Moore's 1987 graphic novel *Watchmen*, Yunior hovers over a panel that Oscar, "who never defaced a book in his life," circled "three times in the same emphatic pen he used to write his last letters home" (*OW*, 331). The panel depicts a postapocalyptic world, after the antihero Adrian Veidt has purportedly saved it from nuclear holocaust by sacrificing millions. "It all worked out in the end," Veidt says, to which Dr. Manhattan replies, "In the end? Nothing ends, Adrian. Nothing ever ends" (*OW*, 331).

Chapter Six

CARCERAL MIGRATION II

The Flores Declarations and
Edwidge Danticat's *Brother, I'm Dying*

> Every day we are locked in the same space nearly all day. The hours here feel eternal.
>
> —PROJECT AMPLIFY, TEMPORARY RESTRAINING ORDER (TRO)
> DECLARATIONS, CHILDREN, JUNE 2019

"It began," writes Jorge Barrera, "with a phone call from a Hollywood actor to a Los Angeles lawyer about his maid whose daughter was detained by U.S. immigration authorities and held in a 1950s-era motel with a drained swimming pool, surrounded by razor wire."[1] The daughter, Jenny Lisette Flores, age fifteen, became the lead plaintiff in a class action suit filed in 1985 by the American Civil Liberties Union, the Center for Human Rights and Constitutional Law, and other activist groups, on behalf of children and youth being held in detention by the U.S. Immigration and Naturalization Service (INS). At the time of the filing, the INS was placing thousands of children in makeshift detention centers, like the motel where Jenny Flores was held, sharing rooms and bathrooms with unrelated adults of both sexes for "weeks or months."[2] Like many other children her age, Jenny was arrested at the border, handcuffed, and strip-searched before being sent to detention. Not only were there no special accommodations for the children (no medical services, schooling, or counseling), but they could not be released to anyone who was not a legal guardian and thus had to remain in detention even if, as was the case with Jenny, they had relatives living in the United States.

After more than a decade of litigation, the U.S. government entered into a settlement, known as the Flores Agreement, "limiting the time children and youth spend in custody by allowing their release into the care of a qualified guardian; ensuring they are held in facilities licensed to care for dependent children; restricting the amount of time they spend in U.S. Border Patrol facilities—72 hours—and ensuring their humane detention in the aftermath of an arrest."[3] The original agreement "was designed to be temporary, pending the issuance of formal regulations," but the governments of the two decades that followed did not issue said regulations. Instead, the INS inconsistently followed the rules of the agreement.[4]

In 2008, Congress passed a bill making provisions for unaccompanied migrant children, who are especially vulnerable to human trafficking.[5] In 2015, a federal judge extended the Flores requirements to "apply to both unaccompanied minors and children apprehended with their parents,"[6] and set a limit to the time that children can spend in detention: twenty days under the watch of the Office of Refugee Resettlement (ORR) or Immigration and Customs Enforcement (ICE). An anti-immigration organization, the Center for Immigration Studies, claims that this 2015 extension of the Flores Agreement constitutes a loophole that is driving the immigration crisis. It argues that "aliens" have "clearly gotten the message that if they ask to be put into asylum proceedings, their children—and often if not usually the adults, too—will be released into the country shortly after they are apprehended as they await their removal proceedings."[7] This kind of thinking produced the 2018 "zero tolerance" policy under the Trump administration that led to the separation of families and to mass criminal prosecutions of immigrants at the United States–Mexico border. Ostensibly lasting from April to June 2018, the "zero tolerance" policy had been in effect for a full year before the announcement and remained ongoing, in one form or another, throughout Trump's presidency.

In August 2019, the Trump administration, claiming to have issued regulations that would satisfy the Flores Agreement, sought to end the agreement altogether and replace it with new policies, called the "Final Rules," which would allow for the indefinite detention of migrant families and eliminate effective ways to report or correct violations in detention facilities. A group of minors, represented by several children's advocacy organizations, challenged this move through the U.S. Court of Appeals for the Ninth Circuit in California, which has had jurisdiction over the Flores case since its beginning. The court concluded that the Final Rules " 'not only do not implement the *Flores* Agreement, they intentionally subvert it," and ordered the continued enforcement of the Flores regulations.[8] Trump's administration challenged this verdict, and, in response, the Constitutional Accountability Center filed an *amici curiae* brief on January 28, 2020, on behalf of 132 members of Congress, who urged the court to affirm the district court's judgment (*Flores v. Barr*). In October 2020, the court denied the government's motion.

Hundreds of sworn declarations from children (some given through representatives or parents on their behalf) were filed in *Flores v. Barr*.[9] The interviews were conducted by a team of investigators, including legal, medical, and mental-health experts, who visited multiple detention centers at the U.S.-Mexican border. Upon witnessing the "deplorable, inhumane, and illegal conditions they found the children in," they decided it was necessary to go public.[10] This brought the national media's attention to the children's suffering.[11] The public learned of the conditions in the *hieleras*, the freezing rooms or "ice boxes," and the cage-like spaces known as "dog pounds"; they also learned about the children who had died under ICE custody (six between September 2018 and May 2019, though the number could be higher). The publicity forced ICE to move some of the children out of Border Patrol stations and into family centers like the one in Dilley, Texas, run by CoreCivic.

After moving the children, ICE opened the Dilley facility to journalists in an effort to curb the public criticism. Matthew Albence, ICE's acting director, who once compared family detention to "summer camp," took pride in showing the facility to news photographers and television cameras, in what was obviously a public-relations event.[12] In fact, as the *New York Times* reported, the Trump administration "want[ed] to expand the system of secure facilities where migrant families [could] be incarcerated for months or longer."[13] The reason for this desire, as I discuss later, had less to do with national security than with the economic profit it could bring to the companies managing the facilities.

News cycles invariably come and go, and the media's focus on the incarceration of children—and of all migrants—ebbs and flows. In the summer of 2018, when the Trump administration had separated more that 2,800 children from their parents, the public outrage both in the country and abroad was intense.[14] In January 2019, the attention paid to migrants hit a high when the Department of Health and Human Services' inspector general admitted that thousands more children than previously known may have been separated "before the accounting required by the court."[15] That year, nearly 7,000 unaccompanied children sought asylum in the United States and were "detained by the U.S. federal government . . . Under the Migration Protection Protocol (MPP), colloquially referred to as the Remain in Mexico program, that figure in Mexico [was] over 15,000 unaccompanied kids."[16] The subsequent outbreak of the COVID-19 pandemic in early 2020 brought fresh attention to the conditions of all migrant detainees since ICE consistently failed to follow public-health protocols in running the detention centers.[17] But the pandemic eventually overshadowed the migrant crisis at the border.

In this chapter, I examine a selection of the Flores declarations, gathered by lawyers and made public by Project Amplify, a national nonprofit campaign launched to establish legal protections for detained children, to amplify their voices and elevate the truth. While collaborating with the photographer Michele Asselin on an art project for a benefit exhibition, I read the interviews taken in June 2019 (Project Amplify has made several months' worth of interviews publicly available, beginning with August 2018).[18] Since the interviews are redacted and focus solely on the conditions of arrest and imprisonment, the children's stories are sparse, anonymous, and centered on everyday life. They are also plotless, or rather they repeat a similar plot—and in so doing they become choral, making them inadvertently echo the novels I have examined in this book.

As sworn statements, the interviews follow legal protocol, laying out facts that are pertinent to legal proceedings and based on individuals' memories. They are signed "under penalty of perjury," after being translated from Spanish to English and read back to the interviewees in Spanish.[19] In short, they are mediated and follow a format. While this makes them different from novels or any artistic rendering of migration, it does not exclude them from being analyzed through a critical perspective, using the lens of migrant aesthetics. Such an analysis demonstrates the fact that migrant aesthetics, beyond being a set of strategies used in fiction, can also be used to apprehend actual experiences of material conditions. The interviews allow us to focus on how incarceration suspends the children, and all other detainees, in time and space, alienating them from teleological time in ways that recall Julie Otsuka's *When the Emperor Was Divine*. More to the point, a critical perspective enables us to create analogies not just across mediums (e.g., novels and real-life documentation) but also across historical experience, so that we can draw into a loose but productive relationship such events as the internment of Japanese Americans during World War II and contemporary migrant detention, with the goal of creating migrant solidarity.

Extending the analogical link, in this chapter I place the Flores declarations in conversation with Edwidge Danticat's book *Brother, I'm Dying* (2007), which testifies to the death of Danticat's uncle, Joseph, while he was being held at Krome, a detention center in Florida with a long record of abuse. In the book, Danticat intertwines her own experiences with a combined biography of her father, Mira, and her uncle (his brother, Joseph) and contextualizes all these threads within the history of Haitian migration to the United States. Yet partly because Danticat is a well-known writer whose successful career seemingly exemplifies the American-dream myth, the testimonial power of *Brother, I'm Dying* has been largely obfuscated by her personal story. Its reception, with reviews focusing on her family's close ties rather than the book's larger discussion of migration, bears this out. The book's genre has also contributed to the public's difficulty in grasping the full implications of the memoir. As I argue throughout this book, (auto)biography in migrant fiction is too compromised, too saturated by the conventions of "immigrant literature," and too often produced and marketed as a conduit for empathy, to make readers think analytically about the socioeconomic and political conditions of forced and carceral migration. In this chapter, by placing *Brother, I'm Dying* in conversation with the Flores testimonies, I hope to recover the book's testimonial power and to highlight Danticat's method of expanding the scale of migration by exploring the history of (neo)colonialism, in particular Haitian migration to the United States. As I show, Danticat's choice of embedding her own migrant aesthetics within the genre of the immigrant memoir compromised her efforts.

EXTRATEMPORALITY

> Inmates of detention centers are suspended in time and place, "disappeared" into a void.
>
> —NICOLE WALLER, "TERRA INCOGNITA"

In chapter 4, we saw how Julie Otsuka in her novels gives aesthetic shape to the experience of time and place within carceral migration. Her use of strategically anonymous and choral narrative voices, her attention to surface and diurnal details, and her fragmented structure not only preemptively block assimilationist readings based on an empathetic model but also enable her to represent the suspension of time in confinement. *When the Emperor Was Divine* makes vivid the visceral modes of carceral time—how the present can expand and feel endless, how the past both contracts and becomes insubstantial, how these two temporal states mix and blur with the elusive, unknown future. That phenomenon creates what Matthew Hart would call the "extratemporality" of settings like the detention center,[20] places that are, in Nicole Waller's words, "neither fully charted in national nor in international territory and jurisdiction."[21]

A critical perspective using migrant aesthetics shows how much the descriptions of carceral time in the Flores testimonies overlap with those in Otsuka's novels. Because of the suffering to which they attest, the Flores statements have great affective intensity, but at the same time, because they are gathered to make a legal case, they are necessarily objective and nonsentimental. They thus thwart readerly empathy, which is not the same as failing to elicit feeling. Repeatedly, one reads the stories of children, ranging from teenagers in their late teens to infants, who have been separated from their parents, guardians, or siblings. Some are parents themselves, fleeing while pregnant or with newborns. Many have been forced to live in *hieleras* or stuffed into "dog pounds," which are so crowded that sometimes there isn't room to sit. They sleep on the floor or on cement benches, often without blankets and under bright lights that are kept on all night and all day. They are forced to eat food that leaves them hungry and sick, and many do not have access to clean water. Others are denied showers, toothbrushes, combs. Most have nothing to occupy them during the endless hours and days; many are not allowed outside for more than brief periods. They are incarcerated, freezing, hungry, sick, afraid, separated from their families, bereft of rights and dignity. These are the conditions described repeatedly in sixty-seven interviews from only one month in 2019, even as the full life story of each child remains obscure.

A representative page from one of the statements (Exhibit 10) shows how the form of the declarations impedes readers' empathetic engagement with individuals by literally blocking out personal details (Figure 6.1).

Recall that the use of migrant aesthetics involves foreclosing empathy by rejecting autobiography and in-depth character development in favor of strategic anonymity, choral or collective narration, and shifting vantage

Declaration of M▮▮ Z▮▮-L▮▮,  and L▮▮ L▮▮-O▮▮ (My Little Sister).

I, M▮▮ Z▮▮-L▮▮, declare under penalty of perjury that the following is true and correct to the best of my knowledge and recollection.

1. My little sister and I came from Honduras. She is six years old and I am eight years old. Our grandmother brought us to the United States so that we can live with our mother because it is not safe for us to stay in Honduras.
2. Our mother lives in Houston. Her name is J▮▮ G▮▮ L▮▮ O▮▮. Her telephone number is ▮▮▮▮▮▮. Our grandmother put our mother's telephone number in my jacket so that we can call her, but we have only spoken to her once in three weeks. One time my sister asked an official if we could please call our mom. The official said we had to wait. We talked to her one week after we got in a truck with border officers. Our stepdad's telephone number is ▮▮▮▮▮▮
3. They took us away from our grandmother and now we are all alone. They have not given us to our mother. We have been here for a long time. I have to take care of my little sister. She is very sad because she misses our mother and grandmother very much.
4. My sister has been very sick. The doctor told her not to cry because if she cries she will get sicker.
5. One of the children in our cell is mean to us and tells us that we can't play and that we will be locked in a dark room here. I believe her and don't want to be locked in the dark room.
6. We sleep on a cement bench. There are two mats in the room, but the big kids sleep on the mats so we have to sleep on the cement bench. We have been sleeping on the cement bench ever since we came here, except when my sister got sick, she was quarantined and she got to sleep on a mat on the floor in another room.
7. We have only been allowed to go outside four times. I have only been allowed to bathe twice since we came here. My sister has only been allowed to bathe once. The water is very cold. Some kids don't mind the cold water, but I wish it is warm. We have only been allowed to brush our teeth twice here. There is no soap except when you take a bath. We have been wearing the same clothes the entire time we have been here and no one has washed them.
8. My sister and I hold a blanket up for one another so no one can see us when we go to the bathroom.

I, M▮▮ Z▮▮-L▮▮, swear under penalty of perjury that the above declaration is true and complete to the best of my abilities. This declaration was read to me in Spanish, a language in which I am fluent.

June 18, 2019

M▮▮ Z▮▮-L▮▮

FIGURE 6.1. Exhibit 10 in the TRO Declarations, Children, June 2019. *Source*: Project Amplify.

points. It also rejects an assimilationist model of relationality by inviting readers to inhabit positions, not persons; it does not purport to give "voice" to the disempowered but rather describes the positions that individuals take in time and space, all with the aim of guarding against the commodification of migrants as racially marked Others.

The sixty-seven Flores statements from June 2019 (and the many hundreds from other months) offer testimony that becomes choral, that forces the reader to think on a broad scale. Most of the interviewed children state that they left their countries of origin because of violence: "We left Guatemala with my uncle because we lived in a dangerous neighborhood filled with gangs and drug dealers" (Exhibit 12). "The main reason I left El Salvador [is] because the gang MS 13 was threatening us" (Exhibit 50). "In El Salvador, I was studying for my bachelor's degree and was doing well. But my father and uncle were soldiers during El Salvador's civil war. They were threatened, and my baby and I were threatened, too" (Exhibit 27). There is an underlying theme in these various reasons for migration: a gang born in Los Angeles (MS 13) that grew into a transnational network due to U.S. immigration policies; the long-lasting effects of United States proxy wars in Central America during the Cold War; narco wars fueled in part by American consumption of drugs and trading in arms. These factors, all linked to U.S. policy, loom large in the children's statements, shaping the political and economic conditions that forced the children and their families to seek asylum in the first place. Some children also report fleeing domestic violence with their mothers, from whom they were then separated; some came from countries with little to no resources to help them.

Their statements produce in the reader a wide range of feelings that spring from a sense of justice, a sense of human decency. But since there are no complete story lines, no consistent trajectories that one can follow, one cannot fully empathize with the subjects. Instead, one looks for patterns, for breaks in those patterns, for exceptional moments, and for ways of reading that respect the subjects, whose pain makes the documents so vivid. A representative passage shows one pattern: the autobiographical format of the statements tends to give way to a collective account of incarceration:

1. I came from El Salvador with my brothers who are 11 and 19 years old. I am 15 years old. My birthday is [redacted]. We came to be with our mother who lives in the United States because the gangs were threatening us. They came to our house and beat up our aunt and so we had to leave before they came back.
2. They took our older brother to another facility and then brought my younger brother and me here to Clint Border Patrol Station two days ago. At first

my brother and I were together, but then they said that he could not be in the same room.
3. A Border Patrol Agent came in our room with a two-year-old boy and asked us, "Who wants to take care of this little boy?" Another girl said she would take care of him, but she lost interest after a few hours and so I started taking care of him yesterday. His bracelet says he is two years old.
4. I feed the 2-year-old boy, change his diaper, and play with him. He is sick. He has a cough and a runny nose and scabs on his lips. He was coughing last night so I asked to take him to see the doctor and they told me that the doctor would come to our room, but the doctor never came.
5. The little boy that I am taking care of never speaks. He likes for me to hold him as much as possible. (Exhibit 41)

The girl being interviewed here begins with her own experience and that of her immediate family, but soon shifts to describe the two-year-old boy who "never speaks." In this way, rather than offering only autobiographical stories, the documents reveal how the children regroup among themselves, forging family-like bonds to survive.

Many of the children in their teens take care of the younger ones to the best of their ability, and testify for them in the interviews:

> I am worried about the very young children here who do not know what country they are from and where they should go. I worry about the many children that do not have passports. There is one very young girl in my room, only six years old, who doesn't know where she is from or where she is supposed to go. I do not know what will happen to her. She arrived here five days ago. When we came here yesterday, I asked who she was with. She said she was with her father but they had been separated. The officials told her that her father would have to come to get her. I do not know if that will happen. (Exhibit 9)

The speaker here is a twelve-year-old girl from Ecuador, who was incarcerated with her eight- and four-year-old sisters. At first, she describes how the Border Patrol officers arrested her, her sisters, and their grandmother—now separated from them—and took "everything from us except our documents. They even took our shoe laces." Then she shifts the attention from her own story, adding that there was a "mother in our group traveling with a very young baby. The officers took her diapers, baby formula, and nearly everything else she had and threw it away. They left her with just two shirts and one pair [of] pants for the baby. The mother really wanted to keep the diapers because her baby was allergic to regular diapers but the officers didn't listen" (Exhibit 9). In another part of her statement, the girl describes other children: "One child was here for 7 days and got sick and has now been here for a very long time. There is a girl here from El Salvador and a boy from Guatemala who have been here for almost a month. They both got infections in their lungs and have had to stay here" (Exhibit 9).

Again and again, the children testify to the conditions of others around them, forcing the reader to think of the detainees in the aggregate, though not as a solid block. One is forced repeatedly to shift perspective, not only throughout the collection but within a single statement. The experience of reading the passages I have presented here mirrors the experience of reading the statements as a group. In all of them, the children's ages, histories, and backgrounds shift continuously, just as these passages come from a five-year-old girl from Honduras, a fifteen-year-old from El Salvador who cares for a "little boy," and an Ecuadorian girl who describes not only herself and her sisters but several other children as well.

As I noted earlier, the Flores declarations also highlight the distorted experience of carceral time that we see in Otsuka's *When the Emperor Was Divine*. One child says that "hours here feel eternal" (Exhibit 14), a recurring statement throughout the testimonies. By law, the children are not supposed to spend more than seventy-two hours at Custom and Border Protection facilities, yet many spend several days or even weeks there ("I have been at the Clint Station for about 17 days," says one child in Exhibit 8).[22] Children are supposed to be sent from detention camps such as the Central Processing Center in McAllen, Texas (commonly known as Ursula) to facilities run by the Department of Health and Human Services. This department then places them in juvenile facilities or foster homes, and often in this process they lose track of their family members, both those already in the United States and those who have traveled with them from their country of origin. In one case, a girl was "separated from her family, shuttled back and forth between shelters and foster homes across the United States, from Oregon to Massachusetts to Texas to Florida, and back to Texas and Oregon again," over the course of seven years; she was ten when she originally presented herself at the border, seeking asylum in late 2013.[23] Meanwhile adult migrants, with or without criminal records, are frequently held captive in detention centers for months or even years.[24]

Many of the detainees give evidence of the psychological repercussions of incarceration, repeating versions of the same phrase: "We spend all day every day in that room. There are no activities, only crying. We eat in the same area. We can only go outside to go to the bathroom" (Exhibit 15). Other children testified:

> During the two weeks we've been here, they have let us outside about 5 times for about 20 minutes each time. Otherwise, there is nothing to do all day but sit in the cell and sleep. (Exhibit 40)

> There are no other activities. We don't have any crafts or indoor games, except for a card game. We don't have any books to read. We don't get anything to draw with or make with our hands. (Exhibit 42)

> They let us out of our cell twice a day for a few minutes, but other than that we just sit there. We cry a lot and the other kids in the cell also cry . . . We spend time just lying down. We watch movies even though the sound is off. We're allowed to go outside to spend time in the sun every few days. I've been outside four times in the 13 days I've been here. (Exhibit 48)

If the present feels eternal for the children, the future is a mystery. Some can talk to their parents or guardians by phone a limited number of times; others lose all contact when they are separated from their older siblings or caretakers. Most do not know what will happen to them: "I have not been told of any release date or any release plan. I do not know when I will be released" (Exhibit 64). "The staff here haven't told me anything about what will happen in my case and whether I'll be able to live with my parents" (Exhibit 42). "We haven't been able to speak to anyone in my family until we met with the lawyer here today. No one from the detention center has tried to make contact with our family. We are all alone. Every time I talk about my family I start to cry" (Exhibit 44). Such comments are reminiscent of the boy in *When the Emperor Was Divine*, pacing the floor, thinking of his father perhaps ill or dead in some other camp. When the boy imprisons and then kills a tortoise, we get a glimpse of the psychological toll it takes on him. But we are left to wonder, how are the children in detention coping with their emotional stress, since they do not even have access to bare necessities like clean water?

While time is both eternal and unknown in detention, space is punishingly cold and constricting: "We live in Room 203 with 25 children. I estimate that it is 10 by 15" (Exhibit 41). "I was put in a cell with a lot of men, too many to tell. It was way too full and extremely cold. There were no beds, no mats, only the concrete floor. The lights were on all night" (Exhibit 58). "My brother and I were taken to a freezer box for about 10 hours where we were only given some cookies to eat. It was cold. My brother was given a blanket, but I was not given one" (Exhibit 12). "They do not treat children well at the Ice Box. They gave us nothing to eat the entire time we were there except a cookie and some water. The water tasted ugly, like chlorine" (Exhibit 52). The children are also subjected to humiliating limitations: they are not allowed to bathe or brush their teeth for weeks; some are forced to use bathrooms that are inside the cells and lack privacy. One testified, "I still have the same clothes on that I came with from Guatemala. When I got arrested, all my other belongings were thrown away. I have not been able to wash my clothes. I have not been given any other clothes" (Exhibit 65). Another said, "I wish I could get clean. I've only been able to take a quick shower, maximum 3 minutes, two times since I've been here. And they let me brush my teeth twice but [then] they took the brush and told me they were throwing it away" (Exhibit 40). Many of the children become ill due to the low temperatures or the close contact with so many people in crowded spaces, and the sick are not always isolated. Most commonly they contract the flu, but chickenpox and measles are also present. In their cells, children with the flu must sleep on benches even as they cough.[25] The COVID-19 pandemic made these conditions even more perilous, with the Center for Disease Control and Prevention reporting that, "as of July 2021, there were more than 8000 COVID-19 cases among unaccompanied minors" in Office of Refugee Resettlement facilities.[26]

In one interview, the speaker, a fifteen-year-old girl who did not feel "comfortable talking about what has happened to [her] since [she] came to America," testified not only for herself but for a little girl, known as "X" in the redacted document (Exhibit 15). She attested to their lack of basic needs, including soap, showers, nourishing food, clean clothing, and beds. Frequently she used the pronoun "we," signaling her bond both with the younger girl and with the many other children in detention. After the interview, she refused to sign the statement, for fear of the repercussions of revealing her name. Whatever other horrors she suffered were thus implicated but not revealed, highlighting the limits of the sworn statements' testimony. Yet her statement (Exhibit 15) *is* signed—by the interviewer, Elora Mukherjee, a graduate from Yale Law School who practices in New York and New Jersey and is a professor of law and the director of the Immigrants' Rights Clinic at Columbia University. The transparency of the interviewer's background, in contrast to the opacity of the speaker's, and the great imbalance of power between the lawyer and the teen girl are thus built into the sworn statement. Such imbalances are particularly stark in those statements that include only short certificates of translation, while also including the interviewers' full names, addresses, and professional affiliations.

Mukherjee's role in the production of Exhibit 15 echoes that of Valeria Luiselli in *Tell Me How It Ends* and of the mother in *Lost Children Archive*. It points to the vast network needed to create and make public the detainees' testimony—the lawyers, the centers for immigrants' rights, the nonprofit agencies like Project Amplify. These mediators of migrant testimony, like Teju Cole, Valeria Luiselli, and the other writers featured in this book—indeed, like the professor writing this book—are those who have "made it," according to the exceptionalist rhetoric of the touted "American dream." And yet these writers, lawyers, and advocates do not focus on their own trajectories; instead, through their own specific modes, they highlight the wider geopolitical scale of migration and the imbrication of all Americans in it.

From this vantage point, one needs to ask, who profits from the detention camps in the United States? Who constitutes that other network, which is working not toward justice but for capital? The short answer is the prison system, specifically the first- and second-largest private prison organizations in the world: CoreCivic, formerly known as Corrections Corporation of America (CCA), which is headquartered in Tennessee, and GEO, a Florida-based company with facilities in North America, Australia, South Africa, and the United Kingdom.[27] While neither company runs the jails that hold children separated from their parents, both of them profit from the detention centers for undocumented immigrant families and from jails for adult migrants. The longer answer to the question of who profits is more complex, but it starts with the legislation that criminalized undocumented migrants and the fact that the United States has a long-standing practice of confining migrant detainees in prisons, a practice that "has been largely banned in most major developed nations."[28] Even a brief review of detention centers in U.S. history shows the deep roots of racism and xenophobia that have shaped the country's immigration and citizenship laws.

THE BIRTH OF THE U.S. DETENTION CENTER

The establishment of an official, law-enforcing border patrol in 1924 transformed unauthorized entry to the United States into a criminal act carrying the risk of deportation. The Immigration Act of 1924 made unlawful entry a misdemeanor and reentry a felony, both subject to high fines and imprisonment. At this time the main function of Ellis Island changed, as the organization's own website stated until recently, "from that of an immigrant processing station, to a center of the assembly, detention, and deportation of aliens who had entered the U.S. illegally or had violated the terms of admittance."[29] In 1952, the Immigration and Nationality Act made it possible for noncitizens to be released from detention based on community ties (but still on bond), a policy that led to a decrease in the numbers of migrants in detention. But the American destabilization of Latin American governments during the Cold War (not to mention the consequences of its long-standing and ongoing imperial practices in the region),[30] coupled with the national origins caps it placed on immigration, favoring Western and Northern Europe, created a decades-long surge in unauthorized immigration. During the Reagan administration, which oversaw the expansion of the detention system as a response to the waves of Haitian migrants escaping the U.S.-backed Duvalier regime, the criminalization of migrants ballooned, intensified by that administration's conflation of drug and immigration enforcement via their interdiction programs.

Going back further, one can see that the entanglement of U.S. immigration and citizenship laws with racism and xenophobia began well before the twentieth century. The 1790 Naturalization Act granted U.S. citizenship to free white persons of "good moral character," excluding Native Americans, slaves, indentured servants, free blacks, and Asians—groups whose "moral character" was presumed to be deficient.[31] While this policy was modified in the years that followed, it was not replaced until the 1952 Immigration and Nationality Act, which effectively retained the "good moral character" qualification of the 1790 act in its codification of the grounds for blocking entry, deporting, or denying citizenship to immigrants. Before the 1952 act, the U.S. Bureau of Immigration often denied applicants whom they deemed deviant, perverse, or undesirable in some way, either sexually or economically, and including those with physical abnormalities. The 1952 act solidified several aspects of this vetting system, explicitly barring aliens alleged to be homosexual from entering or remaining in the country, as well as those suspected of criminal histories or radical political views.[32]

Several additional laws throughout the twentieth century reinforced the racist and bigoted core of the 1790 Naturalization Act. The 1921 Emergency Quota Act established a quota system designed to favor Western European countries and to limit drastically the admission of immigrants from Asia, Africa, the Middle East, and Southern and Eastern Europe. Three years later, the Johnson-Reed Act, also known as the National Origins Act and the Asian Exclusion Act, provided a pathway to citizenship for European immigrants while restricting Asians, Arabs, and most Africans completely. The 1965 Hart-Celler Immigration Act repealed the quota system, replacing it with a preference system based on family reunification and skill-based labor needs, but the new act also placed annual caps on the number of migrants from the Western Hemisphere for the first time. This had disastrous consequences for Latin American migrants since U.S. foreign policy at that time was making the region unlivable. For Mexicans, the introduction of the 1965 act coincided with the phasing out of the Bracero Program, which had created a circular flow of migrants starting in World War II and growing robust through the 1950s and early 1960s, to the great benefit of the economy of the United States. After the 1965 act was ratified, this circular flow was eliminated and illegal migration from the region surged.[33] Thus laws that seemed to rectify the racist and xenophobic codes of the past carried them forward or created new ways of imposing them.

In addition, and as I discuss in chapter 4, migrants in the United States are highly vulnerable to the vicissitudes of global conflicts and their ramifications for the American government. In 1943, just as Japanese Americans became "alien enemies," Chinese immigrants were eligible for naturalization for the first time. Later, when the Cold War unfolded and China became a communist threat, Chinese people, along with Koreans and Vietnamese, replaced the Japanese as "alien enemies." As Josephine Park explains, depending on U.S.-Asian conflicts, "the political designation of enemy or ally" has shifted for Asian Americans, leaving them open to "sudden reversals in domestic political status."[34]

The same holds true for Caribbeans and Latin Americans. After Fidel Castro's communist revolution, the United States, acting in accordance with its Cold War strategy, accepted all refugees from Cuba unconditionally and even established the Cuban Refugee Program, which offered $1.3 billion in direct financial assistance—including public assistance, Medicare, free courses in English, scholarships, and low-interest college loans.[35] During the same period, however, the United States returned most Haitian refugees to Haiti because it considered them to be fleeing poverty rather than political repression—despite the fact that American neocolonial practices had actively contributed to the conditions that led to the vast Haitian migration. Not only had Americans occupied Haiti for decades and kept it under the obligation of a gross debt (see chapter 3), but the U.S. government also supported one of Haiti's most notorious despots, François Duvalier, because he was anti-communist. "Starting in the mid-nineteen-sixties," writes Laurent Dubois, "one U.S. President after another funnelled aid to Duvalier, even as waves of Haitian immigrants fleeing poverty and political oppression arrived in the U.S."[36]

In response to these waves, the Carter administration established a number of detention camps, starting a new phase in the immigration history of the United States.[37] As Carl Lindskoog has described, while Cubans were kept in the same or similar detention centers as the Haitians, most of them "were soon freed from detention to join family and sponsors already in the United States," whereas "the many Haitians who did not have such an established community or were denied authorization to be in the country remained in detention."[38] When Reagan assumed power in 1981, all undocumented Haitians were denied the possibility of bond. The ensuing protests and court battles that were meant to highlight the discriminatory core of such practices, which originally applied only to Haitians, ironically led to the expansion of the exclusion policy, so that "Salvadoran refugees and immigrants and asylum seekers from around the world began to join Haitians in a rapidly expanding detention system."[39] With this massive expansion of the prison-industrial complex, strengthened by fears sparked after 9/11 and stoked by Trump's election, the criminalization of nonwhite migrants attained new levels of potency.

Due to the strain that this long history put on the country's incarceration capacities, the federal government turned in the 1980s to private companies like CoreCivic (formerly CCA), founded in 1983, to run U.S. prisons and detention centers—justifying the decision as a cost-cutting measure.[40] Since those companies' assumption of the role, the criminalization of migrants and the privatized-prison system have both grown exponentially. The so-called 1996 Laws exacerbated the situation by including in the list of "crimes of moral turpitude" any criminal activity, such as minor drug offenses, for which both legal immigrants and undocumented noncitizens could be detained and deported.[41] The massive increase of this system after 9/11, during the Clinton, Bush, and Obama administrations, has made the leaders of CoreCivic and GEO enormously wealthy: according to Livia Luan, the companies "earned [a] combined revenue exceeding $4 billion in F[iscal] Y[ear] 2017."[42]

The U.S. government maintains the world's largest immigration detention system. What does it cost the federal government to imprison migrants?[43] Or, more precisely, what does it cost American taxpayers? According to a 2018 article in *The Week*, ICE pays "private companies at the border $159 per inmate per day, including for detained children. Because subcontractors don't have to follow the same transparency rules as government agencies, it's unclear exactly what services the inmates are getting for that price."[44] We do know, however, that the private companies tasked with providing food, security, and health care at the detention centers cut costs by "hiring fewer guards, paying them less, and giving them less training, as well as by providing fewer educational, medical, and enrichment services to inmates."[45] When they fail to meet their contractual obligations, the companies can be fined by the Bureau of Prisons, but the fines are "so modest," according to the Global Detention Project, that it "often costs less for the centres to pay the penalty than to meet the obligation and hire additional medical staff."[46]

Trump campaigned for the presidency in 2016 on "zero tolerance" for illegal immigration. Soon after his inauguration, the Justice Department began prosecuting every person who entered the country illegally. This policy required the building of more facilities to hold all the detainees, which created yet another boom for the private prison industry. As described by *The Week*, "A month after Trump's inauguration, CoreCivic and GEO

Group stocks shot up by 137 percent and 98 percent, respectively... GEO Group donated heavily to President Trump's campaign, and both GEO and CoreCivic contributed $250,000 to his inauguration committee."[47] CoreCivic also contributed to the campaigns of politicians involved in shaping immigration policy and to state and federal anti-immigration lobbies.[48] Both companies routinely pay counties and states a portion of their gains, in addition to bringing employment to both. When Trump reversed his family-separation policy, the administration sought to house families at private facilities at the border indefinitely. This resulted in huge gains for CoreCivic and the GEO Group.[49] Meanwhile, the conditions at the GEO-run Adelanto detention center in San Bernardino, California, the country's largest privately run adult immigration detention center, have driven several inmates to attempt suicide.[50]

Since private companies are responsible only to their shareholders, not the public, their focus is on raising sales. Who are their shareholders? The major ones are the Vanguard Group, Fidelity/FMR LLC, State Street Corp., Blackrock, and Prudential Financial, Inc. The fact that the first two groups manage several pension plans at my university—Harvard—and have various connections to other universities (including Johns Hopkins and Vanderbilt) demonstrates how these different networks of power intersect. Harvard currently invests in both CoreCivic and GEO through the iShares Core S&P Mid-Cap ETF fund, even as other universities, including Columbia and the University of California in 2015, have divested from such funds after being pressured by student groups.[51] Meanwhile, according to a 2019 *Globe Post* article, JP Morgan "no longer loans to either company," but it still holds "over a million shares in both CoreCivic and GEO."[52] Amazon, Microsoft, and a host of other companies have ties to the prison companies too, as do a large number of small organizations, including the nonprofit, faith-based charity BCFS (Baptist Child and Family Services), which, from December 2013 to August 2014, had received "more than $280 million in federal grants" to operate shelters for migrant children in California and Texas. BCFS, according to a 2014 article in *Time*, is only "one part of a sprawling system of shelters for unaccompanied children across the country."[53] Wayfair, a furniture company based in Boston, came under scrutiny in 2019 because it had a contract with BCFS worth $200,000 for bedroom furniture; the company kept its contract despite employee protests.[54]

Public interest in conditions at detention centers depends largely on media coverage, which rarely even scratches the surface of the history I have sketched here. At the time of this writing, the emphasis in the media is on the increased number of people trying to cross the border in the belief that the Biden administration will be more welcoming than the previous administration. Given this limited perspective, what kind of testimony might provide a sense of scale more appropriate to the history of detention centers in the United States? Edwidge Danticat's 2007 memoir *Brother, I'm Dying* suggests one possibility. The book shows how her father's and uncle's lives were shaped by the American occupation of Haiti and by the rise of the Duvaliers and their paramilitary force, the Tonton Macoute, which kept Haiti under near-constant terror. While these conditions led Danticat's father, Mira, to emigrate to the United States, where he worked as a cab driver to sponsor his family's emigration, his brother, Joseph, remained in Haiti, becoming a pastor and community leader. Yet, at the age of eighty-one, Joseph too was forced to leave Haiti, after war broke out between United Nations peacekeepers and the chimères, local gang members, who were threatening his life. He entered the United States with a valid visa but, when he declared that he was seeking asylum, he was apprehended and taken to the Krome detention center in Florida.[55] He died there two days later, after being denied medical treatment when he collapsed during his "credible fear" interview. At nearly the same time, Mira succumbed to lung cancer. In *Brother, I'm Dying*, Danticat, in what Jess Row describes as "cleareyed prose and unflinching adherence to the facts,"[56] highlights the root of both brothers' tragic ends: the American occupation of Haiti and, before that, the country's long history of oppression and revolt, starting with its fight for independence from French colonial rule.

Danticat was two when her father left Haiti for the United States, and her mother followed him when Danticat was four. Because the author and her brother could not join their parents for eight more years, their uncle Joseph raised them. When Danticat was nine, Joseph lost his voice to throat cancer, making their separation three years later even more heartbreaking because their communication became so much more difficult. The family adapted, however, managing to stay close, even from a distance, until Joseph's tragic death, which coincided both with Mira's death and with the birth of Danticat's first child.

In reviews of *Brother, I'm Dying*, this narrative arc tends to take center stage, with Joseph's story receding into the background, much as the story of Yosef does in Dinaw Mengestu's 2010 novel *How to Read the Air*, which I discussed in the Introduction to this book. Recall also Mengestu's short story "An Honest Exit," published in the same year, in which a young man recounts his father's escape from Ethiopia, first to Sudan, then as a stowaway on a cargo ship to Europe, and eventually to America. As I argue in the Introduction, this story underscores the limits of empathy as a mode of engaging with migrant suffering, and challenges its readers to imagine instead the conditions that led to Yosef's predicament: what prompts him to take a journey so evocative of the Middle Passage? Mengestu wove the same story into *How to Read the Air* but in that context, it becomes the background of a bildungsroman, thus giving readers an out: instead of engaging with Yosef's story on its own terms, readers can focus on the novel's more conventional story of Yosef's son, a first-generation Ethiopian American dealing with identitarian questions born of migrant trauma. The story of Danticat's uncle Joseph suffered a similar fate in reviews of *Brother, I'm Dying*. While reviewers noted that "Uncle Joseph is the heart of the book" and acknowledged the "harrowing immigration horror story"[57] that cut his life short, they tended to fall back on conventional modes of reading migrant fiction to engage with the book, highlighting Danticat's success as a writer and the "family love" in the book that purportedly transcends "exile and loss."[58]

To counteract this tendency, I have abstracted Joseph's story here, placing it by itself in conversation with the Flores testimonies to highlight how Danticat contextualizes his trajectory within European and American imperial rule. In this way, I practice migrant aesthetics as a mode of analysis and recuperate the testimonial power of Joseph's story.

BROTHER, I'M DYING

Her uncle, writes Danticat, like his family across generations, had spent his life in Haiti "watching the strong arm of authority in action, be it the American marines who'd been occupying the country" since 1915, "or the brutal local army they'd trained and left behind to prop up, then topple, the puppet governments of their choice."[59] Observing her uncle's corpse at Krome years later, Danticat wonders what his final thoughts might have been: "Was he afraid? Did he think it ironic that he would soon be the dead prisoner of the same government that had been occupying his country when he was born?" (250). Uncle Joseph's "most haunting childhood memory," she writes, "and the only one he ever described to me in detail, was of the year 1933," when the American occupation was ending, and he was ten years old. Joseph's father, Granpè Nozial, who had been part of the guerilla resistance against the occupation for years, had forbidden him to go near the American marines, for fear they would harm him or conscript him into manual labor (245). Once, the young Joseph disobeyed, seeing a "group of young white men in dark high boots and khakis ... kicking something on the ground" while emitting something like laughter (246–247). The "ball" turned out to be a head "full of black peppercorn hair," with blood "dripping out of the severed neck, forming dusty dark red bubbles in the dirt" (247). Danticat places this story at the end of her narrative, vivifying the memory so that it frames her uncle's death. In essence, she writes, "he was entering and exiting the world under the same flag. Never really sovereign, as his father had dreamed, never really free" (250).

Danticat weaves in the history of Haiti's fight for freedom throughout her memoir. Less than thirty pages in, she provides a history of the neighborhood of Bel Air, specifically the hill where her uncle built his house, because it is the "site of a famous battle between mulatto abolitionists and French colonists," who had "controlled most of the island since 1697 and had imported black Africans to labor on coffee and sugar plantations as slaves" (29). She reminds her readers that, a century later, "slaves and mulattoes joined together to drive the French out" and formed the Republic of Haiti (29). Then, when "World War I dawned and the French, British, and Germans, who controlled Haiti's international shipping, rallied their gunboats to protect their interest," President Woodrow Wilson ordered an invasion; he was trying to protect the United States' interest in, among other entities, "the United Fruit Company" and its "40 percent of the stock of the Haitian national bank" (29). Danticat then depicts her family's migration and the violence that forced Joseph to seek asylum, contextualizing them as consequences of this larger colonial and neocolonial history.

She also describes how Joseph got caught between local gangs and UN peacekeepers, who arrived to stabilize the country after Haiti's first democratically elected president, Jean-Bertrand Aristide, was forced into exile in 2004, by many accounts due to U.S. interference.[60] The gangs accused

Joseph of betraying his community by letting UN soldiers and the Haitian riot police into his church, where the latter shot many innocent people in their attempt to target the gangs. In retaliation, the gangs burned Joseph's church and threatened his life. When he reported the situation to the police, he received no response. Joseph realized how futile his act had been: the police, like the so-called peacekeepers, offered only an "illusion of shelter and protection," while in fact they retained the power to "obliterate" civilians (204).

Joseph's story has clear similarities with the experiences of the children in America's detention camps, as described in the Flores statements, and with those of people all over the world who are threatened by gang members or lack the protection of governments that have been corrupted, directly or indirectly, by (neo)colonial forces. Unlike the other writers examined in this book, however, Danticat—though she offers frequent historical context for Joseph's story—focuses primarily on the narration of his specific experience, making it possible for readers to view his tragic end as a singular case and therefore to lose track of the broader effects of migration and imperialism.

As I noted earlier, the reception of *Brother, I'm Dying* bears this claim out. Reviewers tended to underplay the political history contained in the memoir, focusing instead on how it details one family's survival against great odds. Michiko Kakutani, in the *New York Times*, writes:

> Ms. Danticat not only creates an indelible portrait of her two fathers, her dad and her uncle, but in telling their stories, she gives the reader an intimate sense of the personal consequences of the Haitian diaspora: its impact on parents and children, brothers and sisters, those who stay and those who leave to begin a new life abroad. She has written a fierce, haunting book about exile and loss and family love, and how that love can survive distance and separation, loss and abandonment and somehow endure, undented and robust.[61]

Kakutani isn't wrong in her assessment: the love in the memoir is fierce. But it is marshaled against forces that form part of a much broader story of migration. Junot Díaz's concept of decolonial love works at the scale necessary to fully apprehend the love that Kakutani highlights. To focus only on the family's bonds is to see only part of the story. Yet other reviewers echo Kakutani: "Poignant and never sentimental, this elegant memoir recalls how a family adapted and reorganized itself over and over, enduring and succeeding to remain kindred in spite of living apart."[62] "Through the seemingly effortless grace of Danticat's words," writes Terry Hong, "a family's tragedy is transformed into a promise of collective hope."[63] Jess Row, also reviewing the memoir for the *New York Times*, begins by noting that most of the memoir is dedicated to Uncle Joseph's story and highlights some of Danticat's efforts to gesture toward the broader scale of migration, but ultimately she makes use of another all-too-familiar trope of immigrant literature, the hyphenated identity:

> "He shouldn't be here. If our country were ever given a chance and allowed to be a country like any other, none of us would live or die here." Danticat lets this stand without comment; we are left to imagine how painful it must have been for her and her American-born siblings to hear this sentiment spoken aloud. Are Haitians in America immigrants, and the children of immigrants, or exiles? Do they accept a hybrid identity, a hyphen, or do they keep alive the hope of "next year in Port-au-Prince," so to speak?[64]

Row concludes by wondering how Danticat might reconcile the "feeling of estrangement and alienation within one's adopted culture" with "her own near-miraculous American odyssey," bringing the scale of migration down to Danticat's unique case.[65]

This emphasis in the reviews becomes even more surprising when one considers that, in addition to underscoring how American neocolonial practices have caused Haitian migration, Danticat draws attention in the memoir to Krome, describing the prisoners she encountered there during her visit as a community activist. Krome, she writes, is a "series of gray concrete buildings and trailers" in what seems like "the middle of nowhere, in southwest Miami" (211). Ken Silverstein in the *New Republic* confirms this description: "Krome, like most other detainee facilities, operates far out of range of sustained public and media scrutiny." Though located near the Dolphin Mall and a resort and gambling complex, it remains, like many ICE camps, hard to find: "If you don't have a detained relative or some other reason to know it's there, it's out of sight and out of mind."[66] The men whom Danticat met there during her visit lived in conditions similar to those of the children at ICE facilities: they slept in "rows and rows of bunk beds" or on "thin mattresses on the floor" in overcrowded rooms; they were so cold that they shivered all night; the food they were given "rather than nourish them, punished them, gave them diarrhea and made them vomit" (212). They were sometimes beaten and often driven to despair. One of the men told Danticat, "If I had a bullet, I'd have shot myself" (213). She saw men "who looked too young to be the mandatory eighteen years old for detention at Krome"—a few "looked fourteen or even twelve." When she asked a lawyer how their ages were recorded with no birth certificates and no documents, the lawyer told her that "their ages were determined by examining their teeth," making Danticat think of auction blocks "where mouths were pried open to determine worth and state of health" (212).

Danticat also makes it clear in the memoir that her efforts to get her uncle released were thwarted. After his death, she had to piece together what had happened to him from a few official documents that she procured from the Bureau of Customs and Border Protections. These documents demonstrate both the maddening maze of questionnaires, most of which provide only "yes" or "no" options, and the callousness of Krome's officers, a callousness that became fatal for an elderly man who, aside from requiring medicine for high blood pressure, was also a throat-cancer survivor requiring a voice box to speak. The documents show that an officer who interviewed him checked "no" for health factors, and a medic who arrived at the scene of his collapse claimed that Joseph was "faking" (233).

In an interview after the publication of *Brother, I'm Dying*, Danticat said that she hoped the memoir and other books "like it are used in the training of U.S. customs officers and immigration workers," for, if "they can only remember that they are dealing with human beings at possibly the worst moments of their lives and not mere numbers or so-called 'aliens,' then they would do a better job."[67] Despite Danticat's good intentions, I would argue that this appeal to empathy—and indeed the memoir's overall focus on an individual case—colludes with the standard rhetoric about migration, not only facilitating the kind of public reception that the book did in fact garner but also reducing it to "a handbook," in Nicole Waller's words, "instead of pointing to a larger, systemic problem"—a problem of which Danticat is quite aware.[68] If Americans understood how U.S. foreign policy has shaped Haiti and its diaspora, Danticat said in an interview, "they would understand Iraq a little better," because Haiti "is not independent of Iraq" but part of "policies [that] are cyclical."[69] As Waller argues, *Brother, I'm Dying* exposes how, on the one hand, U.S. policy "utilizes the language and practices of globalization to expand its influence beyond the national borders of other states," while, on the other, it "insists on the inviolability of US national borders."⁷⁰ Yet the autobiographical form of the family memoir paradoxically dwarfs the larger geopolitical discussion in *Brother, I'm Dying*, because of the tenacious readerly expectations of what a migrant narrative should deliver.

Still, readers willing to reach beyond those expectations can find the political core of Danticat's memoir. Nicole Waller's essay "Terra Incognita: Mapping the Detention Center in Edwidge Danticat's *Brother, I'm Dying* and the US Supreme Court Ruling *Boumediene v. Bush*" not only finds that core but goes well beyond Danticat's work to present a case against the American government. Waller notes that many U.S. detention centers "are situated on sites which were originally either prisons or bases for US armed forces," a connection that suggests "both a criminalization of immigrants and their embeddedness in international military conflicts."⁷¹ Using insights derived from *Brother, I'm Dying*, Waller argues that the detention of suspected terrorists at Guantánamo Bay "is not a crucial innovation brought about by exceptional circumstances," namely 9/11, but "a continuation of an earlier US policy developed for the detention of potential immigrants."⁷² Just as the Reagan administration fused the War on Drugs with the criminalization of immigrants, subsequent administrations have intertwined anti-terrorist and anti-immigrant laws, using detention centers as places where they can deny suspected terrorists and migrants (often seen as one and the same) their fundamental human rights:

> Detention centers are in many ways placed outside standard legal and social relations—they figure as blank spaces on the map—and [are] nevertheless circumscribed and controlled by larger constellations of power. The human beings made to inhabit such spaces are often removed from the minimum standards of legal and social embeddedness; they are conceptualized as leading, in the words of Giorgio Agamben, "unclassifiable" lives. At the same time, they are utilized to express the fault lines of political power on our global map.⁷³

This forced liminality, this strategy of placing refugees outside U.S. jurisdiction, in a state of legal limbo, recalls Mae Ngai's account of how the so-called illegal alien was produced as "a social reality and a legal impossibility—a subject barred from citizenship and without rights."[74] It also recalls the "alien citizen," who purportedly has the rights of citizens but remains, in Ngai's words, "alien in the eyes of the nation."[75]

Brother, I'm Dying could have exposed the connections among these different types of "impossible subjects," but instead Danticat used the memoir to zero in on a particular set of circumstances, shaped by larger historical forces. And significantly, unlike the writers I discussed in previous chapters, Danticat did not use migrant aesthetics to guard her memoir against the reception it in fact received: the book lacks the kind of metafictive layering present in the other texts I have examined, which might have prevented a complacent, merely empathetic response from readers. Recall how Dinaw Mengestu undercuts the conventions of reading migrant fiction in "An Honest Exit" and *All Our Names*, or how Teju Cole and Junot Díaz capitalize upon the flexibility of the unreliable narrator to destabilize the idea of the migrant as informant. Consider Julie Otsuka's use of strategic anonymity and choral narration to push back against the empathy model of reading. Her strategies resonate in the Flores interviews, which preempt empty gestures towards feeling and force us to "face the facts" in Mary McCarthy's sense of the phrase. Think of the metafictive flights in the novels of Aleksandar Hemon and Valeria Luiselli, which make readers conscious of migrant aesthetics at work and prevent a passive consumption of migrant suffering. These strategies are missing in Danticat's memoir.

As a result, despite her sharp, often eviscerating depiction of migration as a consequence of empire, reviewers were able to fall back on the tropes of identitarian discourse and transcendence. Their responses exemplify the fact that, as soon as the story of carceral migration is channeled through a single life story or a family tale complete with names and full narrative arcs, as soon as the smallest hint of transcendent resolution is offered (and *Brother, I'm Dying* does not lack in this respect), the narrative in question—no matter what the intentions of its author may be—becomes part of a fantasy of empathetic engagement, substituting in place of the search for truth a much more comfortable illusion: that feeling sorry for the incarcerated migrant is enough.

EPILOGUE

"Chinga La Migra"—Karla Cornejo Villavicencio's *The Undocumented Americans*

When Karla Cornejo Villavicencio was a senior at Harvard, she wrote an anonymous essay for the *Daily Beast* about being undocumented. Literary agents soon found her, asking if she wanted to write a memoir. A news program asked for permission to film her while she packed up her dorm, apparently wanting to show that she was "leaving Harvard without any plans, without even the promise of a career" (this was before the Deferred Action for Childhood Arrivals [DACA], for which she would later qualify).[1] Cornejo Villavicencio rejected these offers to make her a spectacle and instead enrolled in a PhD program in American Studies at Yale, while continuing to write. She wanted to focus on the eleven million undocumented people in the United States, to tell the stories not of exceptional cases but of the "people who work as day laborers, housekeepers, construction workers, dog walkers, deliverymen, people who don't inspire hashtags" (xvi). "I wanted to write about our daily lives," she said in an interview, "how we survive, how we thrive, how we cope."[2] In 2020, she published *The Undocumented Americans*.

Part memoir, part journalistic reporting, part elegiac testament to the undocumented dead, the book intertwines episodes of Cornejo Villavicencio's life and those of her undocumented parents with a kind of migrant ethnography. Over the course of ten years, she conducted interviews with undocumented people all over the country and used the sites she visited as the organizing principle for her book. *The Undocumented Americans* takes us first to Staten Island, New York's whitest, most conservative borough, where Cornejo Villavicencio interviewed day laborers who had to network to protect each other from exploitation. She then describes a support group for undocumented workers from other sections of New York who were struggling with crippling physical and mental illness caused by the toxins they had been exposed to while doing cleanup at Ground Zero after 9/11; then a group of women in Miami seeking medicine from pharmacies and botanicas willing to serve uninsured and undocumented immigrants; then the community of undocumented residents in Flint, Michigan, who endured the brunt of the town's severe lead-poisoning crisis; and finally a group of families in Cleveland and New Haven who were coping with deportation orders; this last group included two fathers who sought sanctuary in churches. Throughout the book, she asks probing questions: What does it take to survive under constant surveillance? How does one make a life when everything one does is technically outside the law? How does one grow up, raise families, keep a job, grow old, stay sane?

Among the works that I have examined in this book, *The Undocumented Americans* is a telling exception. Even more than Danticat, Cornejo Villavicencio embraces memoir as a form of migrant enunciation, and yet, because she practices migrant aesthetics, she is able—at least partly—to preempt the kind of narrowly focused reception that *Brother, I'm Dying* received. My readers might ask at this point, doesn't migrant aesthetics challenge and reject autobiography? As we have seen, Teju Cole simulates aspects of memoir as a ruse in *Open City*: he uses conventions of life writing but only to disabuse readers from the assumption that this is the only mode of representing migration and to redirect their attention to the intimate connection between colonialism and migration. Working toward the same ends, Aleksandar Hemon employs Nabokovian refraction, Valeria Luiselli makes use of echoes to refract and thus abstract her own lived experience, and Junot Díaz manipulates the conventions of the unreliable narrator across decades of interconnected fiction. Other writers explicitly reject autobiographical forms, as we have seen in Dinaw Mengestu's *All Our Names* and in Julie Otsuka's internment novels. In contrast to these authors, Cornejo Villavicencio incorporates her own experiences within a collective portrait of undocumented life. At the same time, she plays with the conventions of the migrant narrator, thereby retrieving the effective use of direct autobiography for migrant aesthetics.

In interviews, in social media, and most potently in her writing, Cornejo Villavicencio exudes a bravura that is strategically at odds with the humility and obsequiousness so often expected from an undocumented migrant, whether she be a servant or a writer. This bravura is how she sabotages efforts to frame her and undocumented immigrants in general as long-suffering victims. This is also how she disrupts the expectations and assumptions that readers are likely to bring to her text. *The Undocumented Americans* has been called by one reviewer an "immigration punk manifesto"[3] because, in the words of another, it "lifts both middle fingers at [so-called] saviors" who pity migrants;[4] a third applauded it for being "willing to stick a thumb in the eye of liberal politicians and prominent Latinx thinkers" and for prose that is "caustic, quick, and simmering with righteous anger [but] leads seamlessly from heartbreak to gut-splitting laughter."[5] Cornejo Villavicencio starts the book "with a three-word declaration of love," writes Myriam Gurba, "'Chinga la migra.' This inscription establishes the book's punk sensibility while el Sagrado Corazón de Jesús (Sacred Heart—a Catholic symbol she baroquely asserts) lays down a beat."[6] Cornejo Villavicencio seems to reveal her own bleeding heart as she writes of her struggles with mental illness, of her parents and their precarious lives, of her efforts to "mak[e] sure they age and die with dignity in a country that has never wanted them," and of the pain and sorrow that she has witnessed in undocumented communities (148). Her bleeding heart, however, is not on display for consumption. Its thorns are meant to prick you.

Cornejo Villavicencio challenges readers to think from the position of undocumented migrants whose stories, aside from the fluctuating attention they receive at the border, are "largely absent from modern journalism and literature."[7] When she writes of her father collapsing after he lost his job as a taxi driver in the aftermath of 9/11—the state "suspended driver's licenses for undocumented immigrants as part of a national security measure"— she does so in the context of the increased vulnerability of undocumented migrants at a time of rabid xenophobia (41). When she writes of how he then became a delivery man, she keeps her focus on his role as part of an invisible workforce. Similarly, when she writes about her mother, she underlines how, like many other women represented in the book, her mother felt stifled by normative gender roles and saw migration, despite its hardships, as an opportunity to get beyond the roles of wife, mother, and homemaker. And when Cornejo Villavicencio writes about her own mental illness, it is with a candor designed to destigmatize a condition shared by countless others, migrant or not.

For at least one critic, the "most memorable and shocking parts of the book are those that deal with [Cornejo] Villavicencio's own experiences and those of her parents."[8] One wonders, on reading this statement, what exactly is "shocking" in their story since, alas, it is far from exceptional. When Cornejo Villavicencio was a toddler, her parents left her with relatives in Ecuador, where she was born. A few years later, when she was five, they brought her to New York and quickly learned that she was a precocious child who excelled in school. What they didn't know, at least initially, was that she also showed signs of mental illness—later diagnosed as "borderline personality disorder, major depression, anxiety, and OCD"—conditions that her doctors traced to her parents' abandonment of her in early childhood (61). "She blames them; she loves them; she wants to protect them. It's a heartbreaking mix," writes the reviewer who found her story "shocking."[9] And yet *The Undocumented Americans* places that "heartbreaking mix" in the context of a broad collectivity, as one experience among many in a wide range of undocumented communities.

Like several of the other authors I've considered in this book, Cornejo Villavicencio highlights the expectations that she is writing against by creating a metafictive discourse in her book about representing undocumented migrants. Like Otsuka, she also creates a choral narration by melding her own experiences with those of the many subjects she interviewed. No story, not even her own, has a full narrative arc. Instead, Cornejo Villavicencio weaves parts of several stories that echo each other while retaining enough specificity to mark them as separate. The result is something like Díaz's use of the short-story form to create plotlines that reverberate and intersect with each other across multiple works, to expand the scale of migration beyond identitarian concerns.

Cornejo Villavicencio pitched a version of the book to Yale as a dissertation project; it was rejected, she says, because it went against the conventions of migration studies:[10]

> I would not ask undocumented subjects why they came to America, no focus on push/pull factors, because I believe migration is a human right. I would

not ask, except in rare cases, how they came to America. No thrilling, explicit, border crossing stories. I would not ask them if they felt American. No apologizing for our illegality. But I would ask them if they had regrets. I would ask them if they had nightmares.[11]

Cornejo Villavicencio took notes during her interviews but destroyed them later; she did not use a recorder. "When you are an undocumented immigrant with undocumented family, writing about undocumented immigrants," she writes, "it feels unethical to put on the drag of a journalist" (xvi). She translated the interviews on the spot, approaching the task in "the way a literary translator would approach translating a poem, not the way someone would approach translating a business letter" (xv). She may or may not have changed the names and physical description of her subjects and the places she visited. In this and other ways, she mixes journalism with fiction to produce what she calls a work of "creative nonfiction" (xvi).

Her methods prompt the question of how her interviewees might "feel about being recreated on the page, and how freely their notes have been transposed."[12] The possible answers to this question have made at least one reviewer feel "ill at ease."[13] But Cornejo Villavicencio didn't write the book to make readers comfortable; as she put it, "I didn't write it for you to *like* it" (xvi, emphasis in the original). She wrote it, instead, to disabuse her readers of certain expectations, like "meaty" and "groveling" explanations for migrating, which would wrongly encourage readers to "judge whether or not" people have sufficient need to migrate in the first place.[14]

Deep into the book, Cornejo Villavicencio reveals that she knows "some Emily Dickinson poems by heart," a fact that lines up with her artistic sensibility (84). Dickinson's poem "My Life Had Stood – a Loaded Gun" imagines the poet as a gun that is aggressively but ecstatically shot by the muse. Cornejo Villavicencio wields her power as a writer similarly. "I have the ability to kill who I have to kill," she said, reflecting on her work, "and resuscitate who I have to resuscitate and that's what I did in this book."[15] Nowhere is this power more in evidence than when she mourns the undocumented dead, with passages that reveal her skill in modulating her narrative voice so that it hits you intensely when you least expect it. Her voice often melds with those of the people she interviews, though she also emphasizes moments when her life story clashes with theirs. All along, she molds her sentences with a style reminiscent of Joan Didion, who provides the book's epigraph—at one point in an interview, Cornejo Villavicencio remarked, "'Three different kinds of flowers amid shards of glass,' that's a Didion turn of phrase"[16]—and trains our attention on how undocumented people shape the world around us.

In the first chapter, Cornejo Villavicencio reveals that, as when Hurricane Katrina hit New Orleans in 2005, many of those who were among the first on the ground after Hurricane Sandy hit Staten Island in 2014 were Latinx, undocumented day laborers. They "cleaned flooded basements, removed fallen branches and trees, repaired fences, waded in dirty waters up to their knees to remove furniture from houses, removed drywall, picked up debris," doing "whatever needed to get done" (25). Unlike other volunteers, day laborers could use their skills in "painting, electrical wiring, and landscaping" to do extensive renovation projects; they worked for free in "hopes of encouraging future working relationships," though "many people just took the free labor" (27). Cornejo Villavicencio decided to document the stories of these laborers to make sure that they, unlike those who helped to clean up after Katrina, were not effaced from public record. "About half of the reconstruction crews in New Orleans were Latinx, and more than half of those were undocumented"—but she writes, this is far from being widespread knowledge (23–24).

At the end of the chapter, Cornejo Villavicencio tells the story of one laborer named Ubaldo Cruz Martinez, who drowned in a basement during Hurricane Sandy "because he was probably drunk" (28). "Ubaldo was found floating in dirty water, and his body was repatriated to his hometown in San Jerónimo Xayacatlán," she writes. "The bell at the church rang at one o'clock in the morning to mark the return of one of their own" (28–29). Many of the laborers with whom Cornejo Villavicencio spoke knew Ubaldo personally, or "knew of him but didn't really want to talk about him," probably because they were "embarrassed by him"; he was an alcoholic who might, they feared, give credence to stereotypes about undocumented people (28). Cornejo Villavicencio imagines how people in his town "gossiped that it was a shame he had died with no friends with nobody to cry over his grave," and she calls on her readers to bear witness to his death (29). We see Ubaldo taking in a wounded squirrel in the hours before he died— nursing it, feeding it "between her bunny teeth" even though he knows that neither he nor she will live past the night, because "no creature should have to die alone" (29).

EPILOGUE

And then comes this passage:

> Did this happen?
> Are we in gangs?
> Do we steal Social Security numbers?
> Do we traffic our own children across the border?
> Is this book nonfiction?
> Can we imagine that he was capable of kindness, even as he was drinking? That he was capable of courage, even as he was wounded?
> What if this is how, in the face of so much sacrilege and slander, we reclaim our dead? (30)

Having created a fictional sentimental atmosphere, Cornejo Villavicencio jolts readers out of it with this barrage of questions, which expose the constructed nature of the representation and the potential biases that readers might bring to her subject and her narrative ("Are we in gangs?" "Is this book nonfiction?"). Cornejo Villavicencio hopes that her book will move nonimmigrant readers "towards something other than pity, or inspiration, or charity, or looking at us and then feeling #blessed about their lot in life."[17] She intertwines Ubaldo's story with those of other men like him, some of whom have become alcoholics because of the loneliness and heartbreak of migrant life—the family separations, the marriage breakups, the constant devaluation of one's life. But she is careful not to explain away or claim authority over Ubaldo's experience. The conditions of his life and death were known only to him; what Cornejo Villavicencio offers instead is a fictionalized eulogy. Like Luiselli, she acts as an Antigone figure, giving burial rites to those exiled by the state from their communities.

In the book's second chapter, she uses this same method to discuss the undocumented migrants who died during the attacks of 9/11. She focuses on those who worked in restaurants, in housekeeping, in security, and she calls out the names of the delivery men who worked graveyard shifts and perished during the attacks but left no legal trace and are thus not included in the official number of the dead. "There is no telling how many were killed because restaurant owners and managers have refused to come forward with the names of the missing people for fear that they will be fined for employing undocumented laborers" (49–50). Nevertheless, since advocacy organizations such as Asociación Tepeyac fielded many calls "from families who had not heard from a loved one," there is a record of at least some of the undocumented people who perished (50). Cornejo Villavicencio calls out some of the names, recalling the rites of burial that "Isaac" conducts in Mengestu's *All Our Names* (54).

She ends the chapter with the story of nineteen-year-old Fernando Jimenez Molinar, who died under the collapsing towers. Shifting almost imperceptibly from fact into fiction, Cornejo Villavicencio imagines him dying with a fake ID between his teeth: "Your flesh may burn but your teeth will remain and the ID will be there" (56). Will the ID allow his loved ones to identify his body? Or is his fate to be among nameless others? "Nobody will ever know you died. Nobody will ever know you lived" (56). Cornejo Villavicencio dedicated *The Undocumented Americans* to the late Claudia Gómez González, a twenty-year-old Indigenous woman from Guatemala who was shot in the head by a Border Patrol agent in 2018. The undocumented dead are a constant underlying theme in the book, though the bulk of it focuses on the living.

One of the most striking aspects of the book, from my perspective, is that its chorus of voices collectively resists what has been my central argument in this work: that the history of empire is key in understanding the roots of migration at a scale appropriate to its global dimensions. For Cornejo Villavicencio, this emphasis on empire threatens to obscure the micro-level decisions and conditions that prompt individuals to migrate and that shape migrant life. In other words, migration at its most visceral is fueled by a person's will, by family life, by gender violence, by local politics, by contingency. I have been arguing that these decisions and conditions are shot through with the marks of empire, but for Cornejo Villavicencio this argument obscures the fact that migration is a human right. We don't need empire to justify migration, she might say, and in *The Undocumented Americans* she writes:

> I personally subscribe to Dr. King's definition of an "unjust law" as being "out of harmony with the moral law." And the higher moral law here is that people have a human right to move, to change location, if they experience hunger, poverty, violence, or lack of opportunity, especially if that climate in their home countries is created by the United States, as is the case with most third world countries from which people migrate. (138)

EPILOGUE

But even as she reminds us here that migration is a human right, Cornejo Villavicencio invokes empire. I am sympathetic to her desire to highlight contingency and agency in the experience of migration. Her granular, micro focus reveals conditions and subjectivities obscured by exceptionalist and spectacle-driven migrant literature. Nevertheless, given the dearth of emphasis on empire in most criticism of migrant literature, I stand by my argument that more attention needs to be paid to its crucial role in causing migration, directly and indirectly.

In some instances, the broader political contexts for individual stories insinuate themselves just slightly beyond Cornejo Villavicencio's focus. Take for instance the story of Paloma, who fled Colombia for economic reasons but also because she was trying to escape an oppressive home life: fleeing an abusive stepfather, she married early but quickly realized that her marriage was another prison. Her flight ended tragically: in 2010, Paloma was diagnosed with breast cancer, which her doctors linked to the cleanup work she had done at Ground Zero (47). Recall Junot Díaz's concept of decolonial love and the connection he makes between colonialism and gender and sexual violence. Paloma's story might be understood in this context. But even without it, Paloma's life is threatened by the radioactive force of Ground Zero, which, after Teju Cole, we can see as a palimpsest of colonial violence. There is also Esme, whom Cornejo Villavicencio met in Miami. A victim of her father's physical abuse, Esme grew up in the late 1970s and 1980s under the dictatorship of Gregorio Álvarez in Uruguay, which, like the dictatorships of nearby Argentina and Chile, demonstrated how easily a state can make civilians disappear. Again, after Díaz, we might see the gender and state violence in Esme's life as connected at the nexus of a colonialist-produced toxicity. Unlike Paloma, however, Esme is not victimized. After migrating to Miami, she became part of a subgroup of the legendary Mothers of the Plaza de Mayo, who have been protesting the disappearance of nearly 30,000 people in Argentina for forty years. Esme's group, You Are Not Alone, watches over the offices of the U.S. Citizenship and Immigration Services in nearby Miramar, ready to testify to the abuse of immigrants who are often treated "like livestock" and shipped "to detention centers, never to be seen again" (78). "*We see you, and you won't get away with this!* the women yell at officers" (79, emphasis in the original).

Cornejo Villavicencio also calls attention to the effects of carceral migration beyond detention camps:

Being deportable means you have to be ready to go at any moment, ready to go with nothing but the clothes on your body. I've learned to develop no relationship to anything, not to photos, not to people, not to jewelry or clothing or ticket stubs or stuffed animals from childhood. Sometimes to prove my ability to let go, I'll write something long and delete it, or go on my phone and delete all the photos I have of happy memories. I've never loved a material object. (60)

When Cornejo Villavicencio describes the two fathers who sought sanctuary in churches, she makes vivid their experience of being suspended in time during their captivity, in much the same way that Otsuka represents internment in *When the Emperor Was Divine*. But she also reminds us that, at the time of her writing, there were only "forty-two individuals in the United States living in churches in defiance of their deportation orders." "It takes a particular kind of person to go into sanctuary," she writes. "They're extraordinary" (137).

The more common experiences are of families being torn apart through migration and deportation. Cornejo Villavicencio follows the fate of several children trying to cope with the disorientation and fear that results from such traumatic events, and she makes explicit the psychological cost, describing her own experience of having been left in Ecuador alongside the experiences of the children she interviewed (and helped in the process).[18] "Researchers have shown," she writes, "that the flooding of stress hormones resulting from a traumatic separation from your parents at a young age kills off so many dendrites and neurons in the brain that it results in permanent psychological and physical changes"—and indeed one psychiatrist told her that her "brain looked like a tree without branches," it was so lacking in dendrites (61). After this description, quickly pivoting from her own experience, she urges us to "think about all the children who have been separated from their parents, and there's a lot of us, past and present": "Some are under more traumatic circumstances than others—like those who are in internment camps right now—and I just imagine us as an army of mutants. We've all been touched by this monster, and our brains are forever changed, and we all have trees without branches in there, and what will happen to us? Who will we become? Who will take care of us?" (61). This dystopian vision calls to mind Díaz's story "Monstro" in its use of sci-fi imagery to ask questions about our common future. While the "we" here clearly refers to a particular community, the questions are posed to a broader "we": how will we *all* face the kind of future we are now building through our current immigration policies? These policies, Cornejo Villavicencio argues, are begetting problems that will inevitably multiply and collide with challenges already confronting all of us, including climate change (hurricanes Katrina and Sandy are but mild foreshadows) and growing class differences that are increasingly shaping global health.

Cornejo Villavicencio wrote *The Undocumented Americans* in the aftermath of the 2016 presidential election, knowing that there would undoubtedly be an increase of xenophobic violence after Trump's inauguration. She wanted to give testimony at a moment of crisis. What she ultimately reveals, however, is how profoundly the conditions that shape undocumented lives affect the lives of all Americans. When she went to Miami in 2017, for instance, the House of Representatives had just voted to replace the Affordable Care Act, stripping an estimated twenty-three million Americans of healthcare and substituting "new legislation that listed cesarean sections, rape, and depression as preexisting conditions" (61). Cornejo Villavicencio notes that both uninsured and undocumented people are vulnerable under such conditions, but there is a key difference between the two groups: undocumented people cannot buy health insurance "even if they can afford it" (62). Absurdly, this inability creates situations that feed one of the "bogeymen of the right, in this country or any Western country . . . the image of the sick immigrant—the supposed strain on the healthcare system, the burden on emergency rooms and taxpayers" (62). That bogeyman not only strengthens prejudice but obscures the vulnerability of all uninsured citizens and distracts the public from the state's systematic assault on all vulnerable communities.

Similarly, regarding the lead poisoning in Flint, Cornejo Villavicencio writes: "The government wanted the people of Flint dead, or did not care if they died, which is the same thing, and set in motion a plan for them to be killed slowly through negligence at the highest levels" (115). During the crisis, Flint's officials made access to clean water contingent upon having a state ID, thus ensuring that survival would become dramatically more difficult for the undocumented. "What I saw in Flint," Cornejo Villavicencio concludes, "was a microcosm of the way the government treats the undocumented everywhere, making the conditions in this country as deadly and toxic and inhumane as possible so that we will self-deport" (115). Yet she also notes that the state often inflicts similar forms of violence on its own citizens. Like Lani Guinier and Gerald Torres, whose influential book *The Miner's Canary* (2003) argues that racial injustice points to underlying societal problems affecting everyone, not just minorities, Cornejo Villavicencio shows how the precarity of undocumented lives exposes the cracks in the American social fabric as a whole—from labor exploitation to healthcare disparities and more. She is not a "native informant" who "gives voice" to the disenfranchised; nor is she a tourist guide allowing the white gaze into highly guarded communities or an activist promoting positive images of migrants. "I'd honestly rather swallow a razor blade than be expected to change the mind of a xenophobe," she writes (62). But, nevertheless, Cornejo Villavicencio *is* out to radicalize migrant literature and, in doing so, to expose how migration shapes our common world.

In an interview, Cornejo Villavicencio noted that the stories that are "popular about immigrants, undocumented or not," are predominantly those told by people who are "grateful to America," whose aim is "to change racist white people's minds about us. And that didn't feel right with me."[19] Witness, for instance, Julissa Arce's memoir *My (Underground) American Dream: My True Story as an Undocumented Immigrant Who Became a Wall Street Executive* (2016). Given its title, it isn't surprising that Donald E. Graham, former chairman and publisher of the *Washington Post*, called this book a "21st-century David Copperfield with its utterly lovable, wildly imperfect heroine" and praised it for a "plot packed with incident; a few villains and many, many heroes."[20] While Arce advocates for DACA citizenship, she also sells her story as an example of the American dream, in order to make migrants more "relatable" to nonmigrants. Other recent memoirs, like *Children of the Land* (2020) by the poet Marcelo Hernandez Castillo or *Dear America: Notes of an Undocumented Citizen* (2018) by the journalist and filmmaker Jose Antonio Vargas, are incisive and well crafted and decidedly not obsequious, but they are still DACA memoirs and thus fall into the exceptionalist category that Cornejo Villavicencio rejects.

Still, Cornejo Villavicencio had to compromise in terms of how her book was marketed. After its release, a *New York Times* reviewer noted that, "read in a certain way, her personal story fits the definition" of the exceptional DACA achiever who is "always grateful, never entitled, burning the midnight oil" to get into "an elite college and, later, a prestigious yet morally laudable career path"; publicity for the book never fails to mention her success.²¹ At best, Cornejo Villavicencio's personal narrative of success acts like a hook, pulling in readers who might not otherwise read a book that so thoroughly rejects American mythmaking. The need for this hook, I would argue, reveals how completely both the literary market and academia depend on the topoi of acculturation and Americanization. Cornejo Villavicencio, declared the *Guardian*'s reviewer, is "the glorious exception that keeps the myth of the American dream alive, the undocumented child of undocumented parents who is, nevertheless, a Harvard graduate, Yale doctoral student and the author of this much-praised book, whose champions include Barack Obama and the *New York Times*."²² Cornejo Villavicencio reluctantly agreed for the book to be marketed in this way for the sake of getting her testimony out into the world.²³ "I don't want all of the images of our people during this period to be of us on our knees or in cages, or begging for soap," she has said. "I want this book to also exist as a snapshot of this period in time, where there are people who are different, who are imperfect, who are weird, who are hardworking, who are just people."²⁴ She sees her work as following the tradition of Latin American *testimonios*—eyewitness accounts of injustice that take a variety of different textual forms.²⁵

The Undocumented Americans was published in the same year as Jeanine Cummins's novel *American Dirt* (2020), which caused a literary scandal by stereotyping migrants and cashing in on their suffering. The fictional story of a Mexican mother and son who journey to the U.S. border after a cartel murders the rest of their family, the novel was the subject of a bidding war between presses. It eventually earned Cummins a seven-figure advance from Flatiron Press, which engaged in a massive publicity campaign, enlisting writers such as Sandra Cisneros and Stephen King to blurb it. The novel debuted at the top of the *New York Times* bestseller list and initially received what the critic Parul Sehgal described as "rapturous and demented praise"—it was "anointed 'The Grapes of Wrath' for our time, 'required reading for all Americans,'" and was promoted by Oprah.²⁶ Its literary merit, however, did not live up to the hype, not least because Cummins relied, in Myriam Gurba's words, on "overly-ripe Mexican stereotypes" to cover what she herself could not imagine, delivering stilted prose and shallow characterization.²⁷

Cummins, who until the publication of the novel identified as white, also seems to have engaged in a performance of brownface while simultaneously embracing the concept of the white savior. She was bothered that "migrants at the Mexican border were being portrayed as a 'faceless brown mass'" (her words) and said "she wanted to give these people a face."[28] (With Toni Morrison's *Playing in the Dark* in mind, one can understand how a lack of racial consciousness can dwarf the imagination and the power of language.) Cummins apparently put in some research—Sehgal notes that she vividly conjures scenes taking place on La Bestia—but she did not bother to hide what Sehgal calls "[her] excited fascination in commenting on gradients of brown skin," which is in evidence throughout the novel.[29] She also, contradicting her own earlier statements, tried to pass for brown, laying emphasis on her Puerto Rican grandmother and allowing the press to report that her husband was undocumented without mentioning the fact that he is Irish. Flatiron Press added to the absurdity by using floral centerpieces wrapped in barbed wire at a dinner party celebrating the book's release; the pieces were apparently meant to echo the "*American Dirt* book cover, which is outlined in barbed-wire and covered in those exact flowers."[30] In an even more vulgar turn of events, Cummins also wore the image in the form of a manicure.[31]

Recall Cornejo Villavicencio's stated goal of creating "a snapshot of this period in time," in which migrants can be recognized as "just people." Cummins paid lip service to this humanizing impulse, but in her book, as Sehgal points out, "the deep roots of these forced migrations are never interrogated; the American reader can read without fear of uncomfortable self-reproach. It asks only for us to accept that 'these people are people,' while giving us the saintly to root for and the barbarous to deplore—and then congratulating us for caring."[32] Cornejo Villavicencio, by contrast, is propelled by the belief that literature can create productive empathy, or at least compassion:

> Art allows us to feel *for* the pain of others who have or will experience pain we cannot imagine or cannot ever happen to us. Even if we cannot *feel it*, or *imagine* it, that's just human limitation. A failure of imagination can be compensated by the construction of a sturdy enough bridge of artistic articulation of that pain, and if it's honest enough, we may not *feel it*—though in some cases we may—but we will feel *for* our fellow humans, and that is the job of the artist.[33]

EPILOGUE

The ambivalence I detect in Cornejo Villavicencio's several qualifications ("we may not *feel it*—though in some cases we may") shows that she is unsure of the power of empathy, of the power of art to facilitate it. Yet she insists that "we will feel *for* our fellow humans," and makes this contingent on how honestly artists can represent pain. But it isn't so simple.

Throughout this book, I have shown the limits of the empathy model of reading and have argued, after Arendt, for the need to make readers *think*, as themselves, from the position of others. Only in this way can we probe the deep imperial roots of forced migration and pay testimony to the innumerable crimes and injustices committed against migrants. Cornejo Villavicencio understands but understates the economic and political roots of migration—she wants the world to see her subjects "as just people," not merely as victims of forces beyond their control. But, as *Migrant Aesthetics* has shown, we also need a broad perspective to apprehend the scale of those forces.

The Undocumented Americans works at a granular level, complementing the work of the other authors I have discussed, to make us think beyond our own narrow confines. It lifts both middle fingers at so-called saviors who pity migrants, while challenging the literary marketplace that peddles migrant suffering to prop up comforting myths. And like all the other texts I discuss in *Migrant Aesthetics*, it mourns the migrant dead, especially those who die anonymously. Recall Luiselli's words in *Tell Me How It Ends*: "Numbers and maps tell horror stories, but the stories of deepest horror are perhaps those for which there are no numbers, no maps, no possible accountability, no words ever written or spoken. And perhaps the only way to grant any justice—were that even possible—is by hearing and recording those stories over and over again so that they come back, always, to haunt and shame us."[34]

NOTES

INTRODUCTION: MIGRANT AESTHETICS

1. Gregory Radick, "Kafka's Wonderful Ape," *Times Literary Supplement* 6048 (March 1, 2019): 8–9.
2. See, for instance, Christopher Watkin, "Kafka's 'A Report to an Academy' and the Authoritative Discourse of the Liminally Human," July 18, 2012, https://christopherwatkin.com/2012/07/18/kafkas-a-report-to-an-academy-and-the-authoritative-discourse-of-the-liminally-human/. See also Yasco Horsman, "Braying, Howling, Growling for Justice: Animal Personhood in Law, Literature, and Cinema," *Law and Literature* 28, no. 3 (November 2016): 319–334.
3. Matthew T. Powell, "Bestial Representations of Otherness: Kafka's Animal Stories," *Journal of Modern Literature* 32, no. 1 (Fall 2008): 129–142.
4. Dagmar C. G. Lorenz, "Transatlantic Perspectives on Men, Women, and Other Primates: The Ape Motif in Kafka, Canetti, and Cooper's and Jackson's King Kong Films," *Women in German Yearbook* 23 (2007): 159.
5. Lorenz, "Transatlantic Perspectives," 157.
6. Samuel J. Spinner, "Plausible Primitives: Kafka and Jewish Primitivism," in "FOCUS: Revisiting the Classics," special issue, *German Quarterly* 89, no. 1 (Winter 2016): 17–35.
7. Franz Kafka, "A Report for an Academy" (1917), trans. Ian Johnston, https://www.kafka-online.info/a-report-for-an-academy.html. First published by Martin Buber in the German monthly *Der Jude* (1917), "A Report to an Academy," like the novella *The Metamorphosis* (1915), is part of what are known as Kafka's animal stories, or fables, in which he fuses human and animal features to challenge accepted ideas of human distinctiveness, animal agency, and the human condition.
8. Kafka, "A Report for an Academy."

INTRODUCTION

9. Immigrant writing has not only been "complicit with but also critical of Americanization, conceived broadly as legal, political, cultural, and popular discourse." See Cristina Stanciu, "Americanization and the Immigrant Novel, Redux: Abraham Cahan's *The Rise of David Levinsky*," *Linguaculture* 12, no. 1 (2021): 29.
10. Dinaw Mengestu, "An Honest Exit," *New Yorker*, June 5, 2010, https://www.newyorker.com/magazine/2010/07/12/an-honest-exit.
11. Mengestu, "An Honest Exit."
12. Deborah Nelson notes that, while we use the term "sympathy" less often because it connotes a power imbalance, "empathy" works in similar ways. Deborah Nelson, "Tough Enough: Arbus, Arendt, Didion, McCarthy, Sontag, Weil," University of Chicago, Division of the Humanities, October 21, 2017, YouTube video, 32:03, https://www.youtube.com/watch?v=IZpz_OXLJfw.
13. Mengestu, "An Honest Exit."
14. These conditions were most famously represented by the engraving of the slave ship *Brookes*. See "Drawing of the Slave Ship 'Brookes,'" British Library, https://www.bl.uk/collection-items/drawing-of-the-slave-ship-brookes.
15. For a reading of this link, see Emma F. Bond, "'Let Me Go Back and Recreate What I Don't Know': Locating Trans-National Memory Work in Contemporary Narrative," *Modern Languages Open* (2016), https://www.modernlanguagesopen.org/article/10.3828/mlo.v0i0.134/.
16. Hannah Arendt, *Between Past and Future: Eight Exercises in Political Thought* (New York: Penguin Books, 1977), 258. As quoted in Namwali Serpell, "The Banality of Empathy," *New York Review of Books*, March 2, 2019, https://www.nybooks.com/online/2019/03/02/the-banality-of-empathy/.
17. Serpell, "The Banality of Empathy."
18. Serpell, "The Banality of Empathy."
19. James Dawes discusses Paul Bloom's *New Yorker* essay "The Baby in the Well" in "Is Empathy Bad?," Harvard University Press Blog, June 3, 2013, https://harvardpress.typepad.com/hup_publicity/2013/06/james-dawes-on-empathy.html.
20. Dawes, "Is Empathy Bad?" See also Paul Bloom, *Against Empathy: The Case for Rational Compassion* (New York: Ecco, 2016), 31–35.
21. Paul Bloom, "The Baby in the Well: The Case Against Empathy," *New Yorker*, May 13, 2013, https://www.newyorker.com/magazine/2013/05/20/the-baby-in-the-well.
22. Bloom, "The Baby in the Well."
23. Deborah Nelson, *Tough Enough: Arbus, Arendt, Didion, McCarthy, Sontag, Weil* (Chicago: University of Chicago Press, 2017), 9.
24. Dawes, "Is Empathy Bad?"
25. Dawes, "Is Empathy Bad?"
26. Bloom, "The Baby in the Well."
27. Susan Lanzoni, "A Short History of Empathy," *The Atlantic*, October 15, 2015, https://www.theatlantic.com/health/archive/2015/10/a-short-history-of-empathy/409912/.
28. As quoted in Lanzoni, "A Short History of Empathy."
29. Nelson, *Tough Enough*, 10, 59.
30. Nelson, "Tough Enough."
31. Serpell, "The Banality of Empathy."
32. Serpell, "The Banality of Empathy."

INTRODUCTION

33. Mae M. Ngai, *Impossible Subjects: Illegal Aliens and the Making of Modern America* (Princeton, NJ: Princeton University Press, 2004), 5.
34. Madelaine Hron, *Translating Pain: Immigrant Suffering in Literature and Culture* (Toronto: University of Toronto Press, 2009), Kindle edition, loc. 334.
35. Perspective by incongruity is produced through "deliberate misfits"—terms that, by virtue of not being usually associated together, challenge or extend our understandings of both. See Kenneth Burke, *Permanence and Change: An Anatomy of Purpose*, 3rd ed. (Berkeley: University of California Press, 1984), 90–91, and Kenneth Burke, *Attitudes Toward History*, 3rd ed. (Berkeley: University of California Press, 1984), 308–309.
36. Hron, *Translating Pain*, loc. 403.
37. William Q. Boelhower, "The Immigrant Novel as Genre," in "Tension and Form," special issue, *MELUS* 8, no. 1 (Spring 1981): 12.
38. Pankaj Mishra and Francine Prose, "Are Categories Like Immigrant Fiction and 'New American' Fiction Valid or Worthwhile?," *New York Times*, July 1, 2014, https://www.nytimes.com/2014/07/06/books/review/are-categories-like-immigrant-fiction-and-new-american-fiction-valid-or-worthwhile.html.
39. Werner Sollors, *Beyond Ethnicity: Consent and Descent in American Culture* (New York: Oxford University Press, 1986), 6–7. See also Sacvan Bercovitch, *The Puritan Origins of the American Self* (New Haven, CT: Yale University Press, 1975).
40. Werner Sollors, "Introduction," in Mary Antin, *The Promised Land* (New York: Penguin Books, 1997 [1912]), xv.
41. Ngai, *Impossible Subjects*, 13.
42. Ngai, *Impossible Subjects*, 3.
43. Ngai, *Impossible Subjects*, 4.
44. "Unlawful entry would be a misdemeanor punishable by $1,000 fine and/or up to 1 year in prison, and unlawful re-entry would be a felony punishable by $1,000 fine and/or up to two years in prison." See "A Short History of Immigration Detention," Freedom for Immigrants, https://www.freedomforimmigrants.org/detention-timeline/, accessed on September 27, 2022.
45. Ngai, *Impossible Subjects*, 13.
46. Ngai, *Impossible Subjects*, 9.
47. In 2011, Bharati Mukherjee noted the emergence of a new body of immigrant literature that could be distinguished from those of earlier periods. She argued that at the time scholars did not recognize "literature of the immigrant experience" as distinct "in its aims, scope, and linguistic dexterity from postcolonial literature, literature of globalization, or diasporic literature," and "misapplied literary theories that are relevant to literatures of colonial damage, nation building, dispersal, exile, voluntary expatriation, and cultural and economic globalization," which "are inappropriate templates for a literature that centers on the nuanced process of *rehousement* after the trauma of forced or voluntary *unhousement*." Mukherjee urged scholars "to come up with a new literary theory that provides a more complete, more insightful entry" into this new body of work. *Migrant Aesthetics*, however, argues that the categorical split Mukherjee makes is not necessary and that, in fact, what we need is a method for seeing how postcolonial and global literatures are inextricably intertwined with the literature of forced migration. See Mukherjee, "Immigrant

Writing: Changing the Contours of a National Literature," *American Literary History* 23, no. 3 (Fall 2011): 683.
48. Mishra and Prose, "Are Categories Like Immigrant Fiction and 'New American' Fiction Valid or Worthwhile?"
49. Malcolm Jones, "Cultural Exchange," *New York Times*, May 19, 2014, https://www.nytimes.com/2014/03/23/books/review/all-our-names-by-dinaw-mengestu.html.
50. Ron Charles, "'All Our Names,' by Dinaw Mengestu," *Washington Post*, March 4, 2014, https://www.washingtonpost.com/entertainment/books/book-review-all-our-names-by-dinaw-mengestu/2014/03/04/e97d0f5e-9f24-11e3-b8d8-94577ff66b28_story.html.
51. Parul Sehgal, "New Ways of Being," *New York Times*, March 10, 2016, https://www.nytimes.com/2016/03/13/books/review/new-ways-of-being.html. In this article, Sehgal reviews both *A Life Apart* by Neel Mukherjee and *The Year of the Runaways* by Sunjeev Sahota.
52. Quoted in Sehgal, "New Ways of Being."
53. Quoted in Sehgal, "New Ways of Being."
54. Hron, *Translating Pain*, loc. 358.
55. Hron, *Translating Pain*, loc. 345.
56. Hron, *Translating Pain*, loc. 358.
57. Hron, *Translating Pain*, loc. 368.
58. Dinaw Mengestu, *How to Read the Air* (New York: Riverhead Books, 2010), 24.
59. Madelaine Hron uses the term "immigrant." See chapter 2 of *Translating Pain*.
60. Hron, *Translating Pain*, loc. 1220.
61. Hron, "For a Responsive Conclusion," in *Translating Pain*, loc. 4529.
62. Susan Stanford Friedman, "Migrations, Diasporas, and Borders," in *Introduction to Scholarship in Modern Languages and Literatures*, ed. David Nicholls (New York: Modern Language Association, 2006), 264.
63. David Cowart, *Trailing Clouds: Immigrant Fiction in Contemporary America* (Ithaca, NY: Cornell University Press, 2006), 8, 7, 12.
64. Cowart, *Trailing Clouds*, 12.
65. Cowart, *Trailing Clouds*, 207. The writers whom Cowart examines include Saul Bellow, Bharati Mukherjee, Ursula Hegi, Jerzy Kosinski, Jamaica Kincaid, Cristina Garcia, Edwidge Danticat, Junot Díaz, Wendy Law-Yone, Mylène Dressler, Lan Cao, Chang-rae Lee, Theresa Hak Kyung Cha, and Nora Okja Keller.
66. See, for instance, Ilan Stavans's *Becoming Americans: Four Centuries of Immigrant Writing* (New York: Library of America, 2009), an anthology that offers eighty-five essays, short stories, novel excerpts, poems, letters, and bits of memoir by immigrant writers from forty-five countries. While rich in content, the book lacks a clear description of the selection process that went into its making. See also Louis Mendoza and Subramanian Shankar, *Crossing Into America: The New Literature of Immigration* (New York: New Press, 2005). *The Penguin Book of Migration Literature: Departures, Arrivals, Generations, Returns*, ed. Dohra Ahmad (New York: Penguin Books, 2019) is an excellent exception; it is organized clearly, in such a way as to "push back against the fallacies that migration is always elective; that migrants are always keen to leave their home countries; that migration is one-way, and

INTRODUCTION

necessarily leads to a better fate." See Parul Sehgal, "A New Collection Upends Conventional Wisdom About Migration," *New York Times*, September 9, 2019, https://www.nytimes.com/2019/09/09/books/review-penguin-book-migration-literature-dohra-ahmad.html.
67. Sollors, *Beyond Ethnicity*, 14.
68. Sollors, *Beyond Ethnicity*, 7–8.
69. Other topics have been important too. Critical attention to globalization has led scholars in diverse fields—literature, anthropology, cultural, and postcolonial studies—to be more attuned to the "porousness of cultural borders of the nation-state" and to how the "history of empire and (post) colonialism binds the literatures of different parts of the world." See Friedman, "Migrations, Diasporas, and Borders," 262. Others have explored changing ideas of America, especially post-9/11, in immigrant fiction. See, for example, Katie Daily's *Rejection and Disaffiliation in Twenty-First Century American Immigration Narratives* (New York: Palgrave Pivot, 2018).
70. Friedman, "Migrations, Diasporas, and Borders," 263.
71. Miguel Á. Hernández-Navarro, "Migratory Aesthetics," in *Encyclopedia of Aesthetics*, ed. Michael Kelly (New York: Oxford University Press, 2014), Oxford Reference.
72. Dalia Kandiyoti, *Migrant Sites: America, Place, and Diaspora Literatures* (Hanover, NH: Dartmouth College Press, 2009), 24.
73. Hernández-Navarro, "Migratory Aesthetics." See also Miguel Á. Hernández-Navarro, "Little Resistances. Contradictions of Mobility," in *2Move: Video Art Migration*, ed. Mieke Bal and Miguel Á. Hernández-Navarro (Murcia: Cendeac, 2008), 83–137.
74. Hernández-Navarro, "Migratory Aesthetics."
75. Hernández-Navarro, "Migratory Aesthetics." I appreciate the fact that Bal and Hernández-Navarro also focus on how migrants aesthetically transform their host societies.
76. Alexander Koch, Chris Brierley, Mark M. Maslin, and Simon L. Lewis, "Earth System Impacts of the European Arrival and Great Dying in the Americas After 1492," *Quaternary Science Reviews* 207 (March 2019): 13. See also David E. Stannard, *American Holocaust: The Conquest of the New World* (New York: Oxford University Press, 1992).
77. Ann Laura Stoler, *Duress: Imperial Durabilities in Our Time* (Durham, NC: Duke University Press, 2016), Kindle edition, loc. 138.
78. Stoler, *Duress*, loc. 116.
79. See the chapter "Colonial Aphasia: Disabled Histories and Race in France" in Stoler's *Duress*.
80. Rabih Alameddine, "Comforting Myths: Notes from a Purveyor," *Harper's Magazine*, June 10, 2018.
81. Alameddine, "Comforting Myths."
82. Viet Nguyen, "The Post-Trump Future of Literature," *New York Times*, December 22, 2020, https://www.nytimes.com/2020/12/22/opinion/fiction-poetry-trump.html.
83. Nguyen, "The Post-Trump Future of Literature."
84. Nguyen, "The Post-Trump Future of Literature."

1. MIGRANT ANONYMITY: STRATEGIC OPACITY IN DINAW MENGESTU AND TEJU COLE

1. See Glenda R. Carpio, "'Am I Dead Yet?': Slapstick Antics and Dark Humor in Contemporary Immigrant Fiction," *Critical Inquiry* 43 (Winter 2017): 345. See also Werner Sollors, *Ethnic Modernism* (Cambridge, MA: Harvard University Press, 2008), 12. Sollors argues that immigrant literature "participated in the development of an American literary modernism" precisely because of its concerns with fragmentation and alienation.
2. Pankaj Mishra and Francine Prose, "Are Categories Like Immigrant Fiction and 'New American' Fiction Valid or Worthwhile?," *New York Times*, July 1, 2014, https://www.nytimes.com/2014/07/06/books/review/are-categories-like-immigrant-fiction-and-new-american-fiction-valid-or-worthwhile.html.
3. Mishra and Prose, "Are Categories Like Immigrant Fiction and 'New American' Fiction Valid or Worthwhile?"
4. Sam Roberts, "More Africans Enter the U.S. Than in Days of Slavery," *New York Times*, February 21, 2005, https://www.nytimes.com/2005/02/21/nyregion/more-africans-enter-us-than-in-days-of-slavery.html. See also Sam Roberts, "Influx of African Immigrants Shifting National and New York Demographics," *New York Times*, September 2, 2014, https://www.nytimes.com/2014/09/02/nyregion/influx-of-african-immigrants-shifting-national-and-new-york-demographics.html.
5. Isidore Okpewho and Nkiru Nzegwu, eds., *The New African Diaspora* (Bloomington: Indiana University Press, 2009).
6. Isidore Okpewho, "Introduction: Can We 'Go Home Again'?," in Okpewho and Nzegwu, *The New African Diaspora*, 6–7.
7. Okpewho, "Introduction: Can We 'Go Home Again'?," 6–7.
8. Taiye Selasi, "Bye-Bye Babar," *LIP#5 Africa*, March 3, 2005.
9. Selasi, "Bye-Bye Babar." Selasi's version of Afropolitanism has been criticized for its focus on a particular class of urban elites, as well as for its collusion with the glossy, consumerist-oriented vision of African cosmopolitanism. See Stephanie Bosch Santana, "Exorcizing the Future: Afropolitanism's Spectral Origins," *Journal of African Cultural Studies* 28, no. 1 (March 2016): 120–126.
10. Achille Mbembe, "Afropolitanism," trans. Laurent Chauvet, in *Africa Remix: Contemporary Art of a Continent*, ed. Njami Simon and Lucy Durán (Ostfildern: Hatje Cantz Publishers, 2005), 26–30. Reprinted in *Nka: Journal of Contemporary African Art* 46 (May 2020): 60.
11. Mbembe, "Afropolitanism," 58.
12. Mbembe, "Afropolitanism."
13. Yogita Goyal, *Runaway Genres: The Global Afterlives of Slavery* (New York: New York University Press, 2019), Kindle edition, loc. 173.
14. Goyal, *Runaway Genres*, loc. 174.
15. As noted earlier, Selasi's version of Afropolitanism has been "associated with elements of pop culture, consumerism, with privileged status, luxury, and carries with it a sense of exclusivity, elitism." See Eleanor T. Khonje, as quoted in Susanne Gehrmann, "Cosmopolitanism with African Roots: Afropolitanism's Ambivalent Mobilities," *Journal of African Cultural Studies* 28, no. 1 (March 2016): 63. Meanwhile, "the marketability of Afropolitan authors—largely sustained by their American

publishing houses' systematic publicity campaigns—points again to its commodification" (66).
16. Harry Harootunian, "Remembering the Historical Present," *Critical Inquiry* 33 (Spring 2007): 474.
17. Dinaw Mengestu, *All Our Names* (New York: Knopf, 2014), 4. All subsequent citations to this work will be made parenthetically in the main text.
18. Giles Foden, *"All Our Names* Review—Dinaw Mengestu's Drama of Displacement," *Guardian*, June 4, 2014, https://www.theguardian.com/books/2014/jun/04/all-our-names-review-dinaw-mengestu-foden.
19. The novel's historical vagueness "too often leaves us with a version of Africa as a place of cyclical violence in which the laws of cause and effect seem ill-defined." See Elizabeth Lowry, "This Is How They Break You," *London Review of Books* 36, no. 11 (June 5, 2014), https://www.lrb.co.uk/the-paper/v36/n11/elizabeth-lowry/this-is-how-they-break-you. Mengestu, by contrast, said in the interview with Lowry: "I could use Kampala—and, by extension, elements of Uganda's history—to ground the characters, but I also needed the freedom to imagine a distinct world for them according to the needs and demands of the story I was imagining." Others have argued that Mengestu's representation of Africa is as problematic as those by V. S. Naipaul. See Ron Charles, "Book Review: 'All Our Names,' by Dinaw Mengestu," *Washington Post*, March 4, 2014, https://www.washingtonpost.com/entertainment/books/book-review-all-our-names-by-dinaw-mengestu/2014/03/04/e97d0f5e-9f24-11e3-b8d8-94577ff66b28_story.html.
20. Joseph H. Carens, "Realistic and Idealistic Approaches to the Ethics of Migration," *International Migration Review* 30, no. 1 (Spring 1996): 158.
21. Doris Sommer, *Proceed with Caution, When Engaged by Minority Writing in the Americas* (Cambridge, MA: Harvard University Press, 1999), 8.
22. Sommer, *Proceed with Caution*, 8, 15.
23. Pieter Vermeulen, "Reading Alongside the Market: Affect and Mobility in Contemporary American Migrant Fiction," *Textual Practice* 29, no. 2 (March 2015): 278.
24. Sommer, *Proceed with Caution*, 15.
25. Vermeulen, "Reading Alongside the Market," 281.
26. Rob Nixon, introduction to *Slow Violence and the Environmentalism of the Poor* (Cambridge, MA: Harvard University Press, 2011).
27. Charles, "Book Review."
28. Charles, "Book Review."
29. The essay was written in part as a response to "one of the most promising of the young Negro poets" (probably Countee Cullen), who claimed that he wanted "to be a poet—not a Negro poet." For Hughes, this position amounted to a rejection of the black artist's responsibility to assert the distinctiveness of black culture. George Schuyler's "The Negro-Art Hokum" (also published in the *Nation*, a week before Hughes's essay) argues against the racial particularity that Hughes highlights.
30. There might be an indirect reference here to how Barack Obama describes the beginning of his parents' romance in *Dreams from My Father* (1995).
31. It is worth stressing that, although Mengestu exposes Helen's naivete, he does not typecast her. Rather, he shows her rising to the challenge of engaging intimately with Isaac beyond the stereotypes and assumptions that at first distort her judgment.

32. Madelaine Hron, *Translating Pain: Immigrant Suffering in Literature and Culture* (Toronto: University of Toronto, 2009), 17.
33. Doris Sommer, "On Not Knowing in Minority Literature," in *Proceed with Caution, When Engaged by Minority Writing in the Americas*, rev. ed. (Cambridge, MA: Harvard University Press, forthcoming).
34. Goyal, *Runaway Genres*, loc. 71.
35. Goyal, *Runaway Genres*, loc. 71.
36. Hron, *Translating Pain*, chap. 1.
37. Hron, *Translating Pain*, loc. 381.
38. Hron, *Translating Pain*, loc. 560.
39. Goyal, *Runaway Genres*, loc. 73.
40. James Wood, "The Arrival of Enigmas: Teju Cole's Prismatic Début Novel, 'Open City,'" *New Yorker*, February 28, 2011, https://www.newyorker.com/magazine/2011/02/28/the-arrival-of-enigmas.
41. Wood, "The Arrival of Enigmas."
42. I owe this observation to my former student George Meyer. In an essay for a course on contemporary immigrant fiction at Harvard College in Fall 2014, George showed that, in his attention to solitude, Teju Cole is in conversation with John Keats, specifically his poem "O Solitude! If I must with thee dwell."
43. Teju Cole, *Open City* (New York: Random House, 2011), 164. All subsequent references to this work will be made parenthetically in the main text.
44. Wood, "The Arrival of Enigmas."
45. Pieter Vermeulen, "Flights of Memory: Teju Cole's *Open City* and the Limits of Aesthetic Cosmopolitanism," *Journal of Modern Literature* 37, no. 1 (2013): 51.
46. Vermeulen, "Flights of Memory," 42.
47. Vermeulen, "Reading Alongside the Market," 283.
48. Morrison offered the phrase "it slaps and it embraces" in an interview with Paul Gilroy, in reference to the effect of black music on listeners. See "Living Memory: A Meeting with Toni Morrison," in *Small Acts: Thoughts on the Politics of Black Cultures* (New York: Serpent's Tail, 1993), 181. Doris Sommer takes Morrison's phrase to argue that minority writers employ diverse formal strategies to "seduce us and to keep us at a distance," thus keeping the reader engaged with difference and preempting the desire to turn reading practices into forms of mastery. See Sommer, "Be-Longing and Bi-Lingual State," in *Grounds for Comparison Around the Work of Benedict Anderson, Pheng Cheah and Jonathan Culler* (New York: Routledge, 2003), 112.
49. Vermeulen, "Reading Alongside the Market," 283.
50. Richard T. Gray, "Sebald's Segues: Performing Narrative Contingency in *The Rings of Saturn*," *Germanic Review: Literature, Culture, Theory* 84, no. 1 (2009): 28. It's also the Belgian beginning of Sebald's novel *Austerlitz* (2001), which Cole riffs on in his Brussels section.
51. Paul Sheehan, "The History of Smoke: W. G. Sebald and the Memory of Fire," *Textual Practice* 26, no. 4 (2012): 737. Roberta Silman's *New York Times* review of Sebald's novel discusses how its flow of connections looks on the page. See Roberta Silman, "In the Company of Ghosts," *New York Times*, July 26, 1998, https://archive.nytimes.com/www.nytimes.com/books/98/07/26/reviews/980726.26silmant.html.
52. W. G. Sebald, *The Rings of Saturn* (New York: New Directions, 1998 [1995]), 118–119. All subsequent citations to this work will be made parenthetically in the main text.

53. The novel's title, however, does refer to the surrender of Brussels to the German occupation troops in World War I.
54. Sheehan, "The History of Smoke," 737.
55. Bernice E. Finney, "The American Colonization Society," *Negro History Bulletin* 12, no. 5 (February 1949): 117. See also "American Colonization Society," *Encyclopedia Britannica*, December 7, 2016, https://www.britannica.com/topic/American-Colonization-Society.
56. "American Colonization Society."
57. Paul Finkelman, ed., *Encyclopedia of African American History* (New York: Oxford University Press, 2006), 2:58.
58. Nasia Anam, "The Migrant's Nervous Condition," *Post45*, January 2017, https://post45.org/2017/01/the-migrants-nervous-condition/.
59. Emphasis in original. As Anam notes, the phrase also alludes to Tsitsi Dangarembga's 1988 coming-of-age novel, *Nervous Conditions*, "in which two young Zimbabwean women experience the turbulent emotional consequences of colonial 'double-consciousness.'" See Anam, "The Migrant's Nervous Condition."
60. Anam, "The Migrant's Nervous Condition."

2. MIGRANT REFRACTION: ALEKSANDAR HEMON'S ANTI-AUTOBIOGRAPHY

1. Aleksandar Hemon, "The Lazarus Project: One Writer's Research," *Paris Review* no. 173 (Spring 2005): 115–129.
2. Geoffrey Johnson, "The Lost Boy," *Chicago Magazine*, May 19, 2009, https://www.chicagomag.com/Chicago-Magazine/May-2009/Lost-Boy/.
3. Aleksandar Hemon, *The Lazarus Project* (New York: Riverhead Books, 2008), 1. All subsequent citations to this work will be made parenthetically in the main text.
4. Per Russian custom at the time, citizens sought letters of good character from the police chief before attempting to travel or find work.
5. Johnson, "The Lost Boy." See also Walter Roth and Joe Kraus, *An Accidental Anarchist: How the Killing of a Humble Jewish Immigrant by Chicago's Chief of Police Exposed the Conflict Between Law & Order and Civil Rights in Early 20th-Century America* (Chicago: Chicago Review Press, 2005).
6. Johnson, "The Lost Boy." As Robert J. Goldstein writes, "[the] fact that there was never any real evidence that a member of the Chicago anarchist movement was responsible for the bombing was disregarded in the hysteria which swept the country, and four leaders of the movement were hanged." Robert J. Goldstein, "The Anarchist Scare of 1908: A Sign of Tensions in the Progressive Era," *American Studies* 15, no. 2 (Fall 1974): 57.
7. As quoted in Johnson, "The Lost Boy."
8. With this act, "Congress banned from entry to the U.S. anarchists or persons who believe in or advocate the overthrow by force and violence of the government of the U.S." Goldstein, "The Anarchist Scare of 1908," 56, 58.
9. Hemon, "The Lazarus Project: One Writer's Research," 115.
10. Hemon, "The Lazarus Project: One Writer's Research," 117.

2. MIGRANT REFRACTION

11. Wendy Ward, "Does Autobiography Matter? Fictions of the Self in *The Lazarus Project*," *Brno Studies in English* 37, no. 2 (2011): 186.
12. Menachem Kaiser, "The Exchange: Aleksandar Hemon," *New Yorker*, June 8, 2009, https://www.newyorker.com/books/page-turner/the-exchange-aleksandar-hemon; emphasis in original.
13. Irina Reyn, "Exile on Any Street," *Guernica*, February 1, 2010, https://www.guernicamag.com/not_melted_into_the_pot/; emphasis in original.
14. Hemon claims not only that he learned English by reading Nabokov but that it was Nabokov's example against which he measured his effort to become a writer in English as a new immigrant in America. See Aleksandar Hemon with Deborah Treisman, "Fiction Podcast: Aleksandar Hemon Reads Vladimir Nabokov," *New Yorker*, December 1, 2014, https://www.newyorker.com/podcast/fiction/aleksandar-hemon-reads-pnin-by-vladimir-nabokov.
15. Vladimir Nabokov, *Speak, Memory* (New York: Vintage, 1989), 171.
16. There are also some key differences: Nabokov styled himself as a Russian émigré who loved the United States, his adopted country for several decades, and hated communism. Hemon belongs to a postsocialist diaspora, is more critical of America, and embraces his status as an immigrant in America. Hemon is also more forthright about his political commitments than Nabokov ever was.
17. Sonia Weiner, "Double Visions and Aesthetics of the Migratory in Aleksandar Hemon's *The Lazarus Project*," *Studies in the Novel* 46, no. 2 (Summer 2014): 218.
18. Weiner, "Double Visions and Aesthetics of the Migratory," 216.
19. See "An Interview with Aleksandar Hemon," BookBrowse, 2008, https://www.bookbrowse.com/author_interviews/full/index.cfm/author_number/1557/aleksandar-hemon.
20. Hemon, "The Lazarus Project: One Writer's Research," 116.
21. Hemon, "The Lazarus Project: One Writer's Research," 116.
22. For a fuller discussion of the role of humor in the novel, see Glenda R. Carpio, "'Am I Dead?': Slapstick Antics and Dark Humor in Contemporary Immigrant Fiction," *Critical Inquiry* 43, no. 2 (Winter 2017): 341–360.
23. "The photos of the dead Lazarus—the heart of the book—are so haunting because they document that he did live and he did die." See "An Interview with Aleksandar Hemon."
24. Hemon, "The Lazarus Project: One Writer's Research," 115–116.
25. "Many of the photographs in Hemon's novel were taken by photographers working for the *Chicago Daily News* and apparently appeared in the press immediately following the shooting at the Shippy residence." Weiner, "Double Visions and Aesthetics of the Migratory," 218.
26. See Lisa Yaszek, "'Them Damn Pictures': Americanization and the Comic Strip in the Progressive Era," *Journal of American Studies* 28, no. 1 (April 1994): 23–38; and Nickie D. Phillips and Staci Strobl, *Comic Book Crime: Truth, Justice, and the American Way* (New York: New York University Press, 2013), 20–39.
27. Mike Romo, "Violence in Comics," iFanboy, April 15, 2009, https://ifanboy.com/articles/violence-in-comics/; emphasis in original.
28. The combination of comic-book detectives and yellow journalists is apt, given the fact that American comics were "invented in 1895 for Joseph Pulitzer's *New York World* . . . with Richard Fenton Outcault's *The Yellow Kid*, which focused on

2. MIGRANT REFRACTION

contemporary urban immigrants and featured an endearing, obnoxious child," whose "recognizable yellow gown" reportedly "gave birth to the term yellow journalism." Pulitzer, who "realized that the strip was a circulation booster," vied with William Randolph Hearst for the distribution of *The Yellow Kid*; the two men's newspapers competed by publishing ever more sensationalist stories about both national life and international conflicts involving the United States. See Hillary Chute, "Comics as Literature? Reading Graphic Narrative," *PMLA* 123, no. 2 (March 2008): 455.
29. Johnson, "The Lost Boy."
30. Greg Beam, "The Rambo Effect," *Medium*, December 7, 2018, https://medium.com/@glandrybeam/the-rambo-effect-67fb887f04d.
31. Weiner, "Double Visions and Aesthetics of the Migratory," 226.
32. Weiner, "Double Visions and Aesthetics of the Migratory," 224.
33. Seymour M. Hersh, "Torture at Abu Ghraib: American Soldiers Brutalized Iraqis. How Far Up Does the Responsibility Go?," *New Yorker*, April 30, 2004, https://www.newyorker.com/magazine/2004/05/10/torture-at-abu-ghraib.
34. Hersh, "Torture at Abu Ghraib."
35. See, for instance, Namwali Serpell, "Becoming a U.S. Citizen in the Age of Trump," *Los Angeles Times*, September 29, 2017, https://www.latimes.com/opinion/op-ed/la-oe-serpell-becoming-an-american-citizen-in-the-age-of-trump-20170921-story.html. "The truth is," she writes, "I felt torn about swearing allegiance to a nation with such a horrific past—slavery, lynching, internment, Hiroshima, deportation, police brutality."
36. According to the Geneva Convention, Vladimir is not a refugee, even though he was stuck in the United States when the war broke out. For a discussion of how *The Lazarus Project* challenges the Geneva Convention's definition of a refugee, see Jessy Carton, "Complicated Refugees: A Study of the 1951 Geneva Convention Grounds in Aleksandar Hemon's *Life Narrative*," *Law and Literature* 30, no. 2 (2018): 331–347.
37. Once free of the police, Olga walks home and out of the pages of the novel. The historical Olga Averbuch returned to Eastern Europe (to Ukraine, then still part of the Russian Empire), where she might have been sent to the Nazi death camps, given the fact that many Jews from her region died in the camps. Miraculously, or perhaps erroneously, her name does not appear among the long list of the dead.
38. Donald E. Pease, "American Exceptionalism," *Oxford Bibliographies*, June 27, 2018, https://www.oxfordbibliographies.com/view/document/obo-9780199827251/obo-9780199827251-0176.xml.
39. Sacvan Bercovitch, preface to *The Puritan Origins of the American Self* (New Haven, CT: Yale University Press, 2011 [1975]), xvi–xvii, xl.
40. Weiner, "Double Visions and Aesthetics of the Migratory," 224.
41. Weiner, "Double Visions and Aesthetics of the Migratory," 227.
42. Weiner, "Double Visions and Aesthetics of the Migratory," 228.
43. Ward, "Does Autobiography Matter?," 194.
44. This echoes the fact that Hemon received a MacArthur grant in 2004.
45. Weiner, "Double Visions and Aesthetics of the Migratory," 227. She notes, for instance, that the frontispiece of the novel includes a photograph "portraying a man with his back turned, whose gaze meets that of the viewer through a mirror reflection," and argues that this establishes the importance in the novel of "reflection, both

in the sense of thought (to reflect) as well as in the sense of 'a reflection,' which implies duality and 'the double,' distance and distortion, and the complexity of distinguishing between the 'copy' and the 'real' or 'original.'" This is all further complicated by the fact that "the man and his reflection are reproduced in a photographic image." Like Ward, Weiner sees Hemon's use of photography as being in conversation with W. G. Sebald, who is "acclaimed for harnessing photographs in his fictional works to evoke the absent, the dispossessed, and the dead, and the worlds they once inhabited." Weiner, "Double Visions and Aesthetics of the Migratory," 220.

46. This offers another connection to Nabokov, who preferred "the bravery of reconstruction" to self-pity and nostalgia. See Michael Wood, *The Magician's Doubts: Nabokov and the Risks of Fiction* (Princeton, NJ: Princeton University Press, 1994), 93.
47. See Werner Sollors, *Beyond Ethnicity: Consent and Descent in American Culture* (New York: Oxford University Press, 1988), chaps. 3 and 4.
48. The play opened in Washington, DC, in 1908 but was published in 1909.
49. Sollors, *Beyond Ethnicity*, 71–72.
50. Weiner, "Double Visions and Aesthetics of the Migratory," 230.
51. Eva Hoffman, "The New Nomads," in *Letters of Transit: Reflections on Exile, Identity, Language, and Loss*, ed. André Aciman (New York: New Press, 1999), 57. As quoted in Weiner, "Double Visions and Aesthetics of the Migratory," 230.
52. Salman Rushdie, *Imaginary Homelands: Essays and Criticism, 1981–1991* (New York: Granta Books, 1992), 10.
53. Rushdie, *Imaginary Homelands*, 20.
54. Richard Rorty, *Contingency, Irony, Solidarity* (Cambridge: Cambridge University Press, 1989), 191–192.
55. Stefanie Stiles, "A Philosophy of Suffering: Redemption, Rorty, and Nathanael West's *Miss Lonelyhearts*," *Interdisciplinary Literary Studies* 16, no. 2 (2014): 254. Rorty took from Judith Shklar's *The Liberalism of Fear* (1989) the definition of a liberal as being someone who thinks that "cruelty is the worst thing we [human beings] do." Rorty, *Contingency, Irony, Solidarity*, xv.
56. Rorty, *Contingency, Irony, Solidarity*, xvi.
57. Rorty, *Contingency, Irony, Solidarity*, xvi.
58. Stiles, "A Philosophy of Suffering," 257.
59. Namwali Serpell, "The Banality of Empathy," *New York Review of Books*, March 2, 2019, https://www.nybooks.com/online/2019/03/02/the-banality-of-empathy/.
60. I'm here invoking Danish immigrant Jacob Riis's famous books of photojournalism, *How the Other Half Lives*, about the squalid living conditions of immigrants in late nineteenth-century New York, which, while bringing attention to the need for reform, also relied on ethnic stereotyping.
61. Namwali Serpell, "The Banality of Empathy."
62. Hannah Arendt, *Between Past and Future* (New York: Penguin, 2006 [1961]), 237.
63. Namwali Serpell, "The Banality of Empathy." See also Matthew Wester, "Reading Kant Against Himself," *Arendt Studies* 2 (2018): 193–214.
64. Hannah Arendt, *Essays in Understanding, 1930–1954* (New York: Harcourt, Brace, 1994), 323.
65. Hannah Arendt, "Reflections on Little Rock," *Dissent* (Winter 1959): 46.

3. MIGRANT SOLIDARITY

66. Franco Palazzi, "Representative Thinking, Paternalism and Invisibility," *Public Seminar*, February 5, 2016, https://publicseminar.org/2016/02/representative-thinking-paternalism-and-invisibility/.
67. Palazzi, "Representative Thinking, Paternalism, and Invisibility."
68. Palazzi, "Representative Thinking, Paternalism, and Invisibility."

3. MIGRANT SOLIDARITY: VALERIA LUISELLI'S ECHO CANYON

1. Gaiutra Bahadur, "Valeria Luiselli Traces the Youngest Casualties of the Border," *New York Times*, March 6, 2019, https://www.nytimes.com/2019/03/06/books/review/lost-children-archive-valeria-luiselli.html.
2. Bahadur, "Valeria Luiselli Traces the Youngest Casualties of the Border."
3. Bahadur, "Valeria Luiselli Traces the Youngest Casualties of the Border."
4. Valeria Luiselli, *Lost Children Archive* (New York: Vintage Books, 2019), 50. All subsequent citations to this work will be made parenthetically in the main text, with the reference *LCA*.
5. Dinaw Mengestu, "A Life in 40 Questions: Harrowing Stories of Child Migration," *New York Times*, April 28, 2017, https://www.nytimes.com/2017/04/28/books/review/tell-me-how-it-ends-valeria-luiselli.html.
6. Mengestu, "A Life in 40 Questions."
7. Valeria Luiselli, *Tell Me How It Ends: An Essay in Forty Questions* (Minneapolis, MN: Coffee House Press, 2017), 45. All subsequent citations to this work will be made parenthetically in the main text, with the reference *TM*.
8. See, for instance, Hannah Dreier, "How a Crack Down on MS-13 Caught Up Innocent High School Students," *New York Times*, December 27, 2018, https://www.nytimes.com/2018/12/27/magazine/ms13-deportation-ice.html.
9. Mengestu, "A Life in 40 Questions."
10. Suketu Mehta, *This Is Our Land: An Immigrant's Manifesto* (New York: Farrar, Straus, and Giroux, 2019), 69–70.
11. Mehta, *This Is Our Land*, 97.
12. Mehta, *This Is Our Land*, 104.
13. "Mission," Coffee House Press, https://coffeehousepress.org/pages/mission, accessed on September 27, 2022.
14. Mary Wang, "Valeria Luiselli: 'There Are Always Fingerprints of the Archive in My Books,'" *Guernica*, February 12, 2019, https://www.guernicamag.com/miscellaneous-files-interview-valeria-luiselli/.
15. The former "has a retro kind of candor, like the grainy Cold War films we watched on VHS": the questions concern possible threats in the form of "polyamorous debauchery, communism, [and] weak morals!" (*TM*, 10). Anyone who has ever applied for permanent residency knows the dark humor of these questions, a humor that is possible only with historical distance (tragedy plus time equals comedy). "'Do you intend to practice polygamy?' and 'Are you a member of the Communist Party?' and 'Have you ever knowingly committed a crime of moral turpitude?'" (*TM*, 10). "The process by which a child is asked questions during the intake interview," by contrast, "is called screening," a term "as cynical as it is appropriate: the child a reel of footage, the translator-interpreter an obsolete apparatus used to

channel that footage, the legal system a screen, itself too worn out, too filthy and tattered to allow any clarity, any attention to detail" (*TM*, 11).
16. Wang, "Valeria Luiselli."
17. Wang, "Valeria Luiselli."
18. Claire Messud, "At the Border of the Novel," *New York Review of Books*, March 21, 2019, https://www.nybooks.com/articles/2019/03/21/valeria-luiselli-border-novel/.
19. In her review, Messud misses the refraction that Luiselli creates between the essay and the novel: "The conceptual overlap between *Tell Me How It Ends* and *Lost Children Archive* is considerable. It is not new for a writer to address a subject in multiple forms. Camus famously did this when grappling with his theory of the absurd, writing three thematically linked but profoundly different works: *The Myth of Sisyphus* (a philosophical essay), *The Stranger* (a novel), and *Caligula* (a play). In his case the works are markedly distinct, however, and each is fully realized on its own terms; whereas here, Luiselli's novel, framed, like the essay, by a family's road trip across the United States from New York to Arizona, repurposes both literal and thematic material in ways that don't feel fully realized in the novel." Messud, "At the Border of the Novel."
20. "Apacheria" was the term used to designate the region inhabited by the Apache people. The earliest written records describe it as a region extending from north of the Arkansas River into what are now the northern states of Mexico, and from central Texas through New Mexico to central Arizona.
21. Since the terms have been defined differently across cultures and disciplines, the International Organization for Standardization offers these definitions of the terms. See https://www.iso.org/obp/ui/#iso:std:iso:12913:-1:ed-1:v1:en. See also Raymond Murray Schafer, *The Soundscape: Our Sonic Environment and the Tuning of the World* (New York: Simon and Schuster, 1993).
22. See Steven Feld, *Sound and Sentiment: Birds, Weeping, Poetics and Song in Kaluli Expression* (Philadelphia: University of Pennsylvania Press, 1982). "I wanted to study ways [that] sound and sounding link environment, language, and musical experience and expression," Feld wrote; see Steven Feld, "From Ethnomusicology to Echo-Muse-Ecology: Reading R. Murray Schafer in the Papua New Guinea Rainforest," *Soundscape Newsletter* 8 (June 1994), https://static1.squarespace.com/static/545aad98e4b0f1f9150ad5c3/t/5465b2bee4b0c4e0caea1605/1415951038575/1993+From+Ethnomusicology+to.pdf.
23. Feld sees his anthropological work in this way: "Our ultimate concern is with people, with adequately and evocatively representing their experiential worlds, their voices, their humanity . . . But deep down we hope that by writing and circulating other peoples' histories, by giving their voices places to speak and shout and sing from, we in some measure combat and counter the longstanding arrogance of colonial and imperial authority, of history written in one language, in one voice, as one narrative." See Feld, "From Ethnomusicology to Echo-Muse-Ecology."
24. Toni Morrison, *Beloved* (New York: Vintage International, 2004 [1987]), 43.
25. Messud, "At the Border of the Novel."
26. Ann Brigham, *American Road Narratives: Reimagining Mobility in Literature and Film* (Charlottesville: University of Virginia Press, 2015), 4. Mobility, in this context, is the "central geographical fact of American life, one that distinguishes

3. MIGRANT SOLIDARITY

Euro-Americans from their European ancestors . . . While Europe had developed through time and in a limited space and had thus become overcrowded and despotic, America could simply keep expanding west." Timothy Cresswell, *On the Move: Mobility in the Modern Western World*, as quoted in Brigham, *American Road Narratives*, 7.

27. Brigham, *American Road Narratives*, 3.
28. Brigham, *American Road Narratives*, 14.
29. Cresswell, as quoted in Brigham, *American Road Narratives*, 7.
30. Farah Griffin, *"Who Set You Flowin'?" The African-American Migration Narrative* (New York: Oxford University Press, 1995). See also John Haber, "Two Nations," HaberArts, 2014, https://www.haberarts.com/evans2.htm. Below a photograph of an American man, whom they had picked up hitchhiking, Ilf and Petrov wrote: "One of our passengers, an out-of-work fellow from Texas. He has a little Indian blood. It's enough to have one drop of Negro blood to ruin a person's entire life. A dash of Indian blood is less destructive."
31. As quoted in James Maher, "A Foreigner's Road Trip—Robert Frank's America," James Mayer Photography, 2017, https://jamesmaherphotography.com/new-york-historical-articles/the-foreigners-road-trip-robert-franks-america/.
32. Quoted in Maher, "A Foreigner's Road Trip."
33. "Domineering edifices loom high within these photographs, invasive roads often divide the frame; oversized billboards fill the skies, and brightly colored cars roam freely throughout the land." Aaron Schuman, "An Autobiography of Seeing: Stephen Shore's Uncommon Places," *Modern Painters* (Spring 2004), available at https://aaronschuman.com/shorearticle.html.
34. James Wood, "Writing About Writing About the Border Crisis," *New Yorker*, February 2, 2019, https://www.newyorker.com/magazine/2019/02/04/writing-about-writing-about-the-border-crisis.
35. The surname Camposanto means "burial ground" in Spanish and Italian and, as Claire Messud notes, it might also refer to W. G. Sebald's posthumous collection of essays, *Campo Santo*. See Messud, "At the Border of the Novel." The reference to Sebald would be apt, for he is, "above all else, an elegist. His lost men, emigrants and wandering solitaries tell of lives ended abruptly or displaced by the inexorable forces of history over which they have no control. Many of the people he writes about exist now only in photographs or as names on gravestones and memorials." Hamish Hamilton, "Notes from a Time Traveller," *Guardian*, February 27, 2005, https://www.theguardian.com/books/2005/feb/27/travel.travelbooks.
36. As Yogita Goyal might argue, this is the twenty-first-century version of what occurred in the eighteenth and nineteenth centuries when slave narrators made use of classic texts in the European tradition to narrate their fugitive subjectivity and thus make it "familiar" to their readers. See Yogita Goyal, *Runaway Genres: The Global Afterlives of Slavery* (New York: New York University Press, 2019).
37. William Golding, *Lord of the Flies* (1954); Cormac McCarthy, *The Road* (2006). Juan Rulfo's novel *Pedro Páramo* (1955) is about a man named Juan Preciado who travels to his recently deceased mother's hometown, Comala, to find his father, only to come across a literal ghost town. See Wood, "Writing About Writing About the Border Crisis."

3. MIGRANT SOLIDARITY

38. As Luiselli notes, Pound's "Canto I" is itself a kind of appropriation, since it is "a *free* translation from Latin, and not from Greek, into English, following Anglo-Saxon accentual verse metrics, of Book XI of the *Odyssey*" (*LCA*, 358).
39. Luiselli lists all the exact lines or words alluded to, and their sources, in a "Works Cited" section in the novel (*LCA*, 357–361).
40. Brian Pijanowski, Luis J. Villanueva-Rivera, Sarah L. Dumyahn, Almo Farina, Bernie L. Krause, Brian M. Napoletano, Stuart H. Gage, and Nadia Pieretti, "Soundscape Ecology: The Science of Sound in the Landscape," *BioScience* 61, no. 3 (March 2011): 203.
41. James F. Knapp, *Ezra Pound* (Boston: G. K. Hall, 1979), 137. "Pound combines borrowings from Homer, the Provençal poet Arnaut Daniel, the history of the Italian Renaissance, President John Adams, Robert Browning, and Chinese poetry . . . with offbeat economic and social theories to relate what he calls 'the tale of the tribe,' that is, the intellectual life of the human race, exemplified in certain key historical or literary moments." Pericles Lewis, *The Cambridge Introduction to Modernism* (New York: Cambridge University Press, 2007), 147.
42. I. A. Richards, as quoted in Lewis, *The Cambridge Introduction to Modernism*, 130.
43. Brett Edward Whalen, review of *The Children's Crusade: Medieval History, Modern Mythistory*, by Gary Dickson, *Reviews in History* (July 2009), https://reviews.history.ac.uk/review/785.
44. Whalen, review of *The Children's Crusade*.
45. Marcel Schwob, *The Children's Crusade*, trans. Kit Schulter (Cambridge, MA: Wakefield Press, 2018 [1896]), 15. The original French text's emphasis on whiteness matches that of the translation; see *La Croisade des Enfants*, La bibliothèque électronique du Québec, https://beq.ebooksgratuits.com/vents/Schwob-croisade.pdf.
46. Schwob, *The Children's Crusade*, 8–9, 44, 8, 39, 19, 20.
47. Schwob, *The Children's Crusade*, 27, 44, 47, 50.
48. See Alan M. Kraut, *Silent Travelers: Germs, Genes, and the "Immigrant Menace"* (Baltimore, MD: Johns Hopkins University Press, 1994).
49. "They just think it's funny. They just do it long enough so everyone can hear, and then we all start laughing." Dan Barry, Miriam Jordan, Annie Correal, and Manny Fernandez, "Cleaning Toilets, Following Rules: A Migrant Child's Days in Detention," *New York Times*, July 14, 2018, https://www.nytimes.com/2018/07/14/us/migrant-children-shelters.html.
50. Wood, "Writing About Writing About the Border Crisis."
51. Wood, "Writing About Writing About the Border Crisis."
52. John B. Vickery, *The Prose Elegy: An Exploration of Modern American and British Fiction* (Baton Rouge: Louisiana State University Press, 2009), 2, 7.
53. Eileen Battersby, "The Triumph of Memory: On Daša Drndić's 'Belladonna,'" *Los Angeles Review of Books*, June 29, 2018, https://lareviewofbooks.org/article/the-triumph-of-memory-on-dasa-drndics-belladonna/. Like *Lost Children Archive*, *Belladonna* is a "densely intertextual, self-referential historical metafiction." See Michele Levy, "*Belladonna* by Daša Drndić," *World Literature Today*, January 2018, https://www.worldliteraturetoday.org/2018/january/belladonna-dasa-drndic.
54. *The Gates of Paradise* was originally published in Polish as *Bramy raju* (1960). I am working from its Spanish translation by Sergio Pitol, *Las Puertas Del Paraíso*

(Valencia: Pre-Textos, 2004), which is also the version Luiselli used. All translations from Spanish to English are mine.
55. See review of "The Gates of Paradise (1960, by Jerzy Andrzejewski, Translated by James Kirkup)," Mimic Hootings, November 28, 2017, https://mimichootings.word press.com/2017/11/28/the-gates-of-paradise-1960-jerzy-andrzejewski-translated -by-james-kirkup/.
56. Review of "The Gates of Paradise."
57. Andrzejewski, *Las Puertas*, 29.
58. Wang, "Valeria Luiselli."
59. Wang, "Valeria Luiselli."
60. Wang, "Valeria Luiselli."
61. Nathaniel Mackey, "Sound and Sentiment, Sound and Symbol," in *Conversant Essays: Contemporary Poets on Poetry*, ed. James McCorkle (Detroit, MI: Wayne State University Press, 1990), 195.
62. Harry Harootunian, "Remembering the Historical Present," *Critical Inquiry* 33 (Spring 2007): 472.
63. Harootunian, "Remembering the Historical Present," 472.
64. Harootunian, "Remembering the Historical Present," 474.
65. Messud, "At the Border of the Novel."
66. Ann Laura Stoler, *Duress: Imperial Durabilities in Our Time* (Durham, NC: Duke University Press, 2016), Kindle edition, loc. 116. See also the chapter "Colonial Aphasia: Disabled Histories and Race in France."
67. "The US-Mexico border has long existed as an unspoken space of exception where human and constitutional rights are suspended in the name of security. Border crosser deaths are justified by a person's lack of citizenship (i.e., exceptional status), his or her commission of a civil offense, and the hypocritical desire to protect the United States." Jason De León, *The Land of Open Graves: Living and Dying on the Migrant Trail* (Oakland: University of California Press, 2015), 68.
68. "What physically happens to the bodies of the people killed by nature and left to decompose in its embrace? What can animals scavenging a corpse tell us about the political nature of migrant fatalities? . . . I argue that the unique deaths that border crossers experience and the ways nature affects their bodies are a form of postmortem violence that developed out of the underlying logic of Prevention Through Deterrence." De León, *The Land of Open Graves*, 72.

4. CARCERAL MIGRATION: JULIE OTSUKA'S INTERNMENT NOVELS

1. Julie Otsuka, *When the Emperor Was Divine* (New York: Knopf, 2002), 48. All subsequent citations to this work will be made parenthetically in the main text.
2. Josephine Park, "Alien Enemies in Julie Otsuka's *When the Emperor Was Divine*," *Modern Fiction Studies* 59, no. 1 (Spring 2013): 135.
3. "Briefly Noted: *When the Emperor Was Divine*," *New Yorker*, October 28, 2002, https://www.newyorker.com/magazine/2002/10/28/when-the-emperor-was -divine.

4. Namwali Serpell, "The Banality of Empathy," *New York Review of Books*, March 2, 2019, https://www.nybooks.com/online/2019/03/02/the-banality-of-empathy/.
5. David Manuel Hernández, "Carceral Shadows: Entangled Lineages and Technologies of Migrant Detention," in *Caging Borders and Carceral States: Incarcerations, Immigration Detentions, and Resistance*, ed. Robert T. Chase (Chapel Hill: University of North Carolina Press, 2019), 57.
6. Hernández, "Carceral Shadows," 58.
7. Hernández, "Carceral Shadows," 58.
8. Dominique Moran, "'Doing Time' in Carceral Space: TimeSpace and Carceral Geography," *Geografiska Annaler. Series B, Human Geography* 94, no. 4 (2012): 309.
9. Andrew Duncan, "Julie Otsuka, Interview," IndieBound, https://www.indiebound.org/author-interviews/otsukajulie, accessed on September 27, 2022.
10. This is partly because, like other Japanese Americans who experienced internment, her family "didn't talk about the internment much," while her "grandfather's FBI file . . . was not too revealing. Which makes sense," she adds, "since not a single Japanese or Japanese-American in this country was ever found guilty of espionage or sabotage." Duncan, "Julie Otsuka, Interview."
11. See Mieke Bal, "Migratory Aesthetics: Double Movement," *Exit* 32 (2008): 156.
12. John Streamas writes, "In early 1942, in a rush to prepare Japanese Americans for their evacuation and imprisonment, the government and military cobbled together several explanatory and instructional pamphlets and short films. The earliest materials called the camps 'colonies' and Japanese Americans 'colonists' . . . The government called Japanese Americans 'pioneers' and the camps their 'frontier.'" John Streamas, "Frontier Mythology, Children's Literature, and Japanese American Incarceration," as quoted in Stephen Hong Sohn, "These Desert Places: Tourism, the American West, and the Afterlife of Regionalism in Julie Otsuka's *When the Emperor Was Divine*," *Modern Fiction Studies* 55, no. 1 (Spring 2009): 179. Emily Hiramatsu Morishima writes, "Initially, the prevailing opinion of the internment during the buildup to the 1942 evacuation order and the early years of WWII was that the removal of Japanese Americans from society was necessary to protect the public from acts of sabotage by Japanese Americans, who were too foreign, not 'real' Americans, and loyal to Japan. Following government public relations efforts to humanize Japanese Americans and prove their loyalty to America in preparation for their eventual release into the outside world, public perception of the camps began to shift gradually; instead of protecting the public, the camps were viewed as protecting Japanese Americans from racism in the outside world, while also having the added benefit of Americanizing them . . . Even as late as the 1990s, there were still many people who asserted that the internment was for the good of Japanese Americans." Emily Hiramatsu Morishima, "Remembering the Internment in Post–World War II Japanese Fiction" (PhD diss., University of California, Los Angeles, 2010), 15–16.
13. Greg Robinson, "Writing the Internment," in *The Cambridge Companion of Asian American Literature*, ed. Crystal Parikh and Daniel Y. Kim (New York: Cambridge University Press, 2015), 49–50. For a list of literary works, including memoirs, novels, poems, and plays, on internment, see Stan Yogi, "Literary Works on Incarceration," *Densho Encyclopedia*, November 14, 2015, https://encyclopedia.densho.org/Literary%20works%20on%20incarceration.

4. CARCERAL MIGRATION

14. Robinson, "Writing the Internment," 49.
15. Robinson, "Writing the Internment," 48.
16. Patricia Wakida, "*Desert Exile* (book)," *Densho Encyclopedia*, February 2, 2018, https://encyclopedia.densho.org/Desert_Exile_(book)/.
17. Robinson, "Writing the Internment," 56.
18. Guterson was able to quit his job as a teacher and dedicate himself full-time to writing after the success of his novel.
19. Robinson, "Writing the Internment," 56.
20. "A 2019 survey of diversity in publishing found that 78 percent of executives, 85 percent of editors, 80 percent of critics and 80 percent of agents are white." Reyna Grande, "'American Dirt' Has Us Talking. That's a Good Thing," *New York Times*, January 30, 2020, https://www.nytimes.com/2020/01/30/opinion/sunday/american-dirt-book-mexico.html. See also Richard Jean So, *Redlining Culture: A Data History of Racial Inequality and Postwar Fiction* (New York: Columbia University Press, 2020).
21. Deborah Nelson, *Tough Enough: Arbus, Arendt, Didion, McCarthy, Sontag, Weil* (Chicago: University of Chicago Press, 2017).
22. Cordelia Palitz, "Q&A with Julie Otsuka," *Student Life*, Washington University of St. Louis, September 16, 2009, https://www.studlife.com/news/2009/09/16/qa-with-julie-otsuka/.
23. Amanda Geller, "Short Takes," *Boston Globe*, October 13, 2002.
24. See Morishima, "Remembering the Internment in Post–World War II Japanese Fiction," 66–68. Morishima attributes the aesthetic choice to Otsuka's "universalism."
25. Serpell, "The Banality of Empathy."
26. "An Interview with Julie Otsuka," BookBrowse, 2002, https://www.bookbrowse.com/author_interviews/full/index.cfm/author_number/807/Julie-Otsuka.
27. Patricia Nelson Limerick, *The Legacy of Conquest: The Unbroken Past of the American West* (New York: Norton, 1987), 18–19.
28. Hong Sohn, "These Desert Places," 175.
29. Tanforan was "one of seventeen temporary detention camps established by the U.S. Army to hold Japanese Americans forcibly removed from the West Coast until more permanent concentration camps could be constructed." For more information about the Tanforan camp, please see, "Tanforan (detention facility)," *Densho Encyclopedia*, January 5, 2021, https://encyclopedia.densho.org /Tanforan_(detention_facility)/.
30. Sandra C. Taylor, *Jewel of the Desert: Japanese American Internment at Topaz* (1993), as quoted in Hong Sohn, "These Desert Places," 173.
31. Hong Sohn, "These Desert Places," 171–172.
32. Hong Sohn, "These Desert Places," 176.
33. Hong Sohn, "These Desert Places," 176.
34. The idea of "scrims" or "latticework" that can hang over the imagination as we read comes from Elaine Scarry's *Dreaming by the Book* (Princeton, NJ: Princeton University Press, 2001), 177.
35. Morishima, "Remembering the Internment in Post–World War II Japanese Fiction," 75.
36. "Topaz History," Topaz Museum, https://topazmuseum.org/topaz-history/, accessed on September 27, 2022.
37. Moran, "'Doing Time' in Carceral Space," 309.

38. Moran, "'Doing Time' in Carceral Space," 309.
39. Moran, "'Doing Time' in Carceral Space," 310.
40. Park, "Alien Enemies in Julie Otsuka's *When the Emperor Was Divine*," 139.
41. Park, "Alien Enemies in Julie Otsuka's *When the Emperor Was Divine*," 142.
42. Park, "Alien Enemies in Julie Otsuka's *When the Emperor Was Divine*," 135–136.
43. Park, "Alien Enemies in Julie Otsuka's *When the Emperor Was Divine*," 137.
44. Morishima, "Remembering the Internment in Post–World War II Japanese Fiction," 67.
45. Emiko Ohnuki-Tierney, "The Emperor of Japan as Deity (Kami)," *Ethnology* 30, no. 3 (July 1991): 212.
46. The novel's title also invokes Japan's own imperial expansion. Occurring from the late nineteenth century through the end of World War II, that expansion killed or deracinated people on a massive scale across Japan's colonies. Min Jin Lee's novel *Pachinko* (2017) dramatizes how a family from one such colony (Korea) is forced to migrate (to Japan and later to Europe and America) because of Japan's expansion, suffering bigotry, economic oppression, and alienation. Published in the United States, *Pachinko* broadens the scale of migration narratives by vivifying imperial rule and forced migration in a context other than the United States or Europe.
47. Park, "Alien Enemies in Julie Otsuka's *When the Emperor Was Divine*," 137.
48. Mae M. Ngai, *Impossible Subjects: Illegal Aliens and the Making of Modern America* (Princeton, NJ: Princeton University Press, 2004).
49. "An Interview with Julie Otsuka."
50. Michiko Kakutani, "War's Outcasts Dream of Small Pleasures," *New York Times*, September 10, 2002, https://www.nytimes.com/2002/09/10/books/books-of-the-times-war-s-outcasts-dream-of-small-pleasures.html.
51. "An Interview with Julie Otsuka."
52. As Issei, the parents could not have become citizens even if they had wanted to, until 1952, when the U.S. Senate and House voted to ratify the McCarran-Walter Act, allowing Japanese immigrants to become naturalized U.S. citizens.
53. While Otsuka concentrates on Japanese picture brides in California, many Japanese and Korean picture brides also came to other regions on the West Coast, as well as to Hawaii and Canada.
54. Julie Otsuka, *The Buddha in the Attic* (New York: Knopf, 2011), 30. All subsequent citations to this work will be made parenthetically in the main text.
55. Ron Charles, "Julie Otsuka's 'The Buddha in the Attic,'" *Washington Post*, November 16, 2011, https://www.washingtonpost.com/entertainment/books/julie-otsukas-the-buddha-in-the-attic-reviewed-by-ron-charles/2011/11/08/gIQAHxqhPN_story.html.
56. Mako Yoshikawa, "The Things They Left Behind: *The Buddha in the Attic* by Julie Otsuka," *Women's Review of Books* 29, no. 1 (January/February 2012): 18.
57. Yoshikawa, "The Things They Left Behind," 18.
58. Yoshikawa, "The Things They Left Behind," 18.
59. Yoshikawa, "The Things They Left Behind," 18.
60. Charles, "Julie Otsuka's 'The Buddha in the Attic.'"
61. Charles, "Julie Otsuka's 'The Buddha in the Attic.'"
62. Yoshikawa, "The Things They Left Behind," 18.

5. APOCALYPSE AND TOXICITY

63. See the acknowledgment page in *The Buddha in the Attic*. The first study "to offer a sociological/historical perspective on these women" was published in 1986. See Evelyn Nakano Glenn, *Issei, Nisei, War Bride: Three Generations of Japanese American Women in Domestic Service* (Philadelphia: Temple University Press, 1986). An oral history of picture wives in Hawaii was published in 2016; see Barbara Kawakami, *Picture Bride Stories*, Latitude 20 (Honolulu: University of Hawai'i Press, 2016).
64. Otsuka does not "give voice" to the silenced but instead creates something like Saidiya Hartman's "critical fabulation" (though the historical record of immigrants, unlike the archive of slavery with which Hartman works, does include some firsthand accounts from migrants like those Otsuka writes about). In "Venus in Two Acts," Hartman argues for historical speculation, or "critical fabulation" as she calls it, as a way of speculating about the inaccessible, silenced voices of the past, to "tell an impossible story" while simultaneously acknowledging the "impossibility of its telling." Saidiya Hartman, "Venus in Two Acts," *Small Axe* 26, no. 12 (June 2008): 11.
65. Charles, "Julie Otsuka's 'The Buddha in the Attic.'"
66. Serpell, "The Banality of Empathy."
67. "Whether cited as a cautionary tale, terrible mistake, or logical outcome," Josephine Park notes, "internment is, over and again, an example." Park, "Alien Enemies in Julie Otsuka's *When the Emperor Was Divine*," 135.
68. Nicole Waller, "Terra Incognita: Mapping the Detention Center in Edwidge Danticat's *Brother, I'm Dying* and the US Supreme Court Ruling *Boumediene v. Bush*," *Atlantic Studies* 6, no. 3 (2009): 359. See also Matthew Hart, *Extraterritorial: A Political Geography of Contemporary Fiction* (New York: Columbia University Press, 2020).
69. Waller, "Terra Incognita," 359.

5. APOCALYPSE AND TOXICITY: JUNOT DÍAZ'S MIGRANT AESTHETICS

1. "Junot Diaz and Hilton Als Talk Masculinity, Science Fiction, and Writing as an Act of Defiance: A Conversation from *Upstairs at the Strand*," Literary Hub, March 18, 2016, https://lithub.com/junot-diaz-hilton-als-talk-masculinity-science-fiction-and-writing-as-an-act-of-defiance/.
2. A recent article reveals that the allegations against Díaz were not "considered charges of sexual misconduct at all" by the law firm assigned to examine them. See Ben Smith, "Junot Díaz in Limbo," *Semafor*, November 27, 2022, https://www.semafor.com/article/11/27/2022/junot-diaz-in-limbo.
3. Junot Díaz, "The Silence: The Legacy of Childhood Trauma," *New Yorker*, April 9, 2018, https://www.newyorker.com/magazine/2018/04/16/the-silence-the-legacy-of-childhood-trauma. See also Lila Shapiro, "Misogyny Is Boring as Hell," *Vulture*, June 2018, https://www.vulture.com/2018/06/misogyny-is-boring-carmen-maria-machado.html.
4. Linda Martín Alcoff, "This Is Not Just About Junot Díaz," *New York Times*, May 16, 2018, https://www.nytimes.com/2018/05/16/opinion/junot-diaz-metoo.html.

5. Alexandra Alter, "Junot Díaz Cleared of Misconduct by M.I.T.," *New York Times*, June 19, 2018, https://www.nytimes.com/2018/06/19/books/junot-diaz-cleared-of-misconduct-by-mit.html.
6. José David Saldívar, "Junot Díaz's Search for Decolonial Aesthetics and Love," in *Junot Díaz and the Decolonial Imagination*, ed. Monica Hanna, Jennifer Harford Vargas, and José David Saldívar (Durham, NC: Duke University Press, 2016), 325.
7. Glenda R. Carpio, "Voyaging Across Arcs: A Conversation with Junot Díaz," *ASAP/Journal* 2, no. 3 (2017): 502.
8. See Junot Díaz, *The Brief Wondrous Life of Oscar Wao* (New York: Riverhead Books, 2007), 97n. All subsequent references to this work will be made parenthetically in the main text, with the reference *OW*.
9. Jennifer Harford Vargas, "Dictating a Zafa: The Power of Narrative Form as Ruin-Reading," in Hanna, Vargas, and Saldívar, *Junot Díaz and the Decolonial Imagination*, 202. Yunior is also sly: while he narrates *The Brief Wondrous Life of Oscar Wao*, for instance, he does not reveal his identity until halfway through the novel, at which point the reader must figure out which of the two Yuniors he is. The question arises because some of the stories in *Drown* (the titular one, for instance) have nameless narrators who may or may not be the Yunior born in the United States.
10. "Junot Diaz and Hilton Als Talk Masculinity, Science Fiction, and Writing as an Act of Defiance."
11. Carpio, "Voyaging Across Arcs," 502.
12. *Drown* culminates with the story "Negocios," which imagines the life of Ramón de las Casas after he has abandoned his wife, Virta, in the Dominican Republic with their children, Yunior and Rafa. Virta writes letters pleading with her husband to come back, while he returns to the United States, struggles to find shelter and work, and eventually decides to marry Nilda, another Dominican immigrant who is a U.S. citizen. Ramón then fathers another Yunior with her. "Invierno" and "Otravida, Otravez," in *This Is How You Lose Her*, offer a follow-up and a second iteration of that story, respectively. In "Invierno," Yunior recounts how his father, having returned to the Dominican Republic to get his first family, settles with them in New Jersey. "Otravida, Otravez," which is narrated from the point of view of a woman named Yasmin, tells the story of a man also named Ramón de las Casas who has abandoned a family in the Dominican Republic but does *not* return to get them; instead, he buys a home and fathers a child with Yasmin. The title of the story, which means "Another Life, Another Time," captures the intertextual fluidity of Díaz's short fiction.
13. As José David Saldívar shows in *Junot Díaz: On the Half-Life of Love* (Durham, NC: Duke University Press, 2022), these intertextual connections have their roots partly in the fact that Díaz drafted many of the stories published in *This Is How You Lose Her* during his MFA years at Cornell.
14. Ross Scarano, "Interview: Junot Díaz Talks Dying Art, the Line Between Fact and Fiction, and What Scares Him Most," *Complex*, December 17, 2012, https://www.complex.com/pop-culture/2012/12/junot-diaz-interview.
15. Díaz told an audience member during the Hals interview: "If I ever write my next book in this series, Yunior will tell that story again," referring to the "foundational myth" of his and his family's immigration story. See "Junot Diaz and Hilton Als Talk Masculinity, Science Fiction, and Writing as an Act of Defiance."

16. The fact that "the most punishing climate horrors will indeed hit those least able to respond" is called "the problem of environmental justice," but it should be called the "climate caste system," as I have done here, for the poor, in countries both poor and rich, are relegated to the "marshes, the swamps, the floodplains, the inadequately irrigated places with the most vulnerable infrastructure... Just in Texas, 500,000 poor Latinos live in shantytowns called 'colonias' with no drainage systems to deal with increased flooding." See David Wallace-Wells, *The Uninhabitable Earth: Life After Warming* (New York: Duggan Books, 2019), 24.
17. Richard Patteson, "Textual Territory and Narrative Power in Junot Díaz's *The Brief Wondrous Life of Oscar Wao*," *Ariel: A Review of International English Literature* 42, no. 3–4 (2012): 8.
18. A. O. Scott, "Dreaming in Spanglish," *New York Times*, September 30, 2007, https://www.nytimes.com/2007/09/30/books/review/Scott-t.html.
19. Paula Moya, "The Search for Decolonial Love: A Conversation Between Junot Díaz and Paula M. L. Moya," in Hanna, Vargas, and Saldívar, *Junot Díaz and the Decolonial Imagination*, 396–397.
20. Moya, "The Search for Decolonial Love," 397. For an extended discussion of decolonial love in Díaz's oeuvre, see chap. 5 of Saldívar, *Junot Díaz: On the Half-Life of Love*.
21. Jennifer Hartford Vargas defines *zafar* as "'to let go of' or 'to release from'...'to liberate one's self from harm.'" See Vargas, "Dictating a Zafa," 204.
22. That pleasure recalls Ishmael Reed's in his novel *Mumbo Jumbo* (1972), which pits "the Wallflower Order," an international conspiracy obsessed with power and profit, against "Jes Grew," a fluid, hybrid, collaborative, decentralized, infectious phenomenon with no true definition, a sort of "anti-plague" that moves people to free forms of expression. The infection starts in colored ghettos and has its source in black culture (but even this is rendered in loose terms, for, like Topsy—who in *Uncle Tom's Cabin* is described as having grown just like a weed, since she had no parents or guardians—the virus "jes grew"). It soon moves across racial divides and threatens to dismantle a world order forged upon the backs of the poor, the dispossessed, and the dark.
23. See, for instance, Katherine Weese, "'Tú no Eres Nada de Dominicano': Unnatural Narration and De-Naturalizing Gender Constructs in Junot Díaz's *The Brief Wondrous Life of Oscar Wao*," *Journal of Men's Studies* 22, no. 2 (Spring 2014): 93.
24. Monica Hanna, "A Portrait of the Artist as a Young Cannibalist: Reading Yunior (Writing) in *The Brief Wondrous Life of Oscar Wao*," in Hanna, Vargas, and Saldívar, *Junot Díaz and the Decolonial Imagination*, 94. Yunior's cannibalizing of Oscar's story might also dramatize a point that Díaz has made about the pariah-like relationship between "many Latinos and black writers who are writing to white audiences, who are not writing to their own people," and the communities that they draw upon to make their art; they "loot them of ideas, and words, and images," Díaz argues, in order to "coon them to the dominant group." See Diógenes Céspedes and Silvio Torres-Saillant, "Fiction Is the Poor Man's Cinema: An Interview with Junot Díaz," *Callaloo* 23, no. 3 (Summer 200): 900.
25. Vargas, "Dictating a Zafa," 202.
26. See Glenda R. Carpio, "'Am I Dead?': Slapstick Antics and Dark Humor in Contemporary Immigrant Fictions," *Critical Inquiry* 43, no. 3 (January 2017): 358.

5. APOCALYPSE AND TOXICITY

27. Patteson, "Textual Territory and Narrative Power in Junot Díaz's *The Brief Wondrous Life of Oscar Wao*," 12.
28. Yunior's last name, de las Casas, speaks to his role as the narrator because it recalls that of Bartolomé de las Casas, a chronicler of the Spanish Conquest who was critical of the Spaniards' cruelty toward indigenous peoples. While originally advocating for the use of enslaved Africans to spare indigenous people, he eventually rejected that position and became an advocate for the end of slavery in the Americas.
29. Danny Méndez, *Narratives of Migration and Displacement in Dominican Literature* (New York: Routledge, 2012), 127, as quoted in Ylce Irizarry, "This Is How You Lose It: Navigating Dominicanidad in Junot Díaz's *Drown*," in Hanna, Vargas, and Saldívar, *Junot Díaz and the Decolonial Imagination*, 156. I drafted this chapter during the Trump presidency, when these words attained an echoing effect.
30. See Erin Blakemore, "The Shocking Photo of 'Whipped Peter' That Made Slavery's Brutality Impossible to Deny," History.com, November 22, 2022, https://www.history.com/news/whipped-peter-slavery-photo-scourged-back-real-story-civil-war. The photograph was taken on April 2, 1863, in Baton Rouge, Louisiana.
31. Díaz's choice of the word "ruination" recalls Michelle Cliff's novel *No Telephone to Heaven* (1987), in which the word also figures prominently. A novel about a mixed-race Jamaican family who immigrates to the United States, *No Telephone to Heaven* similarly explores the intersection of immigration and race in the United States in the context of Caribbean history.
32. Werner Sollors, *Beyond Ethnicity: Consent and Descent in American Culture* (New York: Oxford University Press, 1987), 5–6.
33. Junot Díaz, "Homecoming, with Turtle," *New Yorker*, June 14, 2004, https://www.newyorker.com/magazine/2004/06/14/homecoming-with-turtle.
34. Díaz, "Homecoming, with Turtle."
35. Junot Díaz, *This Is How You Lose Her* (New York: Riverhead Books, 2012), 9. All subsequent references to this work will be made parenthetically in the main text, with the reference *TH*.
36. Díaz deliberately makes Magda Cuban, showing how, among dispersed Caribbeans, the region can stand in for the nation.
37. Carpio, "Voyaging Across Arcs," 499.
38. Carpio, "Voyaging Across Arcs," 506.
39. Carpio, "Voyaging Across Arcs," 499. Designated under the Comprehensive Environmental Response, Compensation, and Liability Act (CERCLA) of 1980, Superfund sites are part of a program that has had more success in raising environmental awareness than in "cleaning up toxic sites and making corporate polluters pay." See Jon Hurdle, "After 40 Years, Superfund Program in NJ Is Still Work in Progress," *NJ Spotlight News*, April 22, 2020, https://www.njspotlightnews.org/2020/04/after-40-years-superfund-program-in-nj-is-still-work-in-progress/.
40. "Permian Extinction," *Encyclopedia Britannica*, September 8, 2022, https://www.britannica.com/science/Permian-extinction.
41. Alexander Koch, Chris Brierley, Mark Maslin, and Simon Lewis, "European Colonisation of the Americas Killed 10% of World Population and Caused Global Cooling," *The Conversation*, January 31, 2019, https://theconversation.com/european-colonisation-of-the-americas-killed-10-of-world-population-and-caused-global

5. APOCALYPSE AND TOXICITY

-cooling-110549. See also, David Stannard, *American Holocaust: The Conquest of the New World* (New York: Oxford University Press, 1992).
42. Koch et al., "European Colonisation."
43. Simon Lewis and Mark Maslin, "Anthropocene Began with Species Exchange Between Old and New Worlds," *The Conversation*, March 11, 2015, https://theconversation.com/anthropocene-began-with-species-exchange-between-old-and-new-worlds-38674. See also Simon Lewis and Mark Maslin, "Defining the Anthropocene," *Nature* 519 (2015): 171–180.
44. Lewis and Maslin, "Defining the Anthropocene," 177.
45. There has been a vibrant debate not only over how to date the beginning of the Anthropocene but over the adequacy of the term itself. As Janae Davis et. al. argues, "Anthropocene is clearly not the product of 'human nature,' or humanity as a whole, but rather interrelated historical processes set in motion by a small minority." See also Janae Davis, Alex A. Moulton, Levi Van Sant, and Brian Williams, "Anthropocene, Capitalocene, . . . Plantationocene? A Manifesto for Ecological Justice in an Age of Global Crises," *Geography Compass* 13, no. 5 (May 2019), https://doi.org/10.1111/gec3.12438.
46. Kathryn Yusoff, "Preface," *A Billion Black Anthropocenes or None* (Minneapolis: University of Minnesota Press, 2018). Available at: https://manifold.umn.edu/read/6b94c453-792a-4a6e-8aea-5a2c8c8155bd/section/b17181bd-c615-4a1b-8cb1-5c0fa03afd74#pref.
47. Yusoff, "Preface."
48. Dana Luciano, "The Inhuman Anthropocene," *Los Angeles Review of Books*, March 22, 2015, https://avidly.lareviewofbooks.org/2015/03/22/the-inhuman-anthropocene/.
49. Junot Díaz, "Apocalypse: What Disasters Reveal," *Boston Review*, May 1, 2011. Reprinted in *Utne Reader: The Best of the Alternative Press* (September–October 2011): 50. All subsequent citations refer to the *Utne Reader* version of the essay.
50. Díaz, "Apocalypse," 52.
51. Díaz, "Apocalypse," 51.
52. Díaz, "Apocalypse," 53.
53. Díaz, "Apocalypse," 51.
54. Díaz, "Apocalypse," 52.
55. In my conversation with Díaz, he described "Central Jersey," where he grew up, as "very Smithson" and identified Smithson's essay specifically as an influence. See Carpio, "Voyaging Across Arcs," 499, 497.
56. Robert Smithson, "A Tour of the Monuments of Passaic, New Jersey" (1967), http://pdf-objects.com/files/Essay_Robert-Smithson-A-Tour-of-the-Monuments-of-Passaic.pdf. Originally published as "The Monuments of Passaic," *Artforum*, December 1967, 52–57.
57. Smithson, "A Tour of the Monuments of Passaic, New Jersey," 3–4.
58. Andrew Menard, "Robert Smithson's Toxic Tour of Passaic, New Jersey," *Journal of American Studies* 48, no. 4 (November 2014): 1029.
59. Menard, "Robert Smithson's Toxic Tour of Passaic, New Jersey," 1019, 1021. The idea of America as Eden has had purchase since at least the so-called discovery of the New World. See also William Cronon, "The Trouble with Wilderness; or, Getting

5. APOCALYPSE AND TOXICITY

Back to the Wrong Nature," in *Uncommon Ground: Rethinking the Human Place in Nature* (New York: W. W. Norton, 1995), 69–90.
60. Menard, "Robert Smithson's Toxic Tour of Passaic, New Jersey," 1029.
61. Menard, "Robert Smithson's Toxic Tour of Passaic, New Jersey," 1024–1025.
62. Menard, "Robert Smithson's Toxic Tour of Passaic, New Jersey," 1029, 1031.
63. Smithson, "A Tour of the Monuments of Passaic, New Jersey," 2.
64. Menard, "Robert Smithson's Toxic Tour of Passaic, New Jersey," 1038.
65. Robert Smithson, *The Collected Writings*, ed. Jack Flam (Berkeley: University of California Press, 1996), 165, as quoted in Menard, "Robert Smithson's Toxic Tour of Passaic, New Jersey," 1022.
66. Junot Díaz, *Drown* (New York: Riverhead Books, 1996), 195. All subsequent references to this work will be made parenthetically in the main text, with the reference *Drown*.
67. See Hurdle, "After 40 Years, Superfund Program in NJ Is Still Work in Progress."
68. Lori M. Hunter, "The Spatial Association Between U.S. Immigrant Residential Concentration and Environmental Hazards," *International Migration Review* 34, no. 2 (Summer 2000): 460. See also Ricardo Rubio, Sara Grineski, Timothy Collins, and Danielle X. Morales, "Ancestry-Based Intracategorical Injustices in Carcinogenic Air Pollution Exposures in the United States," *Society and Natural Resources* 33, no. 8 (August 2020): 987–1005.
69. Carpio, "Voyaging Across Arcs," 506.
70. Edwidge Danticat, "The Long Legacy of Occupation in Haiti," *New Yorker*, July 28, 2015, https://www.newyorker.com/news/news-desk/haiti-us-occupation-hundred-year-anniversary.
71. Michele Wucker, *Why the Cocks Fight: Dominicans, Haitians, and the Struggle for Hispaniola* (New York: Hill and Wang, 1999), 43, as quoted in Danticat, "The Long Legacy of Occupation in Haiti." See also Aida Alami, "Between Hate, Hope, and Help: Haitians in the Dominican Republic," *New York Review of Books*, August 13, 2018, https://www.nybooks.com/online/2018/08/13/between-hope-hate-help-haitians-in-the-dominican-republic/.
72. Lorgia García Peña, "One Hundred Years After the Occupation," North American Congress on Latin America, May 25, 2016, https://nacla.org/news/2016/05/25/one-hundred-years-after-occupation.
73. Rory Fanning, "LBJ's Other War," *Jacobin*, April 28, 2015, https://jacobin.com/2015/04/dominican-republic-occupation-united-states-1965/.
74. His mother's rage and sorrow are only hinted at but remain a subtle constant, barely accessible to young Yunior. Meanwhile, "Negocios" shows us what the absent father might be doing in the United States—he is twenty-four, working menial jobs, living in roach-infested places: the "roaches were so bold in his flat that turning on the lights did not startle them. They waved their three-inch antennas as if to say, Hey puto, turn that shit off" (*Drown*, 179). Unable, and perhaps unwilling, to face his family in the Dominican Republic, he views his life in the United States as a chance to run away but is haunted by guilt. Thus, both Yunior's father and the United States itself represent false promises.
75. "El Cuco," Guide to the Colonial Zone and the Dominican Republic, https://www.colonialzone-dr.com/el-cuco/, accessed on September 27, 2022.

5. APOCALYPSE AND TOXICITY

76. Sonia Shah, *The Next Great Migration: The Beauty and Terror of Life on the Move* (New York: Bloomsbury, 2020), 188.
77. Shah, *The Next Great Migration*, 214.
78. Shah, *The Next Great Migration*, 215.
79. Shah, *The Next Great Migration*, 178.
80. Shah, *The Next Great Migration*, 184.
81. Shah, *The Next Great Migration*, 184.
82. Shah, *The Next Great Migration*, 184.
83. See Alan M. Kraut, *Silent Travelers: Germs, Genes, and the "Immigrant Menace"* (Baltimore, MD: Johns Hopkins University Press, 1995).
84. Díaz, "Apocalypse," 51.
85. Díaz, "Apocalypse." Díaz here quotes sociologist Jan Nederveen Pieterse, "Global Inequities: Bringing Politics Back In," *Third World Quarterly* 23, no. 6 (2002): 1022–1023.
86. Díaz, "Apocalypse," 53.
87. Cressida Leyshon, "This Week in Fiction: Junot Díaz," *New Yorker*, May 27, 2012, https://www.newyorker.com/books/page-turner/this-week-in-fiction-junot-daz-2.
88. Junot Díaz, "Monstro," *New Yorker*, June 4, 2012, https://www.newyorker.com/magazine/2012/06/04/monstro. All subsequent references to the story are to this version of the text.
89. García Peña, "One Hundred Years After the Occupation." See also Alami, "Between Hate, Hope, and Help." Alami writes: "For decades, Haitians living in a country struck by natural disasters and shaken by political instability have looked for work in the Dominican Republic, where a healthier economy and more robust economic growth—and, in turn, a need for low-waged Haitian labor—has created openings. Controlling the movement of people across the border has historically been a challenge for the authorities, as it is relatively easy for Haitians to bribe Dominican border guards to get to the other side. Inside the Dominican Republic, though, Haitians have long suffered abuses. In recent years, thousands have been pressured to leave voluntarily or have been forcibly deported, including documented cases of people of Haitian descent who were actually born in the Dominican Republic."
90. Alami, "Between Hate, Hope, and Help."
91. Alami, "Between Hate, Hope, and Help."
92. Sarah Quesada, "A Planetary Warning? The Multilayered Caribbean Zombie in 'Monstro,'" in Hanna, Vargas, and Saldívar, *Junot Díaz and the Decolonial Imagination*, 307, 309.
93. Quesada, "A Planetary Warning?," 291.
94. Wallace-Wells, *The Uninhabitable Earth*, 7. In a review of Sonia Shah's *The Next Great Migration*, Richard O. Prum tellingly equates human migration with colonization. Criticizing Shah for not addressing "the enormous ecological impact that human migration has already had on the planet," he cites the paleontologist David Steadman, who "has estimated that human colonization of the Pacific Ocean islands between 1,000 and 5,000 years ago resulted in the extinction of approximately 2,000 species of birds—one-fifth of the world's populations. This scale of human-mediated ecological devastation cannot be dismissed as inconsequential." While Prum is right

in arriving at this conclusion, his claim that colonization and human migration are one and the same obfuscates the fact that colonization *causes* human migration and ecological damage. See Richard O. Prum, "Birds Do It. People, Too. Is Migration Simply Natural for All Species?" *New York Times*, June 2, 2020, https://www.nytimes.com/2020/06/02/books/review/next-great-migration-sonia-shah.html.
95. Rob Nixon, *Slow Violence and the Environmentalism of the Poor* (Cambridge, MA: Harvard University Press, 2011).
96. Díaz, "Apocalypse," 54.
97. Díaz, "Apocalypse," 54.
98. Leyshon, "This Week in Fiction: Junot Díaz."

6. CARCERAL MIGRATION II: THE FLORES DECLARATIONS AND EDWIDGE DANTICAT'S *BROTHER, I'M DYING*

1. Jorge Barrera, "How a 35-Year-Old Case of a Migrant Girl from El Salvador Still Fuels the Border Debate," CBC Radio, June 28, 2019, https://www.cbc.ca/radio/day6/detained-migrant-children-resident-orcas-stranger-things-stonewall-at-50-and-more-1.5192640/how-a-35-year-old-case-of-a-migrant-girl-from-el-salvador-still-fuels-the-border-debate-1.5192662.
2. "The History of the Flores Settlement and Its Effects on Migration," NPR, June 22, 2018, https://www.capradio.org/news/npr/story?storyid=622678753.
3. Barrera, "How a 35-Year-Old Case of a Migrant Girl from El Salvador Still Fuels the Border Debate."
4. Veronica Stracqualursi, Geneva Sands, Elizabeth Elkin, and Veronica Rocha, "What Is the Flores Settlement That the Trump Administration Has Moved to End?" CNN, August 23, 2019, https://edition.cnn.com/2019/08/21/politics/what-is-flores-settlement/index.html.
5. The William Wilberforce Trafficking Victims Protection Reauthorization Act (TVPRA) was signed by President George W. Bush. See "Trafficking Victims Protection Reauthorization Act Safeguards Children," National Immigration Forum, May 23, 2018, https://immigrationforum.org/article/trafficking-victims-protection-reauthorization-act-safeguards-children/.
6. Stracqualursi et al., "What Is the Flores Settlement That the Trump Administration Has Moved to End?"
7. Matt Sussis, "The History of the *Flores* Settlement," Center for Immigration Studies, February 11, 2019, https://cis.org/Report/History-Flores-Settlement. "Aliens respond to incentives," further wrote Sussis, assistant director of communications at the Center for Immigration Studies. "*Flores* remains a strong one. After all, if a Central American mother knows that bringing her child means that she can simply show up at a port of entry, claim credible fear, and then quickly be released from detention into the country regardless of the actual validity of her asylum claim, why wouldn't she do so?"
8. Quoted in Elizabeth B. Wydra, Brianne J. Gorod, and Dayna Zolle, "*Flores v. Rosen*," Constitutional Accountability Center, https://www.theusconstitution.org/litigation/flores-v-rosen/, accessed on September 27, 2022.

9. For an explanation of how TRO declarations fit in the Flores case, see "Flores Plaintiffs Seek TRO," Legal NewsRoom, LexisNexis, June 28, 2019, https://www.lexisnexis.com/legalnewsroom/immigration/b/insidenews/posts/flores-plaintiffs-seek-tro.
10. Ruth Noack, curator, "Art Exhibition: When We First Arrived . . .," The Corner at Whitman-Walker, Washington, DC, January 25–March 29, 2020, https://whitmanwalkerimpact.org/2020/02/20/art-exhibition-when-we-first-arrived/. See also "Child Migrants Speak Truth to Power," Project Amplify, https://www.project-amplify.org/declarations.
11. Caitlin Dickerson, "'There Is a Stench': Soiled Clothes and No Baths for Children at a Texas Center," *New York Times*, June 21, 2019, https://www.nytimes.com/2019/06/21/us/migrant-children-border-soap.html.
12. Maria Sacchetti, "ICE's Chief Called Family Detention 'Summer Camp.' Here's What It Looks Like Inside," *Washington Post*, August 25, 2019, https://go.gale.com/ps/i.do?p=AONE&sw=w&issn=&v=2.1&it=r&id=GALE%7CA597423258&sid=googleScholar&linkaccess=abs&userGroupName=anon%7Ea64ac47c.
13. Caitlin Dickerson, "Despite Warnings, Trump Moves to Expand Migrant Family Detention," *New York Times*, December 9, 2019, https://www.nytimes.com/2019/12/09/us/migrant-family-detention-border.html.
14. Reilley Frye, "Family Separation Under Trump's Administration: Applying an International Law Framework," *Journal of Criminal Law and Criminology* 110, no. 2 (2020): 351.
15. "HHS OIG: Many Children Separated from Parents, Guardians Before *Ms. L. v. Ice* Court Order and Some Separations Continue," Office of Inspector General, U.S. Department of Health and Human Services, January 17, 2019, https://oig.hhs.gov/newsroom/news-releases/2019/uac.asp.
16. Noack, "Art Exhibition: When We First Arrived . . ."
17. "*Jenny L. Flores v. William P. Barr*," Network for Public Health Law, https://www.networkforphl.org/resources/jenny-l-flores-v-william-p-barr/, accessed on September 27, 2022.
18. See Project Amplify. DYKWTCA (Do You Know Where the Children Are?), an organization led by the artists and activists Mary Ellen Carroll and Lucas Michael, curated an art exhibition of over one hundred unique artworks that each incorporated or represented an actual account (in whole or in part) from an unaccompanied child detained by the U.S. government. The profits from the sale of the artworks were used to support advocacy of the children's human rights. See Noack, "Art Exhibition: When We First Arrived . . ."
19. Project Amplify, Temporary Restraining Order (TRO) Declarations, Children, June 2019, https://www.project-amplify.org/declarations. Unless otherwise noted, all subsequent citations of the sworn statements are from this source and will be cited parenthetically in the main text. "There are several required elements of a sworn statement that ensure that the statement will be accepted as a legal document. First, it is imperative that a sworn statement be as detailed as possible, and written in the first-person. Exaggerations and opinions should be left out. All a statement should consist of is straight facts, including events listed chronologically. The person writing the statement should use his full, legal name, and he should date the

document with the date he signs it." See "Sworn Statement," *Legal Dictionary*, February 17, 2017, https://legaldictionary.net/sworn-statement/.
20. Matthew Hart, *Extraterritorial: A Political Geography of Contemporary Fiction* (New York: Columbia University Press, 2020), 228.
21. Nicole Waller, "Terra Incognita: Mapping the Detention Center in Edwidge Danticat's *Brother, I'm Dying* and the US Supreme Court Ruling *Boumediene v. Bush*," *Atlantic Studies* 6, no. 3 (2009): 359.
22. There are exceptions. Under U.S. law, some unaccompanied children from Canada or Mexico can be deported upon apprehension at the border.
23. Aura Bogado, "The Disappeared," *Reveal*, February 18, 2020, https://revealnews.org/article/the-disappeared/.
24. Andrea Castillo, "With or Without Criminal Records, Some Immigrants Spend Many Years in Detention," *Los Angeles Times*, November 12, 2018, https://www.latimes.com/local/lanow/la-me-immigrant-detainees-20181112-story.html.
25. "Child Migrants Speak Truth to Power."
26. Carlo Foppiano Palacios, Elizabeth W. Tucker, and Mark A. Travassos, "Coronavirus Disease 2019 Burden Among Unaccompanied Minors in US Custody," *Clinical Infectious Diseases*, August 5, 2022, ciac636, https://doi.org/10.1093/cid/ciac636. Since "the extent of disease among children under the care of the Office of Refugee Resettlement (ORR) has not been well-documented," the figures reported by the Center for Disease Control and Prevention may be higher. See also Jennifer L. Siegel, "The COVID-19 Pandemic: Health Impact on Unaccompanied Migrant Children," *Social Work* 67, no. 3 (July 2022): 218–227, https://doi-org.ezp-prod1.hul.harvard.edu/10.1093/sw/swac014.
27. Dana Nickel, "Who Profits from Migrant Detention in the U.S.?" *Globe Post*, August 19, 2019, https://theglobepost.com/2019/08/19/profit-migrant-detention/.
28. "Unites States Immigration Detention Profile," Global Detention Project, May 2016, https://www.globaldetentionproject.org/wp-content/uploads/2016/06/us_2016.pdf, 6.
29. Quoted in Susan Tamasi and Lamont Antieau, *Language and Linguistic Diversity in the US: An Introduction* (New York: Routledge, 2014), 201.
30. In 1946, for instance, the School of the Americas (SOA) was formed at Fort Benning, Georgia. SOA is "a U.S. military program (still in effect) to exert imperialistic influence over Latin America and train Latin American soldiers in counterinsurgency, counterterrorism, anti-communism, torture, and surveillance techniques. Former Panamanian president Jorge Illueca has called SOA, which has trained over 60,000 foreign soldiers, the 'biggest base for destabilization in Latin America.' It is estimated that hundreds of thousands of Latin Americans have been forcibly displaced by the effects of this program." See "A Short History of Immigrant Detention," Freedom for Immigrants, https://www.freedomforimmigrants.org/detention-timeline, accessed on September 27, 2022.
31. See Marian L. Smith, "Race, Nationality, and Reality: INS Administration of Racial Provisions in U.S. Immigration and Nationality Law Since 1898," *Prologue Magazine* 34, no. 2 (Summer 2002), https://www.ilw.com/articles/2003,0616-smith.shtm. Matthew Frye Jacobson argues that whiteness has been historically a shifting category. Jewish people of diverse nationalities, as well as Irish people, Italians, and Slavs, were not originally categorized as white in America. See Matthew Frye Jacobson,

Whiteness of a Different Color: European Immigrants and the Alchemy of Race (Cambridge, MA: Harvard University Press, 1998).

32. Margot Canaday shows how homosexuality was policed indirectly through the exclusion of sexually "degenerate" immigrants and other regulatory measures aimed at combating poverty, violence, and vice. See Margot Canaday, *The Straight State: Sexuality and Citizenship in Twentieth Century America* (Princeton, NJ: Princeton University Press, 2009).
33. See Douglas S. Massey and Karen A. Pren, "Unintended Consequences of US Immigration Policy: Explaining the Post-1965 Surge from Latin America," *Population and Development Review* 38, no. 1 (2012): 1–29.
34. Josephine Park, "Alien Enemies in Julie Otsuka's *When the Emperor Was Divine*," *Modern Fiction Studies* 59, no. 1 (Spring 2013): 139.
35. Kelly Lopez, "A Brief History of Latino Immigration to the United States," in *The American Latino: Psychodynamic Perspectives on Culture and Mental Health*, ed. Salma Akhtar and Solange Margery Bertoglia (New York: Rowman and Littlefield, 2015), 18.
36. Laurent Dubois, "How Will Haiti Reckon with the Duvalier Years?," *New Yorker*, October 6, 2014, https://www.newyorker.com/news/news-desk/will-haiti-reckon-duvalier-years.
37. "The first office for federal immigration control in the United States was established in 1864. However, it was not until the Immigration Act of 1882, which provided that immigration regulation was the responsibility of the federal government, that operations at the office began in earnest." "United States Immigration Detention Profile," 3. A similar facility opened on Angel Island in the San Francisco Bay in 1910. By the 1950s, detention of immigrants there was deemed inhumane; the American government released immigrants to wait inside the country while their cases were being processed.
38. Carl Lindskoog, "How the Haitian Refugee Crises Led to the Indefinite Detention of Immigrants," *Washington Post*, April 9, 2018, https://www.washingtonpost.com/news/made-by-history/wp/2018/04/09/how-the-haitian-refugee-crisis-led-to-the-indefinite-detention-of-immigrants/.
39. Lindskoog, "How the Haitian Refugee Crises Led to the Indefinite Detention of Immigrants."
40. CCA, which rebranded itself as CoreCivic in 2016 as a response to ongoing scrutiny of the private prison industry, was the first to enter into a contract with the federal government for an immigration detention facility in Texas. It has been cited numerous times for abuses in its prisons.
41. The Antiterrorism and Effective Death Penalty Act (AEDPA) "required the mandatory detention of non-citizens convicted of a wide range of offenses, including minor drug offenses." The Illegal Immigration Reform and Immigrant Responsibility Act of 1996 (IIRIRA) "expanded the list of offenses for which mandatory detention was required," as well as the definition of "aggravated felonies," to include even misdemeanors under state law. See "Analysis of Immigration Detention Policies," American Civil Liberties Union (ACLU), https://www.aclu.org/other/analysis-immigration-detention-policies, accessed on September 27, 2022. "These laws can be applied retroactively, and also impose 3-year, 10-year, and lifetime bars on returning to the U.S. after deportation." See "A Short History of Immigration Detention."

42. Livia Luan, "Profiting from Enforcement: The Role of Private Prisons in U.S. Immigration Detention," *Migration Information Source*, Migration Policy Institute, May 2, 2018, https://www.migrationpolicy.org/article/profiting-enforcement-role-private-prisons-us-immigration-detention.
43. "According to a 2014 study on the history of immigration control policies in the United States, between 1986 and 2012, the United States spent some $187 billion on immigration enforcement. In 2012, the government spent nearly $18 billion on enforcement, 'approximately 24 percent higher than collective spending for the FBI, Drug Enforcement Administration, Secret Service, U.S. Marshals Service and Bureau of Alcohol, Tobacco, Firearms and Explosives.'" See "United States Immigration Detention Profile," 1–2.
44. "The old system of giving migrants alternatives to detention (such as ankle bracelets, the equivalent of parole officers, or just a pledge to show up) cost just $4 a day, while housing them temporarily in local jails cost about $100." See "The Private Prison Industry, Explained," *The Week*, August 6, 2018, https://theweek.com/articles/788226/private-prison-industry-explained.
45. "The Private Prison Industry, Explained."
46. "United States Immigration Detention Profile," 12.
47. "The Private Prison Industry, Explained."
48. "CoreCivic Inc PAC Contributions to Federal Candidates, 2017–2018," Open Secrets, 2018, https://www.opensecrets.org/political-action-committees-pacs//C00366468/candidate-recipients/2018.
49. Jeff Sommer, "Trump Immigration Crackdown Is Great for Private Prison Stock," *New York Times*, March 10, 2017, https://www.nytimes.com/2017/03/10/your-money/immigrants-prison-stocks.html.
50. Miriam Jordan, "Inspectors Find Nooses in Cells at Immigration Detention Facility," *New York Times*, October 2, 2018, https://www.nytimes.com/2018/10/02/us/oig-inspector-general-adelanto-immigrants-nooses.html.
51. "Over 90% of CCA and GEO's stock is owned by institutional investors such as banks, mutual funds and private equity firms—which often invest without their clients knowing where their money is being invested ... Targeting institutional shareholders for divestment has, therefore, become a growing trend." Joe Watson, "Corporations, Colleges and Cities Dump Private Prison Stock," *Prison Legal News*, October 3, 2016, 48, https://www.prisonlegalnews.org/news/2016/oct/3/corporations-colleges-and-cities-dump-private-prison-stock/.
52. Nickel, "Who Profits from Migrant Detention in the U.S.?"
53. Alex Altman and Elizabeth Dias, "This Baptist Charity Is Being Paid Hundreds of Millions to Shelter Child Migrants," *Time*, August 4, 2014, https://time.com/3066459/unaccompanied-minor-immigration-border/.
54. Meghan B. Kelly and Laney Ruckstuhl, "Wayfair Employees Protest Sale of Furniture to Migrant Detention Center," NPR, June 26, 2019, https://www.npr.org/2019/06/26/736308620/wayfair-employees-protest-sale-of-furniture-to-migrant-detention-center.
55. "Krome's broad medical care is horrendous. In addition to being fed terrible food—high-calorie-and-starch institutional fare with little to no nutritional value—detainees face long waits to see doctors and are rarely provided medicines other than Tylenol or other over-the-counter painkillers." Ken Silverstein, "Shock Corridor: The First

Inside Report from an ICE Mental-Health Facility," *New Republic*, August 19, 2019, https://newrepublic.com/article/154616/immigration-customs-enforcement-krome-miami-mental-health-facility-investigation.
56. Jess Row, "Haitian Fathers," *New York Times*, September 9, 2007, https://www.nytimes.com/2007/09/09/books/review/Row-t.html.
57. Nick DiMartino, "Book Review: *Brother, I'm Dying*," Shelf Awareness, September 14, 2007, https://www.shelf-awareness.com/issue.html?issue=516#m3401.
58. Michiko Kakutani, "A Haitian Tragedy: Brothers Yearn in Vain," *New York Times*, September 4, 2007, https://www.nytimes.com/2007/09/04/books/04dant.html.
59. Edwidge Danticat, *Brother, I'm Dying* (New York: Vintage, 2007), 171. All subsequent references to this work will be made parenthetically in the main text.
60. Kevin Moran and Azadeh Shahshahani, "Haiti: US Interference Wins Elections," *The Hill*, October 13, 2015, https://thehill.com/blogs/congress-blog/foreign-policy/256679-haiti-us-interference-wins-elections/.
61. Kakutani, "A Haitian Tragedy."
62. Review of *Brother, I'm Dying*, by Edwidge Danticat, *Publishers Weekly*, September 2007, https://www.publishersweekly.com/978-1-4000-4115-2.
63. Terry Hong, "Review: Edwidge Danticat's 'Brother, I'm Dying,' a Memoir on Death," *SF Gate*, October 9, 2007, https://www.sfgate.com/books/article/Review-Edwidge-Danticat-s-Brother-I-m-Dying-a-2536196.php.
64. Row, "Haitian Fathers."
65. Row, "Haitian Fathers."
66. Silverstein, "Shock Corridor."
67. As quoted in Rose Marie Berger, "Death by Asylum," *Sojourners Magazine* 37, no. 4 (April 2008): 36.
68. Waller, "Terra Incognita," 357–358.
69. As quoted in Waller, "Terra Incognita," 359.
70. Waller, "Terra Incognita," 361.
71. Waller, "Terra Incognita," 362.
72. Waller, "Terra Incognita," 357.
73. Waller, "Terra Incognita," 357–358.
74. Mae M. Ngai, *Impossible Subjects: Illegal Aliens and the Making of Modern America* (Princeton, NJ: Princeton University Press, 2004), 4.
75. Ngai, *Impossible Subjects*, 8.

EPILOGUE: "CHINGA LA MIGRA"—KARLA CORNEJO VILLAVICENCIO'S *THE UNDOCUMENTED AMERICANS*

1. Karla Cornejo Villavicencio, *The Undocumented Americans* (New York: One World, 2020), xiv. All subsequent references to this work will be made parenthetically in the main text.
2. Alexia Arthurs, "A Book About Undocumented Americans That Doesn't Pander to White Expectations," Electric Lit, April 28, 2020, https://electricliterature.com/a-book-about-undocumented-americans-that-doesnt-pander-to-white-expectations/.
3. Andrea Gonzàlez-Ramirez, "'The Undocumented Americans' Is the Immigration Punk Manifesto We Need Today," GEN, March 23, 2020, https://gen.medium.com

/the-undocumented-americans-is-the-immigration-punk-manifesto-we-need-today-f09e01636952.
4. Myriam Gurba, "Why Karla Cornejo Villavicencio's 'The Undocumented Americans' Is a Hardcore Masterpiece," Remezcla, May 28, 2020, https://remezcla.com/features/culture/karla-cornejo-villavicencio-the-undocumented-americans-review-and-interview/.
5. Lucas Iberico Lozada, "Karla Cornejo Villavicencio: DREAMer Memoirs Have Their Purpose. But That's Not What I Set Out to Write," *Guernica*, June 10, 2020, https://www.guernicamag.com/karla-cornejo-villavicencio-dreamer-memoirs-have-their-purpose-but-thats-not-what-i-set-out-to-write/.
6. Gurba, "Why Karla Cornejo Villavicencio's 'The Undocumented Americans' Is a Hardcore Masterpiece."
7. Caitlin Dickerson, "This Is the Face of an Undocumented Migrant. Don't Look Away," *New York Times*, March 24, 2020, https://www.nytimes.com/2020/03/24/books/review/the-undocumented-americans-karla-cornejo-villavicencio.html.
8. Natasha Walter, "The Undocumented Americans by Karla Cornejo Villavicencio Review—Hidden Lives and Human Rights," *Guardian*, June 6, 2020, https://www.theguardian.com/books/2021/jun/06/the-undocumented-americans-by-karla-cornejo-villavicencio-review-hidden-lives-and-human-rights.
9. Walter, "The Undocumented Americans by Karla Cornejo Villavicencio Review."
10. Iberico Lozada, "Karla Cornejo Villavicencio."
11. As quoted in Arthurs, "A Book About Undocumented Americans That Doesn't Pander to White Expectations."
12. Walter, "The Undocumented Americans by Karla Cornejo Villavicencio Review."
13. Walter, "The Undocumented Americans by Karla Cornejo Villavicencio Review."
14. Gonzàlez-Ramirez, "'The Undocumented Americans' Is the Immigrant Punk Manifesto We Need Today."
15. Arthurs, "A Book About Undocumented Americans That Doesn't Pander to White Expectations."
16. In an interview that I conducted with Cornejo Villavicencio, she spoke of Didion as a writer she reads for style, not for political insight, adding that she does not find Didion's reportage, especially in the essays on Central America, particularly illuminating. Interview with the author, May 9, 2021.
17. Arthurs, "A Book About Undocumented Americans That Doesn't Pander to White Expectations."
18. In *The Undocumented Americans*, Cornejo Villavicencio recounts how she raised funds to help children who are left without family breadwinners, and of the mentoring relationship that she and her partner developed with two teenage girls in circumstances like her own.
19. Iberico Lozada, "Karla Cornejo Villavicencio."
20. Praise for Julissa Arce, *My (Underground) American Dream*, Center Street, https://www.centerstreet.com/titles/julissa-arce/my-underground-american-dream/9781455540266/, accessed on September 28, 2022.
21. Dickerson, "This Is the Face of an Undocumented Migrant."
22. Walter, "The Undocumented Americans by Karla Cornejo Villavicencio Review."

23. In an interview, Cornejo Villavicencio stated that she knew, "despite [her] reluctance, this imprint *had* to market [her book in this way], because we needed to sell books." See Iberico Lozada, "Karla Cornejo Villavicencio."
24. Concepción de León, "'I Came from Nothing': An Undocumented Writer Defies the Odds," *New York Times*, October 21, 2020, https://www.nytimes.com/2020/10/21/books/karla-cornejo-villavicencio-undocumented-americans.html.
25. Iberico Lozada, "Karla Cornejo Villavicencio." For an extended definition of the genre, see Laura Webb, "Testimonio: The Assumption of Hybridity and the Issue of Genre," *Studies in Testimony* 2, no. 1 (2019): 3–23, https://studiesintestimony.co.uk/issues/volume-two-issue-one-2019/testimonio-the-assumption-of-hybridity-and-the-issue-of-genre/#easy-footnote-bottom-2-886.
26. Parul Sehgal, "A Mother and Son, Fleeing for Their Lives Over Treacherous Terrain," *New York Times*, January 17, 2020, https://www.nytimes.com/2020/01/17/books/review-american-dirt-jeanine-cummins.html.
27. Myriam Gurba, "Pendeja, You Ain't Steinbeck: My Bronca with Fake-Ass Social Justice Literature," Tropics of Meta, December 12, 2019, https://tropicsofmeta.com/2019/12/12/pendeja-you-aint-steinbeck-my-bronca-with-fake-ass-social-justice-literature/.
28. Gurba, "Pendeja, You Ain't Steinbeck."
29. Sehgal, "A Mother and Son, Fleeing for Their Lives Over Treacherous Terrain."
30. Opheli Garcia Lawler, "'American Dirt' and the Frustrating Use of Mexican Migrants as Props," Mic, January 22, 2020, https://www.mic.com/p/american-dirt-the-frustrating-use-of-mexican-migrants-as-props-21738411.
31. *The American Dirt* controversy died down a year later. While it invigorated the ongoing critique of the racial and class inequalities of the literary world—see Richard So's *Redlining Culture: A Data History of Racial Inequality and Postwar Fiction* (New York: Columbia University Press, 2020)—it also exposed the American appetite for comforting myths about migration to the United States (in Cummins's novel it is portrayed as a "magnetic sanctuary"). See also Gurba, "Why Karla Cornejo Villavicencio's 'The Undocumented Americans' Is a Hardcore Masterpiece."
32. Sehgal, "A Mother and Son, Fleeing for Their Lives Over Treacherous Terrain."
33. Karla Cornejo Villavicencio, as quoted in Arthurs, "A Book About Undocumented Americans That Doesn't Pander to White Expectations."
34. Valeria Luiselli, *Tell Me How It Ends: An Essay in Forty Questions* (Minneapolis, MN: Coffee House Press, 2017), 30.

INDEX

Abu Ghraib prison, 82–83
acculturation: *The Buddha in the Attic* (Otsuka) and, 131; Hemon and, 68, 71, 74–76; *How to Read the Air* (Mengestu) and, 7–8; immigrant literature and, 3–4, 14–15, 16–18, 233; in *The Lazarus Project* (Hemon), 74–76, 83–84; *The Melting Pot* (Zangwill) and, 88; as necessary condition for integration, 47; "A Report for an Academy" (Kafka) and, 1–2, 4–5, 31
Adams, Robert, 107, 108
Addams, Jane, 69
Adichie, Chimamanda Ngozi, 18
aesthetics, 15–16. *See also* migrant aesthetics
Affordable Care Act (ACA, 2010), 231
Afropolitanism, 34–36, 37, 66
After the End (Berger), 177
Against Empathy (Bloom), 9
"Aguantando" (Díaz), 182–84
Alameddine, Rabih, 30–31
Alami, Aida, 191, 263n89
Albence, Matthew, 197
Alien and Sedition Acts (1798), 69–70

aliens: immigration laws and, 17; Japanese Americans as, 137–38, 146–48; undocumented children as, 95, 117; U.S.-Asian conflicts and, 209–10
All Our Names (Mengestu): child-soldier narratives and, 46–47; immigrant literature and, 18–19; metafiction in, 8, 220; migrants as traumatized figures in, 65–66; point of view of the "native" in, 20, 53, 155–56; rejection of autobiography and, 48, 222; rites of burial in, 228; strategic anonymity in, 37–47; writing in, 43, 47–50
Als, Hilton, 159, 258n15
Álvarez, Gregorio, 229
Amazon, 212
American Civil Liberties Union (ACLU), 195–96
American Colonization Society, 61
American Dirt (Cummins), 233–34
American Migrant Fictions (Weiner), 23
American Photographs (Evans), 107–8
American Photographs (Ilf and Petrov), 107–8

INDEX

Americanization, 3–4, 18, 22, 83–84, 233. *See also* acculturation
Americans, The (Frank), 108
Amin, Idi, 37
Anam, Nasia, 66
anarchism, 26, 69–70, 76, 80–82
Anarchist Exclusion Act (1903), 70
Andrzejewski, Jerzy, 110–11, 114, 115, 119–20, 121
anonymity. *See* strategic anonymity
Anthropocene, 24, 162, 174, 175–76, 186
Antin, Mary, 16–17, 18
Antiterrorism and Effective Death Penalty Act (1996), 211
Apache people, 104, 105, 108, 119
apocalypse, 24, 162–63, 164, 174–81, 187–94
"Apocalypse: What Disasters Reveal" (Díaz), 176–78, 181, 188–89, 192–93
Appiah, Kwame Anthony, 36
Arbus, Diane, 134–35
Arce, Julissa, 232
archives, 109–10, 112, 118–19, 122–27
Arendt, Hannah: on "facing reality," 11, 15, 25, 120; on representative thinking, 8–9, 91–94, 136, 235; unsentimentality and, 134–35
Argentina, 229
Aristide, Jean-Bertrand, 215
arms trade, 98
Artforum (magazine), 178
Asociación Tepeyac, 227–28
Asselin, Michele, 198
assimilation: Cole and, 38–39; Díaz and, 160, 164; Flores declarations and, 200–201; Hemon and, 73, 74–76; immigrant literature and, 16–17, 31, 126; Mengestu and, 38–39; Otsuka and, 130, 146, 152, 157, 199–200; Sommer on, 12
Austerlitz (Sebald), 244n50
autobiography: *All Our Names* (Mengestu) and, 48, 222; *Brother, I'm Dying* (Danticat) and, 29, 199, 219–20, 222; Díaz's fiction and, 160–62, 169; Flores Agreement and, 200–204; Hemon and, 71–72; *How to Read the Air* (Mengestu) and, 7–8; immigrant literature and, 14–15, 16–17, 21; migrant aesthetics and, 13, 222–24; Nabokov and, 71–72; *Open City* (Cole) and, 64, 222; Otsuka's novels and, 130–31, 134; *Tell Me How It Ends* (Luiselli) and, 100–101; *The Undocumented Americans* (Cornejo Villavicencio) and, 221–24
autofiction, 109
Averbuch, Lazarus: in *The Lazarus Project* (Hemon), 68–69, 70–71, 74–81, 84–88; murder of, 68–70; photographs of, 70, 77–79, 78, 82–83, 87
Averbuch, Olga: in *The Lazarus Project* (Hemon), 76–80, 86; life of, 69, 70, 247n37

Bahadur, Gaiutra, 95
Bal, Mieke, 23–24, 132
Balaguer, Joaquín, 183
Baldwin, James, 15–16
"Banality of Empathy, The" (Serpell), 9, 12, 91–92, 93, 129, 136, 153
Bannon, Steve, 188
Barrera, Jorge, 195
Batson, C. Daniel, 11
BCFS (Baptist Child and Family Services), 212
Belgium, 55–56, 64–65
Belladonna (Drndić), 110, 118–19
Beloved (Morrison), 105, 171
Bercovitch, Sacvan, 84
Berger, James, 177
Berlant, Lauren, 11, 20
Beyond Ethnicity (Sollors), 17, 22, 171
Biden administration (2021–), 213
Billion Black Anthropocenes or None, A (Yusoff), 175
Blackrock, 212
Bloom, Paul, 9–10, 31
Boelhower, William Q., 16
Bosnian war (1992–1995), 68, 70–71, 81, 83–88
Boukman, Dutty, 60
Bowie, David, 109

INDEX

Božović, Velibor, 71, 87
Bracero Program, 209
Brecht, Bertolt, 93, 115
Brewster, John, Jr., 51, 54
Brief Wondrous Life of Oscar Wao, The (Díaz): apocalyptic historical events in, 162–63; decolonial love in, 166, 216, 229; environmental toxicity in, 181; final chapter of, 193–94; narrative style of, 165–66; refraction in, 162–64; toxic colonial violence in, 166–67, 169–71, 182, 184–85; toxic masculinity in, 167–68, 169–71, 173; writing in, 41, 164–65, 168–69
Brother, I'm Dying (Danticat), 199, 213–20, 222
Brower, David, 187
Brown, Wendy, 20
brownface, 233–34
Brussels, 38, 52, 55–56, 64–65, 244n50
Buddha in the Attic, The (Otsuka): carceral migration and, 148, 155–58, 199; choral or collective narration in, 130–31, 148–53, 155, 199–200, 220, 224; sources of, 152; strategic anonymity in, 131, 148–53, 199, 220; white Americans in, 153–56
Bulawayo, NoViolet, 18
Bureau of Customs and Border Protections, 218
Burke, Kenneth, 15
Bush administration (2001–2009), 147, 178, 211, 264n5
Butler, Octavia, 51–52
Byrne, Monica, 159

Calvino, Italo, 42
Camp of the Saints, The (Raspail), 187–88
Campo Santo (Sebald), 251n35
Canaday, Margot, 267n32
Cane (Toomer), 107–8
Cantos (Pound), 111, 113, 114, 122
carceral migration: concept of, 14, 129–30; *The Buddha in the Attic* (Otsuka) and, 155–58; children in detention centers and, 157–58; Flores declarations and, 198–99, 200, 204–6;

in *The Undocumented Americans* (Cornejo Villavicencio), 229–30; *When the Emperor Was Divine* (Otsuka) and, 128–31, 132, 140–47, 157–58, 198, 199–200, 204, 205–6, 229–30
Carroll, Mary Ellen, 265n18
Carter administration (1977–1981), 210
Cartwright, Rosalind Dymond, 10
Caruth, Cathy, 20
Casas, Bartolomé de las, 260n28
Castro, Fidel, 210
Center for Human Rights and Constitutional Law, 195–96
Center for Immigration Studies, 187, 196
character anonymization. *See* strategic anonymity
Charles, Ron, 50, 149, 151, 152–53, 155
Cheney, Dick, 120
Cheney, Lynne, 120
Chicago Daily News (newspaper), 78, 82, 246n25
Chicago Tribune (newspaper), 69, 80, 86
children in detention centers: carceral migration and, 157–58; Flores Agreement and, 195–207, 201, 216; photographs of, 198; Trump administration and, 196–98; in *When the Emperor Was Divine* (Otsuka), 128. *See also Lost Children Archive* (Luiselli); *Tell Me How It Ends* (Luiselli)
Children of the Land (Hernandez Castillo), 232
Children's Crusade, 110, 115–17, 119–20
Children's Crusade, The (Schwob), 110–11, 114, 115–17, 119
child-soldier narratives, 46–47
Chinese immigrants, 17, 151, 209
choral narration: concept and role of, 13, 160, 200–201; in *The Buddha in the Attic* (Otsuka), 130–31, 148–53, 155, 199–200, 220, 224; in Díaz's fiction, 163; in Flores declarations, 198, 202–4; in Luiselli's writing, 113; in *The Undocumented Americans* (Cornejo Villavicencio), 224–25, 228–32

Christie, Agatha, 115
CIA, 62, 98
Cisneros, Sandra, 233
Citizen 13660 (Okubo), 132–33
City in the Sun (Kehoe), 133
Civil Liberties Act (1988), 132
Clemmons, Zinzi, 159
Cleveland, Ohio, 222
Cliff, Michelle, 260n31
climate change, 98–99, 162–63, 164, 174–80, 192, 231
Clinton administration (1993–2001), 126, 211
Coffee House Press, 99
Cole, Teju: Afropolitanism and, 36, 66; new immigrant literature and, 18; as "time witness," 192. See also *Open City* (Cole)
collective narration. See choral narration
colonialism: Brussels and, 55–56, 64–65; climate change and, 175–76; legacy and effects of, 24–25; in *Lost Children Archive* (Luiselli), 114–17; migrant aesthetics and, 14; migration from Africa and, 34–36; toxic masculinity and, 159–60; toxic violence of, 163–64, 166–67, 169–71, 184–85; *When the Emperor Was Divine* (Otsuka) and, 139–40. See also neocolonialism
Columbia University, 99, 207, 212
Comprehensive Environmental Response, Compensation, and Liability Act (CERCLA) (1980), 260n39
Congo, 6, 34, 56, 60, 65
Conrad, Joseph, 56, 90, 110–11, 114
Constitutional Accountability Center, 196–97
CoreCivic (formerly Corrections Corporation of America, CCA), 197, 207–8, 211–12
Cornejo Villavicencio, Karla: on empathy, 234–35; as "time witness," 192; as undocumented woman, 221, 223. See also *Undocumented Americans, The* (Cornejo Villavicencio)
Corregidora (Jones), 173

Cosmopolitanism (Appiah), 36, 51
Cottrell, Leonard, 10
COVID-19 pandemic, 198, 206
Cowart, David, 21–22
creative nonfiction, 225–28
Cresswell, Timothy, 250–51n26
Cuba, 210
Cuban Refugee Program, 210
Cummins, Jeanine, 233–34

Daily Beast (news website), 221
Danticat, Edwidge, 18, 182–83, 192. See also *Brother, I'm Dying* (Danticat)
Dawes, James, 9–10
De León, Jason, 126, 253n67–68
Dear America (Vargas), 232
decolonial love, 166, 216, 229
Deferred Action for Childhood Arrivals (DACA), 221, 232
Delany, Samuel R., 181
Deleuze, Gilles, 23
Denver (Adams), 108
Department of Health and Human Services, 197–98, 204–5
Desert Exile (Uschida), 134
detention centers: in *Brother, I'm Dying* (Danticat), 199, 213, 214–15, 217–18; early history of, 208–12, 219–20; in *Open City* (Cole), 61; private prison system and, 207–8, 211–12; public interest in, 213. See also children in detention centers
Dhalgren (Delany), 181
Díaz, Junot: apocalypse and, 162–63, 164, 174–81, 188–94; autobiography and, 160–62; on decolonial love, 166, 216, 229; micro and macro historical frames and, 14; new immigrant literature and, 18; refraction and, 160–64, 173–74; short-story form and, 224; as "time witness," 192; toxic masculinity and, 159–62, 163–64, 167–68, 169–73; unrealiable narrator and, 220, 222. See also *Brief Wondrous Life of Oscar Wao, The* (Díaz); *Drown* (Díaz); *This Is How You Lose Her* (Díaz)

INDEX

Dickinson, Emily, 225
Didion, Joan, 134–35, 225–26
Dilley, Texas, 197
disability, 54
Dominican Republic, 159–60, 165–67, 169–71, 178, 182–84, 188–92, 193. *See also* Trujillo, Rafael
Douglas, Ann, 11
Douglass, Frederick, 61
Drndić, Daša, 110, 118–19
Drown (Díaz): apocalypse and, 173–74; environmental toxicity in, 180; poverty in, 182–84; refraction in, 162–64; toxic masculinity in, 167, 171–72; Yunior's father in, 167, 180, 182, 184–85, 258n12, 262n74
drug wars, 98, 202, 208, 219, 267n41, 268n43
Du Bois, W. E. B., 15–16, 193
Dubois, Laurent, 210
Duino Elegies (Rilke), 110–11
Duress (Stoler), 25
Dutch East India Company, 51–52
Duvalier, François ("Papa Doc"), 98, 163, 208, 210, 213
Duvalier, Jean-Claude ("Baby Doc"), 98, 213
DYKWTCA (Do You Know Where the Children Are?), 265n18

Eagle Warriors, 120–21
Echo Canyon (Newton), 122
Ehrlich, Anne, 187
Ehrlich, Paul, 187
Eliot, T.S., 110–11, 114–15
Ellis Island, 58, 208
Ellison, Ralph, 15–16
Emergency Quota Act (1921), 209
empathy: concept of, 9–13; *Brother, I'm Dying* (Danticat) and, 218, 220; Cornejo Villavicencio on, 234–35; Díaz's fiction and, 169–70; Flores declarations and, 200–201, *201*; "An Honest Exit" (Mengestu) and, 214; *How to Read the Air* (Mengestu) and, 7–8; immigrant literature and, 3–4, 12, 14–15, 21, 91, 199; migrant aesthetics and, 13, 160, 220; Nguyen on, 31; *Open City* (Cole) and, 52–55, 168, 169, 220; refugees and, 19–20; vs. representative thinking, 8–9; Serpell on, 9, 12, 129, 153; in *When the Emperor Was Divine* (Otsuka), 154–55
estrangement effect, 93
Evans, Walker, 107–8
extratemporality, 200

Fanning, Rory, 183
Fanon, Frantz, 66
Federation for American Immigration Reform (FAIR), 187
Feld, Steven, 104–5, 122
Felman, Shoshana, 20
Ferris, Joshua, 131
Fidelity/FMR LLC, 212
Flatiron Press, 233–34
Flint, Michigan, 222, 231
Flores, Jenny Lisette, 195–96
Flores Agreement, 195–207, *201*, 216
Flores v. Barr (2020), 197
Foley, James, 69
"1492: A New World View" (Luciano), 176
Frank, Robert, 107–8
Friedman, Susan Stanford, 23

gangs, 96–97, 101, 102, 202, 213, 215, 216, 227
García Peña, Lorgia, 183
Garden of Stones (Littlefield), 134
Gates of Paradise, The (Andrzejewski), 110, 114, 115, 119–20, 121
Geller, Amanda, 136
GEO Group, 207–8, 211–12
Geronimo, 105, 108, 119, 122, 124
Global Detention Project, 211
Globe Post (news site), 212
Golding, William, 109, 111, 115
Goldstein, Robert J., 245n6
Gómez González, Claudia, 228
Goyal, Yogita, 35, 46–47, 251n36
Graham, Donald E., 232
Great Acceleration, 175, 187

INDEX

Great Dying of indigenous peoples (1492–1600), 24, 174–75, 192. *See also* Native American forced migration and genocide
Great Dying (Permian-Triassic extinction), 174–75
Griffin, Farah, 107–8
Ground Zero (New York), 56–57, 62, 222, 229
Guardian (newspaper), 233
Guattari, Félix, 23
Guinier, Lani, 232
Gurba, Myriam, 223, 233
Guterson, David, 134

Haiti: in Díaz's writing, 188–92, 193; Duvalier family dictatorship in, 98, 163, 208, 210; independence of, 97–98; invasion of, 182–83; migration to the United States from, 98, 177–78, 208, 210; in *Open City* (Cole), 60–62. *See also Brother, I'm Dying* (Danticat)
Haiti earthquake (2010), 176–78, 188
Harootunian, Harry, 123–24
Hart, Matthew, 200
Hart-Celler Act (Immigration and Nationality Act, 1965), 33–34, 209
Hartman, Saidiya, 257n64
Harvard University, 30, 212, 221, 233, 244n42
Hearst, William Randolph, 246n28
Heart of Darkness (Conrad), 56, 110–11, 114
Hemon, Aleksandar: acculturation and, 68, 71, 74–76; autobiography and, 71–72; Bosnian war and, 70–71; on "displacement, travails, redemption, success" überplot, 159, 186; as "time witness," 192
Hernandez Castillo, Marcelo, 232
Hernández-Navarro, Miguel Á., 23–24
Hicks, Scott, 134
Himes, Chester, 133
Hirohito, Emperor of Japan, 144
Holloway, Natalee, 9–10
Holocaust, 119, 177
"Homecoming, with Turtle" (Díaz), 172–73

Homer, 54, 111, 119, 122, 252n38
"Honest Exit, An" (Mengestu), 4–7, 8, 15, 214, 220
Hong, Terry, 217
Hong Sohn, Stephen, 138, 139
How to Read the Air (Mengestu), 7–8, 20, 214
Hron, Madelaine, 15, 19, 20–21, 47
Hughes, Langston, 15–16, 43–44
Hull House, 69
human trafficking, 5, 35, 85, 196

Ickes, Harold LeClair, 69–70
Ilf, Ilya, 107–8
Illegal Immigration Reform and Immigrant Responsibility Act (1996), 211
imaginary homeland, 88, 89–90
immigrant(s): vs. refugees, 19, 47; use of term, 15
Immigrant Fictions (Walkowitz), 22–23
immigrant literature: acculturation and, 3–4, 14–15, 16–18, 233; assimilation and, 16–17, 31, 126; assimilationist phase of, 16–17; autobiography and, 14–15; empathy and, 3–4, 12, 14–15, 21, 91, 199; as evolving category, 33–36; methodological approaches to, 20–23; vs. migrant aesthetics, 16–20; multiculturalist phase of, 16–17
immigrant solidarity, 74, 87, 88–94. *See also* migrant solidarity
Immigrants' Rights Clinic (Columbia University), 207
Immigration Act (1929), 17, 208
Immigration Act (Johnson-Reed Act, 1924), 17, 209
Immigration and Customs Enforcement (ICE), 196–98, 211. *See also* detention centers; Flores Agreement
Immigration and Nationality Act (Hart-Celler Act, 1965), 33–34, 209
Immigration and Naturalization Act (1952), 208–9
Immigration and Naturalization Service (INS). *See* detention centers; Flores Agreement

INDEX

Immigration Reform Law Institute, 187
imperialism. *See* colonialism; neocolonialism
International Committee on Stratigraphy, 175
"Invierno" (Díaz), 164, 180–82, 183, 185, 258n12
Invisible Cities (Calvino), 42
Islamophobia, 68, 80–81, 84–85, 128, 143–44, 146

Jackson, Andrew, 124
Japanese American internment: in *The Buddha in the Attic* (Otsuka), 155–57; compulsory acts of loyalty in, 143; in *Open City* (Cole), 51–52; Otsuka's family history of, 131–32; representations of, 128–29, 132–34; Wakasa's murder and, 140; xenophobia and, 133, 137–38, 209. See also *When the Emperor Was Divine* (Otsuka)
Jen, Gish, 18
Jewish diaspora, 2–3, 84
Jimenez Molinar, Fernando, 228
Johns Hopkins University, 212
Johnson, Geoffrey, 80
Johnson-Reed Act (1924), 17, 209
Jones, Gayl, 173
JP Morgan, 212
Justice Department, U.S., 211

Kafka, Franz, 1–3, 4–5
Kakutani, Michiko, 147, 216–17
Kaluli people, 105
Kampala, 37, 42–44, 48–49
Kandiyoti, Dalia, 22, 23
Kant, Immanuel, 92
Kaplan, Amy, 11
Katrina (hurricane), 177–78, 226, 231
Kehoe, Karon, 133
Kerouac, Jack, 106–7
Kindred (Butler), 51–52
King, Stephen, 233
Korean immigrants, 209, 256n46, 256n53
Krome (detention center), 199, 213, 214–15, 217–18

La Bestia (network of freight trains), 104, 117, 126, 137, 234
Labor Appropriation Act (1924), 17
Lahiri, Jhumpa, 18, 19
Lalami, Laila, 18
language: in *The Lazarus Project* (Hemon), 75; Luiselli on, 95–96, 100–104, 112, 125–26; migration and, 13; "A Report for an Academy" (Kafka) and, 2, 5
Lanzoni, Susan, 10
Lazarus Project, The (Hemon): (im)migrant solidarity and, 74, 87, 88–94; autobiography and, 71–72; Bosnian war in, 68, 70–71, 81, 83–88; metafiction in, 72–73, 93–94, 220; photographs in, 70–71, 77–79, 82–83, 87; refraction in, 14, 71–73, 76–77, 80–88, 90, 93–94, 104, 160, 222; repetition in, 84–88; writing in, 41, 68–69, 74–81
Le Pen, Marine, 188
Lee, Chang-Rae, 18
Lee, Min Jin, 256n46
Lewis, Pericles, 252n41
Lewis, Simon, 175–76
Li, Yiyun, 18
Liberia, 34, 60, 61–62, 65
Lindskoog, Carl, 210
Littlefield, Sophie, 134
Locke, Alain, 15–16
Lolita (Nabokov), 79
Lord of the Flies (Golding), 109, 111, 115
Lorenz, Dagmar, 2
Lost Children Archive (Luiselli): archives in, 109–10, 112, 118–19, 122–27; echoes of forced migration across time in, 14, 20, 73, 104–27, 136–37, 222; *Elegies for Lost Children* by Ella Camposanto in, 109–21; on language, 95–96, 102–3, 112; mediators of migrant testimony in, 207; metafiction in, 109, 112, 125, 220; migrant solidarity and, 112, 125, 127; soundscapes in, 104–5, 109, 113–14, 120, 122–24; temporality in, 123–25; trains in, 104, 113, 117–19, 121, 122, 126, 136–37; writing in, 41

Luan, Livia, 211
Luciano, Dana, 176
Luiselli, Valeria: on language, 95–96, 100–104, 112, 125–26; representative thinking and, 93; role of writers and, 99–100, 192–93, 227, 235; as "time witness," 192. See also *Lost Children Archive* (Luiselli); *Tell Me How It Ends* (Luiselli)

Machado, Carmen Maria, 159
Mackey, Nathaniel, 123
Martinez, Ubaldo Cruz, 226–27
masculinity: as toxic, 159–62, 163–64, 167–68, 169–73
Maslin, Mark, 175–76
Mbembe, Achille, 35
McCarthy, Cormac, 109, 111
McCarthy, Mary, 11, 134–35, 220
McKinley, William, 70
Mehta, Suketu, 97–99
Melting Pot, The (Zangwill), 88
Menard, Andrew, 178–79
Méndez, Danny, 170
Mengestu, Dinaw: Afropolitanism and, 36, 37; new immigrant literature and, 18–19; representative thinking and, 93; strategic anonymity and, 37–47, 71, 131; on *Tell Me How It Ends* (Luiselli), 96, 97; as "time witness," 192. See also *All Our Names* (Mengestu); "Honest Exit, An" (Mengestu); *How to Read the Air* (Mengestu)
mental illness, 222, 223, 224, 230
Messud, Claire, 106, 124, 250n19, 251n35
metafiction: concept and role of, 15; in *All Our Names* (Mengestu), 8, 220; in "An Honest Exit" (Mengestu), 6–7; in *The Lazarus Project* (Hemon), 72–73, 93–94, 220; in *Lost Children Archive* (Luiselli), 109, 112, 125, 220; Nabokov and, 72; in *Open City* (Cole), 62–65; in *The Undocumented Americans* (Cornejo Villavicencio), 224
Miami, Florida, 217, 222, 229, 231
Michael, Lucas, 265n18

Microsoft, 212
migrant, use of term, 15
migrant aesthetics: concept of, 4, 13–20, 24, 40–41, 160, 200–201; autobiography and, 13, 222–24; empathy and, 13, 160, 220. See also carceral migration; choral narration; metafiction; migrant solidarity; strategic anonymity; temporality; toxicity
migrant literature, 19. See also immigrant literature
Migrant Sites (Kandiyoti), 22, 23
migrant solidarity: concept of, 160; *All Our Names* (Mengestu) and, 38; in Díaz's fiction, 191–92; Flores declarations and, 198–99; *The Lazarus Project* (Hemon) and, 74, 87, 88–94; *Lost Children Archive* (Luiselli) and, 112, 125, 127; *Open City* (Cole) and, 38; *When the Emperor Was Divine* (Otsuka) and, 136–37
migration: from Africa, 34–36; climate change and, 98–99, 162–63, 164, 174–80, 192; eugenic and xenophobic views of, 117, 186–88, 196–98, 208–12, 219–20, 231 (*see also* detention centers); as global phenomenon, 8, 13–14; from Haiti, 98, 177–78, 208, 210 (see also *Brother, I'm Dying* [Danticat]); as human right, 228–29; language and, 13, 95–96, 100–104, 112, 125–26; neocolonialism and, 125; paleogenetics and, 186–87. See also Native American forced migration and genocide
Migration Protection Protocol (MPP), 198
migratory aesthetics (Bal), 23–24, 127. See also migrant aesthetics
Miller, Judith, 80–81, 86, 91
Miner's Canary, The (Guinier and Torres), 232
Mishra, Pankaj, 16, 33–34
"Monstro" (Díaz), 186, 188–92, 193, 230–31
Moore, Alan, 194

INDEX

Morishima, Emily Hiramatsu, 144, 254n12
Morrison, Toni, 52, 105, 132, 171, 234, 244n48
Mothers of the Plaza de Mayo, 229
Mrs. Dalloway (Woolf), 120
MS-13 (Mara Salvatrucha), 96, 97, 101, 202
Mukherjee, Elora, 207
Muller, Gilbert H., 22
Mumbo Jumbo (Reed), 259n22
Muslim Americans, 68, 80–81, 84–85, 128, 143–44, 146
My (Underground) American Dream (Arce), 232
"My Life Had Stood—a Loaded Gun" (Dickinson), 225

Nabokov, Vladimir, 71–72, 79, 86–87, 168–69
Nation, The (magazine), 43–44
Native American forced migration and genocide: climate change and, 174–75; in Díaz's fiction, 162–63; legacy and effects of, 24–25; in Luiselli's writing, 103–4, 105, 108, 120–21, 122, 124–25; in *Open City* (Cole), 51–52, 58; *When the Emperor Was Divine* (Otsuka) and, 139–40
Naturalization Act (1790), 208–9
Nature (journal), 175
"Negocios" (Díaz), 164, 180, 258n12, 262n74
"Negro Artist and the Racial Mountain, The" (Hughes), 43–44
Nelson, Deborah, 10, 11, 134–35, 136
neocolonialism, 14, 97–98, 125, 177–78
New Haven, Connecticut, 222
new immigrant literature, 16, 18–19
New Jersey, 178–79
New Orleans, Louisiana. *See* Katrina (hurricane)
New Republic (magazine), 217
New Strangers in Paradise (Muller), 22
New West, The (Adams), 108
New York: in *Open City* (Cole), 38, 51–52, 56–62; Sandy (hurricane) in, 226–27;

September 11 attacks (2011) in, 222, 223, 227–28, 229; in *The Undocumented Americans* (Cornejo Villavicencio), 222, 226–27
New York Times (newspaper), 19, 197, 216–17, 232–33
New York World (newspaper), 246n28
New Yorker (magazine), 6, 9–10, 160, 163, 189
Newton, James, 122
Ngai, Mae M., 14, 17, 157, 219–20
Nguyen, Viet, 31
Nietzsche, Friedrich, 20
No Telephone to Heaven (Cliff), 260n31
No-No Boy (Okada), 133
Nunez, Sigrid, 95, 99, 125–26

Obama administration (2009–2017), 211
Odyssey (Homer), 111
Office of Refugee Resettlement (ORR), 196, 206
Ohnuki-Tierney, Emiko, 144
Okada, John, 133
Okpewho, Isidore, 34
Okubo, Miné, 132–33
On the Road (Kerouac), 106–7
Open City (Cole): autobiography and, 222; Conrad and, 56, 114; empathy and, 52–55, 168, 169, 220; metafiction in, 62–65; palimpsestic mode of, 14, 38–40, 55–67, 73, 104, 108, 229; rape in, 40, 52–55, 63–64, 147, 168; representative thinking and, 93; strategic anonymity in, 37–40, 50–53, 71, 131; writing in, 50–52, 222
Operation Jump Start, 120, 126
Orphan Train Movement, 103–4
"Otravida, Otravez" (Díaz), 164, 185, 258n12
Otsuka, Julie: family history of internment and, 131–32; rejection of autobiography and, 222; as "time witness," 192. *See also Buddha in the Attic, The* (Otsuka); *When the Emperor Was Divine* (Otsuka)
Outcault, Richard Fenton, 246n28

INDEX

Pachinko (Lee), 256n46
Palazzi, Franco, 93
paleogenetics, 186–87
Park, Josephine, 143–44, 146, 209–10, 257n67
Patient Protection and Affordable Care Act (2010), 231
Patteson, Richard, 164
Pease, Donald, 83–84
Pedro Páramo (Rulfo), 110–11
perspective by incongruity, 15
Peter (chimpanzee), 2
Petrov, Yevgeni, 107–8
photographs: Abu Ghraib prison and, 82–83; Averbuch's murder and, 70, 77–79, 78, 82–83, 87; of children in detention centers, 198; in Díaz's fiction, 182, 184; Japanese "picture brides" and, 130–31, 149; in *The Lazarus Project* (Hemon), 70–71, 77–79, 82–83, 87; in *Lost Children Archive* (Luiselli), 107–8, 118, 122; "A Tour of the Monuments of Passaic, New Jersey" (Smithson) and, 178–79; in *When the Emperor Was Divine* (Otsuka), 138
play, 72–73, 77–79, 86–87
Playing in the Dark (Morrison), 234
Pnin (Nabokov), 168–69
police brutality: in *The Lazarus Project* (Hemon), 85–86. *See also* Averbuch, Lazarus
Population Bomb, The (Ehrlich and Ehrlich), 187
post-redress internment literature, 132
Pound, Ezra, 111, 113, 114, 122
Prevention Through Deterrence, 126
primitivism, 2–3
prison system, 207–8, 211–12
Proceed with Caution, When Engaged by Minority Writing in the Americas (Sommer), 12
Project Amplify, 198, 207
Promised Land, The (Antin), 16–17
Prudential Financial, Inc., 212
Prum, Richard O., 263n94
Pulitzer, Joseph, 246n28
"Pura Principle, The" (Díaz), 180–81

Qaddafi, Muammar al-, 62
Quesada, Sarah, 191–92

Rahman, Zia Haider, 18
rape: Díaz and, 160; in *Open City* (Cole), 40, 52–55, 63–64, 147, 168
Raspail, Jean, 187–88
Reagan administration (1981–1989), 97, 208, 210, 219
Reed, Ishmael, 259n22
"Reflections on Little Rock" (Arendt), 92–93
refraction: in Díaz's fiction, 160–64, 173–74; *The Lazarus Project* (Hemon) and, 14, 71–73, 76–77, 80–88, 90, 93–94, 104, 160, 222; in Luiselli's writing, 104, 250n19; Nabokov on, 71–72
refugees: in *All Our Names* (Mengestu), 8, 37; from Cuba, 210; empathy and, 19–20; "An Honest Exit" (Mengestu) and, 5–7; *How to Read the Air* (Mengestu) and, 20; vs. immigrants, 19, 47; Jewish diaspora and, 84; language and, 95–96, 101–4, 112; in *Lost Children Archive* (Luiselli), 115–19, 120–21, 136–37; "A Report for an Academy" (Kafka) and, 3, 5
Remain in Mexico program (Migration Protection Protocol, MPP), 198
"Remembering the Historical Present" (Harootunian), 123–24
repetition: in *The Gates of Paradise* (Andrzejewski), 119; in *The Lazarus Project* (Hemon), 84–88; in *Lost Children Archive* (Luiselli), 120, 125; in *When the Emperor Was Divine* (Otsuka), 141
"Report for an Academy, A" (Kafka), 1–3, 4–5, 31
representative thinking, 8–9, 91–94, 136, 235
Richards, I. A., 114
Riis, Jacob, 248n60
Rilke, Rainer Maria, 110–11
Rings of Saturn, The (Sebald), 39, 55–56
Road, The (McCarthy), 109
road-trip genre, 106–9, 120, 125
Robinson, Greg, 133, 134

INDEX

romantic relationships: in Díaz's fiction, 162, 171–73; in *The Lazarus Project* (Hemon), 88–89; *The Melting Pot* (Zangwill) and, 88; Sollors on, 171
Rorty, Richard, 90–91, 92
Rousseau, Jean-Jacques, 9
Row, Jess, 213, 217
ruin reading, 181, 192–93
Rulfo, Juan, 110–11
Rushdie, Salman, 73, 89–90

Said, Edward, 80
Saldívar, José David, 161, 258n13
Sandy (hurricane), 226–27, 231
Sartre, Jean-Paul, 66
Scarry, Elaine, 20, 255n34
Schafer, Raymond Murray, 104–5, 122
School of the Americas (SOA), 266n30
Schuettler, Herman F., 80, 86
Schuyler, George, 15–16
Schwob, Marcel, 110–11, 114, 115–17, 119
Sebald, W. G., 39, 55–56, 244n50, 247n45, 251n35
Sehgal, Parul, 19, 233, 234
Selasi, Taiye, 34–35, 66
September 11 attacks (2011), 55, 223, 227–28, 229
Serpell, Namwali, 9, 12, 91–92, 93, 129, 136, 153
Shah, Sonia, 186, 187
Sheehan, Paul, 55
Shippy, George, 69, 70, 86
Shippy, Harry, 69
Shore, Stephen, 108
short stories, 129, 163, 224
Shteyngart, Gary, 18
Sierra Club, 187
Silent Honor (Steel), 134
Silverstein, Ken, 217
Sisters (Cheney), 120
60 Minutes II (CBS), 82–83
slave narratives, 12, 47
slavery: climate change and, 175; in Díaz's fiction, 162–63, 190–91; in Luiselli's writing, 103–4; in *Open City* (Cole), 51–52, 58–62; sexual legacy of, 171. *See also* transatlantic slave trade

Smithson, Robert, 178–79
Snow Falling on Cedars (1999 film), 134
Snow Falling on Cedars (Guterson), 134
social media, 123
Sollors, Werner, 17, 22, 88, 171
Sommer, Doris, 12, 39–40, 52, 132
Sontag, Susan, 134–35
South Texas Family Residential Center (Dilley, Texas), 197
"Space Oddity" (song), 109
Speak, Memory (Nabokov), 72
State Street Corp., 212
Steel, Danielle, 134
Stoler, Ann Laura, 25, 125
strategic anonymity: concept of, 13, 160, 200–201; in *The Buddha in the Attic* (Otsuka), 131, 148–53; in Díaz's fiction, 258n9; Mengestu and, 37–47, 93, 131; in *Open City* (Cole), 37–40, 50–53, 71, 131; in *When the Emperor Was Divine* (Otsuka), 93, 129, 136, 148–49, 199–200, 220
Streamas, John, 254n12
Summer Nights (Adams), 108
"Sun, the Moon, the Stars, The" (Díaz), 172–73
Sussis, Matt, 264n7
sympathy, 11

Tanton, John, 187–88
Taylor, Charles, 62
Taylor, Moses, 58
Tell Me How It Ends (Luiselli): autobiography and, 100–101; choral or collective narration in, 113; on gangs, 96–97; on language, 95–96, 101–4, 125–26; mediators of migrant testimony in, 109, 207; road-trip genre and, 107; on role of writing, 235
temporality: Bal and Hernández-Navarro on, 23–24; Harootunian on, 123–24; in *Lost Children Archive* (Luiselli), 123–25; migrant aesthetics and, 13–14; in *Open City* (Cole), 14, 38–40, 55–67, 73, 104, 108; social media and, 123. *See also* carceral migration

"Terra Incognita" (Waller), 219
testimonios, 233
This Is How You Lose Her (Díaz): environmental toxicity in, 180–82; refraction in, 162–64; toxic masculinity in, 167, 171–74; Yunior's father in, 167, 181, 185, 258n12
This Land Is Our Land (Mehta), 97–99
Thurmond, Strom, 171
Tienhoven, Cornelis van, 51–52, 58
Time (magazine), 212
Tompkins, Jane, 11
Toomer, Jean, 107–8
Torres, Gerald, 232
"Tour of the Monuments of Passaic, New Jersey, A" (Smithson), 178–79
Toussaint, Pierre, 60–62, 64
toxicity: colonial violence and, 163–64, 166–67, 169–71, 184–85; environment and, 163–64, 178–82; masculinity and, 159–62, 163–64, 167–68, 169–73
Trailing Clouds (Cowart), 21–22
trains: in *The Buddha in the Attic* (Otsuka), 156–57; in *Lost Children Archive* (Luiselli), 104, 113, 117–19, 121, 122, 126, 136–37; Orphan Train Movement and, 103–4; in *When the Emperor Was Divine* (Otsuka), 136–40
transatlantic slave trade: climate change and, 175; empathy and, 12; "An Honest Exit" (Mengestu) and, 5–7; legacy and effects of, 24–25; migrant aesthetics and, 14; in *Open City* (Cole), 58–62; "A Report for an Academy" (Kafka) and, 2–3, 5; vs. voluntary migration from Africa, 34–36. *See also* slavery
transculturation, 1–3. *See also* acculturation
Translating Pain (Hron), 15, 19, 20–21
trauma porn, 12
trauma studies, 10, 20
Trujillo, Rafael, 159–60, 163, 165–67, 169–71, 183
Trump administration (2017–2021), 187, 196–98, 210, 211–12, 231

Uganda, 37, 42–44, 48–49
unaccompanied migrant children, 196
Uncommon Places (Shore), 108
Undocumented Americans, The (Cornejo Villavicencio): autobiography and, 221–24; choral or collective narration in, 224–25, 228–32; as creative nonfiction, 225–28; as elegiac testament to undocumented dead, 221, 225, 228, 235; marketing of, 232–33
undocumented people: Cornejo Villavicencio as, 221, 223 (see also *Undocumented Americans, The* [Cornejo Villavicencio]); representations of, 232. *See also Lost Children Archive* (Luiselli); *Tell Me How It Ends* (Luiselli)
United Fruit Company, 98
United Nations (UN), 192
University of California, 212
unsentimentality: concept of, 11, 134–35; in Flores declarations, 200–201, 201; *When the Emperor Was Divine* (Otsuka) and, 129, 131, 134–36, 146–47
Uruguay, 229
U.S. English (organization), 187
Uschida, Yoshiko, 134

Vanderbilt University, 212
Vanguard Group, 212
vanishing Indian, myth of, 108, 139–40
Vargas, Jose Antonio, 232
Vermeulen, Pieter, 52, 54
Vietnamese immigrants, 209
Voltaire, 115
Vonnegut, Kurt, 115

waiting: carceral migration and, 129–30; in Díaz's fiction, 181; in *When the Emperor Was Divine* (Otsuka), 129, 132, 140–42
Wakasa, James Hatsuaki, 140
Wall Street Journal (newspaper), 51–52
Waller, Nicole, 157–58, 200, 218–19
War on Drugs, 219
War Relocation Authority (WRA), 133, 143

War Worker (magazine), 133
Ward, Wendy, 71, 85, 90
Washington Post (newspaper), 232
"Waste Land, The" (Eliot), 110–11, 114–15
Watchmen (Moore), 194
Wayfair, 212
Week, The (magazine), 211–12
Weil, Simone, 134–35
Weiner, Sonia, 23, 73, 82, 87, 89, 90, 247n45
Weinstein, Cindy, 11
West: in *When the Emperor Was Divine* (Otsuka), 136–37, 138–40. *See also* Native American forced migration and genocide
What We Bought (Adams), 108
When the Emperor Was Divine (Otsuka): carceral migration and, 128–31, 132, 140–47, 157–58, 198, 199–200, 204, 205–6, 229–30; echoes of forced migration across time in, 136–37, 139–40; final chapter of, 147–48; migrant solidarity and, 136–37; Otsuka's family history of internment and, 131–32; post-9/11 xenophobia and, 128, 143–44; repetition in, 141; sources of, 132–33, 134; strategic anonymity in, 93, 129, 136, 148–49, 199–200, 220; title of, 144; trains in, 136–40; unsentimentality in, 129, 131, 134–36, 146–47; waiting in, 129, 132, 140–42

"Who Set You Flowin'?" (Griffin), 107–8
Wood, James, 50–51, 109, 111, 118
Woolf, Virginia, 120
Wretched of the Earth, The (Fanon), 66
Wright, Richard, 15–16, 125
writing: in *All Our Names* (Mengestu), 47–49; in Díaz's fiction, 41, 161, 164–65, 169; in *The Lazarus Project* (Hemon), 41, 68–69, 74–81; in *Lost Children Archive* (Luiselli), 41; in *Open City* (Cole), 50–52, 222; in slave narratives, 47
Wucker, Michele, 183
Wynter, Sylvia, 176

xenophobia: Japanese Americans and, 133, 137–38, 209; in *The Lazarus Project* (Hemon), 26, 81, 90; in *Open City* (Cole), 53; September 11 attacks (2011) and, 55, 68, 128, 143–44, 223 (*see also* Islamophobia); views of migration and, 14, 117, 186–88, 196–98, 208, 208–12, 219–20, 231, 232–33. *See also* detention centers

Yellow Kid, The (Outcault), 246n28
Yoshikawa, Mako, 149–50, 151–52
You Are Not Alone, 229
Yusoff, Kathryn, 175

Zangwill, Israel, 88

GPSR Authorized Representative: Easy Access System Europe, Mustamäe tee
50, 10621 Tallinn, Estonia, gpsr.requests@easproject.com

www.ingramcontent.com/pod-product-compliance
Lightning Source LLC
Chambersburg PA
CBHW022038290426
44109CB00014B/906